Download Forms on Nolo.com

You can download the forms in this book at:

 www.nolo.com/back-of-book/WAGE.html

We'll also post updates whenever there's an important change to the law affecting this book—as well as articles and other related materials.

More Resources from Nolo.com

Legal Forms, Books, & Software
Hundreds of do-it-yourself products—all written in plain English, approved, and updated by our in-house legal editors.

Legal Articles
Get informed with thousands of free articles on everyday legal topics. Our articles are accurate, up to date, and reader friendly.

Find a Lawyer
Want to talk to a lawyer? Use Nolo to find a lawyer who can help you with your case.

NOLO
LAW for ALL

11th Edition

Working for Yourself

Law & Taxes for Independent Contractors,
Freelancers & Gig Workers of All Types

Stephen Fishman, J.D.

NOLO
LAW for ALL

ELEVENTH EDITION	JANUARY 2019
Editor	AMY LOFTSGORDON
Cover Design	SUSAN PUTNEY
Book Design	TERRI HEARSH
Proofreading	ROBERT WELLS
Index	UNGER INDEXING
Printing	BANG PRINTING

ISSN: 2639-3794 (print)

ISSN: 2639-3808 (online)

ISBN: 978-1-4133-2581-2 (pbk)

ISBN: 978-1-4133-2582-9 (ebook)

This book covers only United States law, unless it specifically states otherwise.

Please note

We believe accurate, plain-English legal information should help you solve many of your own legal problems. But this text is not a substitute for personalized advice from a knowledgeable lawyer. If you want the help of a trained professional—and we'll always point out situations in which we think that's a good idea—consult an attorney licensed to practice in your state.

Acknowledgments

Many thanks to:

Marcia Stewart, Barbara Kate Repa, Janet Portman, Amy DelPo, Lisa Guerin, Stephanie Bornstein, and Alayna Schroeder for their superb editing.

Malcolm Roberts, CPA, for reviewing the tax materials.

Gary Gerard for sharing his experiences as an independent contractor.

The many independent contractors throughout the country who permitted me to interview them.

About the Author

Stephen Fishman has dedicated his career as an attorney and author to writing useful, authoritative, and recognized guides on taxes and business law for small businesses, professionals, entrepreneurs, and independent contractors. He is the author of over 20 books and hundreds of articles, and has been quoted in *The New York Times*, *The Wall Street Journal*, *Chicago Tribune*, and many other publications. Among his books are *Deduct It! Lower Your Small Business Taxes*, *Home Business Tax Deductions: Keep What You Earn*, and *Working With Independent Contractors*, published by Nolo.

You can find his website at Fishmanlawandtaxfiles.com.

Table of Contents

Welcome to the World of Self-Employment: Introduction to *Working for Yourself*

Working for yourself can be both financially and emotionally satisfying and give you freedom employees rarely get to experience in their professional careers. However you label yourself—consultant, freelancer, or independent contractor—you have a unique opportunity to choose how you'll do business, where you'll do business, and how you'll handle all the day-to-day details of running your business. This book will help you successfully start and run your operations in a business-like manner.

Working for Yourself is intended for those self-employed people who provide personal services, such as writers, health care consultants, artists, photographers, household movers, lawyers, doctors, Web designers, accountants, quality assurance (QA) testing, and drivers. It includes those who work in the gig economy and sell their services through online hiring platforms like Uber, Upwork, Freelancer, and many others.

Working for Yourself covers all the current legal and tax basics self-employed people need to know, including how to:

- choose the type of business entity that's right for you (sole proprietor, corporation, or LLC)
- obtain business licenses and permits
- insure your business (and yourself)
- price your services and get paid on time
- pay estimated taxes
- keep track of tax-deductible business expenses, including special breaks for home-based businesses
- prepare and sign written client agreements (including special issues with online hiring platforms)
- take steps to ensure that the IRS doesn't view you as an employee if you (or your client) are audited
- set up a good record-keeping and bookkeeping system
- manage employees (if any), and
- deal with any special IP issues that may come up, such as regards ownership of a copyright or patent.

This eleventh edition has been completely updated to reflect all the tax changes under the Tax Cuts and Jobs Act, which took effect in 2018 —changes that are largely beneficial to the self-employed.

Fortunately, *Working for Yourself* is not a book you need to read cover to cover. We know you're a busy person! Exactly what chapters and sections you'll want to read depends on many factors, including whether you're already self-employed or just starting out; whether you work at home or an outside office; whether you are constantly hustling business or have one or two solid clients. We've tried to organize the book so you can easily find the information you need, whether you want trusted advice on whether to form an LLC or operate as a sole proprietor or need a sample client agreement you can tailor for your own business. We provide lots of information on the thicket of tax issues facing the self-employed (especially if you work at home). And remember, you can deduct the cost of buying this book as a business expense!

What's in a Name?

People who work for themselves use a variety of descriptive labels, including:

- self-employed
- freelancer
- consultant
- entrepreneur
- gig worker
- solopreneur
- micropreneur
- mompreneur
- contract worker
- contingent worker
- creative professional
- business owner
- one-person business owner
- microbusiness owner
- home business owner
- independent worker, or
- independent contractor.

Theses labels are often used interchangeably. Some mean different things in different businesses or professions. None has any legal significance except for the last: An "independent contractor" is a worker who is not classified as an employee for tax and other legal purposes (a crucial distinction discussed later in this book). You are free to call yourself anything you want. One recent survey found that a plurality of people who work for themselves (36%) prefer the term "self-employed," followed by "independent contractor" (15%), and "business owner" (13%).

A Golden Age for the Self-Employed

In the past, most people were self-employed. They owned and worked on farms or had their own small businesses. This changed in the 19th century, when the Industrial Revolution created massive factories and offices manned by wage slaves. Now, the process is reversing itself. Indeed, the growth in the number of the self-employed has been dubbed the "Industrial Revolution of our time."

Some of the factors that make being self-employed better than ever before include:

- **More work:** It's common today for businesses of all sizes to hire independent contractors, even those who work out of their homes.
- **The Internet:** The Internet makes it much easier and cheaper for self-employed people to market their services, exchange information, and communicate with clients and customers. Many self-employed people find work through online freelance hiring platforms like Upwork, Freelancer, TaskRabbit, and Guru.
- **Obamacare:** The advent of Obamacare has made it possible for every self-employed person to obtain health insurance coverage, even those with preexisting conditions. This has freed millions of people from "job lock": the inability to leave a job because it provides health insurance.
- **Solo support industry:** A growing solo worker support industry has developed. This includes unions and other organizations for the self-employed (such as the Freelancers' Union), and inexpensive or free software and applications freelancers can use for bookkeeping, invoicing, project tracking, contact creation, and tax preparation.

CAUTION

This book is not intended for businesses that sell goods, such as someone who owns a clothing store or restaurant or sells jewelry on Etsy. In these cases, other Nolo business books may be appropriate, such as Peri Pakroo's *Small Business Start-Up Kit*.

Six Things You May Not Know About the Self-Employed

Welcome to the world of self-employment! You're in good company. Here are some things you may not know about the self-employed:

- **There are lots of them.** According to the Bureau of Labor Statistics, 10.6 million independent contractors work in the United States, representing 6.9% of total employment. In fact, four out of ten adult Americans are either currently working or have worked as independent contractors some time during their careers. Over $1.2 trillion in total income is generated by the self-employed each year.

- **Rich people are more likely to work for themselves.** Self-employed people account for two-thirds of all American millionaires.

- **They tend to be older.** According to a recent survey, 44% of self-employed people are 50 years of age or older. Only 20% are younger than 33.

- **They tend to be happy.** A recent survey found that almost two-thirds of self-employed people were highly satisfied with their situation. Only 9% expressed dissatisfaction with their work situation.

- **They work more hours.** Nearly half of all self-employed Americans work more than 44 hours in a typical workweek, compared to 39% of American workers overall, 38% in government and in private business, and 30% in nonprofit organizations.

- **They work in a variety of fields.** The self-employed work in a wide variety of occupations, including higher-skill knowledge and creative occupations and lower-skill service occupations. According to the Bureau of Labor Statistics, self-employment rates are highest for workers in the arts, entertainment, and media (26.7%); personal care (22.8%); construction and extraction (22.6%); building and grounds cleaning (17.6%); legal (17.2%); management (16.2%); and sales (8.1%).

Get an Independent Contractor Agreement, Useful Forms, and Updates on This Book's Companion Page on Nolo.com

This book includes several useful forms, including an independent contractor agreement you can tailor for your own clients. You can download all the forms in this book at:

www.nolo.com/back-of-book/WAGE.html

When there are important changes to the information in this book, we'll post those updates on the same dedicated page (what we call the book's companion page).

See Appendix A, "Using the Downloadable Forms on the Nolo Website," for a list of all forms and resources available on Nolo.com.

Working for Yourself: The Good, the Bad, and the Ugly

Before you delve into the following chapters, here's a quick overview of the pros and cons of being self-employed as compared to being an employee. It may help you make an informed decision if you're thinking about striking out on your own, or help confirm that you made the right decision if you're already working for yourself.

Working for Yourself: The Good

Being self-employed can give you more freedom and privacy than working for an employer. It can also result in substantial tax benefits—benefits that have increased as a result of the new tax law.

Independence

Most self-employed people bask in the freedom that comes from being in business for themselves and being their own boss. The amount of money you make is directly related to the quantity and quality of your work; unlike most employees, you don't need ask your boss for a raise—you simply go out and find more work.

Likewise, if you're self-employed, you're normally not dependent upon a single company for your livelihood, so the hiring or firing decisions of any one company won't have the same impact on you as on that company's employees.

This sentiment expressed by one self-employed person sums it up: "I can choose how, when, and where to work, for as much or as little time as I want. In short, I enjoy working for myself."

Higher Earning Potential

While how much you're paid is a matter for negotiation between you and your clients you can often earn more when you're self-employed than as an employee for someone else's business (especially if your skills are in great demand).

Tax Benefits

Self-employment also provides many tax benefits that aren't available to employees. Most important, you can take advantage of many tax deductions that are unavailable for employees. When you're self-employed, you can deduct any necessary expenses related to your business from your taxable income, as long as they are reasonable in amount and ordinarily incurred by businesses of your type. This may include, for example, office expenses (including those for home offices), travel and meal expenses, equipment costs, and insurance payments.

In addition, no federal or state taxes are withheld from your paychecks by an employer as they must be for employees. Instead, the self-employed normally pay their own estimated taxes directly to the IRS four times a year. This means you can hold on to your hard-earned money longer. It's up to you to decide how much estimated tax to pay (although there are penalties if you underpay). The lack of withholding combined with control over estimated tax payments can result in improved cash flow for the self-employed.

In contrast to the numerous deductions available to the self-employed, employees are no longer allowed to deduct work-related expenses. The Tax Cuts and Jobs Act eliminated all such deductions by employees for 2018 through 2025. For example, an employee may not deduct work-related driving expenses—but a self-employed person can.

The Tax Cuts and Jobs Act also established a brand new pass-through deduction that enables self-employed taxpayers to deduct up to 20% of their net business income from their income taxes, effectively lowering the tax rate on their business income by 20%. This deduction is not available to employees.

In addition, the self-employed can establish retirement plans, such as SEP-IRAs and solo 401(k) plans, that have tax advantages. These plans also allow them to shelter a substantial amount of their incomes until they retire.

Because of these and other tax benefits described later in this book, the self-employed often ultimately pay less in taxes than employees who earn similar incomes. Indeed, as a result of the changes brought about by the TCJA, the tax advantages of being self-employed are greater than they have ever been.

Working for Yourself: The Bad

Despite its advantages, being self-employed is no bed of roses. Here are some of the major drawbacks:

- **No job security.** When you're an employee, you must be paid as long as you have your job, even if your employer's business is slow. If you're self-employed and don't have business, you don't make money. As one self-employed person says: "If I fail, I don't eat. I don't have the comfort of punching a time clock and knowing the check will be there on payday."

- **No free benefits.** Although not always required by law, employers often provide their employees with health insurance, paid vacations, and paid sick leave. More generous employers may also provide retirement benefits, bonuses, and even employee profit sharing. When you're self-employed, you get no such benefits—for example, you must pay for your own health insurance. (Fortunately, you can obtain health insurance through Obamacare, even if you have preexisting medical condition.) Time lost due to vacations and illness comes directly out of your bottom line. And you must fund your own retirement.

- **No unemployment insurance.** Because hiring firms (companies that hire self-employed people) do not pay unemployment compensation taxes for the self-employed, you cannot collect unemployment benefits when your work for a firm ends.

- **No workers' compensation.** Employers must generally provide workers' compensation coverage for their employees, which provides benefits for injuries that occur on the job (even if the injury was the employee's own fault). In contrast, hiring firms do not provide workers' compensation coverage for the self-employed people they hire. If a work-related injury is a self-employed person's fault, he or she has no recourse against the hiring firm. And even if it's the hiring firm's responsibility, the self-employed person will have to deal with the expense and hassle of a lawsuit.

- **No free office space or equipment.** Employers normally provide their employees with an office or space in which to work and the equipment they need to do the job. This is not usually the case when a company hires a self-employed person, who must normally provide his or her own workplace and equipment.
- **Few or no labor law protections.** A wide array of federal and state laws that protect employees from unfair exploitation by employers (such as wage and hour rules and requirements for family and medical leave) don't typically apply to the self-employed.
- **Complete business responsibility.** When you're self-employed, you won't have a company payroll department to withhold and pay taxes for you. You must run your own business—for example you'll need to have at least a rudimentary record-keeping system or hire someone to keep your records for you for taxes and other purposes.
- **Others may discriminate.** Because you don't have a guaranteed annual income as employees do, insurers, lenders, and other businesses may refuse to provide you with services or may charge you more than employees for similar services. It can be difficult, for example, for a self-employed person to obtain disability insurance, particularly one who works at home. Also, it may be more difficult to buy a house because lenders are often wary of self-employed borrowers. To prove you can afford a loan, you'll likely have to provide a prospective lender with copies of your recent tax returns and a profit and loss statement for your business.

Working for Yourself: The Ugly

Unfortunately, the bad aspects of self-employment discussed above do not end the litany of potential woes. Being self-employed can, in some respects, get downright ugly.

Double Social Security/Medicare Tax

For many, the ugliest and most unfair thing about being self-employed is that you must pay twice as much Social Security and Medicare taxes as employees. Employees pay a 7.65% tax on their salaries, up to a salary amount capped by the Social Security tax limit ($128,400 in 2018). Employers pay a matching amount. In contrast, self-employed people must pay the entire tax themselves—a 12.4% Social Security tax up to the annual ceiling, and a 2.9% Medicare tax on all their income (more if their income is over $200,000/$250,000, as discussed below); this amounts to a whopping 15.3% tax on their income up to the Social Security ceiling. This is in addition to federal and state income taxes. In practice, the Social Security/Medicare tax comes to less than 15.3% because of certain deductions, but it still takes a big bite out of what you earn from self-employment.

As mentioned above, self-employed people must pay Medicare tax on their net self-employment income over the Social Security ceiling. This is a 2.9% tax on income from $128,400 to $200,000 in net self-employment income for singles and $128,400 to $250,000 for married couples filing jointly. High earners will owe a 3.8% tax on all net self-employment income that exceeds these amounts.

Personal Liability for Debts

Employees are not liable for the debts incurred by their employers. An employee may lose his or her job if the employer's business fails but will owe nothing to the employer's creditors.

This is not necessarily the case when you're self-employed. If you're a sole proprietor or partner in a partnership, you are personally liable for your business debts. You could lose much of what you own if your business fails. However, there are ways to decrease your personal exposure, such as obtaining insurance, as discussed in a later chapter.

Deadbeat Clients

Ugliest of all, you could do lots of business and still fail to earn a living. It can be difficult to get clients to pay you on time or at all. When you're self-employed, you bear the risk of loss from deadbeat clients. The government is not going to help you collect on your clients' unpaid bills.

Clients who pay late or don't pay at all have driven some self-employed people back to the ranks of the wage slaves. However, there are many strategies you can use to help alleviate payment problems as discussed in later chapters.

How This Book Will Help You Succeed at Self-Employment

Despite the challenges, millions of people are happily self-employed today. Indeed, most successfully self-employed individuals would never go back to wage slavery.

The purpose of this book is to help you achieve all the financial and personal benefits of working for yourself. We'll show you how to make what's good about self-employment even better, make the bad aspects less daunting, and—hopefully—make the ugly aspects a little more attractive.

Spending a few hours now to learn the legal, tax, and practical nuts and bolts of self-employment will save you countless headaches—not to mention substantial time and money—later on.

Don't worry! The mere fact that you've chosen to take the time and trouble to read this book shows that you have what it takes to be successful working for yourself.

Choosing the Legal Form for Your Business

As a self-employed person, one of the most important decisions you have to make is what legal form your business will take. There are several alternatives, and the form you choose will have a big impact on how you're taxed, whether you'll be liable for your business's debts, and how the IRS and state auditors will treat you.

There are four main business forms that we'll discuss in this chapter:

- sole proprietorship
- corporation
- partnership, and
- limited liability company.

If you own your business alone, you need not be concerned about partnerships; this business form requires two or more owners. If, like most self-employed workers, you're running a one-person business, your choice is between a sole proprietorship, corporation, or limited liability company.

Don't worry too much about making the wrong decision. Your initial choice about how to organize your business is not set in stone. You can always switch to another legal form later. It's common, for example, for self-employed people to start out as sole proprietors, then incorporate or form LLCs later when they become better established and make substantial income.

Sole Proprietorships

A sole proprietorship is a one-owner business. It is by far the cheapest and easiest legal form for organizing your business. You don't have to get permission from the government or pay any fees to be a sole proprietor, except perhaps for a fictitious business name statement or business license. (See Chapter 5.) You just start doing business; if you don't incorporate or have a partner, you are automatically a sole proprietor. If you're already running a one-person business and haven't incorporated or formed an LLC, you're a sole proprietor.

The vast majority of self-employed people are sole proprietors—according to the U.S. Census Bureau, over 86% of all businesses without employees are sole proprietorships. Most sole proprietors run small operations, but a sole proprietor can hire employees and other contractors, too. Indeed, some one-owner businesses are large operations with many employees. If you're already running a one-person business (or thinking about starting one), the sole proprietorship form is a perfectly good choice.

Ways to Organize Your Business

Type of Organization	Main Advantages	Main Disadvantages
Sole Proprietorship	• Simple and inexpensive to create and operate. • Owner reports profit or loss on personal tax return.	• Owner personally liable for business debts. • Not a separate legal entity.
C Corporation	• Clients have less risk from government audits. • Owners have limited personal liability for business debts. • Owners can deduct fringe benefits as business expenses. • Owners can split corporate profit among owners and corporation, for a lower overall tax bill.	• More expensive to create and operate than sole proprietorship or partnership. • Double taxation threat because the corporation is a separate taxable entity. • No beneficial employment tax treatment.
S Corporation	• Clients have less risk from government audits. • Owners have limited personal liability for business debts. • Owners can save on employment taxes by taking distributions instead of salary.	• More expensive to create and operate than sole proprietorship or partnership. • Fringe benefits for shareholders are limited.
Partnership	• Simple and inexpensive to create and operate. • Owners report profit or loss on personal tax returns.	• Owners personally liable for business debts. • Two or more owners required. • No beneficial employment tax treatment.
Limited Liability Company	• Owners have limited liability for business debts if they participate in management. • Profit and loss can be allocated differently than ownership interests.	• More expensive to create and operate than sole proprietorship or partnership. • No beneficial employment tax treatment.

Adapted from *Legal Guide for Starting & Running a Small Business*, by Fred S. Steingold (Nolo).

Tax Concerns

When you're a sole proprietor, you and your business are one and the same for tax purposes. You don't pay taxes or file tax returns separately for your sole proprietorship. Instead, you must report the income you earn or losses you incur on your own personal tax return, IRS Form 1040. If you earn a profit, you add the money to any other income you have, such as interest income or your spouse's income if you're married and file a joint tax return. That becomes the total that is taxed. If you incur a loss, you can use it to offset income from other sources.

Although you are taxed on your total income regardless of its source, the IRS also wants to know about the profitability of your business. To show whether you have a profit or loss from your sole proprietorship, you must file IRS Schedule C, *Profit or Loss From Business*, with your tax return. On this form you list all your business income and deductible expenses. (See Chapter 9.) If you have more than one business, you must file a separate Schedule C for each.

Sole proprietors are not employees of their proprietorships; they are business owners. Their businesses don't pay payroll taxes on a sole proprietor's income or withhold income tax. However, sole proprietors do have to pay self-employment taxes—that is, Social Security and Medicare taxes—on their net self-employment income. These taxes must be paid four times a year (along with income taxes) in the form of estimated taxes. Chapters 10 and 11 cover this in more detail.

Hiring firms don't withhold any taxes from a sole proprietor's compensation, but any firm that pays a sole proprietor $600 or more in a year by cash or check must file Form 1099-MISC to report the payment to the IRS.

> EXAMPLE: Annie operates a consulting business as a sole proprietor. She must report all the income she receives from her clients on her individual tax return, IRS Form 1040, and file Schedule C. She need not file a separate tax return for her business. In one recent year, she earned $50,000 from consulting and had $15,000 in business expenses, leaving a net business income of $35,000. She reports her gross profits from consulting and her business expenses on Schedule C. She must add her $35,000 profit to any other income she has and report the total on her Form 1040. She must pay both income and self-employment taxes on this profit.

Liability Concerns

One concern many business owners have is liability: whether and to what extent they are legally responsible for paying their businesses' debts or judgments entered against their businesses in lawsuits.

Business Debts

When you're a sole proprietor, you are personally liable for all the debts of your business. This means that a business creditor—a person or company to whom you owe money for items you use in your business—can go after all your assets, both business and personal (such as your personal bank accounts, your house). Similarly, a personal creditor (to whom you owe money for personal items) can go after your business assets, such as business bank accounts and equipment.

> EXAMPLE: Arnie, a sole proprietor consultant, fails to pay $5,000 to an office equipment supplier. The supplier sues him in small claims court and wins a $5,000 judgment. As a sole proprietor, Arnie is personally liable for this judgment. This means that the supplier can tap not only Arnie's business bank account, but his personal savings accounts as well. The supplier can also go after Arnie's personal assets, such as his car and home.

Lawsuits

If you're a sole proprietor, you'll also be personally liable for business-related lawsuits, which could result in the following kinds of liability:

- **Premises liability.** Responsibility for injuries or damages that occur at your office, workshop, lab, or other place of business.
- **Infringement liability.** When someone claims that you have infringed on a patent, copyright, trademark, or trade secret.
- **Employer liability.** Liability for injuries or damages caused by an employee while he or she was working for you.
- **Product liability.** Responsibility for injuries or damages caused by a product that you manufacture or sell to the public.
- **Negligence liability.** When someone claims that you failed to use "reasonable care" in your actions, resulting in injuries or damages.

Fortunately, you can obtain insurance to protect yourself against these types of risks. This will be covered in Chapter 6.

Sole Proprietorships for Spouses

Many businesses are co-owned by a husband and wife. Such a business can be organized in a variety of ways—as an S or C corporation, a limited liability company (LLC), or a formal partnership.

If you and your spouse don't take any steps to choose a business form, the IRS will treat your business as a partnership. This results in a complex tax return. You must file IRS Form 1065 (*U.S. Return of Partnership Income*) to report your partnership's income and expenses. Your partnership income and expenses are split between you and your spouse. The partnership must give each spouse a Schedule K-1 showing the spouse's share of these items. All the amounts from both spouses' Schedule K-1s are then recombined and included on their joint Form 1040.

However, spouses who own a business together have another option: They can be taxed as sole proprietors. This does not reduce their overall tax bill, but it does result in a much simpler tax return. More options are available to spouses who live in community property states.

Spouses in all states. Since 2007, spouses in all states who jointly own and manage a business can elect to be taxed as a "qualified joint venture" and treated as sole proprietors for tax purposes. Prior to 2007, spouses who co-owned a business were classified as a partnership for federal tax purposes, unless they formed a corporation or an LLC.

To qualify, the married couple must be the only owners of the business and must both "materially participate" in the business. This means they must both be involved with the business's day-to-day operations on a regular, continuous, and substantial basis. Working more than 500 hours a year in the business meets this requirement. So does working more than 100 hours if no one else works more. Many couples will not be able to satisfy this requirement unless both put substantial time into their businesses.

A couple elects to be treated as a qualified joint venture by filing a joint tax return (IRS Form 1040). Each spouse files a separate Schedule C to report his or her share of the business's profits and losses and a separate Schedule SE to report his or her share of self-employment tax. That way, each spouse gets credit for Social Security and Medicare coverage purposes. If, as is usually the case, each spouse owns 50% of the business, they equally share the business income or loss on their individual Schedule Cs. The couple must also share

Sole Proprietorships for Spouses (continued)

any deductions and credits according to their individual ownership interest in the business. If the business has employees, either spouse may report and pay the employment taxes due on any wages paid to the employees using the EIN of that spouse's sole proprietorship.

Spouses in community property states. There are nine community property states: Arizona, California, Idaho, Louisiana, Nevada, New Mexico, Texas, Washington, and Wisconsin. Spouses in any of these states may elect qualified joint venture status as described above, but they have another option as well. They can choose to classify their business as a sole proprietorship by filing a single Schedule C listing one spouse as the sole proprietor. The requirements to do this may be easier for many couples to satisfy because there is no material participation requirement. The only requirements are:

- The business must be wholly owned by a husband and wife as community property.
- No person other than one or both spouses would be considered an owner for federal tax purposes.
- The business entity is not treated as a corporation. (Rev. Proc. 2002-69.)

One drawback to this election is that only one spouse (the one listed in the Schedule C) receives credit for Social Security and Medicare coverage purposes.

Treating your spouse as your employee. Instead of being co-owners of a business, spouses can have an employer-employee relationship; that is, one spouse solely owns the business (usually as a sole proprietor), which employs the other spouse. In this event, there is no need to worry about having to file a partnership tax return. One Schedule C would be filed in the name of the owner-spouse. The nonowner spouse's income would be employee salary subject to income tax and FICA (Social Security and Medicare) withholding. (See Chapter 8.)

However, a spouse is considered an employee only if there is an employer/employee type of relationship in which the first spouse substantially controls the business and makes management decisions, and the second spouse is under the direction and control of the first spouse. If the second spouse has an equal say in the affairs of the business, provides substantially equal services to the business, and contributes capital to the business, that spouse cannot be treated as an employee.

Audit Concerns

If you are a self-employed person who does work for a client, you are generally considered an independent contractor of the client that hired you. In some cases, however, a self-employed person's relationship to a client will have qualities that make it look more like an employer-employee relationship. When this happens, the government will call you an employee of the client, whether or not you and the client view the relationship that way. This employee label can have serious tax consequences for both you and your client.

Because of these major consequences—which include heavy fines and back taxes—most companies will hire only self-employed people whom they are certain will be viewed by the government as independent contractors and not as employees. One thing the hiring firm will look at is what sort of business entity you are.

A disadvantage of the sole proprietorship business form is that it won't help you establish that you're self-employed in the eyes of the IRS or state auditors. Sole proprietors who provide services can look a lot like employees, especially if they work on their own without assistants and deposit their compensation in a personal bank account. After all, this is exactly what employees do. For this reason, some hiring firms prefer to hire self-employed people who have incorporated their businesses.

RESOURCE
For an overview of what you need to know to establish a sole proprietorship in your state, including how to file a fictitious business name or obtain necessary business licenses, see the "Sole Proprietors" section of Nolo.com.

Corporations

Relatively few self-employed people without employees incorporate—only 6.4% have done so according to a recent survey by the U.S. Census Bureau. Many of these are high-income professionals, such as doctors, lawyers, accountants, architects, and dentists, who have formed professional corporations (see "Professional Corporations" below).

Creating and operating a corporation takes more money, time, and trouble than being a sole proprietor (or a partner in a partnership). But the corporate form can be a good choice if you want to:

- take advantage of the new 21% tax rate on C corporation income
- attract investors or eventually sell your business
- obtain the most "limited liability" you can
- reduce clients concerns about hiring you due to fears that they could get in trouble with the IRS or other agencies
- save on taxes by taking advantage of tax-free employee fringe benefits, or
- reduce your Social Security and Medicare taxes.

RESOURCE

Want more information on business forms for professionals? For detailed guidance on choice of business entity for professionals, see *Tax Deductions for Professionals*, by Stephen Fishman (Nolo).

Overview of Corporations

The word "corporation" usually conjures up images of huge businesses such as WalMart or Apple, Inc. However, a business doesn't have to be large to be a corporation. Virtually any business can be a corporation, even if it has only one owner. Indeed, most corporations have only a few owners; such small corporations are often called "closely held" corporations.

What Is a Corporation?

A corporation is a legal structure you can use to organize and conduct a business. Unlike a sole proprietorship, it has a legal existence distinct from its owners and is considered its own legal "person." That means it can hold title to property, sue and be sued, have bank accounts, borrow money, hire employees, and do anything else in the business world that a human being can do.

In theory, every corporation consists of three groups of people:

- those who direct the overall business, called "directors"
- those who run the day-to-day business affairs, called "officers," and
- those who just invest in the business, called "shareholders."

However, in the case of a small business corporation, these three groups often boil down to the same person: A single person can direct and run the corporation and own all the corporate stock. So, if you want to incorporate your one-person business, you don't have to go out and recruit a board of directors or officers.

A corporation is a creature of state law. You may form a corporation in any state, but it's usually best to do so in the state where you have your main office. A corporation is created by filing Articles of Incorporation with your state Secretary of State or similar official and paying a filing fee, which ranges from $100 to $800 depending on the state. You must also choose a corporate name, appoint directors, adopt bylaws, issue stock, and hold an initial directors' meeting.

For more details on forming a corporation, including state-specific rules, see the "Corporations" section of Nolo.com.

RESOURCE

For a complete step-by-step guide to forming a corporation, see *Incorporate Your Business: A Legal Guide to Forming a Corporation in Your State,* by Anthony Mancuso (Nolo).

Your Employment Status

When you incorporate your business, if you continue to work in the business, you automatically become an employee of your corporation, whether full or part time. This is so even if you're the only shareholder and are not subject to the direction and control of anybody else. In effect, you wear two hats: You're both an owner and an employee of the corporation.

> EXAMPLE: Ellen, an independent truck driver, forms a one-person trucking corporation, Ellen's Trucking, Inc. She owns all the stock and runs the business. The corporation hires her as an employee with the title of president.

When you have incorporated your business, clients hire your corporation, not you personally. You sign any written agreement on behalf of your corporation. When you're paid, the client should issue the check to the corporation and you should deposit it in the corporate bank account, not your personal account. You can then pay the money to yourself in the form of salary, bonus, or dividends. The method you choose to pay yourself can have important tax consequences, discussed below.

You must withhold Social Security and Medicare taxes from any employee salary your corporation pays you, and you must pay this money to the IRS just as an employer would for any employee. However, your total Social Security and Medicare taxes will be about the same as if you were a sole proprietor. They're just paid from two different accounts: Half are paid by your corporation and half are withheld from your salary. Because all the money is yours, there is no real difference here from being a sole proprietor. Some additional state payroll taxes will be due, however (mostly unemployment taxes).

You can also have your corporation provide you with tax-free employee fringe benefits, such as health insurance and pension benefits.

Self-Employed by Any Other Name

Strictly speaking, when you incorporate your business, you are no longer self-employed; you are an employee of your corporation. Legally speaking, your corporation is neither self-employed nor an employee of the clients or customers for whom it provides services. Only individual human beings can be self-employed or employees.

However, people who own single-shareholder corporations and sell services to clients still often refer to themselves as self-employed when they communicate with clients and customers and other self-employed people. This is understandable because their employee status is mainly a legal technicality.

Many Clients Like Hiring Corporations

Many potential clients are fearful of hiring self-employed people because they are afraid they could get in trouble if the IRS audits them and claims that the self-employed workers should have been treated as employees. Firms that hire corporations have a smaller chance of having worker classification problems with the IRS than firms that hire sole proprietors to do the same work. This is because taking the time and trouble to incorporate is strong evidence that a worker is operating an independent business.

Moreover, hiring firms need not report to the IRS on Form 1099-MISC the payments they make to corporations (except for corporations formed by lawyers and doctors). Firms don't like filing such forms because they can lead to IRS audits of their worker classification practices—particularly if they file more such forms than normal for the size and type of business involved.

Because of this clear direction from the IRS, some hiring firms try to avoid hiring sole proprietors or partnerships and deal with incorporated businesses only. Others give preference to a corporation if they have a choice between hiring a sole proprietor and a corporation. The ability to get more business may alone justify the time and expense involved in incorporating.

Incorporating may be particularly helpful if you're a computer programmer, systems analyst, engineer, or drafter, or if you perform similar technical services. Because special IRS rules make it harder for firms that hire such workers to win IRS worker-classification audits, hiring firms generally classify them as employees. But they may make an exception if you're incorporated and they are able to hire your corporation instead of hiring you personally.

However, don't get the idea that you and your clients need not worry about the IRS at all if you incorporate. The IRS also directs that an incorporated worker may be reclassified as an employee of the hiring firm if the worker does not follow corporate formalities or otherwise abuses the corporate form. IRS auditors may disregard your corporate status and find that you're a hiring firm's employee if you act like one by, for example:

- depositing your earnings directly into your personal bank account instead of putting them into a separate corporate account
- failing to file tax returns for your corporation
- not issuing yourself stock, or
- failing to follow other corporate formalities, such as holding an annual meeting or keeping corporate records.

IRS Docks Doc, but Not M.D., Inc.

A case from 1995 shows why many clients prefer to hire corporations rather than sole proprietors. An outpatient surgery center hired two doctors to work as administrators. They both performed the same services. However, one of the doctors had formed a medical corporation of which he was an employee. The surgery center signed a written contract with the corporation, not the doctor. It also paid the corporation, not the doctor. The other doctor was a sole proprietor and had no written contract with the center.

The court concluded that the incorporated doctor was not an employee of the surgery center, but the unincorporated doctor was an employee. As a result, the center had to pay substantial back taxes and penalties for the unincorporated doctor, but not for the doctor who was incorporated. (*Idaho Ambucare Center v. U.S.*, 57 F.3d 752 (9th Cir. 1995).)

Investors Like Corporations

Unlike other business forms, the corporate structure allows a business to sell ownership shares in the company by offering shares of stock. This makes it easier to attract investors and hire and retain key employees who can be provided with stock options. This attribute alone can make forming a corporation a must. On the other hand, the ability to issue stock is unimportant if you will never "go public," or have employees you will want to incentivize with stock options.

Corporations Provide Limited Liability

In theory, forming a corporation provides its owners (the shareholders) with "limited liability." This means that the shareholders are not personally liable for corporate debts or lawsuits. The main reason most small business owners go to the trouble of forming corporations is to obtain such limited liability. However, while incorporating your business can insulate you from liability to a certain extent, the protection is not nearly as great as most people think.

Business Debts

Corporations were created to enable people to invest in businesses without risking their personal assets if the businesses failed or became unable to pay their debts. In theory, corporation owners are not personally liable for corporate debts or lawsuits. That is, they can lose what they invested in the corporations, but corporate creditors can't go after their personal assets such as their personal bank accounts or homes.

This theory holds true for large corporations. If you buy stock in Apple, for example, you don't have to worry about Apple's creditors suing you. But it often doesn't work that way for small corporations. Major creditors (like banks) are probably not going to let you shield your personal assets by incorporating. Instead, they will likely demand that you personally guarantee business loans or extensions of credit by signing a legally enforceable document pledging your personal assets to pay the debt if your business assets fall short. This means that you will be personally liable for the debt, just as if you were a sole proprietor.

> **EXAMPLE:** Lisa forms a corporation to run her part-time home business. She applies for a business credit card from her bank. She reads the application carefully and finds that it contains a clause stating that she will be personally liable for the credit card balance, even though the credit card will be in the corporation's name, not Lisa's own name. Lisa asks the bank to remove the clause. It refuses, stating that its policy is to require personal guarantees from all small, incorporated businesses such as Lisa's. Lisa goes ahead and signs the application. Now, if Lisa's corporation fails to pay off the credit card, the bank can sue her personally and collect against her personal assets, such as her personal bank account.

Not only banks and lenders require personal guarantees; other creditors may as well. For example, you may be required to personally guarantee payment of your office lease or leases for expensive equipment, like a photocopier or truck. Standard forms used by suppliers often contain personal guarantee provisions that make you personally liable when your company buys office equipment or similar items.

You can avoid having to make a personal guarantee for some business debts. These will most likely be routine and small debts. It's not likely, for example, that your office supply store will make you personally guarantee that your corporation will pay for its purchases. But, of course, if it gets wise to the fact that your business is not paying its bills, it won't extend you any more credit.

Lawsuits

If forming a corporation could shield you from personal liability for business-related lawsuits, incorporating would be clearly worthwhile. However, it's important to understand that the small business owner gets relatively little protection from many lawsuits by incorporating, as the following subsections explain.

Personal Liability for Negligence

The people who own a corporation (the shareholders) are *personally liable* for any damages caused by their own "negligence" (carelessness) or intentional wrongdoing in carrying out corporation business. Lawyers are well aware of this rule and will take advantage of it if doing so serves their clients' interests. If you form a corporation that lacks the money or insurance to pay for a legal claim brought against it, you can be certain that the lawyer for the person suing you will seek a way to sue you personally, to collect against your personal assets. Here are some examples of how you could be sued personally even though you've formed a corporation:

- A visitor slips and falls at your place of business and breaks a hip. The visitor's lawyer sues you personally for negligence, claiming you failed to keep your premises safe.
- An employee accidentally injures someone while running an errand for you. The injured person sues you personally for damages claiming you negligently hired, trained, or supervised the employee.
- A product you invented, designed, manufactured, or distributed injures several users. The injured people sue you personally for negligence.
- Someone sues you, claiming you've infringed upon a patent or copyright. Even if you've formed a corporation, you can be personally liable for such claims.

In all these cases, forming a corporation will prove useless to protect you from personal liability.

Piercing the Corporate Veil

Another way you can be personally liable even though you've formed a corporation is through a legal doctrine called "piercing the corporate veil." Under this legal rule, corporate owners risk being reached personally through their corporation's structure if they treat the corporation as their "alter ego," rather than as a separate legal entity; in other words, they behave as if they and the corporation are one and the same, without following the formalities required for corporate status. For example, if they (the corporate owners) fail to contribute money to the corporation or issue stock, they take corporate funds or assets for personal use, they commingle corporate and personal funds, or they don't observe corporate formalities such as keeping minutes and holding board meetings, a court might disregard the corporate form and hold the owners personally liable.

Inactive Shareholders Are Not Liable for Corporate Debts or Wrongs

As discussed above, shareholders who actively participate in the management of a company can be held personally liable, either for their own negligence or wrongdoings, or under the doctrine of piercing the corporate veil. However, shareholders who are not active in the business face no such personal liability unless they provide a personal guarantee. Because they aren't active, they don't commit any personal wrongs for which they could be sued.

The Role of Insurance

If incorporating won't relieve you of personal liability, how can you protect yourself from business-related lawsuits? There's a very simple answer: Get insurance. An insurer will defend you in such lawsuits and pay any settlements or damage awards up to a certain amount, as defined by the insurance policy you choose. All wise business owners—whether sole proprietors, partners, LLC members, or corporation owners—get their businesses insured. Liability insurance and many other forms of business insurance are available to protect you from the types of lawsuits described above. Chapter 6 provides details on obtaining liability insurance.

However, insurance won't protect you from liability for business debts. For example, you'll still be on the hook if you fail to repay a loan or default on a lease.

Tax Savings With Corporations

Forming a corporation rather than running your business as a sole proprietor (or partnership or LLC taxed like a sole proprietorship or partnership) can lower your tax burden.

Corporate Taxation Basics

There are two different types of corporations, for which federal income tax rules differ greatly:

- C corporations, sometimes called regular corporations, and
- S corporations, also called small business corporations.

When you form a corporation, it automatically becomes a C corporation for federal tax purposes. C corporations are treated separately from their owners for tax purposes. C corporations must pay income taxes on their net income and file their own tax returns with the IRS. They also have their own income tax rate, which is lower than individual rates at some income levels.

You always have the option of having your corporation taxed as an S corporation instead of a C corporation by filing an election with the IRS. An S corporation is taxed like a sole proprietorship or partnership. Unlike a C corporation, it is not a separate taxpaying entity. Instead, corporate income or losses are passed through directly to the shareholders: you and anyone else who owns your business along with you. The shareholders must divide the taxable profit according to their shares of stock ownership and report that income on their individual tax returns. An S corporation normally pays no taxes, but must file an information return with the IRS showing how much the business earned or lost and indicating each shareholder's portion of the corporate income or loss.

Each type of corporation has benefits and drawbacks. S corporations have been the most popular type of corporation for one-person businesses, primarily because they can result in reduced Social Security and Medicare taxes. C corporations can be better for successful businesses with substantial profits. This is particularly true today because the Tax Cuts and Jobs Act significantly lowered the income tax rate paid by C corporations. However, a C corporation might not be a good choice if you expect your business to lose money in its first few years of operation, because you can't deduct such losses from any other income you have, such as salary income.

You can start out as an S corporation and switch to a C corporation later, or vice versa. But there can be tax costs if you convert a C corporation to an S corporation or other entity. Consult a tax professional before converting a corporation to another business entity form.

S Corporation Restrictions

There are some IRS restrictions on who can establish an S corporation and how it must be operated. For example:

- An S corporation may have no more than 100 shareholders.
- None of the shareholders may be nonresident aliens (noncitizens who don't live in the United States).
- An S corporation may have only one class of stock. You can't, for example, create preferred stock giving some shareholders special rights.
- The shareholders may only be individuals, estates, or certain trusts; a corporation may not be an S corporation shareholder.

If you are running a one-person business, are a U.S. citizen or live in the U.S., and will be the only shareholder, these restrictions will not affect your S corporation operations in the least.

RESOURCE

For additional information on corporate taxation, see:

- *Tax Savvy for Small Business,* by Frederick W. Daily (Nolo), and
- IRS Publication 542, *Corporations.* You can download it from the IRS website at www.irs.gov.

C Corporation Tax Rate

A C corporation is taxed separately from its owners. Like any other business, a C corporation is entitled to deduct its business expenses. It must then pay income taxes on its net income at the C corporation tax rate and file its own tax return with the IRS, using Form 1120 or Form 1120-A. You pay personal income tax on C corporation income only when it is distributed to you in the form of salary, bonuses, or dividends.

As a result of the Tax Cuts and Jobs Act, starting in 2018, the tax rate for regular C corporations was reduced from a top rate of 35% to a flat tax of 21% on all C corporation income. For the first time in decades, corporate tax rates are substantially lower than the income tax rates paid by higher-income individuals, which can be as high as 37%. However, because of double taxation, this doesn't necessarily mean you'll save on taxes by forming a C corporation for your business. When you're the owner of a C corporation, any direct payment of your corporation's profits to you will be considered a dividend by the IRS and taxed twice. First, the corporation will pay corporate income tax on the profit at the 21% corporate rate on its own return, and then you'll pay personal income tax on what you receive from the corporation.

C corporation dividends are usually taxed at capital gains rates. Higher-income taxpayers must also pay a 3.8% Medicare tax on net dividend and investment income. The tax rates on dividends range from 15% to 23.8% for high-income taxpayers. So, for example, if you pay tax on your corporation's dividends at the 15% rate, the total tax on every $100 distributed to you will amount to $32.85. The effective tax rate is 32.85%: 21% corporate tax rate + (79% x 15% capital gains rate) = 32.85%. And dividend payments are not deductible by the corporation. The effective 32.85% tax rate is higher than what taxpayers in all but the top two individual income tax brackets must pay, as shown in the following chart.

Income: Married Filing Jointly	Income: Individual	Individual Income Tax on Business Income	Combined Tax on C Corp. Distributions (21% C corporation tax + dividend tax)
$0 - $19,050	$0 - $9,525	10%	21%
$19,050 - $77,400	$9,525 - $38,700	12%	21%
$77,400 - $165,000	$38,700 - $82,500	22%	32.85%
$165,000 - $315,000	$82,500 - $157,500	24%	35.85%
$315,000 - $400,000	$157,500 - $200,000	32%	35.85%
$400,000 - $600,000	$200,000 - $500,000	35%	35.85%
over $600,000	over $500,000	37%	39.80%

Moreover, C corporations don't qualify for the new pass-through deduction that enables business owners other than C corporation share-holders to deduct up to 20% of their net business income from their income taxes. (See Chapter 9.) When the loss of this deduction is factored in, C corporations look even less desirable as a tax saving vehicle for most self-employed people.

Saving Tax Through Income Splitting

However, it is possible to save tax with a C corporation through income splitting.

You don't pay personal income tax on income your incorporated business earns until it is distributed to you (as individual income) in the form of salary, bonuses, or dividends. This allows you to split the income your business earns with your corporation.

Such income splitting can save income tax because the 21% C corpora-tion tax rate is lower than all but the bottom two individual tax rates as shown in the chart above. Thus, money kept in your C corporation and taxed only once is taxed less.

You can keep up to $250,000 of your business earnings in your corporate bank account without penalty. (This amount is reduced to $150,000 for professional corporations in the fields of health, law, accounting, architecture, or consulting.) You can use this money to expand your business, buy equipment, or pay yourself employee benefits, such as health insurance and pension benefits. However, if you keep more than $250,000, you'll become subject to an extra 15% tax called the "accumulated earnings tax." This tax is intended to discourage you from sheltering too much of your C corporation's earnings.

There is another substantial tax benefit to income splitting: You don't have to pay Social Security and Medicare taxes, also called employment taxes, on the profits you retain in your corporation. This is a 15.3% tax on salaries paid to employees, including yourself (up to a ceiling amount—$128,400 in 2018). For example, if you retain $10,000 in your corporation rather than paying it to yourself as salary, you'll save $1,530 in employment taxes.

EXAMPLE: Betty, a single taxpayer, owns and operates an incorporated construction contracting business. In one year, the corporation makes a net profit of $50,000, after paying Betty a salary of $120,000. Rather than pay herself the $50,000 in additional salary or bonuses, Betty decides to leave the money in her corporation. She uses the money to buy equipment. The corporation pays only the 21% corporate income tax on these retained earnings. Had Betty taken the $50,000 profit as salary or bonus, she would have had to pay a 32% personal income tax on her earnings.

Of course, income splitting is a viable option only if your business earns enough money for you to leave some in your corporate bank account, rather than distributing it all to yourself in the form of salary, bonuses, and benefits. Many self-employed people don't make enough money to even consider income splitting, particularly when they're starting out.

Tax-Free Fringe Benefits

The other significant tax benefit of forming a C corporation is that your corporation can provide you—its employee—with fringe benefits, which it can then deduct from the corporation's income as a business expense.

Possible employee fringe benefits include:
- health insurance for you and your family
- disability insurance
- reimbursement of medical expenses not covered by insurance
- deferred compensation plans
- group term life insurance
- retirement plans, and
- death benefit payments up to $5,000.

You do not have to include the value of premiums or other payments your corporation makes for your benefits in your personal income for income tax purposes. With health insurance costs skyrocketing, the ability to fully deduct these expenses is one of the best reasons to form a C corporation.

EXAMPLE: Marilyn incorporates her marketing business, of which she is the only employee. Marilyn's corporation provides her with health insurance for her and her family at a cost of $12,000 per year. The entire cost can be deducted from the corporation's income for corporate income tax purposes, but is not included as income on Marilyn's personal tax return.

Sole proprietors, S corporation owners, and partners in partnerships may deduct their health insurance premiums from their personal income tax, including their own health insurance premiums and those for their spouses and dependents. But this is a special personal deduction, not a business deduction. Thus, it doesn't reduce their income for Social Security and Medicare tax purposes.

S corporations can also provide their employees with some of the less popular tax-free fringe benefits, such as dependent care assistance and education assistance. Other business owners get no other tax-advantaged fringe benefits. If the entity provides the owner with another type of fringe benefit, the owner must include its value—and pay income tax on it—on the owner's personal tax return. For example, if an entity taxed as a partnership provides an owner with disability insurance, the owner must include the value of the insurance in his or her taxable income for the year. But there is one way around this: The business owner can hire his or her spouse as an employee and provide the spouse with benefits. (See Chapter 6.)

Saving on Payroll Taxes With an S Corporation

Unlike a C corporation, an S corporation is not a separate taxpaying entity. Instead, all of its profits and losses flow to its shareholders. Thus, there is no such thing as income splitting with an S corporation, nor are tax-free benefits available to the employee-shareholders of S corporations. Nevertheless, S corporations are extremely popular with many small business owners because owners can save significantly on Social Security and Medicare tax. This is a flat 15.3% tax on your first $128,400 in income (in 2018); the taxable income ceiling is adjusted annually for inflation. If you earn more than that amount, you also pay a 2.9% tax on your income up to $200,000 if you're single, or $250,000 if you're married filing jointly. All employee wages or net self-employment income over these amounts is subject to a 3.8% Medicare tax.

If you're a sole proprietor, partner in a partnership, or limited liability company member, all the income you receive from your business is subject to these taxes, called self-employment taxes. (See Chapter 10.) If you incorporate your business and you are an employee of your corporation, the same 15.3% tax must be paid. You pay half out of your employee compensation, and your corporation pays the other half.

Whether you are a sole proprietor, partner in a partnership, limited liability company member, or an employee of your C corporation, you must pay Social Security and Medicare taxes on all the income you take home.

Only S corporations offer you a way to take home some money without paying these taxes. You report your corporation's earnings on your personal tax return, and you must pay Social Security and Medicare taxes on any employee salary your S corporation pays you. You do not, however, have to pay such tax on distributions from your S corporation (the net profits that pass through the corporation to you personally). The larger your distribution, the less Social Security and Medicare tax you'll pay.

> **EXAMPLE:** Mel, a consultant, has formed an S corporation of which he's the sole shareholder and only employee. In one year, his corporation had a net income of $100,000. If Mel pays this entire amount to himself as employee salary, he and his corporation will have to pay a 15.3% Social Security and Medicare tax on all $100,000—a total tax of $15,300.
>
> Instead, Mel decides to pay himself only a $30,000 salary. The remaining $70,000 is passed through the S corporation and reported as an S corporation distribution on Mel's personal income tax return, not as employee salary. Because it is not viewed as employee earnings, Mel does not have to pay Social Security or Medicare tax on this amount. Mel pays only $4,590 in Social Security and Medicare taxes instead of $15,300, for a tax saving of $10,710.

Theoretically, if you took no salary at all, you would not owe any Social Security and Medicare taxes. As you might expect, however, this is not allowed. The IRS requires S corporation shareholder-employees to pay themselves a reasonable salary (at least what other businesses pay for similar services).

Of course, how much Social Security and Medicare tax you'll save with an S corporation depends on how much money your business earns. It's not worth forming an S corporation to save on these taxes if your business earns less than $50,000 or so. If Mel's S corporation in the above example had $40,000 in income instead of $100,000, it would still have had to pay him a reasonable salary—$30,000—leaving only $10,000 to be distributed to him free of Social Security and Medicare taxes. This would save him only $1,530 in such taxes, not enough to make up for the extra costs of incorporating (such as state franchise or corporate taxes, as well as the price of Mel's unemployment insurance and workers' compensation coverage, which the corporation must get for Mel because he's an employee). See "Extra State Taxes and Fees" below.

Avoid Medicare Net Investment Income Tax

The Medicare Net Investment Income (NII) tax is a 3.8% tax on net dividend and investment income earned by taxpayers whose adjusted gross income exceeds $200,000 for single taxpayers, or $250,000 for married couples filing jointly. The tax must be paid on the lower of:

- the amount by which the taxpayer's adjusted gross income (investment income plus other taxable income) exceeds the $200,000/$250,000 threshold, or
- the taxpayer's total net investment income.

The NII tax applies to all dividends issued by regular C corporations to their shareholders. But distributions paid to an S corporation shareholder are not subject to the NII tax, as long as the shareholder "materially participates" in the business. Thus, forming an S corporation also allows you to take money out of your business without having to pay this tax.

Disadvantages of the Corporate Form

Although there can be advantages to incorporating, there are also some disadvantages. You'll have to observe corporate formalities that will take some time and effort. And you'll have to pay some taxes and fees that other business entities don't pay.

Corporate Formalities

The IRS and state corporation laws require corporations to hold annual shareholder meetings and document important decisions with corporate minutes, resolutions, or written consents signed by directors or shareholders. Fortunately, this is not a substantial burden for small businesses with only one or a few shareholders and directors. Such corporations usually dispense with holding real annual meetings. Instead, the secretary of the corporation prepares minutes for a meeting that takes place on paper only. There are also standard minute and consent forms you can use to ratify important corporate decisions.

If you're audited and the IRS discovers that you have failed to comply with corporate formalities, you may face drastic consequences. For example, if you fail to document important tax decisions and tax elections with corporate minutes or signed consents, you may lose crucial tax benefits and risk substantial penalties. Even worse, if you neglect these basic formalities, the IRS or a court may conclude that your corporation is a sham—and you may lose the limited liability afforded by your corporate status. This could leave you personally liable for corporate debts.

In addition, certain institutions—such as banks, trusts, escrow and title companies, and landlords—often insist on a board or shareholder resolution that approves a corporate transaction with the institution— for example, borrowing money or renting property.

RESOURCE
For forms and guidance that will help you handle corporate formalities in a streamlined manner, see *The Corporate Records Handbook: Meetings, Minutes & Resolutions,* by Anthony Mancuso (Nolo).

More Tax on Sales of C Corporation Assets

C corporations face tax disadvantages when the shareholders want to sell their business. Buyers of businesses usually want to purchase a firm's assets, not buy corporate stock. When they buy assets, like equipment and business real estate, they can take depreciation deductions that they can't get when they purchase stock. When a C corporation sells its assets, two layers of tax must be paid. First, the C corporation pays tax at the 21% rate on any profit earned from the sale. Then, the corporate shareholders pay tax at capital gains rates when the proceeds are distributed to them. In contrast, only a single level of tax is paid when an S corporation sells its assets: The S corporation shareholders pay tax at their individual rates on any gain from the sale, but the S corporation itself pays no tax.

More Complex Bookkeeping

It is absolutely necessary that you maintain a separate corporate bank account if you incorporate. You'll need to keep a more complex set of books than you would as a sole proprietor. You'll also need to file a somewhat more complex tax return, or file two returns if you form a C corporation. And because you'll be an employee of your corporation, you'll need to pay yourself a salary and file employment tax returns. (See Chapter 8.) All of this takes time and costs money.

Extra State Taxes and Fees

Forming and running a corporation will require you to pay taxes and fees that you don't have to pay when you're a sole proprietor. How much you'll have to pay depends on your state's rules and how much money your business earns. These extra expenses include:

State corporate formation fees. You'll have to pay at least a few hundred dollars to form your corporation, perhaps more. For 50-state links to secretary of state or business filing offices, see the National Association of Secretaries of State website, www.nass.org.

Unemployment insurance. Because you'll be an employee of your corporation, it will be required to pay for state unemployment insurance for you. For links to all 50 state unemployment insurance agencies, see www.careeronestop.org, a website sponsored by the U.S. Department of Labor (search under the "Find Local Help" tab).

Workers' compensation insurance. In most states, your corporation will also be required to provide you, as its employee, with workers' compensation coverage. For links to all 50 state workers' compensation agencies, see www.workerscompensation.com.

State corporate tax or franchise fees. Most states require corporations doing business there to pay state corporate taxes and/or franchise fees. Some states require corporations to pay a minimum annual tax, no matter how little the corporation earns (or even if it incurs a loss). For example, California imposes a minimum $800 annual franchise tax on all corporations after their first year in business. For links to all 50 state tax agencies, see the IRS website at www.irs.gov/businesses/small-businesses-self-employed/state-links-1.

Special S corporation taxes. S corporations are not taxpaying entities for federal tax purposes, so they usually pay no federal corporate taxes. However, some states impose special state corporate taxes on S corporations. For example, California imposes a 1.5% tax on S corporation profits in addition to a minimum annual franchise tax of $800.

Professional Corporations

As explained above, you may be required to form a special kind of corporation called a "professional" corporation if you're involved in certain types of professions. The list of professionals who must form professional corporations varies from state to state but usually includes:

- accountants
- engineers
- lawyers
- psychologists
- social workers
- veterinarians, and
- health care professionals, such as doctors, dentists, nurses, physical therapists, optometrists, opticians, and speech pathologists.

Check with your state's corporate filing office—usually the office of the secretary of state or corporations commissioner—to see who is covered in your state. Links to each state's office can be found at www.nolo.com/legal-encyclopedia/secretary-state-offices.html.

Ownership Requirements

Typically, a professional corporation must be organized for the sole purpose of performing professional services, and all shareholders must be licensed to render that service. For example, in a medical corporation, all the shareholders must be licensed physicians.

Formation Requirements

You must use special forms and procedures to establish a professional corporation. For example, you might be required to obtain a certificate of registration from the government agency that regulates your profession, such as the state bar association. Also, you must include special language in your articles of incorporation.

Limits on Limited Liability

In most states, you cannot use a professional corporation to avoid personal liability for your own malpractice or negligence (your failure to exercise a reasonable amount of care while carrying out your professional responsibilities).

> EXAMPLE: Janet, a civil engineer, forms a professional corporation of which she is the sole shareholder. She designs a bridge that collapses, killing dozens of commuters. Even though Janet is incorporated, she could be held personally liable (along with her corporation) for any damages caused by her negligence in designing the bridge. Both Janet's personal assets and those of her corporation are at risk.

You can usually obtain additional business insurance to protect you against these types of risks, but it can be expensive. (See Chapter 6.)

However, if you're a professional involved in a group practice with other professionals, incorporating will shield you from personal liability for malpractice committed by other members of the group.

> EXAMPLE: Marcus is a doctor involved in an incorporated medical practice with Susan, Florence, and Louis. One of Louis' patients claims he committed malpractice and sues him personally and the group. Though both the group and Louis can be held liable, Marcus, Susan, and Florence cannot be held personally liable for Louis' malpractice. This means that their personal assets are not at risk.

Partnerships

If you are not the sole owner of your business, you cannot organize as a sole proprietorship. Instead, you automatically become a partner in a partnership unless you incorporate or form a limited liability company. If you co-own a business with one or more people and haven't formed a corporation or LLC, you're in a partnership right now, whether you intended it or not. This can include co-owning a business with your spouse (see "Sole Proprietorships for Spouses," above).

A partnership is much the same as a sole proprietorship except that there are two or more owners. Like a sole proprietorship, a partnership is legally inseparable from the owners (the partners). Ordinarily, a partnership does not pay taxes as an entity, although it files an annual tax form. Instead, partnership income and losses are passed through the partnership to the partners and reported on the partners' individual federal tax returns. Partners must file IRS Schedule E with their returns, showing their partnership income and deductions. However, a partnership has the option of being taxed as a regular C corporation or S corporation. This is done by filing IRS Form 2553, *Election by a Small Business Corporation.* (See the more detailed discussion of this option in "Limited Liability Companies (LLCs)," below.)

Like sole proprietors, partners are neither employees nor independent contractors of their partnership; they are self-employed business owners. A partnership does not pay payroll taxes on the partners' income or withhold income tax. Like sole proprietors, partners must pay income taxes (see Chapter 9) and self-employment taxes (see Chapter 10) on their partnership income.

Ownership

The main difference between a partnership and a sole proprietorship is that one or more people own the business along with you. This means that, among other things, you have to decide:

- how each partner will share in the partnership profits or losses
- how partnership decisions will be made
- what the duties of each partner are
- what happens if a partner leaves or dies, and
- how disputes will be resolved.

RESOURCE

For a detailed discussion of partnerships, including how to write partnership agreements, see *Form a Partnership: The Complete Legal Guide*, by Denis Clifford and Ralph Warner (Nolo).

Although not required by law, you should create a written partnership agreement answering these and other questions.

Personal Liability

Partners are personally liable for all partnership debts and lawsuits, just like sole proprietors. This means that you'll be personally liable for business debts your partners incur, whether or not you know about them.

Limited Partnerships

A limited partnership is a special kind of partnership with two types of partners. One or more "general partners" run the partnership business. The other "limited partners" invest in the partnership but don't help run it. The limited partners are a lot like corporate shareholders in that they aren't personally liable for the partnership's debts. The general partners are treated just like partners in normal partnerships and are liable for all partnership debts and lawsuits.

Limited partnerships are most commonly used to set up real estate and similar investments. Self-employed people rarely form them. If there are people who want to invest in your business but don't want to work in it or have any personal liability, you'd probably be better off forming a corporation and selling them shares. That way, you'll have the limited liability afforded by corporate status.

Registered Limited Liability Partnerships

In all states, professionals may set up a special type of partnership called a "registered limited liability partnership" (RLLP). In some states, including California, Nevada, New York, and Oregon, certain types of professionals are not allowed to form limited liability companies (LLCs, discussed in the next section), so RLLPs were established as an alternative.

RLLPs give their partner-owners the same type of limited liability as owners of professional corporations: The partners remain personally liable for their own malpractice but have limited liability for malpractice by other partners in the firm. In addition, in most states the RLLP partners receive personal liability protection from business debts and other lawsuits, such as slip-and-fall suits.

RLLPs are limited to professionals in certain occupations, typically people who work in the medical, legal, and accounting fields, and a few other professions in which a professional-client relationship exists. The list of professionals who may form an RLLP in a particular state is normally the same as the list of those eligible to form a professional corporation.

You need at least two partners to form an RLLP, and the partners must usually be licensed in the same or related professions. RLLPs are taxed like any other partnership: They are pass-through tax entities. The owners are taxed on all profits on their individual income tax returns at their individual tax rates. The RLLP itself is not taxed on profits.

Limited Liability Companies (LLCs)

The limited liability company, or LLC, is the newest type of business form in the United States. An LLC is taxed like a sole proprietorship or partnership but provides its owners with the same limited liability as a corporation. LLCs have become extremely popular with self-employed people because they are simpler and easier to run than corporations.

LLC Owners

Generally speaking, you are considered a business owner, not an employee, when you form an LLC. If, however, you receive a guaranteed salary or pay from the LLC (instead of or in addition to a share of the LLC's profits), you will be considered an employee of the LLC. For example, if an LLC owner is guaranteed $10,000 per year regardless of the LLC's profits, the owner is treated as an employee of the LLC, which means the $10,000 is subject to income tax withholding and employment taxes.

In some states, people involved in certain professions are not allowed to form regular LLCs. Instead, they must form "professional" LLCs and comply with special rules. Typically, these rules provide that only a licensed professional may own a membership interest in the professional LLC and require each member to carry a specified amount of malpractice insurance. These restrictions usually apply to doctors and other licensed health care professionals, lawyers, accountants, and, in some states, engineers. In a few states, however, such professionals are not allowed to form LLCs at all. Instead, they must form limited liability partnerships, as discussed in the previous section. These states include California and Rhode Island.

Even if you are allowed to form an LLC, doing so may not be advantageous if you are a professional and practice with others, rather than by yourself. This is because LLC laws in most states do not protect an LLC owner from personal liability for the malpractice of another professional in the practice. Thus, if you form an LLC, you could end up being personally liable for the malpractice of your co-owners. You'd be better off forming a professional corporation or an RLLP, both of which will shield you from personal liability for the malpractice of your co-owners.

Tax Treatment

IRS rules permit LLC owners to decide for themselves whether they want their LLC to be taxed as a pass-through entity or as a regular C corporation.

Pass-Through Entity

Ordinarily, LLCs are pass-through entities. This means that they pay no taxes themselves. Instead, all profits or losses are passed through the LLC to be reported on the LLC members' individual tax returns. This is the same as for a sole proprietorship, an S corporation, or a partnership.

If the LLC has only one member, the IRS treats it as a sole proprietorship for tax purposes. The member's profits, losses, and deductions are reported on his or her Schedule C, the same as for any sole proprietor. If the LLC has two or more members, each year it must prepare and file the same tax form used by a partnership—IRS Form 1065, *U.S. Return of Partnership Income*—showing the allocation of profits, losses, credits, and deductions passed through to the members. The LLC must also prepare and distribute to each member a Schedule K-1 form showing the member's allocations.

Changing Your Tax Treatment

Owners of LLCs have the option of being taxed as a C or an S corporation by making an "election" to receive corporation tax treatment with the IRS. Most businesses don't make this election. However, you might choose to be taxed as an S corporation if you want to save on employment taxes. Or, you might want to be taxed as a C corporation because you want to take advantage of the 21% C corporation tax rate, or you want to maximize tax-free employee fringe benefits.

If you want to make an election to change your tax treatment, you simply check the appropriate box on IRS Form 8832, *Entity Classification Election*, and file it with the IRS. The election can be made at any time. Once you file the form, your LLC will be treated exactly like a C corporation by the IRS (most states also recognize the election for state tax purposes). You'll have to file corporate tax returns and will have all the benefits and burdens of C corporation tax treatment described above.

If you want your LLC partnership to be taxed as an S corporation, you may do so by filing an S corporation election with the IRS, IRS Form 2553, *Election by a Small Business Corporation*. But you must meet all the conditions for S corporation status to be treated as one. Your business will still be an LLC for all other nontax purposes. If it turns out you don't like your corporation tax treatment, you can change back to partnership tax treatment by making another election, but ordinarily you must wait five years to do so. (Treas. Reg. § 301.7701-3(c)(1)(iv).)

Choosing to be taxed as a corporation has significant tax consequences, so it's wise to consult a tax pro before making the change. (Partnerships also have the option of choosing corporation tax treatment, as described above.)

Liability Concerns

LLC owners (members) enjoy the same limited liability from business debts and lawsuits as corporation owners.

Pros and Cons of an LLC

LLCs appear to be a clear favorite over partnerships because they offer the same tax benefits but also provide limited liability. They are also a serious alternative to corporations, because they are simpler but offer the same limited liability as corporations and have some tax advantages.

Advantages of LLCs

LLCs provide the same limited liability as corporations. However, as discussed previously, such "limited liability" can be more mythical than real.

Setting up an LLC takes about the same amount of time and money as setting up a corporation, but an LLC is simpler and easier to run thereafter. With a corporation, you must hold and record regular and special shareholder meetings to transact important corporate business. Even if you're the only corporate owner, you need to document your decisions. This isn't required for an LLC.

LLCs also allow more flexibility to allocate profits and losses among the business's owners than corporations do. The owners of an S corporation must pay taxes on profits or get the benefits of losses in proportion to their stock ownership. For example, if there are two shareholders and each owns 50% of the stock, they must each pay tax on 50% of the corporation's profits or get the benefits of 50% of the losses. In contrast, if you form an LLC, you have near total flexibility on how to allocate profits and losses among the owners; for example, one owner could get 75% of the profits and the other 25%. Of course, this will be useful only if two or more people own your business.

Unlike an LLC, a C corporation cannot allocate profits and losses to shareholders at all. Shareholders get a financial return from the corporation by receiving corporate dividends or a share of the corporate assets when it is sold or liquidated.

LLCs don't have to comply with the rules limiting who can form and own an S corporation.

And finally, LLC members are not employees of the LLC, so the LLC doesn't have to pay federal and state unemployment taxes for them. When you form a corporation, you are an employee of the corporation and such taxes must be paid.

Disadvantages of LLCs

Perhaps the biggest drawback of LLCs is that they don't offer the opportunity to save on self-employment taxes, as an S corporation does. LLC members who actively manage the business must pay self-employment tax on all the income they receive from the LLC, whether in the form of salary or distributions. In contrast, you can save on self-employment taxes by forming an S corporation because S corporation distributions—as opposed to salaries—are not subject to self-employment tax.

Moreover, money you retain in an S corporation or C corporation is not subject to self-employment taxes. This is not the case with an LLC that is treated as a pass-through entity. Whether you distribute your LLC profits to yourself or leave them in your company, you must pay self-employment taxes on your entire share of LLC profits.

In addition, firms that hire LLCs and pay them more than $600 per year must file Form 1099-MISC with the IRS to report the amount of the payment. (This requirement doesn't apply if the LLC has opted to be taxed as a corporation.) Generally speaking, hiring firms do not have to file Form 1099-MISC when they hire a corporation. For this reason, some businesses prefer to hire corporations instead of LLCs because they can avoid filing the 1099-MISC form altogether. Firms don't like filing the forms because they often lead to audits.

Forming an LLC

To form an LLC, you must file articles of organization with the appropriate state agency, usually the secretary of state. Your company's name will have to include the words "limited liability company" or "LLC" or a similar phrase as set forth in your state law. You should also create a written operating agreement, which is similar to a partnership agreement.

Nolo Resources for the Self-Employed

Throughout this chapter, we recommend other Nolo books (all available as hard copy and ebook) to help form a corporation, partnership, or LLC. Nolo also publishes a wide variety of other business books and online forms, as well as free information for the self-employed—from writing a business plan and borrowing money to writing contracts of various sorts to handling specific business tasks, such as negotiating a lease. Check out the "Business Formation" and "Small Business" centers on Nolo.com for details, including state-specific rules and resources on forming a corporation, LLC, partnership, or other business entity; taxes; business licenses; and more.

RESOURCE

For a complete explanation of how to form and run limited liability companies, see these Nolo titles:

- *Form Your Own Limited Liability Company,* by Anthony Mancuso
- *Nolo's Guide to Single-Member LLCs,* by David M. Steingold, and
- *Your Limited Liability Company: An Operating Manual,* by Anthony Mancuso.

Choosing a Form of Business

There is no one best business form—and choosing the one that will work best for you can be difficult. It all depends on your goals and preferences. The following chart may help you analyze which business form best furthers your own personal goals.

Goal	Sole Proprietorship	Partnership	LLC	S Corporation	C Corporation
Easiest and cheapest to form and operate	✓	✓			
Simplest tax returns	✓	✓			
Avoid state and federal unemployment taxes	✓	✓	✓		
Deduct losses from your personal taxes	✓	✓	✓	✓	
Distribute high profits	✓	✓	✓	✓	
Limit your personal liability			✓	✓	✓
Added credibility for your business				✓	✓
Save on Social Security taxes				✓	
Retain earnings in business (split income)					✓
Provide tax-deductible benefits to employees, including yourself					✓
Benefit from lower corporate tax rates					✓

Choosing and Protecting
Your Business Name

This chapter will help you choose a name for your business, which you should do shortly after you choose the right legal structure. You'll need to have a business name before you can establish bank accounts and market your business to others.

Naming your business can be confusing because you have the option of using different names in different contexts:

- **Legal name:** This is the official name of the person or entity that owns the business. If you are the only owner of your business, then its legal name is simply your full name. It is the name you must always use when you sign legal documents (for example, contracts), file tax returns, sign leases, apply for bank loans, or file lawsuits.
- **Trade name:** This is the name you use to identify your business to the public, on your business stationery, in advertising, on business cards, in websites, in marketing literature, and so on. Your legal name and your trade name can be, but don't have to be, the same.

Choosing a Legal Name

The legal name you choose will depend in part on what legal form you chose for your business. If, like the majority of self-employed people, you're a sole proprietor, your legal name will be simply your personal name.

> EXAMPLE: Joe Dokes forms his one-person business as a sole proprietorship. Therefore, his business's legal name is "Joe Dokes." This is the name he'll use to sign contracts, file tax returns, and so on.

Things become slightly more complicated if you form a general partnership. In this case, you can use either the last names of all the partners or a name you create as your legal name. If you want to use something other than your last names, you must draft and sign a written partnership agreement that includes your partnership's legal name. (Before you do this, read "Avoiding Conflicts With Other Trade Names," below.) In addition, you must register your partnership's legal name, as described in "Registering a Fictitious Business Name," below.

EXAMPLE: Charles Smith and Mary Jones enter into a partnership to invent and market a new type of can opener. They can call their partnership "Smith and Jones" or "The Smith and Jones Partnership," or they can choose a different name by drafting and signing a written partnership agreement. They decide to do the latter, naming their partnership "The Open Sesame Group."

If you create a corporation or limited liability company (LLC), you must choose its legal name. Like racehorses, corporations must have unique names. Once you decide upon a name, you must get permission to use it by registering the name with the appropriate agency in your state, usually the secretary of state's office.

Choosing a Trade Name

Your trade name is your public name: the moniker customers, clients, and other businesses will use when contacting you. Once you have picked a legal name, you must decide whether you also want to use it as your trade name.

Using Your Legal Name as Your Trade Name

The simplest thing to do is to use your legal name as your trade name. If, like most self-employed people, you're a sole proprietor, this means you'll use your personal name as your trade name. If you're a partnership, an LLC, or a corporation, you'll use the name you've chosen as your legal name (or the last names of the partners).

If you use your legal name as your trade name, you may add words at the end of it to make it clear that you are in business. For example, a sole proprietor consultant named Joe Dokes could use the name "Joe Dokes Consulting." There is no requirement that you do this, but you might find it helpful for marketing or identification purposes.

Depending on the state you live in, you may have to register your name if you add a word to the end. No matter where you live, however, you will always have to register your name if the additional words imply that your sole proprietorship has more than one owner (for example "Joe Dokes and Company").

Using a Made-Up Name as Your Trade Name

Instead of using your legal name as your trade name, you have the option of making up a new name that differs from your legal name.

> EXAMPLE: Roseanne Zeiss quits her job with a public relations firm and sets up her own public relations business as a sole proprietor. The legal name of Roseanne's sole proprietorship is "Roseanne Zeiss." Instead of using this as her trade name, she decides to call her business "AAA Publicity" so she'll come first in her local business directory.

For marketing purposes, self-employed people often prefer to make up names for their businesses rather than use their personal names. A made-up name can sound catchier, help identify what your business does, or make you seem more businesslike. But there is an additional benefit to making up a business name: It can help establish your legal status as an independent contractor. Employees, obviously, don't use business names. We'll discuss why this is so important in Chapter 15.

You can obtain bank accounts in your new name (provided you file a fictitious business name statement, discussed below). To help avoid confusion, if you use a made-up trade name, you'll usually need to provide it along with your legal name when you file lawsuits, apply for loans, and conduct most business transactions.

Avoiding Conflicts With Other Trade Names

Your trade name—regardless of whether it is the same as your legal name—should not be substantially similar to that of another business in your field. If your name is so similar to a name already being used that it may confuse the public, you could be sued under state and federal unfair competition laws. If you lose such a lawsuit, you may be required to change your business's name and even pay money damages.

Before selecting your trade name, conduct a name search. If you find the same or a similar name for a company involved in a field that is the same as or related to yours, it's probably best to choose a different name to avoid potential headaches later on. Similar names used by companies in fields entirely unrelated to yours probably won't pose a problem, unless the name is a famous trademark like McDonald's. For example, even if your name is Joe McDonald, don't name your business "McDonald's Consulting." Companies with famous names are usually fanatical about protecting them.

Here's how to do a quick and free name search:

- Do a Google search with your proposed name or names to see if other people or companies are using similar names.
- Check your county or state fictitious business name database to make sure no one else has already registered the name you want to use. Such databases—often called "fictitious business name indexes"—are usually searchable online.
- Check business directories for the cities in which you plan to do business, as well as surrounding areas.
- Find out if there is a similar federally registered trademark by using the U.S. Patent and Trademark Office (USPTO) website at www. uspto.gov. Choose the link for "Search trademark database." Then click on the button for "Search trademark database" to get free access to records of federally registered marks or marks that are pending. You can also conduct free trademark searches at www.trademarkia.com.
- In addition to checking the federal trademark register, it's a good idea to check your state's trademark database. The state register is often part of the secretary of state's office, though in some states it has a department of its own. Links to the online databases of all Secretary of State offices can be found at www.secstates.com.
- Find out if there is a similar unregistered trademark at the Thomas Register, a comprehensive listing of companies, brand names, products, and services (www.thomasnet.com).
- See if there is a similar Internet domain name by doing a search at any domain name registration website, such as Register.com (www. register.com) or Network Solutions (www.networksolutions.com).

Registering a Fictitious Business Name

In most states, a person or an entity doing business in the state under a name other than its own "true name" must register that business name with the county clerk or secretary of state's office as a "fictitious business name" or a "doing business as" (DBA) name. For a sole proprietorship or partnership, a business name is generally considered "fictitious" unless it contains the last name of the owner or all the general partners and does not suggest the existence of additional owners. Generally, using a name that includes words like "company," "associates," "brothers," or "sons" suggests additional owners and will make it necessary for a business to register.

If you fail to register, you open yourself up to many problems. For example, you may not be able to open a bank account in your business name. You also may be barred from suing on a contract you signed using the business name. And, if you don't register your fictitious name, you aren't putting other businesses on notice that the name is already in use. If a competing business can't find out that you're already using the name, it might take the name—and possibly some of your business—for its own. There is usually a time limit within which you must register your name, often within a month or two after you start doing business.

In most states, fictitious business name registration is handled at the county level. You'll have to register in the county where your business is located; in some states, you must also register in any other counties where you do business.

Procedures vary from state to state and county to county, but it's usually a routine process. Many states require you to begin by searching the county or state fictitious name database to make sure the name you've chosen isn't already being used by someone else. If the name is available, you must obtain a name registration form (over the phone, in person, or from the office's website) and submit it with the correct filing fee, typically $10 to $50.

Some states also require you to publish your fictitious name in a newspaper and then submit an affidavit (sometimes called a proof of publication) to the county clerk or state agency to show that you fulfilled the publication requirement. This makes it easier to track down those who change their business names to confuse and avoid creditors. Some communities have newspapers that specialize in publishing such legal notices. If not, your local newspaper should be able to help you with this filing if your state requires it.

Your fictitious business name registration will be good for a specified period of time after which it must be renewed; five years is a common period. If important facts in your statement change—for example, the number of owners or your business address—you may have to renew your statement before it expires. Check with your county clerk or state agency to find out which types of changes trigger a renewal requirement.

RESOURCE
Need state filing information? For links to fictitious name filing requirements in all 50 states, search "50-State Guide to Establishing a Sole Proprietorship" in the Sole Proprietors section of Nolo.com.

Naming a Corporation or Limited Liability Company

If you form a corporation or an LLC, you must get permission to use your corporate or LLC name by registering it with your state's secretary of state or similar official.

Registering a Corporate Name

To register a corporate name, you must follow these three steps:

1. **Select a permissible name.** Most states require you to include a word or its abbreviation that indicates corporate status, such as "Corporation," "Incorporated," "Company," or "Limited" (or "Corp.," "Inc.," Co.," or "Ltd."). Several states also require that the name be in English or Roman characters.

2. **Clear your name.** Next, you must make sure that your corporate name is distinguishable from any corporate name already registered in your state. Your state won't register a corporate name that too closely mimics a name already on file. The secretary of state or other corporate filing agency will do a search for you prior to authorizing the use of your name. In most states, you can check on the availability of names by using the secretary of state's website or calling its office.

3. **Reserve your corporate name.** A corporation can usually reserve a name before incorporating if the name qualifies for registration otherwise. This freezes out other would-be registrants from claiming the same name or a similar one during the period of reservation, usually 120 days. Most states permit you to extend the reservation for one or more additional 120-day periods for a fee.

The reservation process involves sending an application for reservation to the secretary of state, or the designated office, with a fee. Some states even permit you to reserve a corporate name over the telephone. You can find out about your state's procedures by calling the office of the secretary of state or corporate commissioner.

RESOURCE

Need state information on corporate names? For links to corporation name requirements in all 50 states, search "50-State Guide to Forming a Corporation" in the Corporations section of Nolo.com.

Registering a Limited Liability Company Name

Registering a name for an LLC is very similar to registering a corporate name. You must choose a name that conforms with your state's LLC requirements. Most states require you to use the words "Limited Liability Company," "Limited Company," or their abbreviations ("LLC" or "LC") in your name.

You then call the appropriate state office and ask if the name or names you've chosen are available. Most states allow you to reserve LLC names for 30 to 120 days by paying a small fee, usually no more than $50.

RESOURCE

Need state LLC information? For links to LLC name requirements in all 50 states, search "50-State Guide to Forming an LLC" in the LLCs section of Nolo.com.

Legal Effect of Registering a Name

People often think that once they have complied with all the registration requirements for their trade name, they have the right to use that name for all purposes. This isn't so.

Registering a corporate or an LLC name or registering a trade name by filing a fictitious business name or "doing business as" statement does not make your name a trademark. Though registering a name allows you to do business under that name, it does not give you any ownership right in the name: In other words, it does not allow you to prevent others from using it. If someone else uses your name to identify a product or service to the public before you do, it doesn't make any difference that you registered the name as a legal, trade, corporate, or an LLC name. If they were the first to use the name publicly in the marketplace, they will have the exclusive right to use that name in the marketplace.

Simply put, if the name you have registered was already in use or federally registered as a trademark or service mark, you will have to limit your use of the name to your checkbook and bank account. The minute you try to use the name in connection with marketing your goods or services, you risk infringing the existing trademark or service mark.

If you plan to use your business name in your future marketing plans, in addition to complying with name registration requirements, you must make sure that no one else is using the name as a trademark. If you plan to market your goods or services on the Internet, you'll also want to make sure that no one else has already taken your proposed name as his or her domain name. If so, at the very least, you'll have to use a slightly modified name to do business in cyberspace.

Choosing a Trademark

A trademark is a distinctive word, phrase, logo, or other graphic symbol that's used to distinguish one product from another, such as Ford cars and trucks, Kellogg's cornflakes, Apple computers, and Microsoft software.

A service mark is similar to a trademark, except that trademarks promote products while service marks promote services. Some familiar service marks include: McDonald's (fast-food service), CBS's stylized eye in a circle (television network service), and the Olympic Games' multicolored interlocking circles (international sporting event).

The word "trademark" is also a generic term used to describe the entire body of state and federal law that covers how businesses distinguish their products and services from the competition. Each state has its own set of laws establishing when and how trademarks can be protected. There is also a federal trademark law called the Lanham Act (15 U.S.C. § 1050 and following), which applies in all 50 states.

If, like many self-employed people, you operate within a single state, you'll be covered primarily by your state trademark law should you claim or become subject to a claim of trademark infringement. But if you do business in more than one state, you may be covered by both federal and state law. The various trademark laws don't differ greatly except that some state laws allow trademark owners to collect greater damages from infringers than federal law.

RESOURCE

For a detailed discussion of trademarks, including how to register a trademark or do a trademark search (topics discussed below), see *Trademark: Legal Care for Your Business & Product Name*, by Stephen Fishman (Nolo).

Trade Names Are Not Trademarks

Your trade name is neither a trademark nor a service mark and is not entitled to trademark protection unless you use it to identify a particular product or service that you produce and sell to the public. Businesses often use shortened versions of their trade names as trademarks. For example, Apple Computer Corporation uses the name "Apple" as a trademark on its line of computer products.

A trade name acts like a trademark when it is used in such a way that it creates a separate commercial impression: In other words, when it identifies a product or service. This can be hard to figure out, especially when comparing trade names and service marks, because both often appear in similar places, such as letterheads, advertising copy, signs, and displays. But some general principles apply:

- If the full name, address, and phone are used, it's probably a trade name.
- If a shortened version of the trade name is used, especially with a design or logo beside or incorporating it, the trade name becomes a trademark.

EXAMPLE: Joe, a self-employed website designer, calls his unincorporated business "Acme Website Development." He files a fictitious business name statement with his county clerk. When he uses the name "Acme Website Development" along with his office address on his stationery, it is just a trade name, not a trademark. However, Joe develops a Web design utility program that he calls "Acme Tools" and markets it over the Internet. "Acme Tools" is a trademark.

Selecting a Trademark

Not all trademarks are treated equally by the law. The best trademarks are "distinctive." They stand out in a customer's mind because they are inherently memorable. The more distinctive or "strong" a trademark is, the more legal protection it will receive. Less distinctive or "weak" marks may be entitled to little or no legal protection. Obviously, it is much better to have a strong trademark than a weak one.

Good examples of distinctive marks are arbitrary, fanciful, or coined names such as "Kodak" and "Xerox." Examples of poorly chosen marks include the following:

- personal names, including nicknames, first names, surnames, and initials
- marks that describe the attributes of the product or service or its geographic location. For example, marks such as "Quick Printing" or "Oregon Marketing Research" are initially weak and subject to few legal protections until they have been in use long enough to be easily recognized by customers.
- names with bad translations, unfortunate homonyms (soundalikes), or unintended connotations. For example, a French soft drink called "Pschitt" had to be renamed for the U.S. market.

Selecting a mark usually begins with brainstorming for general ideas. After you have selected several possible marks, your next step may be to use formal or informal market research techniques to see how the potential marks will be accepted by consumers. Then, you have to conduct a trademark search, to find out whether the same or similar marks are already being used.

Registering a Trademark

If you use all or part of your business name or any other name as a trademark or service mark, consider registering it as such (in addition to your state trade or corporate name registration). Trademark registration is not mandatory, but it's a good idea: It makes it easier for you to protect your mark against would-be copiers and puts others on notice that the mark is already taken.

If you do business only in one state, register your mark with your state trademark office. Most local service businesses that don't do business across state lines or sell to interstate travelers fall into this category. If you do business in more than one state, register with the USPTO in Washington, DC. To register, you must fill out an application and pay a fee. Be prepared to work with your state or federal trademark officials to get your registration approved.

The USPTO has a useful website at www.uspto.gov that contains information about trademarks and trademark registration. You can register your trademark online using the Trademark Electronic Application System (TEAS). TEAS allows you to fill out a trademark registration form and check it for completeness over the Internet. You then submit the form directly to the USPTO over the Internet, making an official filing online.

"Intent to Use" Registration

If you intend to use a trademark for a product or service sold in more than one state in the near future, you can reserve the right to use the mark by filing an "intent to use" registration with the USPTO.

If the mark is approved, you have six months to actually use the mark on a product sold to the public and file papers with the USPTO describing the use, accompanied by a $100 fee. If necessary, you may extend this period up to five times, for six months at a time, if you have a good explanation (and pay $150) for each extension. The ownership becomes effective when you put the mark in use and complete the application process, but ownership will be deemed to have begun on the date you filed the application.

You should file an intent to use registration as soon as you have decided on a trademark for a forthcoming product. Don't delay: Your competitors are trying to come up with good trademarks too, and may be considering using a mark like the one you want to use.

Using a Trademark Notice

The owner of a trademark that has been registered with the USPTO is entitled to use a special symbol along with the trademark. This symbol notifies the world of the registration. Use of trademark notices is not mandatory but makes it much easier for the trademark owner to collect damages in case of infringement. It also deters others from using the mark.

The most commonly used notice for trademarks registered with the USPTO is an "R" in a circle, or ®, but "Reg. U.S. Pat. & T.M. Off." may also be used. The "TM" superscript, or ™, may be used to denote marks that have been registered on a state basis only or marks that are in use but have not yet been officially registered with the USPTO. Do not use the copyright symbol, or ©, as it has nothing to do with trademarks.

Enforcing Trademark Rights

Depending on the strength of the mark and whether and where it has been registered, a trademark owner may be able to bring a court action to prevent others from using the same or similar marks on competing or related products.

Trademark infringement occurs when an alleged infringer uses a mark that is likely to cause consumers to confuse the infringer's products with the trademark owner's products. A mark need not be identical to one already in use to infringe upon the owner's rights. If the proposed mark is similar enough to the earlier mark to risk confusing the average consumer, its use will likely be an infringement.

Choosing an Internet Domain Name

Most self-employed people who market their services or products to the public have a website of some kind. Of course, to have a website, you must choose and register a domain name: the unique address in cyberspace at which your website is located.

Because each domain name must be unique, no two different businesses can have the same domain name. If somebody is already using a name you want, you probably won't be able to use it.

It's easy to find out if someone is already using a domain name you want to use. Go to any domain registration website and type in the name you want to use. Then click on "Search." The website will tell you if the name is available or if it is already taken, in which case it will suggest alternatives. To find out who owns the name you want, go to www.whois.net. Type the domain name in the search field and you can see the registration records for the domain name, including the name and contact information for the name owner. If you have your heart set on a particular domain name that is already taken, you can try to purchase the name from the person or company that owns it.

If you register your domain name, no one else can use it for the same purpose on the Internet.

Registering a domain name is very easy. There are several private companies that will register a name for you for a small fee. You just go to one of their websites, type in the name you want, and provide your contact information and a credit card number.

The registration fees these services charge vary, so you might want to check several to see which will give you the best deal. To help you comparison shop, a list of approved domain name registries is available at www.internic.net/regist.html.

Conducting a Name Search

Before choosing a trademark or domain name, conduct a name search to see if someone in a related business is already using the same or a similar name. If the name you want is already in use, choose a different name. Obviously, you don't want to spend money on marketing and advertising a name or mark only to discover that it infringes another name or mark and you must change it.

Doing a Search on Your Own

As with searching for conflicts with your trade name, many resources are available to help you do all or part of a trademark search yourself, including:

- the USPTO online trademark database, which may be accessed for free from the USPTO website at www.uspto.gov (from the home page, select "Search trademark database," then click on the "Search trademark database" button), and
- numerous fee-based trademark search engines that can also be used for a search: these include CompuMark (www.compumark.com) and LegalZoom (www.legalzoom.com). You can find others by performing a Google search for trademark services.

In addition to checking for federally registered trademarks, it's a good idea to check your state's trademark database. The state trademark database is often part of the secretary of state's office, though in some states it has a department of its own. You can also check one of several sites that search for trademarks registered in all 50 states. This is an especially good idea if you'll be doing business in more than one state.

You should also do an Internet search to see how and where the name you want is being used. Searching for unregistered trademarks is important because, even if a trademark hasn't been registered, its existence could prevent you from registering the trademark in your own name or from even using the trademark legally. You can search domain names in use by Web-based businesses at any domain name registrar. You can find a list of domain name registrars at ICANN, the organization that administers registrations, www.icann.org.

Hiring a Search Firm

If your preliminary search does not turn up any similar marks (referred to as "potential conflicts"), you can, if you wish, hire a professional search firm to prepare a complete report of any similar federal, state, common law, or if desired, international trademarks. These searches are expensive (often $300–$500).

Two companies that perform professional searches are Thompson CompuMark (http://trademarks.thomsonreuters.com) and Trademark Express (www.tmexpress.com). ●

Home Alone or Outside Office

When you're self-employed, you have the option of working from home or from an outside office. This chapter covers the pros and cons of each choice, including the special tax deductions available for home office expenses.

Pros and Cons of Working at Home

Legally, it makes little difference where you do your work. The basic legal issues discussed in this book (such as deciding on a legal form and name for your business and collecting from clients) are the same whether you run your business from your garage or from the top floor of a high-rise office building. Your choice may affect whether you can deduct your office expenses; otherwise, your taxes will be the same regardless of where you work.

For the most part, the issues to consider when deciding whether to work at home are more practical than legal: whether you can afford to pay office rent, whether a home office is more convenient (for child care or to avoid a commute, for example), whether working at home will disrupt your home or neighborhood, and so on.

Benefits of Working at Home

Working at home is popular among the self-employed because it can save time and money and improve productivity.

No Office Rent Expenses

For many self-employed people, the greatest benefit of working at home is that you don't have to pay rent for an office. Office rents vary enormously depending upon the area, but you'll likely have to pay several hundred dollars per month for even a small office. In large cities, you may have to spend much more. Look online at craigslist.org to get an idea of going rates.

If you work at home, you can use the money you save in office rent to expand your business or pay your living expenses. And while you can deduct your office rent as a business expense, you may also be able to deduct home office expenses.

One way to reduce the cost of office space is to obtain it from a client that hires you. Many hiring firms are willing to provide independent contractors with desk space. This is particularly likely if having you around will make life easier for them. Some firms may even offer to provide you with office space at no cost to you. However, to safeguard your self-employed status, it's best that you pay something for the space. It doesn't have to be much, and you can charge the client slightly more for your services to cover the cost. Your client shouldn't mind arranging things this way, because it will help the client if the IRS conducts an audit and questions your status.

No Commuting Time or Expenses

Working at home means you don't have to commute to an outside office every day. The American Automobile Association estimated that it cost 56.5¢ per mile to drive a car 15,000 miles in 2017. Using this figure, if working at home allows you to drive 6,000 fewer miles per year (500 miles per month), you'd save $3,390 per year.

Not having to commute also saves you time. If you commute just 30 minutes each day, you're spending 120 hours each year behind the wheel of your car. That's three full 40-hour weeks that you could use earning money in your home office.

You Can Deduct Some Commuting Costs

When you have an outside office, you can't deduct your commuting expenses: what it costs to get from your home to your office and back again. However, if your main office is at home, you may deduct the cost of driving from home to meet clients or to other locations to conduct business.

You Can Deduct Home Office Expenses

If you arrange things correctly, you can deduct your home office expenses, including a portion of your home rent or mortgage payment, utilities, and other expenses. The home office deduction is covered in detail later in this chapter.

The home office deduction is particularly valuable if you rent your home. It enables you to deduct a portion of what is likely your largest single expense (your rent), an item that is not ordinarily deductible from your personal income tax.

Benefits Other Than Money

Of course, the benefits of working at home are not just monetary. For many self-employed people, other factors are equally valuable, such as the increased flexibility they have over their daily schedule. You can, if you wish, work late at night in your pajamas, which can be difficult to do if you're renting an office!

When you work at home, it's also easier to deal with child care issues and household chores and errands. You may also have more contact with your family.

Drawbacks of Working at Home

There are, however, potential drawbacks to working from home. Fortunately, there are usually things you can do to avoid or ameliorate the problems.

Some Clients Don't Take You Seriously

Although working at home has become very common for all types of service providers, some self-employed people who work at home say that clients don't take them seriously. Some clients may be reluctant to deal with a home-based businessperson. This can make it harder for you to get your business established.

There are many things you can do to help create and maintain a professional image. For example:

- Obtain and use professional-looking business cards, envelopes, and stationery.
- Create a professional-looking website for your business.
- Hold meetings at clients' offices or temporary office space, rented by the hour, instead of at your home.
- Rent a mailbox to receive your business mail instead of using your home address.
- Use an assumed name for your business rather than your own name (see Chapter 3).
- Consider incorporating or forming a limited liability company so that clients will be hiring a business, not you personally (see Chapter 2).

You can also rent a "virtual office." For one monthly fee, you can get a professional mailing address, mail forwarding, answering services, business meeting space, and even casual workspace if you get tired of working at home. Such services are usually far cheaper than renting a "real" office.

Restrictions on Home-Based Businesses

Another major problem for the home-based self-employed is restrictions on home businesses imposed by cities, condominium associations, and deed restrictions. It may actually be illegal for you to work at home. These restrictions are explained later in this chapter.

Lack of Security

Your home is likely not as secure as an office building that is filled with people, has burglar alarms, employs security guards, or has security cameras. If you're handling large amounts of cash or other valuable items, you may prefer to work in a more secure environment than your home.

However, there are many commonsense precautions you can take to make your home office more secure. For example:

- Rent a post office box to receive your mail instead of having it delivered to your home.
- Refuse to let equipment servicers or vendors visit without an appointment.
- Obtain good locks and use them.
- Exercise caution when communicating about your absence (for example, don't announce on your Facebook page that you're going out of town).

Isolation, Interruptions, and Other Factors

Some people have trouble adapting to working at home because of the isolation. They miss the social interaction of a formal office setting. However, renting an outside office where you'll be all by yourself won't necessarily end the isolation problem.

In contrast, other self-employed people find it difficult to get any work done at home because of a lack of privacy or interruptions from children and other family members. Others gain weight because the refrigerator is always nearby or end up watching television instead of working.

Most of the millions of self-employed people who work at home, however, are not fazed by these problems.

Businesses Well Suited to Home Offices

Home offices can work well for any business that is normally done in a simple office setting. This includes a multitude of service businesses, such as:

- website design
- accounting or bookkeeping
- computer programming
- consulting
- writing or editing
- telemarketing
- graphic artwork, and
- financial planning.

A home office is also an ideal choice for businesses that do work primarily at clients' offices or other outside locations, including:

- building contracting
- traveling sales
- house and carpet cleaning
- home repair work
- courier or limousine service
- piano tuning
- pool cleaning
- hazardous waste inspection, and
- catering.

Businesses Poorly Suited to Home Offices

Any business that will disrupt your household or neighborhood is not well suited for the home. These include businesses that generate substantial amounts of noise, pollution, or waste.

A home office is not your best choice if substantial numbers of clients or customers must visit you in your office. This could create traffic and parking problems in your neighborhood and cause neighbors to complain. One possible solution to this problem is to rent an office part time or by the hour just to meet clients. Such rentals are available in many cities and will be cheaper than renting a full-time office.

You may also have problems if your business requires you to store a substantial amount of inventory. However, you can still spend most of your time at home by renting a separate storage space for your inventory.

Finally, a home office may not work well if you need to have several employees working with you. This could cause parking problems in your neighborhood and space problems in your home. Moreover, many local zoning laws prevent home businesses from having more than one or two employees. One way around this problem is to allow your employees to work from their own homes, too.

Restrictions on Home-Based Businesses

If you decide to work at home, you may have issues with local zoning laws, business or land use restrictions in your lease, or condominium rules. You should investigate these potential problems before you open your home office. Even if your community is unfriendly to home offices, there are many things you can do to avoid problems before they arise.

Zoning Restrictions

Municipalities have the legal right to establish rules on the types of activities you can conduct in their different geographical areas. For example, they often establish commercial zones for stores and offices, industrial zones for factories, and residential zones for houses and apartments.

Though some communities have no zoning restrictions at all (for example, Houston), most do. These restrictions often include laws that limit the kind of business you can conduct in a residential zone. The purpose of these restrictions is to help maintain the peace and quiet of residential neighborhoods.

Fortunately, while some communities remain hostile to home businesses, the growing trend across the country is to permit them. Many cities—Los Angeles and Phoenix, for example—have updated their zoning laws to permit many home businesses.

Research Your Local Zoning Ordinance

Your first step to determine whether you might have a problem working at home is to read your local zoning ordinance carefully. Get a copy from your city's or county's website, your city or county clerk's office, or your public library.

Zoning ordinances that limit businesses in residential areas are worded in many different ways. Some are extremely vague, allowing "customary home-based occupations." Others allow homeowners to use their houses for a wide but unspecific array of business purposes, such as "professions and domestic occupations, crafts, and services." Still others contain a detailed list of approved occupations, such as "law, dentistry, medicine, music lessons, photography, [and] cabinetmaking."

Ordinances permitting home-based businesses typically include detailed regulations on how to carry out business activities. These regulations vary widely, but the most common ones limit your use of on-street signs, car and truck traffic, and the number of employees who can work at your house on a regular basis (some prohibit employees altogether). Some ordinances also limit the percentage of your home's floorspace that you can devote to your business. Study your ordinance carefully to see how these rules apply to you. If you still aren't sure whether your business is allowed, you may be tempted to discuss the matter with zoning or planning officials. However, until you figure out the rules and politics of your locality, gather information without identifying or calling attention to yourself. For example, have a friend who lives nearby make general inquiries.

Hard Lobbying Can Pay Off

If your town has an unduly restrictive zoning ordinance, you can try to get it changed. For example, a self-employed person in the town of Melbourne, Florida, was surprised to discover that his local zoning ordinance barred home-based businesses. He decided to try to change the law.

He sent letters to his local public officials but got no response. He then reviewed the zoning ordinances favoring home offices from nearby communities and drafted an ordinance that he presented to the city council. He enlisted support from a local home business association and got a major story about his battle printed in the local newspaper. After several hearings, the city council voted unanimously to amend the zoning ordinance to allow home offices.

Determine Local Attitudes on Enforcement

Even if your locality has restrictive zoning laws, you won't necessarily have problems with your home business. In most communities, such laws are rarely enforced unless one of your neighbors complains to local officials. Neighbors usually complain because you make a lot of noise or have large numbers of clients, employees, or delivery people coming and going, causing parking or traffic problems. If you're unobtrusive—for example, you work quietly in your home office all day and rarely receive business visitors—it's unlikely that your neighbors will complain (or even notice).

Unfortunately, some communities are extremely hostile toward home businesses and actively try to prevent them. This is most likely to be the case if you live in an upscale, purely residential community. Even if you're unobtrusive, these communities may bar you from working at home if they discover what you're up to. If you live in such a community, you'll really need to keep your head down to avoid discovery if you decide to work at home.

To determine your community's enforcement style, talk to your local chamber of commerce and other self-employed people in your town. Friends or neighbors who are actively involved with your local government may also be good resources.

Keeping Your Home Business Unobtrusive

There are many ways to keep your home business unobtrusive so as to ward off neighbor complaints. If you get a lot of deliveries, arrange for mail and packages to be received by a private mailbox service such as Mail Boxes, Etc. Don't put your home address on your website, stationery, or business cards. Also, try to visit your clients in their offices instead of having them come to your home office.

A husband and wife team of psychiatrists who ran a 24-hour group therapy practice in a quiet neighborhood of Victorian homes provides a perfect example of how to get neighbors to complain about a home office: They paved every inch of their yard for parking and installed huge lights to illuminate the entire property.

Inform Your Neighbors

Good neighbor relations are the key to avoiding zoning problems. You may want to tell your neighbors about your plans to start a home business so they'll know what to expect and will have the chance to air their concerns to you directly. Explain that there are advantages for them to your working at home, including having someone home during the day could improve security for the neighborhood. You might even offer to meet a neighbor's repairperson or accept his or her packages. If any of your neighbors stay home during the day, try to be particularly helpful to them because they are more likely to complain about a home office than neighbors who spend their days at work.

On the other hand, if your relations with your neighbors are already shaky or you happen to be surrounded by unreasonable people, you may be better off not telling them you work at home. If you're inconspicuous and do not cause problems, they may never know what you're doing.

If Your Neighbors Complain

If your neighbors complain about your home office, you'll probably have to deal with your local zoning bureaucracy. If local zoning officials decide you should close your home business, they'll first send you a letter ordering you to do so. If you ignore this and any subsequent letters, they may file a civil lawsuit against you seeking an injunction: a court order that enjoins (stops) you from operating your home business in violation of the zoning ordinance. If you violate such an injunction, a judge can fine you or even put you in jail.

Immediately after receiving the first letter from zoning officials, talk with the person at city hall who administers the zoning law, usually someone in the zoning or planning department. City officials may drop the matter if you'll agree to make your home business less obtrusive.

If this doesn't work, apply to your planning or zoning board for a "variance": an exception that lets you violate the zoning ordinance. To obtain a variance, you'll need to show that your business does no harm to your neighborhood and that relocation would deprive you of your livelihood. Be prepared to answer the objections of unhappy neighbors who may loudly oppose the proposed variance at the planning commission meeting.

You can also try to get your city council or zoning board to change the local zoning ordinance. To do this, you'll probably have to lobby some city council members or planning commissioners. It will be useful to enlist the support of the local chamber of commerce and other business groups. Try to get your neighbors to help as well. For example, have as many of them as possible sign a petition favoring the zoning change. Many people with home offices are organizing on local, state, and national levels to lobby for new zoning laws that permit home offices.

Finally, you can take the matter to court, claiming that the local zoning ordinance is invalid or that the city has misinterpreted it. You'll probably need the help of a lawyer familiar with zoning matters to do this.

> RESOURCE
> **For detailed guidance on how to handle neighbor disputes,** including disputes over home-based businesses, see *Neighbor Law: Fences, Trees, Boundaries & Noise*, by Emily Doskow and Lina Guillen (Nolo).

Private Land Use Restrictions

The government uses zoning laws to restrict how you can use your property. However, there may also be private restrictions on how you can use your home. Restrictions are commonly found in:

- property deeds
- homeowner association rules, or
- leases.

Property Deed Restrictions

Some property deeds contain restrictions, called "restrictive covenants," limiting how you can use your property. Restrictive covenants often bar or limit home-based businesses.

You can find out if your property is subject to such restrictions by reading your title insurance policy or deed. If your neighbors believe you're violating these restrictions, they can take action in court to stop you. Such restrictions are usually enforced by the courts unless they are unreasonable or the character of the neighborhood has changed so much since they were written that it makes no sense to enforce them. For example, a court might refuse to enforce such a restriction if all you do is work alone in your home office all day without bothering anybody.

Homeowners' Association Rules

One in five Americans lives in a planned community that has a home-owners' association. When you buy property in such a development, you automatically become a member of the homeowners' association. You also become subject to its rules, which are usually set forth in a lengthy document called "covenants, conditions, and restrictions" (CC&Rs). CC&Rs often regulate, in minute detail, what you can do on, in, and to your property. The homeowners' association is in charge of modifying and enforcing these rules.

The CC&Rs for many developments specifically bar home-based business offices. The homeowners' association may be able to impose fines and other penalties against you if your home business violates the rules. It could also sue you in court to get money damages or other penalties. Some homeowners' associations are very strict about enforcing their rules against home businesses while others are less so.

Carefully study the CC&Rs before you buy into a condominium, planned development, or cooperative to see if home-based business offices are prohibited. If so, you may want to buy somewhere else.

If you're already in a development that bars home-based business offices, you may be able to avoid problems if you're unobtrusive and your neighbors are unaware that you have a home office. However, the best course may be to seek to change the CC&Rs. Most homeowner associations rule through a board of directors whose members are elected by all the members of the association. Lobby members of the board about changing the rules to permit home offices. If that fails, you and like-minded neighbors could try to get seats on the board and gain a voice in the association's policy making.

Lease Restrictions

If you're a renter, check your lease before you start your home business. Many standard lease forms prohibit a tenant from conducting a business on the premises or prohibit certain types of businesses. Your landlord could evict you if you violate such a lease provision.

Most landlords don't want to evict their tenants. Many don't care what you do on your premises as long as it doesn't disturb your neighbors or cause damage. Keep up good neighbor relations to prevent complaints.

However, if you have business visitors, your landlord may require you to obtain liability insurance in case a visitor has an accident, such as a trip or fall on the premises. (See Chapter 6.)

Deducting Your Home Office Expenses

If you elect to work from home, the federal government allows you to deduct your home office expenses from your income taxes. This is so whether you own or rent your home. Although this tax deduction is commonly called the "home office deduction," it is not limited to home offices. You can also take it if, for example, you have a workshop or studio at home.

Because some people claim that the home office deduction is an audit flag for the IRS, many self-employed people who may qualify for it are afraid to take it. The IRS denies that taking the home office deduction increases your audit risk, and there is no empirical evidence that it does so. Also, you have nothing to fear from an audit if you're entitled to the deduction.

However, if you intend to take the deduction, you should also make the effort to understand the requirements and set up your home office in a way that meets them.

Sideline Business May Qualify for Home Office Deduction

You don't have to work full time in a business to qualify for the home office deduction. If you satisfy the requirements, you can take the deduction for a sideline business you run from a home office. However, the total amount you deduct cannot exceed your income from the business.

EXAMPLE: Barbara works full time as an editor for a publishing company. She also spends about 15 hours a week writing a freelance articles. She does all of her freelance work from an office in her apartment. Barbara may take the home office deduction. But she can't deduct more than she earns as income from freelancing.

Regular and Exclusive Business Use

You can't take the home office deduction unless you *regularly use* part of your home *exclusively* for a trade or business.

Unfortunately, the IRS doesn't offer a clear definition of "regular use." The only guidance the agency offers is that you must use a portion of your home for business on a continuing basis, not just for occasional or incidental business. You'll likely satisfy this test if you use your home office a few hours each day.

"Exclusive use" means that you use a portion of your home *only* for business. If you use part of your home as your business office and also use that part for personal purposes, you cannot meet the test of exclusive use and cannot take the home office deduction.

> EXAMPLE: Johnny, an accountant, has a den at home furnished with a desk, chair, bookshelf, filing cabinet, and sofa. He uses the desk and chair for both business and personal reasons. The bookshelf contains both personal and business books, and the filing cabinet contains both personal and business files. He does both business and personal reading on the sofa. Johnny cannot claim a business deduction for the den because it is not used exclusively for business purposes.

You needn't devote an entire separate room in your home to your business. But some part of the room must be used exclusively for business.

> EXAMPLE: Paul, an accountant, keeps his desk, chair, bookshelf, and filing cabinet in one part of his den and uses them exclusively for business. He uses the remainder of the room—one-third of the space—to store a bed for houseguests. Paul can take a home office deduction for the two-thirds of the room used exclusively as an office.

As a practical matter, the IRS isn't going to make a surprise inspection of your home to see whether you're complying with these requirements. However, complying with the rules from the beginning avoids having to lie to the IRS if you are audited.

This means, simply, that you'll have to arrange your furniture and belongings so as to devote a portion of your home exclusively to your home office. The more space you use exclusively for business, the more your home office deduction will be worth.

Although not required by law, it's a good idea to physically separate the space you use for business from the rest of the room. For example, if you use part of your living room as an office, separate it from the rest of the room with room dividers or bookcases.

Qualifying for the Deduction

Unfortunately, satisfying the requirement of using your home office regularly and exclusively for business is only half the battle.

You must also meet one of these three requirements:

- Your home office must be your principal place of business.
- You must meet clients or customers at home.
- You must use a separate structure on your property exclusively for business purposes.

Ways to Solidify the Home Office Deduction

Here are some ways to convince the IRS that you qualify for the home office deduction:

- Take a picture of your home office and draw up a diagram showing your home office as a portion of your home.
- Have all your business mail sent to your home office.
- Use your home office address on all your business cards, stationery, and advertising; but not if you want to keep your home business unobtrusive so as to ward off neighbor complaints.
- Obtain a separate phone number for your business. You can deduct the monthly fee for a second phone numbers (including a cell phone) if you use it for business. You can't deduct the monthly fee for a single phone number, even if you use it partly for business, although you can deduct the cost of business calls you place from that number.
- Encourage clients or customers to regularly visit your home office and keep a log of their visits (but not if it will upset your neighbors).
- To make the most of the time you spend in your home office, communicate with clients by phone or email instead of going to their offices.
- Keep a log of the time you spend working in your home office. This doesn't have to be fancy: Notes on your calendar will do.

Home as Principal Place of Business

The most common way to qualify for the home office deduction is to use your home as your principal place of business. Indeed, most self-employed people will be able to qualify for the home office deduction on this basis.

If You Do Most of Your Work at Home

If, like many self-employed people, you do all or most of your work in your home office, your home is your principal place of business. You should have no trouble qualifying for the home office deduction. This would be the case, for example, for writers who do most of their writing at home or telemarketers who make most of their sales calls from home.

If You Do Only Administrative Work at Home

Of course, many people who work for themselves spend the bulk of their time working away from home. This is the case, for example, for:

- building contractors who work primarily on building sites
- travelling salespeople who visit clients at their places of business, and
- house painters, gardeners, and home repair people who work primarily in their customers' homes.

Fortunately, even if you work primarily outside your home, your home office will qualify as your principal place of business if both of the following are true:

- You use the office to conduct administrative or management activities for your business.
- There is no other fixed location where you conduct such activities.

What this means is that to qualify for the home office deduction, your home office does not need to be the place where you generate most of your business income. It's sufficient that you use it regularly to administer or manage your business (for example, to keep your books, schedule appointments, do research, and order supplies). As long as you have no other fixed location where you regularly do such things (an outside office), you can take the deduction.

> **EXAMPLE:** Sally, a handyperson, performs home repair work for clients in their homes. She also has a home office that she uses regularly and exclusively to keep her books, arrange appointments, and order supplies. Sally is entitled to a home office deduction.

You don't have to personally perform at home all the administrative or management activities your business requires to qualify for the home office deduction. Your home office can qualify for the deduction even if:

- You have others conduct your administrative or management activities at locations other than your home (for example, another company does your billing from its place of business).
- You conduct administrative or management activities at places that are not fixed locations for your business, such as in a car or a hotel room.
- You occasionally conduct minimal administrative or management activities at a fixed location outside your home, such as your outside office.

Meeting Clients or Customers at Home

Even if your home office is not your principal place of business, you may deduct your expenses for the part of your home used exclusively to meet with clients, customers, or patients. You must physically meet with others at home; phoning them from home is not sufficient. And the meetings must be a regular part of your business; occasional meetings don't qualify.

There is no numerical standard for how often you must meet clients at home for those meetings to be considered regular. However, the IRS has indicated that meeting clients one or two days a week is sufficient. Again, exclusive use means that you use the space where you meet clients only for business. You are free to use the space for business purposes other than meeting clients, such as doing your business bookkeeping or other paperwork. But you cannot use the space for personal purposes, such as watching television.

> EXAMPLE: June, an attorney, works three days a week in her city office and two days in her home office, which she uses only for business. She meets clients at her home office at least once a week. Because she regularly meets clients at her home office, it qualifies for the home office deduction, even though her city office is her principal place of business.

If you want to qualify for this deduction, encourage clients or customers to visit you at home. Keep a log or an appointment book showing all their visits.

Using a Garage or Another Separate Structure for Business

You can also deduct expenses for a separate freestanding structure, such as a studio, garage, or barn, if you use it exclusively and regularly for your business. The structure does not have to be your principal place of business or a place where you meet patients, clients, or customers.

As always, when the home office deduction is involved, exclusive use means you use the structure only for business. For example, you can't also use the space to store gardening equipment or as a guest house. Regular use is not precisely defined but it's probably sufficient for you to use the structure ten or 15 hours a week.

> **EXAMPLE:** Deborah is a freelance graphic designer. She has her main office in an industrial park but also works every weekend in a small studio in her backyard. Because she uses the studio regularly and exclusively for work, it qualifies for the home office deduction.

Storing Inventory or Product Samples at Home

You can take the home office deduction if you're in the business of selling retail or wholesale products and you store inventory or product samples at home. To qualify, you can't have an office or other business location outside your home. And you must store your inventory at a particular place in your home, such as a garage, closet, or bedroom. You can't move your inventory from one room to another. You don't have to use the storage space exclusively to store your inventory to take the deduction. It's sufficient that you regularly use it for that purpose.

> **EXAMPLE:** Janet sells costume jewelry door to door. She rents a home and regularly uses half of her attached garage to store her jewelry inventory. She also uses it to park her Harley Davidson motorcycle. Janet can deduct the expenses for the storage space even though she does not use her garage exclusively to store inventory. Her garage accounts for 20% of the total floor space of her house. Because she uses only half of the garage for storing inventory, she may deduct one half of this, or 10%, of her rent and certain other expenses.

Amount of Deduction

There are now two ways to calculate the home office deduction. You can use the standard method discussed below. Alternatively, you may use a new simplified method. (See "Optional Simplified Home Office Deduction Method," below.)

To figure out the amount of the home office deduction using the standard method, you need to determine what percentage of your home you use for business. To do this, divide the square footage of your home office by the total square footage of your home. For example, if your home is 1,600 square feet and you use 400 square feet for your home office, you use 25% of the total area for business.

If all the rooms in your home are about the same size, you can figure the business portion by dividing the number of rooms used for business by the number of rooms in the home. For example, if you use one room in a five-room house for business, you use 20% of the area for business. Claiming 20% to 25% of your home as a home office is perfectly acceptable. However, claiming more than 40% will likely raise questions with the IRS (unless you store inventory at home).

The home office deduction is not one deduction, but many. First, you are entitled to deduct from your gross income the percentage you use for your home office of:

- your rent if you rent your home, or
- depreciation, mortgage interest, and property taxes if you own your home.

Whether or not you have a home office, you can deduct your monthly mortgage interest and property tax payments as a personal itemized income tax deduction on your Schedule A. However, starting in 2018 and continuing through 2025, the itemized deduction for property taxes is limited to $10,000 per year. Also, for homes purchased in 2018 through 2025, the deduction for home mortgage interest is limited to acquisition loans for a main and second home totaling a maximum of $750,000. The amount is $1 million for homes purchased before 2018. If you deduct the home office percentage of your mortgage interest and property tax payments as part of your home office deduction, these amounts don't count toward the mortgage and property tax limits. If you do this, you don't deduct these amounts on your Schedule A (because you can't deduct the same item twice).

In addition, you may deduct this same percentage of other expenses for keeping up and running an entire home. The IRS calls these indirect expenses. They include:

- utility expenses for electricity, gas, heat, and trash removal
- homeowner's or renter's insurance
- home maintenance expenses that benefit your entire home, including your home office (for example, roof and furnace repairs or exterior painting)
- condominium association fees
- snow removal expenses
- casualty losses if your home is damaged (for example, in a storm), and
- security system costs.

You may also deduct the entire cost of expenses solely for your home office. The IRS calls these direct expenses. They include, for example, painting your home office or paying someone to clean it. If you pay a housekeeper to clean your entire house, you may deduct your business use percentage of the expense.

EXAMPLE: Jean rents a 1,600-square-foot apartment and uses a 400-square-foot room as a home office for her consulting business. Her percentage of business use is 25% (400 ÷ 1,600). She pays $12,000 in annual rent and has a $1,200 utility bill for the year. She also spent $200 to paint her home office. She is entitled to deduct 25% of her rent and utilities ($3,300) plus the entire cost of painting her office, for a total home office deduction of $3,500.

Be sure to keep copies of all your bills and receipts for home office expenses, including:

- IRS Form 1098 (sent by whoever holds your mortgage), showing the interest you paid on your mortgage for the year
- property tax bills and your canceled payment checks
- utility bills, insurance bills, and receipts for repairs to your office area and your canceled payment checks, and
- your lease and your canceled rent checks, if you're a renter.

The home office deduction can be very valuable if you're a renter because you get to deduct part of your rent: a substantial expense that is not ordinarily deductible.

If you own your home, the home office deduction is worth less because you're already allowed to deduct your mortgage interest and property taxes from your income tax. But taking the home office deduction will allow you to deduct these items from your self-employment taxes. You'll save $153 in self-employment taxes for every $1,000 in mortgage interest and property taxes you deduct. You'll also be able to deduct a portion of repairs, utility bills, cleaning and maintenance costs, and depreciation.

Depreciating Office Furniture and Other Personal Property

Whether or not you qualify for or take the home office deduction, you can deduct the cost of office furniture, computers, copiers, and other personal property you use for your business in your home office. You deduct these costs directly on your Schedule C, *Profit or Loss From Business*. You do not have to list them on the special tax form used for the home office deduction.

If you use the property for both business and personal reasons, the IRS requires you to keep records showing when the item was used for business and when for personal reasons (see Chapter 14 for details).

Optional Simplified Home Office Deduction Method

You have the option of using a much simpler method to calculate your home office deduction. Using this method, you just deduct $5 for every square foot of your home office. All you need do is get out your measuring tape.

For example, if your home office is 200 square feet, you'll get a $1,000 home office deduction. That's all there is to it. You need not figure out what percentage of your home your office occupies. You also don't need to keep records of your direct or indirect home office expenses, such as utilities, rent, mortgage payments, real estate taxes, or casualty losses. These expenses aren't deductible when you use the simplified method. Nor do you get a depreciation deduction for your home office.

Sounds great, but what's the catch? The catch is that when you use the simplified method your home office deduction is capped at $1,500 per year. You'll reach the cap if your home office is 300 square feet. Even if your home office is 400 square feet, you'll still be limited to a $1,500 home office deduction if you use the simplified method. You can't carry over any part of the deduction to future years. Moreover, if you use the simplified method, you can't deduct amounts carried over from past years.

If you're thinking about using the optional method, you should figure your deduction using both methods to see which gives you the larger deduction. The regular method does require more record keeping than the optional method, but you probably keep these types of records anyway. Doing the required calculations and filling out the form can be challenging, but will be much easier if you use tax preparation software.

Profit Limit for Deductions

There is an important limitation on taking the home office deduction: It may not exceed the net profit you earn from your home office in that year. If you run a successful business out of your home office, this limitation isn't a problem, because your profits will exceed your deductions. But if your business earns very little money or even loses money, this could prevent you from deducting part or all of your home office expenses in a given year.

If your deductions exceed your profits in a particular year, you can, however, deduct this excess in the following year and in each succeeding year until you deduct the entire amount. There is no limit on how far into the future you can deduct these expenses: You can claim them even if you are no longer living in the home where they were incurred.

So, whether or not your business is making money, you should keep track of your home office expenses and claim the deduction on your tax return. You do this by filing IRS Form 8829. When you plug in the numbers for your business income and home office expenses and complete the form, it will show you how much you can deduct in the current year and how much you must carry over to the next year.

This limitation applies to the home office deduction only; it does not apply to business expenses that you can deduct under other provisions of the tax code. Your "net profit" for calculating your home business deduction limit is the gross income you earn from your business minus your business deductions other than your home office deduction. You must also subtract the home office portion of any mortgage interest, real estate taxes, and casualty losses you incurred.

Special Concerns for Homeowners

In the past, homeowners who took the home office deduction were subject to a special tax trap: If they took a home office deduction for more than three of the five years before they sold their home, they had to pay capital gains taxes on the home office portion of the profit they made from the sale. For example, if you made a $50,000 profit on the sale of your house, but your home office took up 20% of the space, you would have had to pay this tax on $10,000 of your profit (20% × $50,000 = $10,000).

Fortunately, IRS rules no longer require this if you can exclude your profit from tax. As long as you live in your home for at least two of the five years before you sell it, the profit you make on the sale—up to $250,000 for single taxpayers and $500,000 for married taxpayers filing jointly—is not taxable. However, you will have to pay a capital gains tax on the depreciation deductions you took after May 6, 1997, for your home office. This is taxed at a 25% rate (unless your income tax bracket is lower than 25%).

> EXAMPLE: In 2009, Sally bought a home for $200,000 and used one of the rooms as her home office. She sells her home this year for $300,000, realizing a $100,000 gain (profit). The depreciation deductions she had taken for her home office amounted to $2,000. She must pay a tax of 25% of $2,000, or $500.

IRS Reporting Requirements

If you qualify for the home office deduction and are a sole proprietor or partner in a partnership, you must file IRS Form 8829, *Expenses for Business Use of Your Home*, along with your personal tax return. The form alerts the IRS that you're taking the deduction and shows how you calculated it. You should file this form even if you're not allowed to deduct your home office expenses (because your business had little or no profits). By filing, you can apply the deduction to a future year in which you earn a profit.

There is an important exception to this requirement: If you use the optional simplified method to calculate your deduction, you need not file Form 8829 (the optional method may be used only for tax years 2013 and later). This is one of the major advantages of the simplified method. Filing Form 8829 calls your home office deduction to the attention of the IRS. If you can avoid filing it, you are less likely to face an audit.

RESOURCE

For additional information, see IRS Publication 587, *Business Use of Your Home.* You can obtain this and all other IRS publications from the IRS website at www.irs.gov.

Pros and Cons of an Outside Office

While there are obviously benefits to having a home office, there are also benefits to having an outside office. It can help establish your credibility and provide a more professional setting for meeting clients or customers than a home office. And, it can help you keep your home and work lives separate. It may even enable you to work more efficiently. Renting an outside office will also help establish that you are self-employed if you're audited by the IRS or your state tax department. (See Chapter 15.)

The drawbacks of having an outside office are the flipside of the benefits of having a home office. You must pay rent for your office and drive to and from it every day. You won't be entitled to a home office deduction, although you can deduct your outside office rent, utilities, and other expenses. You also lose much of the flexibility afforded by a home office.

The Coworking Revolution

Instead of leasing traditional offices, many self-employed people use coworking spaces shared by numerous individuals. The space is usually communal, although there may be individual offices available as well.

Coworking is ordinarily much less formal than renting a traditional office, as well as much less expensive. You typically pay a set fee per month or day, usually without any fixed rental term. The money you spend to rent a coworking space is a tax deductible expense if you use the space for business purposes.

You do not sign a traditional commercial office lease, although you may be required to agree to some sort of written rental or membership agreement. Be sure to read it carefully.

For more information on coworking, including a list of active coworking spaces throughout the world, visit the Coworking WIKI at wiki.coworking.com.

Leasing a Workplace

If you decide against working at home, you'll most likely have to rent an outside office or workspace. If you rent a space for your business activities, you'll be renting commercial property, not residential property, and you'll be signing a commercial lease. Renting commercial space is not like renting an apartment or a house; it's a business transaction. As a businessperson, you are presumed to be an adult and able to protect yourself. For this reason, few of the consumer protection laws that protect residential tenants— for example, caps on security deposits—apply to commercial leases.

Despite what a prospective commercial landlord might say, there are no "standard" commercial lease forms. This means that you can negotiate virtually every term in the lease to suit your needs. This section provides an overview of the key elements you will need to negotiate with the landlord before you sign a commercial lease. For a detailed, step-by-step explanation of everything you should know, refer to *Negotiate the Best Lease for Your Business*, by Janet Portman and Fred Steingold (Nolo).

Rent

Probably foremost in your mind is the amount you will have to pay for your workspace. Depending on the commercial rental market in your area, your rent may be highly negotiable. Commercial rent is typically charged by the square foot. When negotiating your rental, find out how the square footage for which you will be charged is determined. For example, does it include common areas, such as hallways, elevators, and restrooms?

In addition to negotiating the amount of rent and square footage, you should understand exactly what your rent will cover. There are two basic types of commercial leases: a net lease and a gross lease. In a net lease, your rent pays for your right to occupy the space only; you must pay for maintenance, insurance, and property taxes separately. In a gross lease, your payment to the landlord covers all of these things: rent, maintenance, insurance, and taxes.

Often a commercial lease includes a formula for increases to your rent. For example, your rent may increase by a set amount each year or an increase may be tied to the Consumer Price Index (CPI).

Term

You can also negotiate the "term," or how long the lease will last, usually anywhere from 30 days to many years. A short-term lease of no more than six months to one year is probably best when you're starting out. If you think you might want to stay longer but want to play it safe, you can include an option to renew if you choose to stay after the term expires. That way, the landlord can't evict you merely because you reached the end of your lease term.

Security Deposit

Just as you would for an apartment, you will have to provide a security deposit for your commercial space. You should negotiate the amount of the deposit and when it will be returned to you. Try to get the landlord to agree to a lease provision that returns a portion of the deposit to you if you pay rent on time for one year.

Permitted Uses

Commercial leases typically include a clause that provides how you may use the property. Again, like the other clauses discussed in this section, you can negotiate this clause so that the permitted uses suit your needs.

A permitted-uses clause is written in one of two ways: Either it lists everything you're forbidden to do, which means you're free to do anything not on the list, or it lists all the ways you are permitted to use the property, which means your intended use must be specifically mentioned in the lease.

If you're going to be storing waste products or your work may create a good deal of noise, odors, vibrations, or other types of environmental pollution, make sure the landlord is aware of this and specifically permits it in the lease.

Improvements

Is the space you want to lease going to be improved or modified in any way? If so, by whom? Will new fixtures be installed? If so, make sure the lease states who will pay for such changes and who will own any new fixtures when the lease ends. Usually, the landlord ends up owning improvements.

Maintenance

The lease should also specify who will maintain and repair the leased space. Some leases state that the landlord will provide basic maintenance services. Others make the tenant pay for everything, including cleaning, building security, heating, and maintenance of the air-conditioning system.

Insurance

If you're signing a net lease, you'll be required to help the landlord pay for property and liability insurance on the premises. (In a gross lease, insurance costs are figured into your rent amount.) If there are multiple tenants, the landlord will often obtain the insurance and require you to contribute to the cost. Your contribution should be based on how much space you use. For example, if you're renting 10% of the building, you should pay only 10% of the insurance costs. If you are the only tenant, you may have to obtain and pay for the insurance yourself.

If the landlord gets the insurance for the premises, make sure you are listed on the policy as an additional insured. This will make it easier for you to deal with the insurance company if you make a claim or share in a payout.

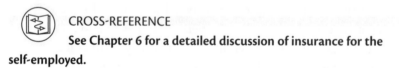 CROSS-REFERENCE
See Chapter 6 for a detailed discussion of insurance for the self-employed.

Termination Clause

Make sure the lease includes a clause that details what happens if you end the lease early. In some leases, you have no right to terminate before the lease term ends, so you will be on the hook for the rent until the end of the rental term. In others, you can terminate the lease early, but only if you pay a penalty to the landlord. It's always in your interest to be able to get out of a lease as easily, quickly, and cheaply as possible.

Sublease Clause

If you may want to rent part or all of the space you lease to someone else, you will want to include a "sublease clause." The right to sublease benefits you if you no longer need all the space you've rented or if you want, but are not allowed, to terminate your lease early. Most leases allow you to sublease only if you get prior permission from the landlord. Some leases permit the landlord to withhold permission for any reason. If the lease allows the landlord to deny you permission to sublease, make sure the landlord may do so only if he or she has a "reasonable basis."

Dispute Resolution

Finally, you should negotiate how you and the landlord will resolve any disputes that may arise. Some leases require the parties to submit to mediation or arbitration instead of allowing them to file a lawsuit, while others don't.

Deducting Your Outside Office Expenses

Virtually all the expenses you incur for an outside office or other workplace that you rent for your business are deductible, including:

- rent
- utilities
- insurance
- repairs
- improvements
- real estate broker fees and commissions to obtain the lease
- fees for option rights, such as an option to renew the lease
- burglar alarm expenses
- trash and waste removal
- security expenses
- parking expenses
- maintenance and janitorial expenses
- lease cancellation fees, and
- attorneys' fees to draft a lease.

If you sign a net lease, you'll have to pay part (or all) of the landlord's maintenance expenses, property taxes, insurance, and maybe even mortgage payments. For tax purposes, these payments are treated the same as rent.

A rental deposit is not deductible in the year it is made if it is to be returned at the end of the lease. However, if the landlord applies the deposit to pay rent you owe, make repairs, or because you've breached the lease, you may deduct the amount in that year.

None of the rules applicable to the home office deduction apply to outside offices. Thus, there is no profit limit on deductions for outside rental expenses: You get your entire deduction even if it exceeds the profits from your business. You report rental expenses for an outside office just like any other business expense. You don't have to file IRS Form 8829, which is required when sole proprietors take the home office deduction.

Obtaining Licenses, Permits, and Identification Numbers

Once you've chosen a name, decided how to structure your business, and figured out where you will work, you'll need to obtain any necessary licenses, permits, and identification numbers. You may have to fill out paperwork and pay some fees, but it's well worth the effort. You can face fines and other penalties if you don't satisfy government requirements for your business.

Also, having all required business licenses helps you look like an independent businessperson instead of an employee. Potential clients may even ask you for copies of your licenses, permits, or numbers before agreeing to hire you because this information will help them if they're audited.

Business Licenses

The type of business licenses and permits that you need (if any) depends on the kind of work you do and where you do it. You may be required to get licenses or permits from federal, state, and local governments. Professional organizations, other self-employed people, and your local chamber of commerce are all good sources information on licensing requirements for your business.

Federal Licenses and Permits

The federal government doesn't require licenses or permits for most small businesses. One notable exception, however, is the trucking industry. Trucking companies must be licensed by the Federal Motor Carrier Safety Administration (www.fmcsa.dot.gov). License requirements are also imposed on investment advisors by the Securities and Exchange Commission (www.sec.gov). For a list of all federally licensed businesses and links for further information, visit this website maintained by the U.S. Small Business Administration: https://business.usa.gov/start-a-business.

State Requirements

A few states require all businesses to obtain state business licenses (in addition to any local licenses required). These states include Alabama, Alaska, Delaware, Florida, Ohio, Nevada, and Washington. For detailed information on obtaining state business licenses in these states, see the "50-State Guide to Business License Requirements" in the "Business Name, Location & Licenses" section of Nolo.com.

Most states don't issue or require general business licenses. However, all states require special licenses for people who work in certain occupations. Doctors, lawyers, architects, nurses, and engineers must be licensed in every state. Most states require licenses for other occupations that require extensive training or that expose consumers to potential hazards or fraud. For example, most states license food service businesses, barbers, bill collectors, building contractors, tax preparers, insurance agents, cosmetologists, real estate agents or brokers, and auto mechanics. Your state may require licenses for other occupations, too.

Procedures for obtaining a license vary from state to state and occupation to occupation. You may have to meet specific educational requirements or have training or experience in the field. You may even have to pass a written examination. Of course, you'll have to pay a license fee. Some states may also require that you have liability insurance before you can be issued a license. (See Chapter 6.)

If your state government discovers that you're doing business without a required license, a variety of bad things can happen to you. You'll undoubtedly be ordered to stop doing business. You may also be fined. And depending on your occupation, failure to obtain a license may be a crime.

All states have websites designed to help new businesses obtain the proper licenses and permits. The U.S. Small Business Administration maintains a comprehensive collection of links to these sites at http://business.usa.gov/start-a-business.

Local Requirements

Many cities, counties, and municipalities require business licenses or permits for all businesses, even one-person, home-based operations. Usually, you just have to pay a fee to get such a licenses. Other cities have no license requirements at all or exempt very small businesses.

If you're doing business within a city's limits, you'll need to contact your city government to find out about licensing requirements. If you're in an unincorporated area, you'll need to contact your county government. If you're doing business in more than one city or county, you may have to get a license for each one.

To find out what to do, contact the appropriate local official in charge of business licensing. This is often the city or county clerk, planning or zoning department, city tax office, building and safety department, or public works department. You may need more than one local license, so you may have to deal with more than one local agency. The U.S. Small Business Administration's website can help you find the right agency (search "State Licenses and Permits" at www.sba.gov). You can input your zip code and obtain links to your city, county, and other local licensing agencies, at https://business.usa.gov/start-a-business. Your local chamber of commerce may also be able to direct you to the right agency or contact person.

To obtain a license, you'll be required to fill out an application and pay a fee. Fees vary by locality, ranging from as little as $15 to several hundred dollars. Fees are often based on your projected gross revenues (for example, ten cents per $1,000 of revenue projected). Periodically, you'll be required to renew your license and pay an additional fee, usually every year. You also may be required to post your license at your place of business.

Many self-employed people, particularly those who work at home, never bother to get a local business license. If your local government discovers you're running an unlicensed business, it may fine you and bar you from doing business until you obtain a license.

Blogging Without a License

In this era of tight local budgets, many cities and counties are stepping up enforcement of their business license requirements in an effort to raise more money. Unfortunately, some cities have gone to ridiculous extremes. One case in point: Philadelphia. The city requires all local businesses to obtain a "commercial activity license" for $300. The city demanded that the operator of a small, low-traffic blog featuring occasional posts about green living obtain a license and pay the fee, even though she had earned only $50 from the blog. The city claimed the blog was a business because, like any blog, it had the potential to earn a profit from the sale of ads. Philadelphia also sent letters to numerous other bloggers demanding that they pay up.

CAUTION
Watch out for zoning restrictions. If you work at home, be careful about applying for a local business license. You'll have to provide your business address to obtain one. Before granting a license, many cities first check to see whether the area in which your business is located is zoned for business. If your local zoning ordinance bars home-based business offices in your neighborhood, you could be in for trouble. (See Chapter 4.)

Employer Identification Numbers (EINs)

A federal employer identification number, or EIN, is a nine-digit number the IRS assigns to businesses for tax filing and reporting purposes. The IRS uses the EIN to identify the taxpayer.

When an EIN Is Required

Use your EIN on all business tax returns, checks, and other documents you send to the IRS. Your state tax authority may also require your EIN on state tax forms.

Sole Proprietors

If you're a sole proprietor, you must have an EIN to:
- hire employees
- have a Keogh or solo 401(k) retirement plan (see Chapter 16)
- buy or inherit an existing business that you operate as a sole proprietorship
- incorporate or form a partnership or limited liability company (LLC), or
- file for bankruptcy.

Also, some banks require you to have an EIN before they'll set up a bank account for your business.

You can obtain an EIN even if it is not required, or you can use your Social Security number. Even if you don't have to get an EIN, there are two good reasons to obtain one and use it instead of your Social Security number:

- **Avoid identity theft.** Theft of taxpayer's identities has become a widespread problem. Identity thieves steal taxpayers' Social Security numbers and use them to file fraudulent tax returns and obtain tax refunds. For this reason, it's wise to keep your personal Social Security number as private as possible. If you perform personal services as an independent contractor, you must provide an EIN or Social Security number to your clients, or the clients will be required to withhold 28% of your payments. Obtaining an EIN allows you to avoid having to provide your Social Security number to clients and other members of the public.
- **Help establish IC status.** Using an EIN on your tax returns and payments also helps to show that you're an independent businessperson. In other words, it demonstrates that you are an independent contractor and not an employee; this can make you more attractive to prospective clients.

Corporations, Partnerships, and Limited Liability Companies

You must have an EIN if you form a corporation, partnership, or limited liability company, even if you were formerly a sole proprietor.

Obtaining an EIN

The fastest and easiest way to obtain an EIN is to apply directly through the IRS website by going to www.irs.gov/businesses/small-businesses-self-employed/apply-for-an-employer-identification-number-ein-online. You can fill out an interview-style online application. As long as you pass the system's automatic validity checks, you will immediately be issued an EIN. If your application doesn't pass the validity checks, you will have the opportunity to review and correct it.

Otherwise, simply print out a copy of the confirmation notice for your records and begin using your new EIN immediately.

Sales Tax Permits

Almost all states and many municipalities impose sales taxes of some kind. The only states without a sales tax are Alaska, Delaware, Montana, New Hampshire, and Oregon. However, Alaska permits local sales taxes, while Delaware imposes a rental and service tax. In addition, the other three states impose sales-type taxes on certain types of business transactions.

In some states, sales tax is imposed on sellers, who then have the option of passing the tax along to their purchasers. In other states, the tax is imposed directly on the purchaser, and the seller is responsible for collecting the tax and remitting it to the state. In a few states, sellers and purchasers split the sales tax.

Selling Products or Services

If you sell tangible personal property—things you can hold in your hand or physically touch—to the public, you'll most likely have to pay sales taxes. All states that have sales taxes impose them on sales of goods or products to the public.

On the other hand, if you only provide services to clients or customers —that is, you don't sell or transfer any type of personal property—you probably don't have to worry about sales taxes because most states either don't tax services at all or tax only certain services. Notable exceptions are Hawaii, New Mexico, South Dakota, and West Virginia which impose sales taxes on all services, subject to certain exceptions. Due to budget constraints, however, more and more states are starting to impose sales taxes on more and more services.

Determining whether you're selling property or providing a service can be difficult because the two are often involved in the same transaction. For example, a piano tuner may have to replace some piano wire to tune a piano, or a dentist may provide a patient with a gold filling in the process of filling a tooth. In these instances, many state taxing authorities look at the true object of the transaction to determine whether sales tax will be assessed. That is, they look at whether the main purpose of the transaction is to provide the consumer with a service or to sell property. It seems clear that the main purpose of hiring a piano tuner or dentist is to obtain a service: the tuning of the piano or filling of the tooth. The property used to provide the service is incidental.

Taxes on Internet Sales

If you sell goods over the Internet, and you're not otherwise exempt, you can be required to collect state and local sales taxes in the state of delivery. The United States Supreme Court has held that this is so even if your business doesn't have a physical presence in the state of delivery, such as a store, office, or warehouse. All that is required is that you have a "substantial nexus" with the state of delivery—that is, you have sufficient sales in the state to make it reasonable to require you to collect and pay its sales taxes. (*South Dakota v. Wayfair, Inc.*, 585 U.S. ____ (2018).) So, for example, California can require a business located in Colorado to collect California sales tax on orders it ships to California, whether the order was made over the Internet or by some other means.

CAUTION
Contact state sales tax departments. Each state's sales tax requirements are unique. A product or service taxable in one state might be tax-free in another. Contact the state sales tax department to find out if the products or services you provide are subject to sales taxes. You can find the state sales tax agencies at www.irs.gov/businesses/small-businesses-self-employed/state-links-1. If you don't understand the requirements, seek help from a tax professional. A commercial service can also calculate, collect, and pay sales taxes on your behalf.

Obtaining a State Sales Tax Permit

If the products or services you provide are subject to sales tax, you'll have to fill out an application to obtain a state sales tax permit. Complete and mail the application before you make a taxable sale. Many states impose penalties if you make a sale before you obtain a sales tax permit. Generally, you pay sales taxes four times a year, but you might have to pay them monthly if you make a lot of sales. Be sure to collect all the taxes due. If you fail to do so, you can be held personally liable for the full amount of uncollected tax.

CAUTION
Watch out for rule changes. States constantly change their sales tax laws, so be on the lookout for changes that affect how you do business. Professional organizations and your state chamber of commerce can be good sources of information on your state's sales tax rules.

Insuring Your Business and Yourself

Many employees don't worry much about health, liability, or property insurance; their employers take care of their insurance needs. Unfortunately, this is not the case when you're self-employed. Self-employed people must purchase all their insurance themselves and usually need more types of coverage than employees.

The Affordable Care Act ("Obamacare")

When you own your own business, you don't have an employer to provide you with health insurance. Unless you're married and can obtain coverage through your spouse's health insurance plan, you must obtain health insurance and pay for it (and other health care costs) on your own (also, individuals under 26 years of age may obtain coverage through their parents' health insurance plan). In the past, obtaining health insurance was one of the greatest challenges faced by the self-employed, particularly those with preexisting medical conditions. Many self-employed people could afford only limited major medical coverage or went without health insurance entirely. One survey found that 24% of self-employed people lacked health insurance.

However, things have changed as a result of the Patient Protection and Affordable Care Act enacted by Congress in 2010—commonly referred to as "Obamacare."

Obamacare affects all businesses, no matter how large or small. However, it is particularly significant for the self-employed, particularly those who may have had trouble obtaining affordable health insurance in the past. Congress has tweaked Obamacare and eliminated one of its major provisions—the individual mandate—starting in 2019. Otherwise, despite campaign promises to "repeal and replace" the program, Obamacare remains in place. (Though, this could change in the future).

Here are the key things to know about Obamacare:
- It requires most individuals to obtain health insurance for themselves and their dependents during 2018 or pay a penalty.
- It imposes minimum standards for health coverage.
- Health insurers are not allowed to deny coverage due to preexisting conditions or to base their insurance rates on health status.
- Self-employed people and small businesses may purchase health insurance through state health insurance exchanges.

- Moderate and low-income individuals and families may qualify for tax credits to help pay for their health insurance.

RESOURCE

Need to know more about Obamacare? To get more information on every aspect of the health care reform law, check out the government's dedicated site, www.healthcare.gov.

Individual Health Insurance Mandate

Since 2014, one of Obamacare's principal features has been the individual health insurance mandate. Subject to certain exceptions, all Americans have been required to obtain at least minimal comprehensive health insurance coverage or pay a penalty to the IRS. Congress effectively eliminated the individual mandate starting in 2019 by reducing the penalty for noncompliance to zero. So, during 2019 and later, individuals who fail to obtain health coverage will not be penalized. Starting in 2019, an individual's decision whether to obtain health insurance will be purely voluntary, just as it was before Obamacare was enacted.

However, the penalty—and the individual mandate—remains in place for 2018. It applies to the self-employed, as well as everybody else—whether you're a self-employed sole proprietor, a partner in a partnership or limited liability company, or an employee of your own small corporation. Unless you're exempt, if you failed to purchase adequate health insurance for yourself and your dependents for more than three months during 2018, you could have to pay a penalty to the IRS. For most taxpayers, the penalty is $695 per uncovered adult and $347.50 per child under 18 (up to a maximum of $2,085 per family). The penalty amount is prorated based on the number of months during the year that you were uninsured.

You could be exempt from the mandate and not have to pay for failing to get coverage during 2018. You may be eligible for an exemption if any of the following apply to you:

- you were uninsured for no more than two consecutive months during the year
- you cannot afford coverage

- obtaining coverage would result in certain hardships for you
- you are not a U.S. citizen, U.S. national, or an alien lawfully residing in the U.S.
- you don't have to file a tax return for the year because your income is below the tax filing threshold (for the current income tax filing thresholds, see IRS Publication 501, *Exemptions, Standard Deduction, and Filing Information,* available at IRS.gov)
- you are unable to qualify for Medicaid because your state has chosen not to expand the program
- you participate in a health care sharing ministry or are a member of a recognized religious sect with objections to health insurance, or
- you are a member of a federally recognized Indian tribe.

The most significant exemptions are based on income. Anyone who would have to pay more than 8.13% of his or her household income to obtain the minimal coverage required by law is exempt.

For more details about exemptions, including an online questionnaire that can help to determine if you qualify for one, see www.healthcare.gov/health-coverage-exemptions/exemptions-from-the-fee.

If you or anyone in your family qualifies for an exemption, you must file IRS Form 8965, *Health Coverage Exemptions,* with your income tax return. However, to obtain some types of exemptions, you must first apply through your state health insurance exchange. For more details on how to claim exemptions with your tax return, see the IRS website at www.irs.gov/affordable-care-act/individuals-and-families/aca-individual-shared-responsibility-provision-exemptions.

The Employer Mandate

Obamacare's employer mandate has not changed. Businesses with at least 50 full-time employees (or a combination of full-time and part-time employees that's "equivalent" to at least 50 full-time employees), must provide at least 95% of their full-time employees (those who work at least 30 hours a week) and their families with minimum essential health care coverage or pay a tax penalty equal to $2,320 per employee, excluding the first 30 employees. Employees can be required to help contribute toward their coverage, but the amount of any employee contribution is capped at 9.5% of household income.

Smaller employers—those with fewer than 50 full-time equivalent employees—are not subject to the employer mandate. However, if they choose to provide their employees with health coverage, they may qualify for tax credits. (See "Small Business Health Care Tax Credit," in Chapter 9.)

Smaller employers can purchase coverage through state small business health insurance exchanges (also called "SHOP exchanges"). This can help keep their costs down because they become part of a much larger risk pool. If you have employees, including your spouse (or yourself if you've formed a corporation), you can obtain coverage through your state's SHOP exchange. You may also qualify for a small business health care tax credit worth up to 50% of your premium costs, but only if you have one or more employees who are not related to you (see Chapter 9). You can still deduct from your taxes the portion of your premium costs not covered by the tax credit. If you're self-employed with no employees, you can get coverage through your state individual health insurance exchange, but not through SHOP. For more information on the SHOP exchanges, visit www.healthcare.gov/small-businesses/employers.

Obamacare Health Insurance Requirements

To help everyone obtain coverage, Obamacare imposed some revolutionary reforms on all health insurers and the coverage they provide. The self-employed, particularly those with preexisting conditions, are among the chief beneficiaries of these changes.

No Preexisting Condition Exclusions

Health insurers are not allowed to deny you coverage based on your health status. This means you can purchase health insurance regardless of any current or past health conditions. This requirement applies only during health insurers' open enrollment periods, unless you have a "qualifying event," such as a job loss, birth, marriage, or divorce.

Insurance Premium Rates

Insurers may vary their premiums based on the following factors only:
- your age (older people may be charged up to 300% more than the young)
- tobacco use

- where you live, and
- the number of family members covered.

Premiums also depend on the level of coverage you choose. As noted above, however, you may not be charged more based on your health status.

Minimal Comprehensive Coverage

All health insurers must offer comprehensive health insurance coverage that provides at least the following ten essential health benefits:

- ambulatory ("walk in") patient services
- emergency services
- hospitalization
- maternity and newborn care
- mental health and substance use disorder services (including behavioral health treatment)
- prescription drugs
- rehabilitative and habilitative services and devices
- lab services
- preventive and wellness services and chronic disease management, and
- pediatric services (including oral and vision care).

No Rescission

Your insurer can't cancel your insurance if you get sick.

No Dollar Caps

Health insurers may not impose lifetime or annual dollar limits on their coverage. This means that no matter how much your health care costs, your insurer must pay all of your expenses once you've paid your total annual out-of-pocket limit.

State Health Insurance Exchanges

To help individuals and small businesses obtain health coverage, each state has a health insurance exchange (also called a health insurance marketplace). Some states have established their own exchanges; others have exchanges run by the federal government.

Purchasing Insurance Through the Exchanges

If you're self-employed and have no employees, you may purchase your health insurance through your state exchange. This is true whether you're a sole proprietor, a partner in a partnership, or a member of a limited liability company.

These exchanges are like virtual malls where you can buy health insurance from different insurers who have negotiated with the mall to set up shop. The state exchanges were specifically designed to help people who currently buy individual policies on their own, the uninsured, and small businesses with fewer than 50 full-time employees.

You aren't required to obtain your health insurance through your state's exchange. However, you won't qualify for health insurance premium credits unless you get your insurance through your state exchange.

RESOURCE

Get in touch with your state exchange. Each state health insurance exchange has an extensive website and a call center for those who prefer to obtain information from a human over the phone. Links to all 50 state exchanges are available at: www.healthcare.gov/get-coverage.

Open Enrollment

Open enrollment for health insurance coverage through the exchanges for 2019 began on November 1, 2018 and runs through December 31, 2018. However, some states have longer open enrollment periods. Coverage can start as soon as January 1, 2019. After the open enrollment period ends, you won't be able to obtain health insurance through your state exchange for that year unless a "qualifying life event" occurs (for example, you lose your job and health coverage, you move to another state your existing insurer doesn't cover, your insurer goes out of business, you get divorced or married, or you have a child).

Association Health Plans

The Trump Administration enacted new rules that allow self-employed individuals and small businesses to obtain health insurance coverage through association health plans. These plans are offered through professional and trade organizations or other associations formed to provide members with such health coverage. Under the new rules, the plans don't have to comply with all the Obamacare coverage requirements discussed above—for example, they don't have to provide coverage for prescription drugs or maternity coverage. Though, association health plans aren't allowed to deny coverage or charge higher rates to individuals with preexisting medical conditions. Because these plans provide less coverage, they should be cheaper than more comprehensive individual coverage obtained through the Obamacare health exchanges.

Health Insurance Premium Tax Credits

Health insurance is available through the state exchanges to everyone who can't get coverage elsewhere. To help moderate- and low-income people afford this coverage, a premium assistance credit is available to those who purchase health insurance from a state exchange. The credits ensure that lower-income people don't have to spend more than a specified percentage of their household income on health insurance. These percentages range from 3.0% to 9.5%.

You're eligible for the premium credit if:

- your household income is between 100% and 400% of the federal poverty level (FPL)
- you are not eligible for other affordable coverage
- you obtain your health insurance through your state exchange, and
- you file a joint tax return (if you're married).

Almost half of American households have household incomes below 400% of FPL and may qualify for these credits.

Based on the 2018 FPL, the credit would be available in 2019 to individuals with household incomes below $48,240, and to families of four with incomes below $98,400. The IRS has created an interactive online questionnaire you can use to see if you qualify for the premium tax credit. It is available at www.irs.gov/uac/am-i-eligible-to-claim-the-premium-tax-credit. Use the Kaiser Health Insurance Marketplace Calculator (www.kff.org/interactive/subsidy-calculator) to get an estimate of what your credit will be.

Although they are called credits, these payments are really a government-funded subsidy. You don't need to owe any income taxes to receive the credit. Moreover, the federal government pays the full credit amount for the year directly to your health insurance company when you enroll in your health insurance plan. In other words, you don't need to wait until your taxes have been filed and processed to receive the credit.

Determining Your Household Income

To qualify for an Obamacare tax credit, you have to estimate your household income for the following year in your application. You can base this amount on your most recently filed tax return, taking into account any changes you expect for the following year. When you fill out your application, you must use your "modified adjusted gross income" (MAGI). MAGI is generally your household's adjusted gross income plus any tax-exempt Social Security, interest, and foreign income you have. For the great majority of self-employed individuals, their MAGI is the same as their adjusted gross income (AGI). Your AGI consists of all your income minus certain deductions, including those for IRA and retirement plan contributions, the self-employed health insurance deduction, and health savings account deduction.

When you file your tax return the following year, you have to reconcile the MAGI you actually earned with the amount of credits you received. If you earned more than you listed on your application, you may have to pay all or part of your credit payments back to the federal government. On the other hand, if you earned substantially less, you may be entitled to additional credits.

It can be tough to forecast your annual income accurately when you're self-employed. If you earn more (or less) money than you thought you would when you applied for coverage, you should notify your state exchange, which will adjust your credit amount.

You also have the option of paying all of your health insurance premiums out of your own pocket, and then applying for the credit when you file your tax return for the year. You can then use the credit to reduce your income taxes due for the year or to get a refund. You could also apply it to your next year's taxes. Alternatively, you could apply for the credit, but only have a portion of it paid in advance. Either method can help you avoid owing money to the IRS at tax time if your income is likely to rise.

Useful Health Care Websites

There are hundreds of websites providing information about health insurance and health care issues. You can even get health insurance quotes online. Some of the most helpful websites include:

- **www.healthcare.gov.** This site, managed by the U.S. Department of Health and Human Services, is the single best source of online information about health care.
- **www.ahirc.org.** The Artists' Health Insurance Resource Center provides a comprehensive database of health care resources for artists, performers, freelancers, and other self-employed people.
- **www.kff.org.** The Henry J. Kaiser Family Foundation website contains a wealth of information about all aspects of health care, especially Obamacare.
- **www.legalconsumer.com/obamacare**. This site provides detailed local information on Obamacare, including available plans, pricing, tax credits, exemptions, and more.
- **www.healthfinder.gov.** A website sponsored by the Department of Health and Human Services' Office of Disease Prevention and Health Promotion (ODPHP). It is a gateway consumer health information website.
- **www.naic.org.** The website of the National Association of Insurance Commissioners provides links to all 50 state insurance departments.
- **www.nahu.org.** The site of the National Association of Health Underwriters, which you can use to locate a licensed insurance broker or agent in your area.

Ensuring Your AGI Is Within Premium Credit Limits

As discussed above, the key to obtaining health care premium credits is to keep your AGI below the 400% FPL threshold for a family of your size. When you're self-employed, you have many ways to control the size of your AGI each year and ensure you qualify for the credit. For example, you could:

- work less
- avoid billing clients for work you do later in the year until the following year

- don't attempt to collect on overdue accounts until the following year
- make tax deductible contributions to retirement plans such as a solo 401(k); such contributions can be substantial and will reduce your AGI (see Chapter 16), or
- increase deductible business expenses by buying equipment or other things you need for your business.

However, before you go to the trouble of rearranging your finances, check the premium calculator at your state health insurance exchange website to see how much you will save based on your AGI and age. (Links to your state exchange are at www.healthcare.gov.) Your credit may be too small to justify the time and expense involved.

Health Savings Accounts

Many self-employed people can afford or obtain only health insurance with high deductibles. If you're in this boat, you should think about getting a health savings account (HSA). HSAs are like medical IRAs: tax-exempt accounts you can use to save money for future health costs.

Contrary to what some feared, HSAs were not eliminated under Obamacare. In fact, HSA-qualified health plans can be offered on the state health exchanges. Because they have high deductibles, such HSA-qualified plans are among the cheapest available on the health exchanges. You can use the money you save on premiums to fund your HSA account. If you need to pay for health care during the year, you can withdraw funds from your HSA account to do so. If you don't see the doctor much, your HSA funds will grow each year—money that belongs to you, not a health insurance company.

RESOURCE
You can get more information on HSAs from IRS Publication 969, *Health Savings Accounts and Other Tax-Favored Health Plans,* which you can obtain from the IRS website at www.irs.gov.

The health savings account concept is very simple: Instead of relying on health insurance to pay for small or routine medical expenses, you pay for them yourself. To help you do this, you establish an HSA with a health insurance company, bank, or another financial institution. Your contributions to the account are tax deductible and you don't have to pay tax on the interest you earn on the money in your account. You can withdraw the money in your HSA to pay for almost any health-related expense without having to pay tax on the withdrawals.

In case you or a family member develops a serious health problem, you must also obtain a health insurance policy with a high deductible—for 2018, at least $1,350 for individuals and $2,700 for families. You can use the money in your HSA to pay this large deductible and any co-payments you're required to make.

Using an HSA can save you money in two ways. First, you can take a tax deduction for the money you deposit in your account. Second, you can save money on your health insurance premiums with your high-deductible health insurance policy, which should cost less than a traditional comprehensive or HMO coverage policy.

To participate in the HSA program, you need two things:

- a high-deductible health plan that qualifies under the HSA rules, and
- an HSA account.

Obtaining an HSA-Qualified Health Plan

To set up an HSA, you must first obtain health care coverage from an HSA-qualified plan: a bare-bones health plan that meets HSA criteria (most health insurers and HMOs offer HSA-qualified plans). There are two requirements:

- **The plan must have a high deductible.** Your plan must have a $1,350 minimum annual deductible if the plan is for yourself or a $2,700 minimum deductible if it is for you and your family.
- **The plan must cap the annual out-of-pocket payments it can require you to make each year.** Out-of-pocket payments include deductibles, co-payments, and other amounts (other than insurance premiums) you must pay for benefits covered by your health plan. As of 2018, the maximum annual out-of-pocket payments that your insurer can require are $6,650 for individuals and $13,300 for families.

You can get an HSA-qualified high-deductible plan through the state health insurance exchanges mandated by Obamacare or outside of the exchanges.

Opening an HSA Account

Once you are covered by an HSA-qualified health insurance policy, you may open your HSA account. You must establish your HSA with a "trustee" who keeps track of your deposits and withdrawals, produces annual statements, and reports your HSA deposits to the IRS. Your trustee can be your health insurer, a bank, or another financial institution.

Making Contributions to Your HSA

Once you set up your HSA-qualified health plan and HSA account, you can start making contributions to your account. There is no minimum amount you are required to contribute each year; you may contribute nothing if you wish. But there are maximum limits on how much you may contribute (and thus deduct from your federal income taxes) each year:

- If you have individual coverage, the maximum you may contribute to your HSA each year is $3,450.
- If you have family coverage, the maximum you may contribute to your HSA each year is $6,900.

These maximums are for 2018; they are adjusted for inflation each year.

People who are 55 to 65 years old have the option of making additional tax-free catch-up contributions to their HSA accounts of $1,000.

Withdrawing HSA Funds

If you or a family member needs health care, you can withdraw money from your HSA to pay your deductible or any other medical expenses. You pay no federal tax on HSA withdrawals used to pay qualified medical expenses. Qualified medical expenses are broadly defined to include many types of expenses ordinarily not covered by health insurance, such as acupuncture, chiropractors, eyeglasses and contact lenses, dental care, fertility treatment, laser eye surgery, and treatment for learning disabilities. This is one of the great advantages the HSA program has over traditional health insurance. (You can find a complete list of qualified medical expenses in IRS Publication 502, *Medical and Dental Expenses*, available online at www.irs.gov.)

Tax-Free Withdrawals

Generally, if you withdraw funds from your HSA to use for something other than qualified medical expenses, you must pay regular income tax on the withdrawal plus a 20% penalty. For example, if you were in the 25% federal income tax bracket, you'd have to pay a 45% tax on your nonqualified withdrawals.

Once you reach the age of 65 or become disabled, however, you can withdraw your HSA funds for any reason without penalty. If you use the money for nonmedical expenses, you will have to pay regular income tax on the withdrawals. When you die, the money in your HSA account is transferred to the beneficiary you've named for the account. The transfer is tax free if the beneficiary is your surviving spouse. Other transfers are taxable.

Are HSAs a Good Deal?

Should you get an HSA? It depends. HSAs are a good deal if you're young or in good health and you don't go to the doctor often or take many expensive medications. You can purchase a health plan with a high deductible, pay substantially lower premiums, and have the security of knowing you can dip into your HSA if you get sick and have to pay the deductible or other uncovered medical expenses. You also get the benefit of deducting your HSA contributions from your income taxes. And you can use your HSA funds to pay for many health-related expenses that aren't covered by traditional health insurance.

If you don't tap into the money you put in your HSA, it will keep accumulating free of taxes. If you enjoy good health while you have your HSA, you may end up with a substantial amount in your account that you can withdraw without penalty for any purpose once you turn 65. Unlike all other existing tax-advantaged savings or retirement accounts, HSAs provide a tax break when funds are deposited and when they are withdrawn. No other account provides both a front-end and back-end tax break. With IRAs, for example, you must pay tax either when you deposit or when you withdraw your money. This feature can make your HSA an extremely lucrative tax shelter, a kind of super IRA.

On the other hand, HSAs are not for everybody. You could be better off with traditional comprehensive health insurance if you or a member of your family has substantial medical expenses. When you're in this situation, you'll likely end up spending all or most of your HSA contributions each year and earn little or no interest on your account (but you'll still get a deduction for your contributions). Of course, whether traditional health insurance is better than an HSA depends on its cost, including the deductibles and co-payments you must make.

In addition, depending on your medical history and where you live, the cost of an HSA-qualified health insurance plan may be too great to make the program cost-effective for you. However, if your choice is an HSA or nothing, get an HSA.

Disability Insurance

Disability insurance is designed to replace the income you lose if you become so sick or injured that you're unable to work for a period of time or never able to work again.

Disability insurance pays you a regular benefit during the time you're unable to work. The cost of disability insurance depends on many factors:

- **The amount of coverage you obtain.** The maximum benefit you can obtain is usually 60% of your income. You can also obtain a smaller benefit and pay a smaller premium. At a minimum, try to obtain a benefit large enough to pay your monthly mortgage costs or rent and other fixed expenses.
- **The term of your coverage.** Some disability insurance plans offer only short-term benefits; the periods range from 13 weeks to five years. More expensive long-term plans pay you until you turn 65 or pay indefinitely. If you can afford it, a long-term policy is best.
- **The elimination period.** Most policies require you to wait a while after you become disabled before you start getting benefits. These elimination periods range from 30 to 730 days. A 90-day period is most common.

- **The nature of your work.** The amount of your premiums will also depend on the nature of your work. People in hazardous occupations—construction, for example—pay more than people with relatively safe jobs.
- **How your policy defines "disability."** More expensive "own occupation" plans pay you full benefits if you can't work in your particular occupation, even if you may be able to do other types of work. Less expensive "any occupation" plans pay you only if you are unable to work in any occupation for which you're suited.
- **Your health.** Your current health is also an important factor. Usually, some type of physical exam will be required. If you smoke or suffer from a preexisting medical condition, be prepared to pay more and search harder for coverage.
- **Renewability.** Try to get a policy that is guaranteed renewable. This means that as long as you make your payments, the company has to renew your policy and can't change the terms or premiums.

How Important Is Disability Insurance?

Disability insurers have compiled some very scary statistics in an attempt to show that disability insurance is absolutely essential. But is it really? If you work in a physically demanding occupation, such as homebuilding or roofing, you may have a good chance of injuring yourself some time during your working life. But if you do office work, your chances of being disabled to such an extent that you are unable to work at all for an appreciable period of time are much lower, particularly if you work at home and don't commute. Only you can decide whether to get disability insurance. But most self-employed people do just fine without it.

Unfortunately, it can be difficult for self-employed people to obtain disability insurance. Many disability insurers don't like to issue policies to the self-employed because their incomes often fluctuate dramatically and they may not be able to pay their premiums. Also, because the self-employed don't have employers to supervise them and verify they're disabled, it can be difficult for an insurer to know for sure whether they're really unable to work. This is a particular problem if you work at home. Some insurers won't issue a disability policy to anyone who works more than half time at home.

California State Disability Insurance Program

California has a state disability insurance program ("SDI") that provides benefits to disabled workers. The SDI program is mandatory for California employees and funded through employee payroll deductions made by employers. Four other states (Hawaii, New Jersey, New York, and Rhode Island) have similar programs. However, California is the only state that gives self-employed residents without employees the option to enroll in its disability program. Self-employed individuals who elect to enroll and become disabled may receive benefits for up to 39 weeks. For more information, see www.edd.ca.gov/disability/self-employed.htm.

Also, many insurers will not issue you a policy until you've been self-employed for at least six months. They want to see how much money you've earned during this period so they'll know whether you can afford the cost of their premiums.

You'll have an easier time obtaining disability coverage if you can show an insurer that you're operating a successful, established business. For example, an insurer may be more willing to cover you if you have:
- employees
- long-term contracts with clients
- a detailed financial forecast statement showing how much money you expect your business to earn in future years, and
- good credit references.

If you're still employed, try to obtain an individual disability policy before you quit your job and become self-employed.

If you're already self-employed, try to obtain group coverage though a professional organization or trade group. If this doesn't work, you'll have to obtain an individual policy.

Business Property Insurance

Business property insurance helps compensate for loss to your business assets: computers, office furniture, equipment, and supplies. If, for example, your office burns down or is burglarized and all your business equipment is lost, your business property insurance will pay you a sum of money. Business owners can buy commercial property insurance whether they own or lease the building where their business is located. Three main factors determine the cost of such insurance: policy limits, value of coverage, and scope of coverage.

Policy Limits

All policies have a maximum limit on how much you will be paid, no matter how great your loss. The greater your policy limit, the more expensive the insurance will be.

Value of Coverage

Property insurance can pay you the cost of replacing your property or its actual present cash value. A "replacement cost" policy will replace your property at current prices regardless of what you paid for it. An "actual cash value" policy will pay you only what your property was worth when it was lost or destroyed. If the item has depreciated in value, you may obtain far less than the amount needed to replace it. A replacement cost policy is always preferable, but it costs more than a cash value policy.

Scope of Coverage

Business property insurance comes in one of two forms: "named peril" (also called "basic form") or "all risk" (also called "special form"). Named peril policies cover you only for the types of harm listed in the policy. For example, the cheapest type of named peril policy covers only losses caused by fire, lightning, explosion, windstorm, hail, smoke, aircraft, vehicles, riot, vandalism, sprinkler leaks, sinkholes, and volcanoes. In contrast, an all risk policy will cover you for anything except for certain perils that are specifically excluded (for example, earthquakes). All risk form policies cost somewhat more.

Before you purchase business property insurance, take an inventory of all your business property and estimate how much it would cost you to replace it if it was lost, destroyed, damaged, or stolen. Obtain replacement value business property coverage with a policy limit equal to this amount. If you can't afford that much coverage, consider a policy with a higher deductible. This is usually much wiser than obtaining coverage with a lower policy limit. If you insure your property for less than its full value, you won't be covered if you suffer a total loss.

Losses from earthquakes and floods aren't normally covered by business property policies. You can obtain earthquake insurance through a separate policy or as an "endorsement" (or enhancement) to your business property coverage. Flood insurance is usually handled through a separate policy called "difference in conditions." Unfortunately, if you live in a part of the country where these hazards are common, such insurance can be expensive.

Cheap Insurance for Your Electronic Equipment

If the only valuable business equipment you have is electronic equipment, such as a computer tablet, or smartphone, you may need only computer insurance. A company called Safeware will insure your electronic equipment against any type of loss except theft of electronic equipment left in an unattended car. The rates are based on the replacement cost of your property, not its present cash value. You can contact Safeware by telephone at 800-800-1492 or online at www.safeware.com.

If You Work at Home

If you work at home, there are several ways to obtain insurance coverage for your business property:

- **Homeowner's policies.** Your homeowner's insurance policy may provide you with a limited amount of insurance for business property (usually no more than $2,500 for property damaged or lost in your home and $250 away from your home). If you have very little business property, this might be enough coverage for you. But note that computer equipment may not be covered at all.

- **Homeowner's insurance endorsements.** You can double the amount of business property covered by your homeowner's policy by purchasing an endorsement. For example, you could increase your coverage from $2,500 to $5,000. The cost is usually only about $25 to $50 per year. However, these endorsements are usually available only for businesses that generate $5,000 or less in annual income. If business visitors occasionally come to your home, you can obtain a "rider" (or add-on) to your homeowner's policy that covers your liability should a visitor be injured while there. The cost is very modest, usually around $50 per year.

- **In-home policies.** The insurance industry has created a special policy for people who work at home. These in-home business policies insure your business property at a single location for up to $10,000. The cost is usually around $200 per year. For an additional premium, the policy includes liability coverage ranging from $300,000 to one million dollars. Liability premium costs are based on how much coverage you buy. There's also coverage available to protect against lost valuable papers, records, accounts receivable, off-site business property, and equipment.

- **BOP policies.** Business owners' policies (BOPs) are for businesses not based at home or for larger home-based businesses. Such policies combine both property and liability coverage in a single policy. BOPs are more expensive than in-home policies but provide the most comprehensive coverage available for small businesses.

- **Business property policies.** Some policies just cover your business property. This might be a good idea if you have extremely valuable business equipment.

If You Rent an Office

If you rent an office outside your home, read your lease carefully to see if it requires you to carry insurance. Many commercial landlords require their tenants to carry insurance to cover any damage the tenant does to the premises or injuries suffered by clients or visitors.

The lease may specify how much insurance you must carry. Your best bet is probably to get a BOP policy providing both property and liability coverage. Your landlord may require you to submit proof that you have insurance, such as a copy of the first page of your policy.

Even if your lease says nothing about property insurance, you may want to obtain coverage anyway. Remember, a building owner's property insurance policy usually doesn't cover the building tenants' property.

Liability Insurance

Liability insurance protects you when you're sued for something you did (or failed to do) that injures another person or damages property. It pays the legal fees to defend you against a lawsuit as well as any settlement or judgment against you up to the policy limit. Liability insurance also pays an injured person's medical bills. In our lawsuit-happy society, such insurance is often a must.

There are two different types of liability insurance:

- general liability insurance, and
- professional liability insurance.

You may need both types of coverage.

Some clients may require you to have liability insurance before they will hire you. Fortunately, such insurance is usually relatively inexpensive. Moreover, the cost is always tax deductible.

 CROSS-REFERENCE

Gig Workers: If you're a gig worker, the online hiring platform you contract with may provide you with some liability insurance coverage. See Chapter 16 for a detailed discussion.

Incorporating Provides Some Lawsuit Protection

Incorporating your business gives you some protection from lawsuits, but not as much as you may think. For example, incorporating may protect your personal assets from lawsuits by people who are injured on your premises, but it won't protect you from personal liability if someone is injured or damaged because of your malpractice or negligence: your failure to exercise your professional responsibilities with a reasonable amount of care.

Also, unless you have a decent insurance policy, all the assets of your incorporated business—which will probably amount to a large portion of your net worth—can be taken to satisfy a court judgment an injured person obtains against you. (See Chapter 2.)

General Liability Insurance

General liability insurance provides coverage for the types of lawsuits any business owner could face. For example, this type of insurance protects you if a client visiting your home office slips on the newly washed floor and breaks an arm, or if you knock over and shatter an heirloom vase while visiting a client at his or her home.

You definitely need this coverage if clients or customers visit your office. If you already have a homeowners' or renters' insurance policy, don't assume you're covered for these types of claims. Such policies ordinarily don't provide coverage for injuries to business visitors unless you obtain and pay for a special endorsement.

You also need general liability insurance if you do any part of your work away from your office, including in clients' offices or homes. You could injure someone or damage property while working there.

On the other hand, if you have little or no contact with the public, you may not need such insurance. For example, a freelance writer who works at home and never receives business visitors probably wouldn't need general liability coverage.

However, whether you want it or not, some clients may require you to carry liability insurance as a condition of doing business with you. Many clients are afraid that if you injure someone while working for them and you don't have insurance, the injured person will sue them instead. This fear is well founded: Lawyers tend to go after the person with the most money or insurance to pay a judgment. You might think this means you'd be better off with no insurance at all because people won't sue you, but this is not necessarily the case. If you have any money or property, there's a good chance you'll get sued. Liability insurance will protect you from losing everything you own.

Luckily, general liability insurance is not terribly expensive. You can usually obtain it for a few hundred dollars per year. You can purchase coverage:

- as part of a package policy such as a BOP, or
- by obtaining a separate general liability insurance policy known as a "commercial general liability" (CGL) policy, which may cost the most but will give you more coverage.

If you work at home, you may also be able to add an endorsement to your homeowners' policy to cover injuries to business visitors.

Professional Liability Insurance

General liability insurance does not cover professional negligence: claims for damages caused by a mistake you made or something you failed to do when performing professional services. You need a separate professional liability insurance policy, also known as "errors and omissions," or E & O, coverage. Some types of workers—doctors and lawyers, for example—are required by state law to obtain such insurance.

> **EXAMPLE:** Susan, an architect, designs a factory building that collapses, costing her client a fortune in damages and lost business. The client claims that Susan's design for the building was faulty and sues her for the economic losses it suffered. Susan's general liability policy won't cover such a claim. She needs a special E & O policy for architects.

Home-Based Architect Gets Liability Insurance

Mel, an architect, recently left a job with a large architectural firm in San Francisco to set up his own architecture business, designing homes and small commercial offices. He works out of an office in a detached studio in his backyard. Mel needs liability insurance.

First, Mel needs general liability insurance because clients, delivery people, and other business visitors come and go from his home office every week. Mel could be subject to a huge lawsuit if, for example, a client was injured after slipping on a roller skate left by Mel's son. Mel calls his homeowners' insurer and obtains an endorsement to his existing homeowners' policy that covers injuries to business visitors and insures up to $25,000 worth of his business equipment. He has to pay an additional $150 annual premium for $500,000 in liability coverage.

Mel also needs E & O insurance because he could be subject to a lawsuit for professional negligence if a problem occurs with one of his buildings. He shops around and decides to purchase coverage through the American Institute of Architects in Washington, DC, a leading membership organization for architects. Mel obtains a $1 million architect liability policy for $3,300 per year.

Professional liability insurance policies commonly cover the following types of workers:

- accountants
- architects
- attorneys
- doctors
- engineers
- insurance agents and brokers
- pension plan fiduciaries, and
- stockbrokers.

You can obtain E & O coverage for many other occupations as well if you're willing to pay the price. Because of the growing number of professional negligence suits and the huge costs of litigation, such insurance tends to be expensive, ranging from several hundred to several thousand dollars per year. The premiums you'll have to pay depend on many factors, including the following:

- **The claims history for your type of business.** Insurance costs more for businesses that generate lots of lawsuits.
- **The size of your business.** The more work you do, the more opportunity there is for you to make a mistake resulting in a lawsuit.
- **Your knowledge and experience in your field.** Less experienced self-employed people are more likely to make mistakes.
- **The size of your clients' businesses.** Mistakes involving large businesses will likely result in larger lawsuits than those involving small businesses.

If you need E & O insurance, the first place to look is a professional association. Many of them arrange for special deals with insurers offering lower rates, and those that don't can at least direct you to a good insurer.

Umbrella Coverage

Another type of liability insurance policy is called "umbrella coverage." An umbrella policy is designed to supplement regular liability insurance. It protects you if you suffer a major liability loss that exceeds the limits of your regular liability policy. For example, if you have a general liability insurance policy with a limit of $1 million and are sued for $2 million and lose, an umbrella policy will pay the $1 million not covered by your regular liability policy.

Umbrella coverage is relatively inexpensive because it merely supplements your regular insurance. You must have a regular liability policy before you can obtain umbrella coverage. There are no standard umbrella policies. Ideally, you want a policy that pays for all defense costs over your regular policy's limits, with no cap. Your regular liability coverage and umbrella coverage should run concurrently; in other words, they should cover the same time periods. This avoids unintended coverage gaps.

Car Insurance

If, like most self-employed people, you use your automobile for business as well as personal use—for example, visiting clients or transporting supplies—you need to be certain that your automobile insurance will protect you from accidents that may occur while on business. The personal automobile policy you already have may cover your business use of your car. On the other hand, it may specifically exclude coverage if you use your car for business.

Review your policy and discuss the matter with your insurance agent or auto insurer. You may need to purchase a separate business auto insurance policy or obtain a special endorsement covering your business use. Whatever you do, make sure your insurer knows that you use your car for business purposes (in addition to personal use and driving to and from your office). If you do not inform your insurer about this, it may cancel your coverage if a claim occurs that reflects a business use (for example, if you get into an accident while on a business trip).

If you keep one or more cars strictly for business use, you will definitely need a separate business automobile policy. You may be able to purchase such a policy from your personal auto insurer.

CROSS-REFERENCE

Gig Workers: If you're a gig worker who drives for Uber or Lyft or another ridesharing company, you need to pay special attention to your auto insurance coverage. Both Uber and Lyft provide auto insurance coverage; but you may need to supplement it with your own ridesharing coverage. See Chapter 16 for a detailed discussion.

Workers' Compensation Insurance

Each state has its own workers' compensation system that is designed to provide replacement income and cover medical expenses for employees who suffer work-related injuries or illnesses. Employers are required to pay for workers' compensation insurance for their employees, through either a state fund or a private insurance company.

Before the first workers' compensation laws were adopted about 80 years ago, an employee injured on the job had only one recourse: to sue the employer in court for negligence. This was often a difficult, time-consuming, and expensive process. The workers' compensation laws changed all this by establishing a no-fault system. Injured employees gave up their rights to sue in court. In return, employees became entitled to receive compensation without having to prove that the employer caused the injury. In exchange for paying for workers' compensation insurance, employers were spared from having to defend themselves against lawsuits by injured employees (and the resulting money damages).

Restricted to Employees

Workers' compensation is for employees, not self-employed people or independent contractors. If you are determined to be an independent contractor under your state's workers' compensation insurance law, your clients or customers need not provide you with workers' compensation coverage. Each state has its own test to determine if a worker qualifies as an employee or independent contractor for workers' compensation purposes.

 RESOURCE
For detailed information on how states classify workers for workers' compensation purposes, see *Working With Independent Contractors*, by Stephen Fishman (Nolo).

You should meet your state's definition for an independent contractor if you act to preserve your status as an independent contractor. (See Chapter 15.) However, whether you're an independent contractor or employee for workers' compensation purposes is the hiring firm's determination to make, not yours.

Your Worker Status

Not having to provide you with workers' compensation coverage saves your clients a lot of money but also presents them with a problem: If you're injured while working on a client's behalf, you could file a workers' compensation claim and allege that you're really the client's employee. If you prevail on your claim, you can collect workers' compensation benefits even if your injuries were completely your own fault. The state workers' compensation agency can also impose fines and penalties against your client if it determines that the client misclassified you as an independent contractor.

Many hiring firms respond to these fears by requiring you to obtain your own workers' compensation coverage, even if you choose not to. They're afraid that if you don't have your own coverage, you'll file a workers' compensation claim against them if you're injured on the job. Also, many workers' compensation insurers require hiring firms to pay additional premiums for any independent contractors they hire who don't have their own workers' compensation coverage.

If You Have Employees

Even if your clients don't require you to have it, you must obtain workers' compensation coverage if you have employees, depending on the state you live in and the number of employees you have. The workers' compensation laws of about one-fourth of the states exclude many small employers. Talk to an attorney to find out the laws in your state.

Many knowledgeable clients will want to see proof that you have workers' compensation insurance for your employees before they hire you because your state law will probably require your client to provide the insurance if you don't. The purpose of these laws is to prevent employers from avoiding paying for workers' compensation insurance by subcontracting work out to independent contractors who don't insure their employees.

After An Injury: Suing a Client for Negligence

Even if you have your own workers' compensation insurance, you can still sue a hiring firm for damages if its negligence caused or contributed to a work-related injury. Because you're not the hiring firm's employee, the workers' compensation provisions barring lawsuits by injured employees won't apply to you. The damages available through a lawsuit may far exceed the modest workers' compensation benefits to which you may be entitled.

EXAMPLE: Trish, a self-employed trucker, contracts to haul produce for the Acme Produce Co. Trish is self-employed and Acme does not provide her with workers' compensation insurance. At Acme's insistence, however, Trish obtains her own workers' compensation coverage. Trish loses her little finger when an Acme employee negligently drops a load of asparagus on her hand. Because Trish is self-employed, she can sue Acme in court for negligence even though she has workers' compensation insurance. If she can prove Acme's negligence, Trish can collect damages for her lost wages, medical expenses, and pain and suffering. These damages could far exceed the limited workers' compensation benefits Trish may be entitled to for losing her finger.

However, if you receive workers' compensation benefits and also obtain damages from the person that caused the injury, you may have to reimburse your workers' compensation insurer for any amounts it paid for your medical care. Your insurer might also be able to bring its own lawsuit against the firm that hired you.

Obtaining Coverage

Most small businesses buy workers' compensation insurance through a state fund or from a private insurance carrier. A few states require businesses to purchase coverage from a state fund; others allow businesses to choose between purchasing from a state fund or a private insurer. If private insurance is an option in your state, you may be able to save money on premiums by coordinating your workers' compensation insurance with your property damage and liability insurance.

Cost of Coverage

The cost of workers' compensation varies from state to state. What you will have to pay depends upon a number of factors, including:
- the size of your payroll
- the nature of your work, and
- how many claims your employees have filed in the past.

As you might expect, it costs far more to insure employees in hazardous occupations, such as construction, than to insure those who work in relatively safe jobs, such as clerical work. It might cost $200 to $300 a year to insure a clerical worker but perhaps ten times as much to insure a construction worker or roofer.

RESOURCE
Need more information on workers' comp? For links to all state workers' compensation agencies, state laws, insurers, and much other useful information, refer to www.workerscompensation.com.

Other Types of Insurance

There are several other types of insurance policies that may be useful for self-employed people:
- business interruption insurance, to replace the income you lose if your business property is damaged or destroyed due to fire or other disasters and you're forced to close, relocate, or reduce your business while you recover and rebuild
- electronic data processing (EDP) insurance, to compensate you for the cost of reconstructing the data you lose when your computer equipment is damaged or destroyed, and
- product liability insurance, which covers liability for injuries caused by products you design, manufacture, or sell.

If you're interested in any such coverage, talk to several agents who have experience dealing with self-employed people in your field. Professional and trade organizations may also be able to offer help.

Ways to Save on Insurance

There are a number of things you can do to make it easier to pay for insurance.

Comparison Shop

Insurance costs vary widely from company to company. You may be able to save a lot by shopping around. Today, it's easy to shop around for insurance online and obtain quotes for various types of coverage. You can obtain insurance quotes online from multiple insurers through websites such as www.insure.com, www.smallbusinessquote.com, www.netquote.com, and many others. Professional, trade, and other membership organizations may also help you find the insurance you need. You may also wish to contact an independent insurance broker or agent to help you comparison shop. If you don't know one, you can find a broker in your area through the website www.independentagent.com.

Also, review your coverage and rates periodically as insurance costs go up and down. If you're shopping for insurance during a time when prices are low, try locking in a low rate by signing up for a contract for three or more years.

Increase Your Deductibles

Your premiums will be lower if you obtain policies with high deductibles. For example, the difference between obtaining a policy with a $250 or a $500 deductible may be 10% in premium costs, and the difference between a $500 and $1,000 deductible may save you an additional 3% to 5%.

Find a Comprehensive Package

It's often cheaper to purchase a comprehensive insurance package that contains many types of coverage than to buy coverage piecemeal from several companies. Many insurers offer special policies or packages for small business owners that combine liability coverage for injuries to clients or their property while on your premises with fire, theft, and business interruption insurance.

Check on an Insurer's Financial Health

Several insurance companies have gone broke in recent years. If this happens and you have a loss covered by a policy, you may receive only a small part of the coverage you paid for, or none at all. The best way to avoid this is to obtain coverage from an insurer that is in good financial health.

Four independent agencies rate the financial health of insurance companies. Each has its own ratings scale and standards. They can disagree with each other, so look at the ratings from at least two agencies. These ratings agencies are:

- A.M. Best Company, www.ambest.com
- Moody's Investor Services, www.moodys.com/researchandratings
- Standard & Poor's Global Ratings, www.standardandpoors.com/en_US, and
- Fitch Ratings, www.fitchratings.com.

To use these websites, you have to register, but the ratings service is free. Insurance rating information can also be found at www.insure.com.

Deduct Your Business Insurance Costs

You can deduct the premiums for any type of insurance you obtain for your business from your taxable income. This includes business property insurance, liability insurance, insurance for business vehicles, and workers' compensation insurance. Car insurance and homeowners' or renters' insurance premiums are deductible to the extent you use your car or home for business. (See Chapter 9.)

The premiums for health insurance you obtain for yourself are deductible if you're a sole proprietor, partner in a partnership, or an S corporation owner. They are also deductible if you form a C corporation that provides insurance for you as its employee. (See Chapter 2.)

You may not deduct premiums for life or disability insurance for yourself. But if you become disabled, the disability insurance benefits you receive are not taxable.

Pricing Your Services and Getting Paid

Two difficult questions self-employed workers face are how much to charge clients and how to make sure they get paid for their services. This chapter will help you figure out how to set your fees and give you ideas about what to do when clients or customers don't pay what they owe you.

Pricing Your Services

New and experienced self-employed people alike are often perplexed about how much to charge. No book can tell you how much your services are worth, but this section gives you some factors to consider in making this determination.

How the Self-Employed Are Paid

There are no legal rules controlling how (or how much) you are paid. It is entirely a matter for negotiation between you and your clients. Some clients insist on paying all self-employed people they hire by the same method (for example, a fixed fee or an hourly rate). Others are more flexible. Many self-employed people also have strong preferences for particular payment methods; for example, some insist on being paid by the hour.

If you're a gig worker who obtains work through online hiring platforms, you may have little choice about what to charge. Some platforms, like Uber and Lyft, dictate how much you may charge for your services. Others, however, permit you to set your fees.

When you're first starting out, you may wish to try several different payment methods with different clients to see which works best for you. However, if the customary practices in your field dictate a particular payment method, you may have no choice in the matter. Other self-employed colleagues and professional organizations can give you information on the practices in your particular field.

This section provides an overview of the most common payment methods for the self-employed. However, these are by no means the only ways you can be paid. Certain fields may use other methods. For example, freelance writers are often paid a fixed amount for each word or article they write.

RESOURCE

For more information on payment methods and setting fees, see:

- *Consulting Fees: A Guide for Independent Consultants,* by Andrea Coutu (Consultant Journal Guides), and
- *What to Charge: Pricing Strategies for Freelancers and Consultants,* by Laurie Lewis (Outskirts Press).

Fixed Fee

In a fixed-fee agreement, you charge a set amount for an entire project. Your fixed fee can include all your expenses—for example, materials costs and travel expenses—or you can bill them separately to the client.

Most clients like fixed-fee agreements because they know exactly what they'll have to pay for your services. However, fixed fees can be risky for you. If you underestimate the time and expense required to complete the project, you could earn much less than your work was worth or even lose money. Some self-employed people refuse to use fixed-fee agreements for this reason. For example, one self-employed technical writer always charges by the hour because she says she's never had a project that didn't last longer than both she and the client anticipated.

> EXAMPLE: Ellen, a graphic artist, agrees to design a series of book covers for the Scrivener & Sons Publishing Co. Her fixed-price contract provides that she'll be paid $10,000 for all the covers. Ellen estimates that the project will take 75 hours at most, so she would earn at least $132 per hour, more than her normal hourly rate of $100 per hour.
>
> However, due to the publisher's exacting standards and demands for revisions, the project ends up taking Ellen 125 hours. As a result, she earns only $80 per hour for the project, far less than what she would have charged had she billed by the hour.

Although fixed-fee agreements can be risky, they can also be very rewarding if you work efficiently and accurately estimate how much time and money a project will take. Surveys of the self-employed have consistently found that fixed-fee agreements are more profitable than other types of contracts. For example, one study found that self-employed people who charged fixed fees earned on average 150% more than those who charged by the hour for the same services. A similar survey found that self-employed people charging fixed fees earned 95% more than their colleagues who charged by the hour or day.

Reducing the Risks of Fixed Fees

There are several ways to reduce the risks involved in charging a fixed fee: Carefully define the scope of the project in writing before determining your fee. If this will take a substantial amount of time, you may wish to charge the client a flat fee or an hourly rate to compensate you for the work involved in this assessment process.

- Leave some room for error or surprises when you calculate your fee, by charging the client as if the project will take a bit longer than you think it will.
- Consider placing a cap on the total number of hours you'll work on the project. Once the cap is reached, you and the client must negotiate new payment terms. For example, the client might increase your fixed fee or agree to pay you by the hour until the project is finished.
- Make sure your agreement with the client contains a provision allowing you to renegotiate your price if the client makes changes or the project takes longer than you estimated. (See Chapter 19.)

Unit of Time

It's safer for you to be paid for your time—that is, by the number of hours or days you spend on a project—rather than a fixed fee. This is especially true if you are unsure how long or difficult the project will be or if the client is likely to demand substantial changes midstream. Many self-employed people refuse to work any other way. This method of payment is customary in many fields, including law and accounting.

However, clients are often nervous about paying by the hour, afraid you'll spread out the project for as long as possible to earn more money. Clients will often seek to place a limit on the total number of hours you can spend on the project to limit the total amount they'll have to spend. Others will require you to provide a time estimate. If you do this, be sure to call the client before spending more time on the project than you estimated.

As with fixed fees, it's a good idea to leave some margin for error when you provide a time estimate. One self-employed person says she determines how many hours a job will take by first deciding how long it should take, doubling that number and then adding 25%. You may not need to go to this extreme, but it's wise to be conservative when estimating the time any project will require.

Fixed and Hourly Fee Combinations

You can also combine a fixed fee with an hourly payment to reduce the risk that you'll be underpaid. If you can't accurately estimate how much time or effort some part of the project might take, charge by the hour for the indeterminable portion and charge a fixed fee for the rest of the project. For example, if your work involves some tasks that are essentially mechanical and others that are highly creative, you can probably accurately estimate how long the mechanical work will take but may have great difficulty estimating how much time the creative work will require. You can reduce the risk of underpayment by charging a fixed fee for the mechanical work and billing by the hour for the creative work.

> EXAMPLE: Bruno, a freelance graphic artist, is hired by Scrivener & Sons Publishing Co. to produce the cover for its new detective thriller *And Then You Die*. Bruno has absolutely no idea how long it will take him to come up with an acceptable design for the cover. He charges Scrivener $75 per hour for this design work. Once a design is accepted, however, Bruno knows exactly how long it will take him to produce a camera-ready version. He charges Scrivener a fixed fee of $1,000 for this routine production work.

Retainer Agreements

With a retainer agreement, you receive a fixed fee up front in return for promising to be available to work a certain number of hours for the client each month or to perform a specified task. Often, the client pays a lump sum retainer fee at the outset of the agreement. Or, you can be paid on a regular schedule (for example, monthly, quarterly, or annually).

> EXAMPLE: Jean, an accountant, agrees to perform up to 20 hours of accounting services for Acme Co. every month, for which Acme pays her $1,500 per month.

Many self-employed people like retainer agreements because they provide a guaranteed source of income. But in return for this security, you usually have to charge somewhat less than you do when paid on a per-project basis. Also, retainer agreements can contradict your work status. If you spend most of your time working for a single client, the IRS may view you as that client's employee. (See Chapter 15.)

Performance Billing

Perhaps the riskiest form of billing is performance billing, also known as charging a contingency fee. Basically, this means you get paid according to the value of the results you achieve for a client. If you get poor results, you may receive little or nothing. Clients generally favor this type of arrangement because they don't have to pay you if your services don't benefit them. Using this type of fee arrangement can help you get business if a client is skeptical that you'll perform as promised or if you're providing a new service with benefits that are not generally understood.

This type of fee arrangement is used most often for sales or marketing projects in which the fee is based on a percentage of the increased business.

> EXAMPLE: Alice, a marketing consultant, contracts to perform marketing services for Acme Co. to help increase its sales. Acme agrees to pay her 25% of the total increase in gross sales over the next 12 months. If sales don't go up, Alice gets nothing.

Some self-employed people reduce the risks involved in performance billing by requiring their clients to pay them a minimum amount regardless of the results they achieve. For example, a contract might provide that a sales trainer would receive $5,000 for providing training services plus 10% of the increase in the client's sales for a specified number of months after the training program.

If you use a performance contract, don't tie your compensation to the client's profits. Clients can easily manipulate their profits—and therefore reduce your compensation—through accounting gimmicks. Use a standard that is easier to measure and harder to manipulate, such as the client's gross sales or some measurable cost saving.

Commissions

Self-employed people who sell products or services are often paid by commission, receiving a set amount for each sale they make. Many independent sales representatives, brokers, distributors, and agents are paid on a commission basis.

> EXAMPLE: Mark is a self-employed salesperson who sells industrial filters. He receives a commission from the filter manufacturer for each filter he sells. The commission is equal to 20% of the price of the filter.

If you're a good salesperson, you can earn far more on commission than with any other payment method. But if business is poor, your earnings will suffer.

Determining Your Hourly Rate

However you're paid, you need to determine how much to charge per hour. This is so even if you're paid a fixed fee for an entire project. To determine the fixed fee you should charge, you must estimate how many hours the job will take, multiply the total by your hourly rate, then add your expenses. Knowing how much you should earn per hour will also help you know whether using a retainer agreement or performance billing is cost-effective or whether a sales commission is fair.

If you're experienced in your field, you probably already know what to charge because you are familiar with market conditions: how much demand for and supply of your services exists and how much others in your field charge. However, if you're just starting out, you may have no idea what you can or should charge. If you're in this boat, try using a two-step approach to determine your hourly rate:

1. Calculate what your rate should be, based on your expenses.
2. Investigate the marketplace to see if you should adjust your rate up or down.

Hourly Rate Based on Expenses

A standard formula for determining an hourly rate requires you to add together your labor and overhead costs, add the profit you want to earn, then divide the total by your hours worked. This is the absolute minimum you must charge to pay your expenses, pay yourself a salary, and earn a profit. Depending on market conditions, you may be able to charge more for your services or you might have to charge less.

To determine how much your labor is worth, pick a figure for your annual salary. This can be what you earned for doing similar work when you were an employee, what other employees earn for similar work, or how much you'd like to earn.

Next, compute your annual overhead. Overhead includes all the costs you incur to do business, such as those for:

- rent and utilities
- business insurance
- website expenses
- stationery and supplies
- postage and delivery
- office equipment and furniture
- clerical help
- travel expenses
- professional association memberships
- legal and accounting fees
- telephone expenses
- business-related meals and entertainment
- advertising and marketing (for example, the cost of an online ad or a brochure), and
- your fringe benefits, such as medical insurance, disability insurance, your retirement fund contribution, and your income and self-employment taxes.

If you're just starting out, you'll have to estimate these expenses or ask other self-employed people to give you some idea of their overhead costs.

You're also entitled to earn a profit over and above your labor and overhead expenses. Your salary is part of your costs; it does not include profit. Profit is the reward you get for taking the risks of being in business for yourself. It also provides money you can use to expand and develop your business. Profit is usually expressed as a percentage of total costs. There is no standard profit percentage, but a 10% to 20% profit is common.

Finally, you must determine how many hours you'll work during the year. Assume you'll work a 40-hour week for purposes of this calculation, although you may choose to work less or end up working more. If you want to take a two-week vacation, you'll have a maximum of 2,000 billable hours (50 weeks × 40 hours). If you want more time off, you'll have fewer billable hours.

However, you'll probably spend at least 25% to 35% of your time on tasks such as bookkeeping and billing, marketing your services, upgrading your skills, and doing other things you can't bill to clients. Assuming a 40-hour workweek and two weeks of vacation away from work, this means you'll likely have at most 1,300 to 1,500 hours for which you can get paid each year.

> EXAMPLE: Sam, a self-employed Web designer, earned a $100,000 salary as an employee and wants to receive at least the same salary. He estimates that his annual overhead amounts to $20,000 per year. He wants to earn a 10% profit and estimates he'll have 1,500 billable hours each year. To determine his hourly rate, Sam must:
>
> 1. Add his salary and overhead together $ 100,000
>   +   20,000
> $ 120,000
> 2. Multiply this total by his 10% profit margin   x   10%
>   and add the amount to his salary and overhead $ 12,000
>   120,000
> $ 132,000
> 3. Divide the total by his annual billable hours   ÷   1,500
> $ 88
>
> Sam determines that his hourly rate should be $88. He rounds this off to $90. However, depending on market conditions, Sam might end up charging more or less.

Hourly Rate Worksheet

You can use the worksheet below to calculate your hourly rate. There are also numerous online calculators and apps you can use, such as the BeeWits Hourly Rate Calculator at https://hourlyrate.beewits.com.

Hourly Rate Worksheet

Yearly overhead expenses

    Marketing

    Travel   _____

    Legal and accounting costs   _____

    Insurance   _____

    Supplies   _____

    Rent   _____

    Utilities   _____

    Telephone   _____

    Professional association memberships   _____

    Business meals and entertainment   _____

    Benefits   _____

    Taxes   _____

    Other   _____

    Total overhead expenses   _____

Total overhead expenses	$_____	
Annual salary you want to earn	+ _____	
Total expenses	$_____	
Total expenses	$_____	
Desired profit %	x _____%	
Profit	$_____	
Profit	$_____	
Total expenses	+ _____	
Target revenue	$_____	
Target revenue	$_____	
Billable hours	÷ _____	
Hourly rate	$_____	

A Calculating Shortcut

An easier but less accurate way to calculate your hourly rate is to find out what hourly salary you'd likely receive if you were to provide your services as an employee in someone else's business and multiply this by 2.5 or 3. This is a much more crude measure that business management experts have developed to calculate how much money you must earn to pay your expenses and salary plus earn a profit.

> EXAMPLE: Betty, a freelance paralegal, knows that employees performing the same work receive $25 per hour. She should charge $62.50 to $75 per hour.

You can find out what many companies pay employees who do work similar to yours on websites like www.salary.com, www.glassdoor.com, and www.payscale.com.

You can also obtain salary information for virtually every conceivable occupation from *The Occupational Outlook Handbook*, published by the U.S. Department of Labor and available at www.bls.gov/oco.

Investigate the Marketplace

It's not enough to calculate how much you'd like to earn per hour. You also have to determine whether this figure is realistic. This requires you to do a little sleuthing to find out what other self-employed people are charging for similar services and what the clients you'd like to work for are willing to pay. There are many ways to gather this information, such as the following: Contact a professional organization or trade association for your field. It may be able to tell you what other self-employed people are charging in your area.

- Some professional organizations even publish pricing guides. For example, the Graphic Artists Guild puts out a *Handbook of Pricing & Ethical Guidelines* for freelance graphic artists.
- Ask self-employed colleagues what they charge. You can communicate about pricing with other self-employed people on the Web. Some freelancers list the fees they typically charge on their websites.

- Talk with potential clients and customers—for example, attend trade shows and business conventions.
- Take a look at websites, such as Upwork.com and Freelancer.com, that post freelance jobs and display bids by site visitors. Keep in mind, however, that bids by people outside the U.S. can be ridiculously low.

Your investigation will likely reveal that there is a wide range of fees charged by people who sell services in your field.

Experimenting With Charging

Pricing is an art, not an exact science. There are no magic formulas, and sayings such as "Charge whatever the market will bear" are not very helpful. The best way—indeed, the only way—to discover how to charge and how much to charge is to experiment. Try out different payment methods and fee structures with different clients and see which work best for you.

The Self-Employed Should Be Paid More Than Employees

Don't be afraid to ask for more per hour than employees earn for doing similar work. It's not unreasonable for self-employed people to be paid a higher hourly rate than employees. Hiring firms do not provide the self-employed with employee benefits, such as health insurance, vacations, sick leave, or retirement plans. Nor do hiring firms have to pay payroll taxes for them. This saves a hiring firm a bundle: Employee benefits and payroll taxes add at least 20% to 40% to employers' payroll costs. Hiring firms often hire independent contractors because they cost less than employees.

In addition, in our economic system, people in business for themselves are supposed to earn more than employees because they take much greater risks. They have many business expenses employees don't have, such as office rent, supplies, and marketing costs. Unlike most employees, self-employed workers don't get paid if business is bad. It's only fair, then, that they should be paid more than employees when business is good.

You may discover that you are not able to get your ideal hourly rate because other self-employed people are charging less in your area. However, if you're highly skilled and performing work of unusually high quality, don't be afraid to ask for more than other self-employed people with lesser skills charge. Lowballing your fees won't necessarily get you business. Many potential clients believe they get what they pay for and are willing to pay more for quality work.

One approach is to start out charging a fee that is at the lower end of the spectrum for self-employed people performing similar services, then gradually increase it until you start meeting price resistance. Over time, you should be able to find a payment method and fee structure that enables you to get enough work and that adequately compensates for your services.

Getting Paid

Hiring firms normally pay their employees like clockwork. Employers know that if they don't pay on time, their employees can get the state labor department to investigate and fine them. Also, employers usually depend upon their employees for the daily operation of their businesses, so they need to keep the workforce as content as possible.

Unfortunately, no similar incentives encourage hiring firms to pay the self-employed. Many self-employed people have trouble getting paid by their clients. Some hiring firms feel free to pay outside workers late; some never pay at all. Sometimes this is because of cash flow problems, but often it's because hiring firms know that the self-employed don't always have the time, money, or will to force them to pay on time. One consultant complains that delaying payment is an almost automatic response for a lot of companies: "They seem to figure that if you don't nag, you don't really want to get paid."

As an independent businessperson, it's entirely up to you to take whatever steps are appropriate and necessary to get paid. No government agency will help you. Here are some strategies you can use to get clients to pay on time (or at least eventually).

CROSS-REFERENCE

Gig Workers: If you're a gig worker, your billings and payments will be processed through the online hiring platform you contract with. You'll ordinarily have to utilize the platform's procedures if you have trouble getting paid. See Chapter 16 for a detailed discussion.

Avoid Payment Problems

Taking a healthy dose of preventive medicine before you sign on with a client can help you eliminate, or at least reduce, payment problems.

Use Written Agreements

If you have only an oral agreement with a client who fails to pay you, it can be very hard to collect what you're owed. Without a writing, the client can claim you didn't perform as agreed or can easily dispute the amount due. Unless you have witnesses to support your version of the oral agreement, it will be your word against the client's. At the very least, you should have something in writing that describes the services you agree to perform, the deadline for performance, and the payment terms. (See Chapter 19.)

Find Out If a Purchase Order Is Required

A purchase order is a document a client uses to authorize you to be paid for your services. (See "Client Purchase Orders" in Chapter 20.) Some clients will not pay you unless you have a signed purchase order, even if you already have a signed contract. Find out whether your client uses purchase orders and obtain one before you start work to avoid payment problems later on.

Ask for a Down Payment

If you're dealing with a new client or one who has money problems, ask for a down payment before you begin work. Some self-employed people refer to such a payment as a "retainer." This will show that the client is serious about paying you. And even if the client doesn't pay you in full, you'll at least have obtained something. Some self-employed people ask for as much as one-third to one-half of their fees in advance.

> ### If You Deal With a Client by Email Only
>
> If you deal with a client solely by email, make sure you have a physical address for the client before you start work. Otherwise, you may have trouble tracking the client down if it fails to pay. Also, if the client is located out of state or in another country, be aware that it may not be economically feasible to bring a collection lawsuit. This means you should get as much money as possible up front.

Use Periodic Payment Schedules

For projects lasting more than a couple of months, try using payment schedules that require the client to pay you in stages. For example, you might ask for one-third when you begin work, one-third when you complete half your work, and one-third when you finish the entire project. Complex projects can be divided into phases or milestones with a payment due when you complete each phase.

If a client misses a payment, you can stop work. If you're never paid in full, you'll at least have obtained partial payment, so the entire project won't be a loss. A staged payment schedule will also improve your cash flow.

Make It Easy for the Client to Pay You

You'll get paid more quickly if you make it as easy as possible for the client to get money into your hands. For example, you could accept electronic payments from online payment services such as PayPal. You could also have clients pay your bank account directly by electronic funds transfer. If you have a business checking account, your bank may offer online invoicing and payment services. Accepting credit or debit card payments can also speed up payment.

Check the Client's Credit

The most effective way to avoid payment problems is to avoid clients with bad credit histories. A company that habitually fails to pay other creditors will likely give you payment problems as well. If you're dealing with a well-established company or government agency that is clearly solvent, you may forgo a credit check. But if you've never heard of the company, a credit check is prudent.

The most effective way to check a client's credit is to obtain a credit report from a credit reporting agency. Dun & Bradstreet, the premier credit reporting agency for businesses, maintains a database containing credit information on millions of companies. You can obtain a credit report on any company in Dun & Bradstreet's database at www.dandb.com, or by calling 800-700-2733. A basic business credit report costs $62 (as of 2018).

A basic Dun & Bradstreet credit report contains information on the company's payment history and financial condition. It will also tell you whether the company has had any lawsuits, judgments, or liens filed against it and whether it has ever filed for bankruptcy. Dun & Bradstreet also assigns a credit rating to help you predict which companies will pay slowly or not at all. Before taking on a large project that may require weeks or months of your time, this might be a good investment.

A cheaper but more time-consuming way to check a potential client's credit is to ask the client to provide you with credit information and references. This is better than nothing but may not give you an accurate picture; potential clients may try to avoid tipping you off about their financial problems by giving you the names of references who have not had problems with them.

Credit checks are routine these days, so your request for credit credentials is not likely to drive away business. Be wary of any potential client that refuses to give you credit information.

Contact the accounting department of the credit references provided and ask if the company has experienced any payment problems with the client. Accounting departments are typically asked for this information and will usually provide it freely. A Google search for the client's name may also uncover financial problems.

If a credit report or your own investigation reveals that a potential client has a bad credit history or is in financial trouble, you may prefer not to do business with that client. However, you may not be able to afford to work only for clients with perfect credit records. If you want to go ahead and do the work, obtain as much money up front as possible and be on the lookout for payment problems. If the client is a corporation or limited liability company, you may seek to have its owners sign a personal guarantee, discussed below.

Check the Form of Ownership

Your investigation of a potential client should include determining how its business is organized legally. This could have a big impact on your ability to collect a judgment against the client if it fails to pay you.

What's in a Name? A Lot

Often, you can tell how a potential client's business is organized legally just by looking at its name. If it's a corporation, its name will normally be followed by the word "Incorporated," "Corporation," "Company," or "Limited," or the abbreviation "Inc.," "Corp.," "Co.," or "Ltd." Partnerships often have the word "Partnership" or "Partners" in their names, but not always. A limited liability company will usually have the words "Limited Liability Company," "Limited Company," or the abbreviation "L.C.," "LLC," or "Ltd. Co." in its name. Sole proprietors often use their own names, but they don't have to do so. They may use fictitious business names or DBAs that are completely different from their own names.

If you win a lawsuit against a client that fails to pay you, the court will order the client to pay you a specified sum of money. This is known as a court judgment. Unfortunately, if the client fails or refuses to pay the judgment, the court will not help you collect it. You've got to do it yourself or hire someone to help you. However, there are many legal tools you can use to collect a court judgment. For example, you can file liens on the client's property that make it impossible for the client to sell the property without paying you, tap the client's bank accounts, and even have business or personal property, such as the client's car, seized by local law enforcement and sold.

Your ability to collect a court judgment may be helped—or severely hindered—by the way the client's business is organized legally:

- If the client is a sole proprietorship—that is, owns the business individually—he or she is personally liable for any debts the business owes you. This means that both the proprietor's business assets and his or her own personal assets are available to satisfy the debt. For example, both the proprietor's business and personal bank accounts may be tapped to pay you.

- If the client is a partner in a partnership, you can go after the personal assets of all the general partners. Be sure to get all their names before you start work. If the partnership is a limited partnership, you can't touch the assets of the limited partners, so don't worry about getting their names.
- If the client is a corporation, you could have big problems collecting a judgment. Normally, you can't go after the personal assets of a corporation's owners, such as the personal bank accounts of the shareholders and officers. Instead, you're limited to collecting from the corporation's assets. If the corporation is insolvent or goes out of business, there may be no assets to collect.
- If the client is a limited liability company (LLC), normally its owners will not be personally liable for any debts the business incurred, just as if it were a corporation.

Obtain a Personal Guarantee

If you're worried about the creditworthiness of a new or small incorporated client or limited liability company, you may ask its owners to sign a personal guarantee. A person who signs a personal guarantee, known as a "guarantor," promises to pay someone else's debt. This is the same as cosigning a loan. A guarantor who doesn't pay can be sued for the amount of the debt by the person to whom the money is owed.

You can ask for a personal guarantee from the officers or owners of a company you're afraid will not pay you. The guarantee legally obligates them to pay your fee if the company does not. This means that if the client fails to pay you, you can sue not only the client but the guarantors as well; and, you can go after their personal assets if you obtain a court judgment.

> EXAMPLE: Albert, a self-employed consultant, contracts to perform services for Melt, Inc., a company involved in the ice cream business. Melt is a corporation owned primarily by Barbara, a multimillionaire. Albert's contract contains a personal guarantee requiring Barbara to pay him if the corporation doesn't.

Melt goes broke when botulism is discovered in its ice cream, and the company fails to pay Albert. Albert files a lawsuit against Barbara and easily obtains a judgment on the basis of the personal guarantee. When Barbara refuses to pay, Albert gets a court order enabling him to tap into one of her hefty personal bank accounts and is paid in full.

Having a personal guarantee will not only help you collect a judgment, it will also help prevent payment problems. The guarantors will have a strong incentive to make sure you're paid in full and on time. By doing so, they safeguard their personal assets.

Not many self-employed people ever think about asking for personal guarantees, so some clients may be taken aback if you do so. Explain that you need the added protection so you can extend the credit the client seeks. Also, note that signing a guarantee presents no risk at all to the business's owners as long as you're paid on time. You might also give the client a choice: The business's owners can either provide you with a personal guarantee or give you a substantial down payment up front.

A personal guarantee can be a separate document, but the easiest way to create one is to include a guarantee clause at the end of your contract with the client.

EXAMPLE: Andre Bocuse, a self-employed consultant, agrees to perform consulting services for Acme Corp., a one-person corporation owned by Joe Jones. Because Andre has never worked for Acme before and is worried about being paid, he asks Joe Jones to sign a personal guarantee. This way, he knows he can go after Jones's personal assets if Acme doesn't pay up. He adds the following clause to the end of his contract with Acme and has Jones sign it:

In consideration of Andre Bocuse's entering into this Agreement with Acme Corporation, I personally guarantee the performance of all of the contractual obligations undertaken by Acme Corporation, including complete and timely payment of all sums due Andre Bocuse under the Agreement.

Joe Jones
Joe Jones

Send Invoices to Your Clients

Send invoices to your clients as soon as you complete work. You don't have to wait until the end of the month. Create a standard invoice to use with all your clients. Accounting or invoice software can create invoices for you. There are also many online services, such as *QuickBooks, FreshBooks,* and *Zoho,* online, that you can use to create and send invoices. The bank where your have your business bank account may also offer online invoicing services. Such services can track clients' billing information, monitor balances, and track overdue payments. You can also choose to have your own invoices printed.

Your invoice should contain:

- your company name, address, phone number, and email address
- the client's name and address, and the name of the contact person for your account
- an invoice number
- the date
- the client's purchase order number or contract number, if any
- the terms of payment
- the time period covered by the invoice
- an itemized description of the services you performed (if you're billing by the hour, list the number of hours expended and the hourly rate)
- if you're billing separately for expenses or materials, the amounts of these items
- the total amount due, and
- your signature.

Find out ahead of time how you should submit your invoices. Most clients will accept emailed invoices. Others may want paper invoices sent by mail. If you send the invoice by postal mail, include a self-addressed return envelope with your invoice. This tiny investment can help speed up payment.

Make at least two copies of each invoice: one for the client and one for your records. You may also want to make a third copy to keep in an unpaid invoices folder so you can keep track of when payments are overdue.

An example of a self-employed worker's invoice is provided below.

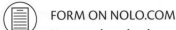 **FORM ON NOLO.COM**
You can download a copy of the Invoice form from this book's
companion page on Nolo.com. For details on finding this and other forms on
Nolo.com, which you can tailor to your own use, see "List of Forms Available on
the Nolo Website" at the end of Appendix A of this book.

Number Your Invoices

Assigning numbers to all your invoices will help you keep track of them. Your
invoices should be numbered in chronological order using a commonsense
system. There are various numbering systems you can use. You can number
your invoices by year (for example, 2019-20 would be the 20th invoice you
sent during 2019). Another common system is to create a unique code for
each project (for example, ACME 2019-03 would be the third invoice for the
Acme project sent during 2019).

Terms of Payment

The terms of payment are one of the most important items in your invoice.
It sets the ultimate deadline by which the client must pay you. This varies
from industry to industry and will also vary from client to client. Thirty
days is common, but some clients will want 45, 60, or even 90 days.

Obviously, the shorter the payment period, the better off you'll be.
This is something you should discuss with the client before you agree to
take a job. Some self-employed people ask for payment within 15 days
or immediately after the services are completed. However, some clients'
accounting departments aren't set up to meet such short deadlines. If you
have a written client agreement, it should indicate how long the client has
to pay you.

The standard way to indicate the payment terms in your invoice is to
use the word "Net" followed by the number of days the client has to pay
after receipt of the invoice. For example, "Net 30" means you want full
payment in 30 days. However, not everybody understands what "net"

Sample Invoice for Self-Employed Worker

Invoice

John Smith
1000 Grub Street
Marred Vista, CA 90000
999-555-5555
Smith@Smith.com

Date: 4/30/20xx

Invoice Number: 103

Your Order Number: 2019-20

Terms: Net 30

Time period of: 4/1/20xx–4/30/20xx

To: Susan Elroy
Accounting Department
Acme Widget Company
10400 Long Highway
Marred Vista, CA 90000

Services:
Consulting services of John Smith on thermal analysis of
Zot2 650 control unit. 50 hours @ $100.00 per hour.

Subtotal: $5,000

Material Costs: None

Expenses: 0

TOTAL AMOUNT OF THIS INVOICE: $5,000

Signed by: *John Smith*

means in this context. So, if you're dealing with a less sophisticated client, you'll be better off using clearer language, such as "payment is due ten days after receipt of our invoice." If you want immediate payment, you should say "Payment is due on receipt of this invoice."

Some self-employed people offer discounts to clients or customers that pay quickly. A common discount is 2% for payment within ten days after the invoice is received. If such a discount can get a slow-paying client to pay you quickly, it's worth it. You're always better off getting 98% of what you're owed right away than having to wait months for payment in full.

The traditional way to note a discount on your invoice is to include the percentage followed by the number of days the client has to pay to receive the discount. For example, "2% 10" means that the client can deduct 2% of the total due if it pays you within ten days. State your discount before the normal payment terms. For example, "2% 10 Net 30" means the client gets a 2% discount if it pays within ten days, but the full amount must be paid within 30 days. A less traditional, but also less cryptic, way to express a discount is to say something like, "You may discount the amount of this bill by ____% if we receive payment within ____ days of the invoice date."

Charge Late Fees

One way to get clients to pay on time is to charge late fees for overdue payments. One consultant was experiencing major problems with late-paying clients; 40% of his clients were over 30 days late in paying him. After he began charging a late fee, the number dropped to 5%. One recent survey by the electronic invoicing company FreshBooks found that freelancers who charged a late fee were not paid any more quickly than those who did not. However, more of them were paid eventually.

However, late fees don't always work; some clients simply refuse to pay them. Not paying a late fee when required in your invoice is a breach of contract by the client, but it's usually not worth the trouble to go to court to collect a late fee.

If you wish to charge a late fee, make sure it's mentioned in your agreement. You should also clearly state the amount of your late fee on all your invoices. For example, your invoices should include the phrase: "Accounts not paid within terms are subject to a ____% monthly finance charge."

The late fee is normally expressed as a monthly interest or finance charge. For example, 1.5% per month (18% per year) is a commonly charged late fee. However, depending on your state, this fee could be in excess of your state usury law. One way to deal with this is to use a clause like the following: "All overdue payments will be subject to a late fee of _____% per month, or the legally allowable maximum, if that amount is less."

> ⊘ CAUTION
> **Some states restrict late fees.** Your state might limit how much you can charge as a late fee. You'll have to investigate your state laws to find out. State usury laws are notoriously complicated, with numerous exceptions and exemptions. Usually, these laws allow different interest rates for consumer and business loans. Charging a late fee to a business to which you've provided professional services may not come within your state's usury law at all. This is the case, for example, in California, where businesses are free to agree to any late fee interest rate. You can find links to the usury law of your state at www.loanback.com/category/usury-laws-by-state. Your professional or trade organization may also have helpful information on this issue.

Collecting Overdue Accounts

If your invoice isn't paid on time, act quickly to collect. Clients who consistently pay late or do not pay at all can put you out of business. Moreover, often the longer a client fails to pay, the less likely it is that you'll ever be paid.

When an Account Is Overdue

Money that your client or customer owes you is called an "account receivable." Keep track of the age of your accounts receivable so you know when a client's payment is late and how late it is. Accounting software can keep track of the age of your accounts receivable.

However, there is a simple way to do this without a computer. Make an extra copy of each of your invoices and keep them in a folder or notebook marked "Unpaid Invoices." When a client pays you, discard the extra copy of the applicable invoice. By looking in this notebook, you can tell exactly which clients haven't paid and how late their payments are.

Consider a client late if it fails to pay you within ten days after the due date on your invoice. At this point, you should contact the client and find out why you haven't been paid.

Don't delay making your first collection call in the hope that a check will soon arrive in the mail. Chances are good that the check isn't in the mail—and won't get there until the client gets your call.

CAUTION
Find out where clients bank. If a client pays you by check, make a note of the name and address of the bank and the account number and place it in your client file. This information will come in handy if you ever have to collect a judgment against the client.

Communicating With Deadbeat Clients by Email

Many self-employed people communicate with their clients primarily (or solely) by email. When it comes to collecting overdue accounts, it's best not to rely solely on emails. These are easily overlooked, or a client can claim he or she never received your email. Settlements or final demands should always be confirmed by postal mail, which can be sent return receipt requested or by certified mail to ensure that they are received by the client.

Contact the Client

Don't rely on collection letters or collection emails. A phone call will have far more impact. Unfortunately, it can often be hard to get clients to return your collection calls. To reduce the time you spend playing phone tag, ask what time the client will be in and call back then. If you leave a phone message, state the time of day you receive return calls (for example, every afternoon from 1 p.m. to 5 p.m.).

Your First Collection Call

During your first collection call, you want to either solve a problem that has arisen or handle a stalled payment. Write down who said what during this and each subsequent phone call.

Prepare before you make your call. You should know exactly how much the client owes you and have a copy of your invoice and any purchase order in front of you when you dial the number. Also, make sure you speak with the appropriate person. In large companies, this may be someone in the accounts payable or purchasing departments; in small companies, it could be the owner.

Politely inform the client that the payment is past due. About 80% of the time, late payments are caused by problems with invoices. For example, your client may not have received an invoice or may have misplaced or misunderstood it. You may simply have to send another invoice or provide a brief explanation of why you charged as you did.

Sample Confirming Letter #1

April 15, 20xx

Sue Jones, President
Acme Corporation
123 Main Street
Marred Vista, CA 90000

Re: Your contract # 1234
    Invoice # 102

Dear Sue:

Thank you for your offer to submit $500 per month to pay off your company's outstanding balance of $2,000 on the above account.

As agreed, I am willing to accept $500 monthly payments for four months until this debt is satisfied. The payments are due on the first of each month, beginning May 1, 20xx, and continuing monthly through August 1, 20xx.

As long as the payments are made on time, I will withhold all further action.

Thank you for your cooperation.

Very truly yours,

Andre Bocuse

On the other hand, some clients may refuse to pay you because they are dissatisfied with your services or charges. In this event, schedule a meeting with the client as soon as possible to work out the problem. If the client is dissatisfied with only part of your work, ask for partial payment immediately.

Other clients may be satisfied with your services but not have the money to pay you. They may want an extension of time to pay or ask to work out a payment plan with you, such as paying a certain amount every two weeks until the balance is paid. If such a client seems sincere about paying you, try to work out a reasonable payment plan. You are likely to get paid eventually this way. You may also get repeat business from the client. If you agree to any new payment terms, set them forth in a confirming letter and send it to the client. The letter should state how much you'll be paid and by when. Keep a copy in your files.

Some clients may offer to pay a part of what they owe if you'll accept it as full payment. Although it may be galling to agree to this, it may make more economic sense than fighting with the client for full payment. If you agree to this orally, send the client a confirming letter setting forth the new payment terms. Keep a copy for yourself.

Sample Confirming Letter #2

August 1, 20xx

John Anderson
200 Grub Street
Albany, NY 10000

Re: My Invoice # 102

Dear John:

You have an outstanding balance on your account of $5,000. As we agreed over the telephone, I'm willing to accept $4,500 as a full and complete settlement of your account.

This sum must be paid by September 1, 20xx, or this offer will become void.

Thank you for your cooperation, and I look forward to receiving payment.

Very truly yours,

Yolanda Allende

Beware of "Payment in Full" Checks

Be careful about accepting and depositing checks that have the words "Payment in Full" or something similar written on them. If there's a dispute about how much the client owes you, depositing a full-payment check usually means that you accept the check in complete satisfaction of the debt. Crossing out the words "Payment in Full" generally won't help you. You'll still be prevented from suing for the balance once you deposit the check. If you don't want to accept the check as payment in full, return it to the client promptly, along with a letter stating that the amount is unacceptable as full payment.

However, in some states, you can cash a full-payment check and still preserve your right to sue for the balance by writing the words "Under Protest" or "Without Prejudice" on your endorsement.

Subsequent Collection Efforts

If you haven't received payment after more than a month despite a first reminder, send the client another invoice marked "Second Notice." Call the client and send invoices monthly. If you've been dealing with someone other than the owner of the company, don't hesitate to call the owner. Explain that cash flow is important to your company and that you can't afford to carry this receivable any longer.

Be persistent. When it comes to collecting debts, the squeaky wheel usually gets the money. A client with a faltering business and many creditors who has the money to pay just one debt will likely pay the creditor who has made the most fuss.

At this point, you should feel free to stop all work for the client and not hand over any work you've completed but not yet delivered. You'll go broke fast if you keep working for people who don't pay you.

If a Client Won't Pay

If a client refuses to pay or keeps breaking promises to pay, you must decide whether to write off the debt or take further action. If the client has gone out of business or is unable to pay you anything, either now or in the future, your best option may be to write off the debt. There's no point in spending time and money trying to get blood from a turnip.

But if the client is solvent, you should seriously consider:

- taking legal action against the client yourself
- hiring an attorney to take legal action against the client, or
- hiring a collection agency.

Don't Harass Deadbeat Clients

No matter how angry you are at a client who fails to pay you, don't harass him or her. Harassment includes:

- threatening or using physical force if the client doesn't pay
- using obscene or profane language
- threatening to sue the client when you don't really intend to do so
- threatening to have the client arrested
- phoning the client early in the morning or late at night
- causing a phone to ring repeatedly or continuously to annoy the client, or
- communicating with the client unreasonably often.

Federal and state laws prohibit these types of collection practices. A client could sue you for engaging in this kind of activity. Use your common sense and deal with the client in a businesslike manner, regardless of how much he or she owes you, and however agitated that debt makes you feel.

Sending a Final Demand Letter

Before you start any type of legal action against a client, send a final demand letter to the client stating that you will sue if you don't receive payment by a certain date. Many clients will pay you voluntarily after receiving such a letter. They don't want to be dragged into court and have their credit ratings damaged if you obtain a judgment against them.

In your letter, state how much the client owes you and inform the client that you'll take court action if full payment isn't received by a specific date. Here is an example of such a letter.

Sample Final Demand Letter

April 24, 20xx

Dick Denius
123 Grub Street
Anytown, AK 12345

Re: Your account #678

Dear Mr. Denius:

Your outstanding balance of $6,000 is over 120 days old.

If you do not make full payment by 5/15/20xx, a lawsuit will be filed against you. A recorded judgment will be a lien against your property and can have an adverse effect on your credit rating.

I hope to hear from you immediately so that this matter can be resolved without filing a lawsuit.

Very truly yours,

Natalie Kalmus

Suing in Small Claims Court

All states have a wonderful mechanism that helps businesses collect small debts: small claims court. Small claims courts are set up to resolve disputes involving relatively modest amounts of money. The limit is normally between $5,000 and $15,000, depending on the state in which you file your lawsuit. If you're owed more than the limit, you can still sue in small claims court for the limit and waive your right to collect the rest.

Small claims court is particularly well suited to collecting small debts because it's inexpensive and usually fairly quick. In fact, debt collection cases are by far the most common type of cases heard in small claims court.

You don't need a lawyer to go to small claims court. Indeed, a few states—including California, New York, and Michigan—bar you from bringing a lawyer to small claims court.

RESOURCE
For detailed advice about how to handle a small claims court suit, see *Everybody's Guide to Small Claims Court,* by Cara O'Neill (Nolo), and *Everybody's Guide to Small Claims Court in California,* by Ralph Warner (Nolo).

You begin a small claims lawsuit by filing a document called a "complaint" or "statement of claim." These forms are available from your local small claims court clerk and are easy to fill out. You may also be asked to attach a copy of your written agreement, if you have one. You then notify the client, now known as the "defendant," of your lawsuit. Depending on your state, the notice can be delivered by certified mail or by a process server. Many clients pay up when they receive a complaint because they don't want to go to court.

A hearing date is then set. If the client doesn't show up in court, you'll win by default. A substantial percentage of clients don't contest claims for unpaid fees in court because they know they owe the money and can't win. If your client attends the court session, you present your case to a judge or court commissioner under rules that encourage a minimum of legal and procedural formality. Be sure to bring all your documentation to court, including your invoices, client agreement, and correspondence with the client.

Unfortunately, getting a small claims judgment against a client doesn't guarantee you'll be paid. Many clients will automatically pay a judgment you obtain against them, but others will refuse to pay. The court will not collect your judgment for you. You've got to do it yourself or hire someone to help you.

Suing in Other Courts

If the client owes you substantially more than the small claims court limit for your state, you may wish to sue in a formal state trial court, usually called the "superior court" or "municipal court." Debt collection cases are usually very simple, so you can often handle them yourself or hire a lawyer for the very limited purpose of giving you advice on legal points or helping with strategy. In truth, few collection cases ever go to trial. Usually, the defendant either reaches a settlement with you before trial or fails to show up in court and loses by default.

Big Fee, Small Claim

Gary, a freelance translator, recently contracted with the San Francisco office of a national brokerage firm to perform translating services on a rush basis. He completed the work on time and sent it to the company with his invoice. The client failed to pay the invoice within 30 days.

Over the next three months, Gary sent the company a stream of collection letters demanding payment, but never heard a word. He finally got sick of waiting and decided to sue the client. He was owed $3,000 (well within the California small claims court limit), so he filed his suit in the San Francisco small claims court.

He then had the San Francisco County Sheriff's Department serve his complaint on the client at its office. The next day he received a fax from the company's legal department at its New York headquarters apologizing for the delay in payment and promising to pay at once. He received a check within a few days.

RESOURCE

For detailed guidance on how to represent yourself in courts other than small claims courts, see *Represent Yourself in Court: How to Prepare & Try a Winning Case,* by Paul Bergman and Sara J. Berman (Nolo). This book explains how to handle a civil case yourself, without a lawyer, from start to finish.

Arbitration

Before you think about suing the client in court, look at your contract to see whether it contains an arbitration clause. If your contract has such a clause, you'll be barred from suing the client in small claims or any other court. This is not necessarily a bad thing. Arbitration is similar to small claims court in that it's intended to be speedy, inexpensive, and informal. The main difference is that a private decision maker paid for by the two parties, called an "arbitrator," not a judge, rules on the case. An arbitrator's judgment can be entered with a court and enforced just like a regular court judgment.

Hire an Attorney

Hiring an attorney to sue a client for an unpaid bill is usually not worth the expense involved unless the debt is very large and you know the client can pay. However, it can be effective to have a lawyer send a letter to a client. Some clients take communications from lawyers more seriously than they take a letter you write on your own. Some lawyers are willing to do this for a nominal charge.

Hire a Collection Agency

Collection agencies specialize in collecting debts. You don't pay them anything. Instead, they take a slice of the money they collect. This can range from 15% to 50% depending on the size, age, and type of debts involved. Collection agencies can be particularly good at tracking down "skips": people who hide from their creditors.

Siccing a collection agency on a client will likely alienate the client and mean that you will not get any repeat business from him or her. Use this alternative only if you don't want to work for a particular client again.

You may have trouble finding an agency to deal with you if you have only a few debts, particularly if they're small. Try to get a referral to a good collection agency from colleagues or a professional organization or trade group. The agency should have Errors and Omissions (E & O) insurance and be duly licensed. Ask for references before hiring any agency and call them to make sure the agency checks out. It's also advisable to get a fee agreement in writing. Chapter 11 includes detailed advice on paying estimated taxes.

RESOURCE
Guides to debt collection. For more guidance on how to collect business debts, refer to the following helpful guides:
- *Collections Made Easy*, by Carol Frischer (Career Press)
- *Credit & Collections Kit for Dummies*, by Steven A. Harms and Aaron Larson (Wiley), or
- *The Guide to Getting Paid: Weed Out Bad Paying Customers, Collect on Past Due Balances, and Avoid Bad Debt*, by Michelle Dunn (Wiley).

New York City Enacts Freelance Isn't Free Law

New York City has enacted a new law intended to help the self-employed get paid. The Freelance Isn't Free Act, the first law of its kind in the nation, requires that:

- anyone who hires an independent contractor (self-employed person) for work worth over $800 must have a written contract that sets forth the scope of the work, payment rate, method of payment, and payment due date
- clients cannot require a contractor to accept less than the amount called for in the contract in exchange for timely payment, and
- if the contract doesn't specify when the contractor will be paid, payment must be received no later than 30 days after the work is completed.

An independent contractor who is not paid in a timely manner by a hiring firm can file a lawsuit against the firm and obtain damages equal to twice the amount owed plus attorney fees. Complaints may also be filed with the Office of Labor Policy and Standards within the New York Department of Consumer Affairs. Hiring firms that repeatedly violate the Act can be fined up to $25,000. Hiring firms that retaliate against workers who use the law can also be sued. Retaliation includes denial of future work opportunities because the worker made a complaint under the law.

The Act doesn't apply to sales representatives, lawyers, or licensed medical professionals. And it applies only in New York City. For more details, visit www1.nyc.gov/site/dca/about/freelance-isnt-free-act.page.

For more information on the Freelancer's Union Freelance Isn't Free initiative, visit www.freelancersunion.org/advocacy.

Deducting Bad Debts From Income Taxes

In a few situations, you can deduct the value of an unpaid debt from your taxable income. This is called a "bad debt deduction." Unfortunately, if you're like the vast majority of self-employed people—a cash basis taxpayer who sells services to your clients—you can't claim a bad debt deduction if a client fails to pay you. Because you don't report income until it is actually received, you aren't considered to have an economic loss when a client fails to pay. This rule seems absurd—you've lost the value of your time and energy when a client fails to pay you for your services—but it's strictly enforced by the IRS.

> EXAMPLE: Bill, a self-employed consultant, works 50 hours for a client and bills $2,500. The client never pays. Bill cannot deduct the $2,500 loss from his income taxes. Because Bill is a cash basis taxpayer, he never reported the $2,500 as income because he never received it. As far as the IRS is concerned, this means Bill has no economic loss.

The only time a business can deduct a bad debt is if it actually lost cash on the account or it previously reported income from selling the item. Few self-employed people give out cash, and only businesses using the accrual method of accounting report income from a sale for which no payment is received. There's no point in trying to switch to the accrual method to deduct bad debts. You won't reduce your taxes because the bad debt deduction merely wipes out a sale you previously reported as income.

Taxes and the Self-Employed

mployees don't need to worry much about taxes: All or most of their taxes are withheld from their paychecks by their employers and paid directly to the IRS and state tax department. The employer calculates how much to withhold. The employee's only responsibility is to file a tax return with the IRS and state tax department each year.

But when you become self-employed, your tax life changes dramatically. You have no employer to pay your taxes for you; you must pay them directly to the IRS and your state. This requires periodic tax filings you probably never made before. You you will also have to calculate how much you owe. To make these filings, you'll need to keep accurate records of your business income and expenses. And the tax return you must file each year will likely be more complicated than the ones you filed when you were an employee.

This chapter provides an overview of the new world of taxation you enter as a self-employed worker and explains some ways to navigate it.

Tax Basics for the Self-Employed

All levels of government—federal, state, and local—impose taxes. You need to be familiar with the requirements for each.

Federal Taxes

The federal government takes the biggest tax bite our of your earnings. When you're in business for yourself, the federal government may impose a number of taxes on you, including:

- income taxes
- self-employment taxes
- estimated taxes, and
- employment taxes.

Income Taxes

Everyone who earns more than a minimum amount must pay income taxes. Unless you're one of the few self-employed people who have formed a C corporation, you'll have to pay personal income tax on the profits your business earns. Fortunately, you may be able to take advantage of a number of business-related deductions to reduce your taxable income when you're self-employed. (See Chapter 9.)

By April 15 of each year, you'll have to file an annual income tax return with the IRS showing your income and deductions for the previous year and how much estimated tax you've paid. You must file IRS Form 1040 and include a special tax form in which you list all your business income and deductible expenses. Most self-employed people use IRS Schedule C, *Profit or Loss From Business.*

Tax matters are more complicated if you incorporate your business. If you form a C corporation, it will have to file its own tax return and pay taxes on its profits. Then, as an employee of your corporation, you'll have to file a personal tax return and pay income tax on the salary your corporation paid you.

Self-Employment Taxes

Self-employed people are entitled to Social Security and Medicare benefits when they retire, just like employees. And just like employees, they have to pay Social Security and Medicare taxes to help fund these programs. These taxes are called "self-employment taxes," or SE taxes. You must pay SE taxes if your net yearly earnings from self-employment are $400 or more. When you file your annual tax return, you must include IRS Form SE, showing how much SE tax you were required to pay. Chapter 10 provides more detail on self-employment taxes.

Estimated Taxes

Federal income and self-employment taxes are pay-as-you-go taxes: You must pay these taxes as you earn or receive income during the year. Unlike employees, who usually have their income and Social Security and Medicare taxes withheld from their pay by their employers, self-employed people normally pay their income and Social Security and Medicare taxes directly to the IRS. These tax payments, called "estimated taxes," are usually made four times every year on IRS Form 1040-ES. They are due on April 15, June 15, September 15, and January 15. You have to figure out how much to pay; the IRS won't do it for you. Chapter 11 includes detailed advice on paying estimated taxes.

Employment Taxes

Finally, if you hire employees to help you in your business, you'll have to pay federal employment taxes for your employees. These consist of half of your employees' Social Security and Medicare taxes and all of their federal unemployment tax. You must also withhold the other half of your employees' Social Security and Medicare taxes and all of their income taxes from their paychecks. You must pay these taxes monthly or bimonthly by electronic deposit to the IRS. You'll have to keep records and file quarterly and annual employment tax returns with the IRS.

When you hire other self-employed people, however, you don't have to pay any employment taxes. You need only report payments over $600 by cash or check for business-related services to the IRS and to your state tax department if your state has income taxes.

State Taxes

To complicate things further, you must pay state taxes in addition to federal taxes.

Income Taxes

All states except Alaska, Florida, Nevada, South Dakota, Texas, Washington, and Wyoming impose their own income taxes on the self-employed. New Hampshire and Tennessee impose income taxes on dividend and interest income only. Most states charge a percentage of the income shown on your federal income return. Depending on the state in which you live, these percentages range anywhere from 3% to 12%. If you're incorporated, your corporation will likely have to pay state income taxes and file its own state income tax return, too.

In most states, you have to pay your state income taxes during the year in the form of estimated taxes. These are usually paid at the same time you pay your federal estimated taxes. You'll also have to file an annual state income tax return with your state tax department. In all but five states— Delaware, Hawaii, Iowa, Louisiana, and Virginia—the return must be filed by April 15, the same deadline as your federal tax return.

Each state has its own income tax forms and procedures. Contact your state tax department to learn about your state's requirements and obtain the necessary forms. You can find your state's tax agency on the IRS website at www.irs.gov/businesses/small-businesses-self-employed/state-links-1.

Employment Taxes

If you live in a state with income taxes and you have employees, you'll likely have to withhold state income taxes from their paychecks and send the money to your state tax department. You'll also have to provide your employees with unemployment compensation insurance by paying taxes to your state unemployment compensation agency.

Sales Taxes

Almost all states and many municipalities impose sales taxes of some kind. The only states without a sales tax are Alaska, Delaware, Montana, New Hampshire, and Oregon.

All states that have sales taxes impose them on sales of goods or products to the public. If you only provide services to clients or customers, you probably don't have to worry about sales taxes, because most states either don't tax services at all or tax only certain specified services. Notable exceptions are Hawaii, New Mexico, South Dakota, and West Virginia all of which impose sales taxes on all services, subject to certain exceptions.

If the products or services you provide are subject to sales tax, you'll have to fill out an application to obtain a state sales tax permit, discussed in Chapter 5. Many states impose penalties if you make a sale before you obtain this permit. Generally, you pay sales taxes four times a year, but you might have to pay monthly if you make a lot of sales.

Other State Taxes

Various states impose a hodgepodge of other taxes on businesses, too numerous and diverse to explain here. For example:

- Nevada imposes a modified business tax on businesses with employees.
- Hawaii imposes a general excise tax on businesses based on their gross receipts.
- Washington state has a business and occupation tax on the gross revenues of all businesses; however, service businesses with less than $56,000 in revenue are exempt.

Contact your state tax department for information on these and other similar taxes your state might impose.

Local Taxes

You might have to pay local business taxes in addition to federal and state taxes. For example, many municipalities have their own sales taxes that you may have to pay to a local tax agency.

Some cities and counties also impose property taxes on business equipment or furniture. You may be required to file a list of such property with local tax officials, along with cost and depreciation information. Some cities also have a tax on business inventory. This is why many retail businesses have inventory sales: They want to reduce their stock on hand before the inventory tax date.

About 5,000 cities, counties, and other local jurisdictions impose their own income taxes. New York City is the most famous example. Some also charge annual business registration fees or business taxes. Check your local government's website to determine if it imposes such taxes. Your local chamber of commerce should also be able to give you good information on your local taxes.

Calendar of Important Tax Dates

The calendar below shows you important tax dates during the year. If you're one of the few self-employed people who uses a fiscal year instead of a calendar year as your tax year, these dates will be different. If you have employees, you must make additional tax filings during the year.

The dates listed below represent the last day you have to take the action described. If any of the dates fall on a holiday or weekend, you have until the next business day to take the action.

Handling Your Taxes

Self-employed people commonly take care of their taxes in one of three ways. Your approach will depend on how complex your tax affairs are and whether you have the time, energy, and desire to do some or all of the work yourself.

Tax Calendar	
Date	**Action**
January 15	Your last estimated tax payment for the previous year is due.
January 31	• If you file your tax return by now, you don't have to make the January 15 estimated tax payment. (See Chapter 11.) • If you hired independent contractors last year, you must provide them and the IRS with Form 1099-MISC.
March 15	• S corporations must file federal information returns. • Partnerships and multimember LLCs taxed as partnerships must file federal information returns.
April 15	• You must file your individual tax return with the IRS and pay any tax due. Or, you can pay the tax due and file for an extension of time to file your return. • You must make your first estimated tax payment for the year. • C corporations must file federal income tax returns • Individual income tax returns due in all states except Delaware, Hawaii, Iowa, Louisiana, and Virginia.
April 20	Individual income tax returns due in Hawaii.
April 30	Individual income tax returns due in Delaware and Iowa.
May 1	Individual income tax returns due in Virginia.
May 15	Individual income tax returns due in Louisiana.
June 15	Make your second estimated tax payment for the year.
September 15	Make your third estimated tax payment for the year.

Self-employed people whose tax affairs are relatively simple can do their tax work themselves, particularly if they're comfortable using accounting and tax preparation software.

EXAMPLE: Steve, a freelance writer, does all of his taxes himself. He is a sole proprietor who works alone—he does not hire employees or independent contractors. As a writer, he works at home and doesn't need much in the way of equipment or supplies. He has few business expenses other than his home office expenses.

Steve keeps track of his income and expenses using simple accounting software. He also uses software to prepare his tax returns. He estimates that it takes him no more than one hour per month to do his bookkeeping and five hours to prepare his annual tax return.

Self-employed people with larger businesses often hire tax pros to do all the work for them. This may be a particularly good idea if you incorporate your business or have employees.

EXAMPLE: Carol, a software tester, has formed a C corporation and has two employees. Her tax affairs are much more complicated than Steve's. She must file tax returns both for herself and her corporation. She must also withhold employment taxes from her own pay and her employees' pay and file quarterly and annual employment tax returns with the IRS and the state of California. Her bookkeeping requirements are more complex than those of a sole proprietor like Steve.

Carol does none of her tax work herself. She hires an accountant to do her bookkeeping and prepare her tax returns and uses a payroll service to calculate and pay employment taxes for herself and her employees.

Some self-employed people combine doing their taxes themselves with getting professional tax help. Even if you have a fairly complex tax return and want a tax pro to prepare it for you, you can still save money by doing some work, such as routine bookkeeping, yourself.

EXAMPLE: Gary, a self-employed translator, is a sole proprietor like Steve. However, unlike Steve, he hires independent contractor translators to work for him. He has to keep track of his payments to the independent contractors and report them to the IRS and his state tax department. He also rents an outside office and must track this and other business expenses. A trained engineer with a mathematical bent, he does all his bookkeeping himself using a manual system. However, he hires an accountant to prepare his annual tax return that includes some rather complex business deductions.

Doing the Work Yourself

The more tax work you do yourself, the less you'll have to pay a tax pro, such as an enrolled agent or a certified public accountant (CPA), to help you. This not only saves you cash but also gives you more personal control over your financial life. This section describes the variety of tasks that you can do some or all of yourself.

Bookkeeping

Even if you hire a tax pro to prepare your tax returns, you'll save money if you keep good records. Tax pros have many horror stories about clients who come in with plastic bags or shoe boxes filled with a jumble of receipts and canceled checks. As you might expect, these people end up requiring more of the tax pro's time and paying much more than those who have a complete and accurate set of income and expense records. It is not difficult to set up and maintain a bookkeeping system for your business. You should do so when you first start business. (Chapter 14 describes a simple bookkeeping system adequate for many self-employed people, while Chapter 9 provides an overview of the business tax deductions you'll need to track.)

Paying Estimated Taxes

If your business makes money, you'll need to pay estimated taxes throughout the year. It's usually not too difficult to calculate what you owe and send in your money. You may have to make estimated tax payments soon after you start doing business, so don't delay this task. (See Chapter 11.)

If you live in one of the 43 states with income taxes—that is, all states but Alaska, Florida, Nevada, South Dakota, Texas, Washington, and Wyoming—check with your state tax department to find out whether you must make estimated tax payments. (You can find your state's tax agency on the IRS website at www.irs.gov/businesses/small-businesses-self-employed/state-links-1.)

Paying State and Local Taxes

If you have to pay various state and local taxes, such as a gross receipts tax, sales tax, or personal property tax, seeking guidance from a tax pro can be very helpful, particularly if the expert is familiar with businesses similar to yours. Otherwise, you'll need to check with your state tax department and local tax office for information. However, once you learn about the requirements and obtain the proper forms, it's usually not difficult to compute these taxes on your own.

Filing Your Annual Tax Returns

The most difficult and time-consuming tax-related task you'll face is filing your annual tax return. This involves figuring out and calculating all your deductible expenses for the year and subtracting them from your gross income to determine your taxable income.

As you probably know, your federal tax return is due by April 15. If you live in a state that has income taxes, you'll have to file a state income tax return as well. These are also due by April 15 except in the states that have later dates. (See "Tax Calendar," above.)

One way to make your life easier is to hire a tax pro to prepare your returns the first year you're in business. You can then use those returns as a guide to do your own returns in future years.

Paying Employment Taxes

If you have employees, your tax life will be much more complicated than if you work alone or hire independent contractors. You'll need to file both annual and quarterly employment tax returns. You're also required to withhold part of your employees' pay and send it to the IRS along with a contribution of your own.

This is an area in which many business owners seek outside help, because calculating tax withholdings can be complex. Many use an accountant or payroll tax service to perform these tasks. However, accounting software, such as *QuickBooks* and *Sage 50,* can calculate your employee withholdings and prepare employment tax returns.

There are also many low-cost online payroll tax accounting services. To find a list, search "payroll service providers" on the IRS website at www.irs.gov.

The IRS also has publications on every conceivable tax topic. These are free, but are sometimes difficult to understand. IRS Publication 910, *Guide to Free Tax Services*, contains a list of these publications; many of the most useful ones are cited in this book. One publication you should get is Publication 334, *Tax Guide for Small Business*. You can obtain these and all other IRS publications by downloading them from the IRS's website at www.irs.gov.

Tax Preparation Software

Many self-employed people do their tax returns themselves. If your business is small, it's usually not that difficult. This task is made much easier by the availability of excellent tax preparation software.

Several tax preparation software packages are available that contain all the necessary forms. The programs automatically put the information and numbers you type into the proper blanks on the forms. When you're done, the program prints out your completed tax forms. Most tax packages also have add-ons you can purchase for your state taxes.

These programs not only do all your tax calculations for you, but they also contain online tax help and questionnaires that help you figure out what forms to use. Two of the most highly regarded tax preparation programs are *TurboTax* and *H&R Block*. There are versions specially designed for small business owners.

If you don't want to shell out the money for commercial tax preparation software, you can prepare your taxes for free. If your income is $66,000 or less, you can participate in the IRS's free file program that enables you to use brand-name tax preparation software tax and e-filing services. It's available only through the IRS website; go to www.irs.gov/uac/free-file-do-your-federal-taxes-for-free.

If your income is more than $66,000, you can use the IRS's Free File Fillable Forms. These are online versions of the paper tax forms. The forms perform some basic calculations, but don't provide the type of help you can get from commercial tax preparation software. Thus, they work best for people who are comfortable preparing their return themselves. Fillable Forms do not support state income tax preparation, nor can they be used if you file certain tax forms. For more information, go to www.irs.gov/uac/free-file-do-your-federal-taxes-for-free.

RESOURCE

If you handle your taxes yourself, you'll likely want to obtain a more detailed book on taxes specifically. Many excellent books are available, including these Nolo books by Stephen Fishman:

- *Deduct It! Lower Your Small Business Taxes*
- *Home Business Tax Deductions,* and
- *Tax Deductions for Professionals.*

Hiring a Tax Pro

Instead of doing it yourself, you can hire a tax professional to perform some or all of the work for you. A tax pro can also provide guidance to help you make key tax decisions, such as choosing the best setup for your business and helping you deal with the IRS if you get into tax trouble.

Types of Tax Pros

There are several types of tax pros, each with different training, experience, and cost.

Tax preparers. As the name implies, tax preparers prepare tax returns. The largest tax preparation firm is H & R Block, but many smaller operations open for business in storefront offices during tax time. Tax preparers focus on individuals and lack the training or experience to handle taxes for businesses, so a tax preparer is probably not a wise choice.

Enrolled agents. Enrolled agents, or EAs, are tax advisors and preparers who are licensed by the IRS. They must have at least five years of experience and pass a difficult test. EAs are often the best choice for self-employed workers. They usually can do as good a job as a certified public accountant, but charge less. Many also offer bookkeeping and accounting assistance.

Certified public accountants. Certified public accountants, or CPAs, are licensed and regulated by each state. They undergo lengthy training and must pass a comprehensive exam. CPAs represent the high end of the tax pro spectrum. In addition to preparing tax returns, they perform sophisticated accounting and tax work. Large businesses routinely hire CPAs for tax help.

However, if you're running a one-person business, you may not require a CPA's expertise; you might do just as well with a less expensive EA.

Tax attorneys. Tax attorneys are lawyers who specialize in tax matters. The only time you'll ever need a tax attorney is if you get into serious trouble with the IRS or a state tax agency and need legal representation. Some tax attorneys also give tax advice, but they are usually too expensive for small businesses. You're probably better off hiring a CPA if you need specialized tax help.

Finding a Tax Pro

The best way to find a tax pro is to obtain referrals from business associates, friends, or professional associations. If none of these sources can give you a suitable lead, check the website of the National Association of Enrolled Agents at www.naea.org; select "Find a Tax Expert" from the home page. Local CPA societies can give you referrals to local CPAs.

Your relationship with your tax pro will be one of your most important business relationships, so be selective about the person you choose. Talk with at least three tax pros before hiring one. You want a tax pro who takes the time to listen to you, answers your questions fully and in plain English, is knowledgeable, has experience with small businesses, and makes you feel comfortable. It can also be helpful if the tax pro already has clients in businesses similar to yours. A tax pro familiar with the tax problems posed by your type of business can often give you the best advice for the least amount of money.

Tax Pros' Fees

Ask about a tax pro's fees before hiring him or her and, to avoid misunderstandings, obtain a written fee agreement before he or she begins work.

Most tax pros charge by the hour. Hourly rates vary widely depending on where you live and on the type of tax pro you hire. Some tax pros charge a flat fee for specific services, such as preparing a tax return.

These fees are rarely set in stone, so you can usually negotiate. You'll be able to get the best possible deal if you hire a tax pro after the tax season when he or she is less busy—that is, during the summer or fall.

IRS Audits

You can report any income and claim any deductions you want to take on your tax return—after all, you (or your tax preparer) fill it out, not the government. However, the income and deductions listed on your tax return are subject to review by the IRS. This review is called a tax "audit." If an IRS auditor determines that you didn't pay enough tax, you'll have to pay the amount due plus interest and penalties.

You Are the IRS's Number One Target

The unfortunate fact is that self-employed people are the IRS's number one target. Every year, the IRS releases statistics about who got audited the previous year. Below are the most recent available audit statistics.

IRS Audit Rates	
	2017 Audit Rate
Sole Proprietors	
Income under $25,000	0.9%
$25,000 – $100,000	1.3%
$100,000 – $200,000	2.1%
More than $200,000	1.9%
Partnerships (includes most LLCs)	0.4%
S Corporations	0.3%
C Corporations	
Assets under $250,000	0.5%
$250,000 – $1 million	1.1%
$1 million – $5 million	0.9%
$5 million – $10 million	1.3%

This chart shows that sole proprietors have a much greater chance of being audited by the IRS than businesses operated through partnerships or corporations. In 2017, 1.9% of sole proprietors earning more than

$200,000 from their businesses were audited. In contrast, only 0.3% of S corporations and 0.5% of C corporations with less than $250,000 in assets were audited. Only corporations with assets worth more than $10 million were audited at rates comparable to sole proprietors.

These statistics undoubtedly reflect the IRS's belief that sole proprietors habitually underreport their income, take deductions to which they are not entitled, or otherwise cheat on their taxes. The lesson these numbers teach is that you need to take the IRS seriously. This doesn't mean that you shouldn't take all the deductions you're legally entitled to take, but you should understand the rules and be able to back up the deductions you do take with proper records.

Audit Time Limit

As a general rule, the law allows the IRS to audit a tax return up to 36 months after it's filed. This means you normally don't have to worry about audits for tax returns you filed more than three years ago. The IRS calls the years during which it can audit you "open years."

Types of Audits

There are three types of audits:

- **Correspondence audits.** As the name indicates, correspondence audits are handled entirely by mail. These are the simplest, shortest, and most common type of IRS audit, usually involving a single issue. They account for about 71% of all individual audits. The IRS sends you written questions about a perceived problem and may request additional information and/or documentation. If you don't provide satisfactory answers or information, you'll be assessed additional taxes. Correspondence audits are often used to question a home business about unreported income: income the IRS knows the taxpayer received because an IRS Form 1099 listing the payment was filed by a client or customer of the taxpayer.
- **Office audits.** Office audits take place face-to-face with an IRS auditor at one of the 33 IRS district offices. These are more complex than correspondence audits, often involving more than one issue or more than one tax year.

- **Field audits.** The field audit is the most comprehensive IRS audit, conducted by an experienced revenue officer. In a field audit, the officer examines your finances, your business, your tax returns, and the records you used to create the returns. As the name implies, a field audit is normally conducted at the taxpayer's place of business; this allows the auditor to learn as much about your business as possible. Field audits are ordinarily reserved for taxpayers who earn a lot of money.

What the Auditor Does

When auditing you as a self-employed business owner, the IRS is most concerned about whether you have done any of the following things:

- **Underreported your income.** Unlike employees who have their taxes withheld for them by their employers, sole proprietors have no automatic withholdings and many opportunities to underreport how much they earned, particularly if they run a cash business.
- **Claimed tax deductions to which you were not entitled.** For example, you claimed that nondeductible personal expenses, such as a personal vacation, were deductible business expenses.
- **Not documented the amount of your deductions.** If you don't have paperwork to back up the amount of a deduction, the IRS may reduce it, either entirely or in part. Lack of documentation is the main reason small business owners lose deductions when they get audited.
- **Taken business deductions for a hobby.** If you continually lose money or are involved in a fun activity such as art, photography, crafts, or writing that doesn't earn profits every year, the auditor may also question whether you are really in business. If the IRS claims you are engaged in a hobby, you could lose every single deduction for the activity. (See Chapter 9 for more on the hobby loss rule.)

An IRS auditor is entitled to examine the business records you used to prepare your tax returns, including your books, check registers, canceled checks, and receipts. The auditor can also ask to see records supporting your business tax deductions, such as a mileage record if you took a deduction for business use of your car. The auditor can also get copies of your bank records, either from you or your bank, and check them to see whether your deposits match the income you reported on your tax return. If you deposited a lot more money than you reported earning, the auditor will assume that you didn't report all of your income, unless you can show that the deposits you didn't include on your tax return were not income. For example, you might be able to show that they were loans, inheritances, or transfers from other accounts. This is why you need to keep good financial records.

Handling Audits

You have the legal right to take anyone along with you to help during an audit, including a bookkeeper, tax pro, or even an attorney. If you've hired a tax pro to prepare your returns, it can be helpful for him or her to attend the audit to help explain your business receipts and records and how the returns were prepared. Some tax pros include free audit services as part of a tax preparation package.

However, if you prepared your tax returns yourself, you can probably deal with an office audit yourself. It could cost more to hire a tax pro to represent you in an office audit than the IRS is likely to seek from you. If you're worried that some serious irregularity will come to light—for example, you've taken a huge deduction and can't produce a receipt or canceled check to verify it—consult with a tax pro before the audit.

For a field audit, however, it usually makes sense to have a tax pro represent you no matter who prepared your tax returns. Field audits can result in substantial assessments.

RESOURCE

Want more information on IRS small business audits? Pick up a copy of *Tax Savvy for Small Business,* by Frederick W. Daily (Nolo).

Eight Tips to Avoid an Audit

Here are eight things you can do to minimize your chances of getting audited.

Be Neat, Thorough, and Exact

If you file by mail, submit a tax return that looks professional. This will help you avoid unwanted attention from the IRS. Your return shouldn't contain erasures or be difficult to read. Your math should be correct. Avoid round numbers on your return (like $100 or $5,000). This looks like you're making up the numbers instead of taking them from accurate records. You should include, and completely fill out, all necessary forms and schedules. Moreover, your state tax return should be consistent with your federal return. If you do your own taxes, using a tax preparation computer program will help you produce an accurate return that looks professional.

Don't File Early

Unless you're owed a substantial refund, you shouldn't file your taxes early. The IRS generally has three years after April 15 to decide whether to audit your return. Filing early just gives the IRS more time to think about whether you should be audited. You can reduce your audit chances even more by getting an automatic extension to file until October 15. Note, however, that filing an extension does not extend the date by which you have to pay any taxes due for the prior year: These must still be paid by April 15.

Form a Business Entity

The audit rate statistics above show that partnerships and small corporations are audited far less often than sole proprietors. Incorporating your business or forming a limited liability company will greatly reduce your audit risk. However, you must balance this against the time and expense involved in forming a corporation or an LLC and having to complete more complex tax returns. Moreover, in some states—most notably California—

corporations and LLCs have to pay additional state taxes. (See Chapter 2 for a detailed discussion of business entities.)

Explain Items the IRS May Question

If your return contains an item that the IRS may question or that could increase the likelihood of an audit, include an explanation and documentation to prove everything is on the up and up. For example, if your return contains a substantial bad debt deduction, explain the circumstances to show that the debt is a legitimate business expense. This won't necessarily avoid an audit, but it may reduce your chances. Here's why: If the IRS computer chooses your return as a candidate for an audit, an IRS classifier screens it to see whether it really warrants an audit. If your explanations look reasonable, the screener may decide you shouldn't be audited after all.

You can make such explanations ("disclosures" in tax parlance) on plain white paper and attach them to your return, or you can use special IRS forms. IRS Form 8275, *Disclosure Statement*, can be used to explain or disclose any information that there isn't room to include on your other tax forms. Another IRS form, Form 8275-R, *Regulation Disclosure Statement*, must be used to disclose tax positions that are contrary to IRS regulations or other rules. You shouldn't file Form 8275-R without professional help.

Avoid Ambiguous or General Expenses

Don't list expenses under vague categories, such as "miscellaneous" or "general expenses": Be specific. IRS Schedule C lists specific categories for the most common small business expenses. If an expense doesn't fall within one of these classifications, create a specific name for it.

Report All of Your Income

The IRS is convinced that self-employed people, including many home business owners, don't report all of their income. Finding such hidden income is a high priority. As mentioned above, IRS computers compare 1099 forms with tax returns to determine whether there are any discrepancies.

Watch Your Income-to-Deduction Ratio

A statistical analysis of 1,200 tax returns concluded that the key factor leading to an audit was the ratio of a taxpayer's expenses to his or her income. This study found that if your total business expenses amount to less than 52% of your gross business income, you are "not very likely" to be audited. If your business expenses are 52% to 63% of your business income, there is a "relatively high probability" that the IRS computer will tag you for an audit. Finally, if your expenses are more than 63% of your income, the analysis claims you are "certain to be computer tagged for audit." Of course, this doesn't necessarily mean that you *will* be audited. Less than 10% of returns that are computer tagged for audit are actually audited. But being tagged considerably increases the odds that you'll be audited.

Whether the study's precise numbers are correct or not is anyone's guess. However, its basic conclusion—that your income-to-deduction ratio is an important factor in determining whether you'll be audited—is undoubtedly true.

Beware of Abnormally Large Deductions

It is not just the total amount of your deductions that is important: Very large individual deductions can also increase your audit chances. How much is too much? It depends in part on the nature of your business. A $50,000 deduction for equipment would likely look abnormal for a psychologist who works from home, but not for a construction contractor.

Reducing Your Income Taxes

I f you're like the vast majority of self-employed people, you must pay personal federal income tax on the net profit you earn from your business activities. This is true whether you're legally organized as a sole proprietor, S corporation, partnership, or limited liability company. The only exception is if you've formed a C corporation.

The key phrase here is "net profit." You are entitled to deduct your business-related expenses from your gross income, which is all the money or the value of other items you receive from your clients or customers. You pay income tax on your resulting net profit, not your gross self-employment income.

> EXAMPLE: Karen, a sole proprietor, earned $75,000 this year from her consulting business. Fortunately, she doesn't have to pay income tax on the entire $75,000. She qualifies for several business-related tax deductions, including a $5,000 home office deduction and a $10,000 deduction for equipment expenses. She deducts these amounts from her $75,000 gross income to arrive at her net profit: $60,000. In addition, Karen qualifies for the 20% pass-through tax deduction that took effect in 2018; this enables her to deduct an additional $12,000 from her income taxes. As a result, she pays income tax on only $48,000.

This chapter provides an overview of the many business-related federal income tax deductions that are available to reduce your gross profits and, therefore, reduce the amount of income tax you have to pay. As a result of the Tax Cuts and Jobs Act, which took effect in 2018, the vast majority of self-employed people will pay less income tax than they have in past years. The Act reduced individual tax rates and largely left business deductions intact, while adding a new 20% pass-through deduction for which many self-employed taxpayers will qualify. The Tax Cuts and Jobs Act also made it easier for all business owners to deduct the full cost of business equipment and other long-term property in a single year. Good record keeping is key to maximizing your deductions (see Chapter 14 for details on this topic). Although this chapter is a good introduction to the complex subject of tax deductions, you may need more detailed information.

RESOURCE

Want more detailed treatment of income taxes? See these Nolo books:

- *Deduct It: Lower Your Small Business Taxes*, by Stephen Fishman
- *Home Business Tax Deductions: Keep What You Earn*, by Stephen Fishman, and
- *Tax Deductions for Professionals*, by Stephen Fishman.

Many IRS publications dealing with income tax issues are mentioned below. You can obtain a free copy of any IRS publication from the IRS website at www.irs.gov.

CAUTION

Most states have income taxes, too. All states except Alaska, Florida, Nevada, South Dakota, Texas, Washington, and Wyoming also impose personal state income taxes on the self-employed. (New Hampshire and Tennessee impose state income taxes only on dividend and interest income.) If you're incorporated, your corporation will likely have to pay state income taxes as well. Contact your state tax department for income tax information and the appropriate forms.

Reporting Your Income

Employers deduct income taxes from their employees' paychecks, which they remit and report to the IRS. They give all their employees an IRS Form W-2, *Wage and Tax Statement*, showing wages and withholding for the year. Employees must file a copy of the W-2 with their income tax returns so that the IRS can compare the amount of income employees report with the amounts their employers claim they paid.

When you're self-employed, no income tax is withheld from your compensation and you don't receive a W-2 form. However, this does not mean that the IRS doesn't have at least some idea of how much money you've made. Depending on how (and how much) you're paid, your client or the entity that processes your payments may have to report payments to the IRS.

Payments by Check, Direct Deposit, or Cash

If a client pays you $600 or more over the course of the year by check, direct deposit to your bank, or cash, the client must complete and file IRS Form 1099-MISC to report the payments. The 1099-MISC must be filed by January 31 with:

- the IRS
- your state tax office (if your state has income tax), and
- you.

Only payments made by check, cash, or direct deposit need be reported on Form 1099-MISC by your clients. Your clients have no duty to report payments they make to you electronically as described below.

There are two exceptions to the 1099-MISC reporting requirements. First, your clients need not file a 1099-MISC form if you've incorporated your business and the client hires your corporation, rather than hiring you personally. This is one reason historically clients have often preferred to hire incorporated businesses. The IRS uses Form 1099-MISC as an important audit lead.

But there are two exceptions to this exception: A Form 1099-MISC must still be filed to report payments to incorporated lawyers and doctors for professional services provided to a business. For example, a 1099-MISC is required if a company hires a doctor to examine an employee so the company can purchase "key man" life insurance, or hires a lawyer to defend the business in a lawsuit.

In addition, a 1099-MISC form need not be filed to report payments to you solely for merchandise or inventory.

1099s May Be Sent Electronically

Hiring firms may send Form 1099s to independent contractors by email. But they may do this only if the independent contractor agrees to it. If not, the firm must deliver them by mail or in person. There is no disadvantage to getting your forms electronically. You'll probably get your Form 1099s faster. Indeed, you may wish to ask your clients to send your forms by email yourself, and they will probably be glad to comply. Be sure to save your Form 1099s.

What to Do With Your 1099-MISC Forms

You should receive all your 1099-MISC forms for the previous year by January 31 of the current year. Make sure the hiring firms you worked for all have your current address, or the forms might not arrive on time (or at all). Even if they have your correct address, not all clients file their 1099s on time: You could end up receiving 1099s in February, March, or even later. On the other hand, not all hiring firms wait until the January 31 deadline to send you a 1099. Some will send you a 1099 along with your payment so that they won't have to send you the 1099 form later. This means you may receive 1099 forms throughout the year, as you finish projects.

Check the amount of compensation your clients say they paid you in each Form 1099 against your own records, to make sure they are consistent. If there is a mistake, contact the client immediately and request a corrected Form 1099. You don't want the IRS to think you were paid more than you really were. The 1099-MISC form has a special box that should be checked to show that the it is correcting a prior 1099 form.

You don't have to file your 1099 forms with your tax returns. Just keep them in your records.

If You Don't Receive a Form 1099

It's not unusual for clients to fail to file required 1099-MISC forms. This may be unintentional. For example, the client may not understand the rules or may just be late in filing them. On the other hand, some clients purposefully fail to file 1099 forms because they don't want the IRS to know they're hiring independent contractors.

If you do not receive a 1099 you're expecting from a hiring firm that has your correct address, should you contact the firm and ask for it? No. It's not your duty to see that 1099 forms are filed. This is your client's responsibility. The IRS will not impose any fines or penalties on you if a client fails to file a Form 1099. It may, however, impose a $250 fine on the client and exact far more severe penalties if an IRS audit reveals that the client should have classified you as an employee.

Whether or not you receive a Form 1099, it is your duty to report all the self-employment income you earn each year to the IRS. If you're audited by the IRS, it will, among other things, examine your bank records to make sure you haven't underreported your income. If you have underreported, you'll have to pay back taxes, fines, and penalties.

Electronic Payments

If a client pays you by credit card, debit card, or by using a third-party settlement organization (TPSO) like PayPal or Payable, the client need not file a 1099-MISC with the IRS. This is so even if the client pays you more than $600 during the year. This relieves clients of an administrative burden, so many prefer to pay independent contractors electronically.

Expense Reimbursements Included in 1099-MISC

If a client reimbursed you for expenses such as travel, be sure to check and see if the Form 1099-MISC the client provides you includes this amount. Some clients routinely include expense reimbursements on their 1099 forms; others do not.

If a Form 1099-MISC includes expenses, you must report the entire amount as income on your tax return. You then deduct the amount of the expense reimbursement as your own business expense on your Schedule C. This way, your net self-employment income will come out right, without raising a red flag for the IRS.

The same holds true if you obtain work through online hiring platforms like Upwork, Uber, Fivver, or freelancer.com. Ordinarily, the clients you work for through these platforms pay you electronically via the hiring platform, which processes your payments. Such clients need not provide you with a 1099-MISC.

However, the electronic payments you receive may have to be reported to the IRS by the payment processor or online hiring platform on IRS Form 1099-K, *Payment Card and Third Party Network Transactions*. Whether this is so depends on how you're paid and how much.

Beware: Income Reported on 1099-MISC and 1099-K

Some clients are unaware that they need not report electronic payments to ICs on Form 1099-MISC. As a result, it's possible that the same payment will be reported by a client on Form 1099-MISC and included in a 1099-K filed by a payment processor. Such duplicate 1099 reporting can lead the IRS to believe you earned more income during the year than you actually did.

You should keep careful track of how much each client pays you during the year. Create your own spreadsheet or other record of all your business income. Note which clients pay you by check which pay electronically. Match what each client paid you with the 1099 forms you receive. This way, you'll be able to tell if the same income was double reported on both Form 1099-MISC and 1099-K.

Also, inform your clients that they need not provide you with a 1099-MISC if they pay you electronically, whether through a payment processor like PayPal or by credit card. Most clients will be happy to know they don't have to file this form. If they don't believe you, tell them to read the Form 1099-MISC instructions, which clearly provide that "[p]ayments made with a credit card or payment card and certain other types of payments, including third-party network transactions, must be reported on Form 1099-K ... and are not subject to reporting on Form 1099-MISC." (2016 Instructions to Form 1099-MISC.)

What if your income was double reported to the IRS? First, you never have to pay tax on more than you actually were paid, regardless of what the 1099 forms sent to the IRS say. You have a couple of options when you file your tax return: You can report your actual income on your Schedule C, and ignore the fact that some income was double reported. However, the IRS may send you a letter stating that your reported income doesn't match the 1099s it received. You'll have to explain what happened. Alternatively, you can list your business income on three lines in your Schedule C instead of one:

- one line for income reported on 1099-MISC
- one line for 1099-K income, and
- one for income reported on neither.

Then, you should deduct the amount of any income that was reported on both 1099-MISC and 1099-K by adding a deduction for "Duplicate 1099 income" in the Other Expenses section of your Schedule C. This way, your net income will not include the amount that was double reported.

Third-Party Network Payments

If a client pays you through a third-party network like PayPal or Payable, or through an online hiring platform like Uber or Upwork, the network or platform must file a 1099-K with the IRS if you are paid over $20,000 and have more than 200 transactions during the calendar year. Copies of the form are sent by the processing company to the IRS, you, and your state tax department. The deadline for filing is January 31 of the year following the year the payments were made.

If you are paid less than $20,000 or have fewer than 200 transactions, a 1099-K need not be filed. As a result, there is a substantial income "reporting hole": The IRS will not receive a 1099 if you do not exceed the annual reporting thresholds. It's important to understand, however, that whether or not the IRS receives a 1099-K or any other form reporting your income to the IRS, you're supposed to report all of your income in your annual tax return.

Payment Cards

If you have a credit card merchant account and directly accept payment from a client's credit card or debit card, the bank or other financial institution that pays you must report the payment to the IRS on Form 1099-K. There is no dollar threshold for such reporting—that is, a 1099-K must be filed no matter how little you're paid during the year.

Income Tax Deduction Basics

A deduction is an expense or the value of an item that you can subtract from your gross income to determine your taxable income: the amount you earn that is subject to taxation. The more deductions you have, the lower your taxable income and the less income tax you pay. When people speak of taking a deduction or deducting an expense from their income taxes, they mean that they subtract it from their gross income.

Most of the work involved in doing your taxes will go into determining what deductions you can take, how much you can take, and when you can take them. You don't have to become an income tax expert. But even if you have a tax pro prepare your tax returns, you need to have a basic understanding of what expenses are deductible so that you can keep proper records. This takes some time, but it's worth it. There's no point in working hard to earn a good income only to miss deductions to which you are entitled and turn over more of your income to the government than required.

What You Can Deduct

Virtually any expense is deductible as long as it is:
- ordinary and necessary
- directly related to your business, and
- for a reasonable amount.

Ordinary and Necessary Expenses

An expense qualifies as ordinary and necessary if it is common, accepted, helpful, and appropriate for your business or profession. An expense doesn't have to be indispensable to be necessary; it need only help your business in some way, even in a minor way. It's usually fairly easy to tell if an expense passes this test.

EXAMPLE 1: Bill, a freelance writer, hires a research assistant for a new book he's writing about ancient Athens and pays her $25 an hour. This is a deductible business expense. Hiring research assistants is a common and accepted practice among professional writers. The assistant's fee is an ordinary and necessary expense for Bill's writing business.

EXAMPLE 2: Bill, the freelance writer, visits a masseuse every week to work on his bad back. Bill claims the cost as a business expense, reasoning that avoiding back pain helps him concentrate on his writing. This is not an ordinary or customary expense for a freelance writer, so the IRS would not likely allow it as a business expense.

Expense Must Be Related to Your Business

An expense must be related to your business to be deductible. That is, you must use the item you buy for your business in some way. For example, the cost of a personal computer is a deductible business expense if you use the computer to write business reports.

You cannot deduct purely personal expenses as business expenses. The cost of a personal computer is not deductible if you use it just to play computer games. If you buy something for both personal and business reasons, you may deduct the business portion of the expense. For example, if you buy a cell phone and use it half the time for business calls and half the time for personal calls, you can deduct half the cost of the phone as a business expense.

However, the IRS requires you to keep records showing when the item was used for business and when for personal reasons. One acceptable form of record would be a diary or log with the dates, times, and reason the item was used. This kind of record keeping can be burdensome and may not be worth the trouble if the item isn't very valuable.

To avoid having to keep such records, try to use items either only for business or only for personal use. For example, if you can afford it, purchase two computers and use one solely for your business and one for playing games and other personal uses.

Deductions Must Be Reasonable

There is usually no limit on how much you can deduct as long as it's not more than you actually spend and the amount is reasonable. Certain areas are hot buttons for the IRS, especially local and long distance travel and meal expenses. The IRS won't allow such expenses to the extent it considers them lavish.

Also, if the amount of your deductions is very large relative to your income, your chance of being audited goes up dramatically. You're relatively safe as long as your deductions don't exceed about half of your revenue. If you have extremely large deductions, make sure you can document them in case you're audited.

Common Deductions for the Self-Employed

Self-employed workers are typically entitled to take a number of income tax deductions. The most common include:
- advertising costs, such as the cost of an online advertisement, brochure, or business website
- attorneys' and accounting fees for your business
- bank fees for your business bank account

- business start-up costs
- car and truck expenses
- costs of renting or leasing vehicles, machinery, equipment, and other property used in your business
- cost of your iPhone or other smartphone (100% deductible if you use it just for business, otherwise you can deduct the business use percentage)
- depreciation of business assets
- education expenses, such as the cost of attending professional seminars or classes required to keep up a professional license
- expenses for the business use of your home
- fees and commissions you pay to online hiring platforms like Uber or Upwork (however, don't deduct any fees such a platform takes directly from your pay and doesn't include in the compensation listed on your 1099 form)
- fees you pay to other self-employed workers you hire to help your business, such as the cost of paying a marketing consultant to advise you on how to get more clients
- health insurance for yourself and your family
- insurance for your business, including liability, workers' compensation, and business property insurance
- interest on business loans and debts—for example, interest you pay for a bank loan you use to expand your business
- license fees, such as fees for a local business or occupational license
- office expenses, such as office supplies
- office utilities
- PayPal and/or credit card transaction fees you pay
- postage
- professional association dues
- professional or business books you need for your business
- repairs and maintenance for business equipment, such as a photocopier or computer
- retirement plan contributions
- software you buy for your business
- subscriptions for professional or business publications
- business travel, meals, and entertainment, and
- wages and benefits you provide your employees.

If Your Client Reimburses You for Expenses

Many self-employed people, especially professionals such as attorneys and accountants, typically have all or some of the expenses they incur while working for a client reimbursed by their clients or customers. This is particularly common for local and long-distance travel expenses.

Obviously, if you incur a deductible expense while performing services for a client, and the client does not reimburse you, you may deduct the expense on your own return. Your client gets no deduction for the expense, because it didn't pay for it.

If your client reimburses you for an expense, your client gets the deduction, not you. However, you need not include the reimbursement in your income if you provide an adequate accounting of the expenses to your client. If the reimbursement is for entertainment expenses, the client must keep your records documenting each element of the expense. The reimbursement should not be included in any 1099-MISC form the client files with the IRS reporting how much you were paid for the year.

> EXAMPLE: Jason, an attorney based in Chicago, is hired by Acme Corp. to handle a trial in Albuquerque, New Mexico. He incurs $5,000 in travel expenses, which he fully documents. Acme reimburses Jason for the $5,000 expense. Jason need not include this amount in his income for the year. Acme may deduct it as a business expense.

To adequately account for an expense, you must comply with all the documentation requirements for the expense and provide your expense records to the client in a timely manner. An accounting is timely if it is made within 60 days after an expense is incurred. You must also return any payments from a client that exceed your actual expenses within 120 days after they are made.

If you do not adequately account to your client for these expenses, the client still gets to deduct the expense, but *you must pay tax on the reimbursement.* Moreover, the client must include the amount of the reimbursement in any 1099-MISC it files with the IRS reporting how much it paid you for your services.

> **EXAMPLE:** Assume that Jason doesn't keep proper records of his travel expenses, but is still reimbursed $5,000 by Acme. Acme must include the $5,000 payment in the 1099-MISC form it files with the IRS reporting how much it paid Jason. Jason will have to pay tax on the $5,000.

For simplicity in bookkeeping, some self-employed people routinely deduct all expenses they incur, even those that were reimbursed by clients. But they also include the amount of all the reimbursements they receive from their clients in their income and pay tax on them. This is fine with the IRS. What you cannot do is deduct an expense and not report as income a reimbursement you received for it.

When to Deduct

Some expenses may be deducted all at once; others have to be deducted over a number of years.

Current Expenses

The cost of anything you buy for your business that has a useful life of less than one year must be fully deducted in the year it is purchased. This includes, for example, rent, telephone and utility bills, photocopying costs and postage, and other ordinary business operating costs. Such items are called "current expenses."

Capital Expenses

Capital assets are things you buy for your business that have a useful life of more than one year, such as land, buildings, equipment, vehicles, books, furniture, machinery, and patents you buy from others. These costs, called capital expenses, are considered part of your investment in your business, not day-to-day operating expenses.

The cost of business real estate—buildings and building components—must always be deducted over many years, in a process called depreciation. Commercial real estate is depreciated over 39 years. However, the cost of personal property used in business—computers, for example—can usually be deducted in a single year using 100% bonus depreciation (available through 2022) or Section 179 of the tax code.

Pass-Through Tax Deduction

Self-employed individuals (other than those who have formed a C corporation) may qualify for a special pass-through tax deduction starting in 2018 through 2025. This enables them to deduct up to 20% of their net business income from their income taxes. Certain limitations and requirements must be met to qualify for this 20% pass-through deduction. (See below for more information.)

> **EXAMPLE:** Cary, a sole proprietor, earned $100,000 in net profit from his consulting business during the year (and had $120,000 in taxable income.) By claiming the pass-through deduction, Cary may deduct 20% of this amount ($20,000), from his income taxes.

Inventory

Special rules apply to when you may deduct the cost of inventory. Inventory consists of the goods and products that a business keeps on hand to sell to customers in the ordinary course of business. It includes almost any tangible personal property that a business offers for sale. It makes no difference if you make the goods yourself or buy them from others to resell.

Before 2018, you had to deduct inventory costs separately from all other business expenses—you deducted the costs as you sold the inventory. But starting in 2018, smaller businesses have the option to deduct inventory: (1) as nonincidental materials and supplies, or (2) in accordance with their accounting method, enabling cash method businesses to deduct inventory in the year it's paid for.

 RESOURCE
For more information on inventories, refer to the "Cost of Goods Sold" section in Chapter 7 of IRS Publication 334, *Tax Guide for Small Business*, and IRS Publication 538, *Accounting Periods and Methods*.

Businesses That Lose Money

If the money you spend on your business exceeds your business income for the year, your business incurs a loss. There is a bright side: You can use a business loss to offset other income you may have, such as interest income or your spouse's income if you file jointly. You can even accumulate your losses and apply them to reduce your income taxes in future or past years.

RESOURCE

Want detailed information on deducting business losses?
See IRS Publication 536, *Net Operating Losses (NOLs) for Individuals, Estates, and Trusts.* You can obtain this and all other IRS publications from the IRS website at www.irs.gov.

Recurring Losses

If you keep incurring losses year after year, you need to be very concerned about running afoul of what is known as the "hobby loss rule." This rule could cost you a fortune in additional income taxes.

The IRS created the hobby loss rule to prevent taxpayers from entering into ventures primarily to incur expenses they could deduct from their other incomes. The rule allows you to take a business expense deduction only if your venture qualifies as a business. Ventures that don't qualify as businesses are called hobbies. If the IRS views what you do as a hobby, there will be severe limits on what expenses you can deduct.

A venture is a business if you engage in it to make a profit. It's not necessary that you earn a profit every year. All that is required is that your main reason for doing what you do is to make a profit. A hobby is any activity you engage in mainly for a reason other than making a profit (for example, to incur deductible expenses or just to have fun).

The IRS can't read your mind to determine whether you want to earn a profit. And it certainly isn't going to take your word for it. Instead, it looks to see whether you do actually earn a profit or behave as if you want to earn a profit. It uses two tests to make this determination: the profit test and the behavior test.

Profit Test

If your venture earns a profit in three out of five consecutive years, the IRS presumes that you have a profit motive. The IRS and courts look at your tax returns for each year you claim to be in business to see whether you turned a profit. Any legitimate profit—no matter how small—qualifies; you don't have to earn a particular amount or percentage. Careful year-end planning can help your business show a profit for the year. If clients owe you money, for example, you can press for payment before the end of the year. You can also put off paying expenses or buying new equipment until the next tax year.

Even if you meet the three-of-five-years profit test, the IRS can still claim that your activity is a hobby, but it will have to prove that you don't have a profit motive. In practice, the IRS usually doesn't attack ventures that pass the profit test unless the numbers have clearly been manipulated just to meet the standard.

The presumption that you are in business applies to your third profitable year and extends to all later years within the five-year period beginning with your first profitable year.

> EXAMPLE: Tom began working at home as a self-employed graphic designer in 2014. Due to economic conditions and the difficulty of establishing a new business, his income varied dramatically from year to year. However, as the chart below shows, he managed to earn a profit in three of the first five years that he was in business.

Year	Losses	Profits
2014	$10,000	
2015		$5,500
2016		$9,000
2017	$6,000	
2018		$18,000

> If the IRS audits Tom's taxes for 2018, it must presume that he was in business during that year. Tom earned a profit during three of the five consecutive years ending with 2018, so the presumption that Tom is in business extends through 2020, five years after his first profitable year (2015).

Behavior Test

If you keep incurring losses and can't satisfy the profit test, you by no means have to throw in the towel and treat your venture as a hobby. You can continue to treat it as a business and fully deduct your losses. However, you must take steps to convince the IRS that your business is not a hobby in case you're audited.

You must be able to convince the IRS that earning a profit—not having fun or accumulating tax deductions—is the primary motive for what you do. This can be particularly difficult if you're engaged in an activity that could objectively be considered fun—for example, creating artwork, photography, or writing—but it can still be done. People who have incurred losses for seven, eight, or nine years in a row have convinced the IRS that they were running a businesses.

You must show the IRS that your behavior is consistent with that of a person who really wants to make money. There are many ways to accomplish this.

First and foremost, you must show that you carry on your enterprise in a businesslike manner. For example, you:

- maintain a separate checking account for your business
- keep good business records
- make some effort to market your services (for example, have a business website, business cards, and, if appropriate, a yellow pages or similar advertisement)
- have business stationery and cards printed
- obtain a federal employer identification number
- secure all necessary business licenses and permits
- have a separate phone line for your business if you work at home (this can be a cell phone)
- join professional organizations and associations, and
- develop expertise in your field by attending educational seminars and similar activities.

You should also draw up a business plan with forecasts of revenue and expenses. This will be helpful if you try to borrow money for your business.

> **RESOURCE**
>
> **Want detailed guidance on how to create a business plan?**
> See *How to Write a Business Plan,* by Mike McKeever (Nolo).

The more time and effort you put into the activity, the more it will look like you want to make money. So try to devote as much time as possible to your business and keep a log showing the time you spend on it.

It's also helpful to consult with experts in your field and follow their advice about how to modify your operations to increase sales and cut costs. Be sure to document your efforts.

> **EXAMPLE:** Otto, a professional artist, has incurred losses from his business for the past three years. He consults with Cindy, a prominent art gallery owner, about how he can sell more of his work. He writes down her recommendations and then documents his efforts to follow them. For example, he visits art shows around the country and talks with a number of gallery owners about representing his work.

You'll have an easier time convincing the IRS that your venture is a business if you earn a profit in at least some years. It's also very helpful if you've earned profits from similar businesses in the past.

Tax Effect

An IRS determination that a venture is a hobby is a true tax disaster. As a result of the Tax Cuts and Jobs Act, hobby expenses are not deductible during 2018 through 2025. But hobbyists still have to report and pay tax on any income they earn from their hobby.

> **EXAMPLE:** Charles runs a yacht charter business using his personal yacht. During 2018, he incurred $10,000 in expenses and earned $5,000 in income from the activity. The IRS determines that this activity is a hobby. As a result, his $10,000 in expenses cannot be deducted but he must still report and pay income tax on the $5,000 in income he earned from his hobby.

Deducting Business Losses From Your Taxes

If, like most self-employed people, you're a sole proprietor, you may deduct any loss your business incurs from your other income for the year (including income from a job, investment income, or your spouse's income, if you file a joint return). If your business is an LLC, an S corporation, or a partnership, your share of the business's losses pass through the business to your individual return, and you may deduct them from your other personal income in the same way as a sole proprietor. However, if you operate your business as a C corporation, you can't deduct a business loss on your personal return. It belongs to your corporation.

If your losses exceed your income from all sources for the year, you have a "net operating loss" (NOL). While it's not pleasant to lose money, an NOL can provide important tax benefits: You can use it to reduce your tax liability.

In the past, business owners could "carry a loss back"—that is, they could apply an NOL to past tax years by filing an application for refund or amended return. This enabled them to get a refund for all or part of the taxes they paid in prior years. NOLs could generally be carried back two years and then carried forward to up to 20 future years. These rules remain in place for NOLs occurring in 2017 and earlier. However, the Tax Cuts and Jobs Act eliminated carrybacks for NOLs occurring in 2018 and later. Starting in 2018, an NOL may only be deducted against the current year's taxes. Moreover, taxpayers may deduct NOLs only up to 80% of taxable income for the year (not counting the NOL deduction). Any unused NOL amounts may be carried forward and deducted in any number of future years.

The Tax Cuts and Jobs Act also limits deductions of "excess business losses" by individual business owners. Married taxpayers filing jointly may deduct no more than $500,000 per year in total business losses. Individual taxpayers may deduct no more than $250,000. Unused losses may be deducted in any number of future years as part of the taxpayer's net operating loss carryforward. This limitation is in effect for 2018 through 2025.

RESOURCE
Need to know more about NOLs? Refer to IRS Publication 536, *Net Operating Losses,* for more information. You can download it from the IRS website at www.irs.gov.

Tax Savings From Deductions

Because tax deductions are subtracted from income before the income is taxed and not from the taxes you owe, only part of any deduction will end up as an income tax saving. For example, a $5,000 tax deduction will not result in a $5,000 income tax savings; instead, it will lower your taxable income by $5,000.

How much you'll save depends on your tax rate. The tax law assigns a percentage income tax rate to specified income levels. People with high incomes pay income tax at a higher rate than those with lower incomes. These percentage rates are called "tax brackets."

To determine how much income tax a deduction will save you, you need to know your "marginal tax bracket." This is the tax bracket in which the last dollar you earn falls. The income tax brackets are adjusted each year for inflation.

RESOURCE
For the current brackets, see IRS Publication 505, *Tax Withholding and Estimated Tax.* You can obtain this and all other IRS publications from the IRS website at www.irs.gov.

As a result of the Tax Cuts and Jobs Act, starting in 2018, there are seven different tax rates, ranging from 10% of taxable income to 37%. (See the chart below.) For example, if you're single and earn $75,000 in 2018, your marginal tax bracket is 22%. This means you have to pay 22 cents in income tax for every additional dollar you earned.

2018 Personal Income Tax Rates		
Rate	**Married Filing Jointly**	**Individual Return**
10%	$0 - $19,050	$0 - $9,525
12%	$19,050 - $77,400	$9,525 - $38,700
22%	$77,400 - $165,000	$38,700 - $82,500
24%	$165,000 - $315,000	$82,500 - $157,500
32%	$315,000 - $400,000	$157,500 - $200,000
35%	$400,000 - $600,000	$200,000 - $500,000
37%	over $600,000	over $500,000

To determine how much tax a deduction will save you, multiply the amount of the deduction by your marginal tax bracket. If your marginal tax bracket is 24%, you will save 24 cents in income taxes for every dollar you are able to claim as a deductible business expense.

> **EXAMPLE:** Barry, a single, self-employed consultant, earns $75,000 in 2018 and is, therefore, in the 22% marginal tax bracket. He was able to take a $5,000 home office deduction. His actual income tax saving was 22% of the $5,000 deduction, or $1,100.

You can also deduct most business-related expenses from your income for self-employment tax purposes. (See Chapter 10.) The effective self-employment tax rate is 15.3% on net self-employment income up to the Social Security tax cap ($128,400 in 2018). (See Chapter 10.)

In addition, you may deduct your business expenses from your state income taxes. State income tax rates vary, but they average about 6%. (However, Alaska, Florida, Nevada, South Dakota, Texas, Washington, and Wyoming don't have state income taxes.)

When you add all this together, you can see the true value of a business tax deduction. For example, if you're in the 24% federal income tax bracket, all the tax deductions you can obtain for business-related expenses add up to about 45% of what you spend (24% + 15% + 6% = 45%). So you end up deducting about 45% of the cost of your business expenses from your state and federal taxes. If, for example, you buy a $1,000 computer for your business, you may end up deducting about $450 of the cost from your taxes. That's a whopping tax savings. In effect, the government is paying for almost half of your business expenses. This is why it's so important to take all the business deductions to which you're entitled.

Business Use of Your Home

Many self-employed people work from home, particularly when they're starting out. If you can meet some strict requirements, you're allowed to deduct your expenses for the business use of part of your home using what's known as the "home office deduction." For a detailed discussion of the home office deduction, see Chapter 4.

Cost of Business Assets

One of the nice things about being self-employed is that you can deduct the money you spend for things you use to make money in your business, such as computers and office furniture. You can take a full deduction whether you pay cash for an asset or buy on credit.

Due to recent changes in the tax laws, you can currently deduct in one year the full cost of most personal property you buy for your business. This is much better than having to deduct the cost a portion at a time over several years—a process called depreciation. You can currently deduct the full cost of business property by using one of the following tax rules:

- the "de minimis" safe harbor
- deduction for materials and supplies
- 100% bonus depreciation, or
- Section 179 expensing.

If you can't currently deduct an expense, you'll have to depreciate the cost as described below.

Property Costing $2,500 or Less: The De Minimis Safe Harbor

The de minimis safe harbor ("de minimis" is Latin for minor or inconsequential) allows most businesses to currently deduct the cost of personal property items that cost up to $2,500 apiece. This can result in a substantial deduction. Indeed, it may enable you to currently deduct all or most of the property you buy for your business.

To use this deduction, you must file an annual election with your tax return—something that is easy to do. When you make this election, it applies to all expenses you incur that qualify for the de minimis safe harbor. You cannot pick and choose which items you want to include. You must also include items that would otherwise be deductible as materials and supplies.

The de minimis safe harbor can't be used to deduct the cost of land, inventory (items held for sale to customers), certain spare parts for machinery or other equipment, or amounts that you pay for property that you produce or acquire for resale.

You may use the de minimis safe harbor only for property whose cost does not exceed $2,500 per invoice, or $2,500 per item as substantiated by the invoice. If the cost exceeds $2,500 per invoice (or item), no part of the cost may be deducted by using the de minimis safe harbor.

> EXAMPLE: Alice purchases the following items for her consulting business from a local computer supply store:
> - printer for $250
> - paper shredder for $100
> - two tablets for $500 each
> - office chair for $1,500, and
> - office desk for $3,000.
>
> Alice's total bill is $5,850. However, she applies the de minimis safe harbor rule item-by-item as shown on the invoice. Each item is less than the $2,500 de minimis safe harbor limit except the desk. Thus, Alice may immediately deduct $2,850 of the total using the safe harbor. She can't use the safe harbor to deduct the $3,000 cost of the desk. Instead, she may deduct the desk in one year using Section 179 or depreciate it over five years.

Since the $2,500 de minimis limit is based on the cost of an item as shown on the invoice, you might be tempted to artificially break an item down into separate costs on the invoice, each of which is less than the limit. However, the IRS does not allow this. You cannot break into separate components property that you would normally buy as a single unit. Be sure to save all your receipts and/or invoices for property you deduct using the de minimis safe harbor.

To qualify for this de minimis expensing safe harbor, a taxpayer must:

- establish before the first day of the tax year (January 1 for calendar year taxpayers) an accounting procedure requiring it to expense amounts paid for property either (1) costing less than a certain dollar amount, and/or (2) with an economic useful life of 12 months or less, and
- actually treat such amounts as currently deductible expenses on its books and records.

You do not need to put your procedure in writing (although you may do so). But it should still be in place before January 1 of the tax year. Here is an example of such a written procedure:

De Minimis Safe Harbor Procedure

Effective January 1, 20xx, XYZ hereby adopts the following policy regarding certain expenditures: Amounts paid to acquire or produce tangible personal property will be expensed, and not capitalized, in the year of purchase if: (1) the property costs less than $500, or (2) the property has a useful life of 12 months or less.

To take advantage of the de minimis safe harbor, you must file an election with your tax return each year, using the following format:

Section 1.263(a)-1(f) De Minimis Safe Harbor Election

Taxpayer's name: _____

Taxpayer's address: _____

Taxpayer's identification number: _____

The taxpayer is hereby making the de minimis safe harbor election under Section 1.263(a)-1(f).

Deducting Materials and Supplies

Items that fall within the definition of materials and supplies in IRS regulations may be currently deducted. However, many small businesses won't need (or be able) to use this deduction because these items can usually be deducted using the de minimis safe harbor.

"Materials and supplies" are tangible property used or consumed in your business operations that fall within any of the following categories:

- any item of tangible personal property that cost $200 or less
- any item of personal property with an economic useful life of 12 months or less, and
- components acquired to maintain or repair a unit of tangible property—that is, spare parts.

The cost of such items may be deducted the year the item is used or consumed in your business—which may be later than the year purchased. To use this deduction, you are supposed to keep records of when such items are used or consumed in your business—something few small business owners do in practice. For this reason, this deduction may be useless for most small businesses. Fortunately, they can use the de minimis safe harbor discussed above instead to deduct materials and supplies.

"Incidental" materials and supplies are personal property items that are carried on hand and for which no record of consumption is kept or for which beginning and ending inventories are not taken. In other words, these are inexpensive items not worth keeping track of. Examples include pens, paper, staplers, toner, and trash baskets. Costs of incidental materials and supplies are deductible the year they are paid for, not when the items are used or consumed in the business.

> **EXAMPLE:** John, a professional writer, purchases two packs of pens and three boxes of paper clips he plans to use for his writing activity over the next two years. The cost was minimal and he does not keep inventory of each pen or paperclip. These are incidental compared to his business and deductible the year he paid for them.

Bonus Depreciation

If you're unable to deduct in one year the cost of personal property using the de minimis safe harbor, you'll likely be able to do so using bonus depreciation. Bonus depreciation enables you to deduct in a single year a specified percentage of a long-term asset's cost. For property placed into service starting September 28, 2017 through December 31, 2022, the percentage is a whopping 100%—in other words, you can deduct in one year the entire cost of property using bonus depreciation. This makes bonus depreciation the go-to method for deducting personal property during these five-plus years.

Unlike the de minimis safe harbor, bonus depreciation is not limited to items that cost $2,500 ($5,000 for businesses with financial statements). Nor is it limited to your annual net income, as is the case with Section 179 expensing discussed below. You can deduct any amount of eligible property using bonus depreciation, even it results in your business incurring a loss for tax purposes.

Bonus depreciation is optional—you don't have to take it if you don't want to. But if you want to get the largest depreciation deduction you can in the year you buy personal property for your business, you will want to take advantage of it whenever possible.

Property That Qualifies for Bonus Depreciation

You can use bonus depreciation to deduct any property you acquire by purchase that has a depreciation period of 20 years or less—this includes all types of tangible personal business property and off-the-shelf software (but not custom software). The property may be used or new, but you must not have used it before acquiring it. So, you can't convert property you previously used for personal use to business use and deduct the cost with bonus depreciation.

You can use bonus depreciation only for property that you purchase—not for leased property or property you inherit or receive as a gift. You also can't use it for property that you buy from a relative or a corporation or an organization that you control. Special rules apply to cars.

Bonus depreciation cannot be used for:

- land
- permanent structures attached to land (except for certain improvements; see below)
- inventory (see Chapter 6)
- intangible property such as patents, copyrights, and trademarks, or
- property used outside the United States.

You can use bonus depreciation to deduct listed property only if you use the property at least 51% of the time for business use. For example, you may deduct a video camera with bonus depreciation only if you use it over 50% of the time for your business, not for personal use. If your business use falls below 51% during the asset's depreciation period (usually five or seven years) you have to give back the bonus depreciation you claimed the first year—a process called recapture (see below).

Calculating the Bonus Amount

You use bonus depreciation to figure out your depreciation deduction for the first year that you own an asset. You figure the deduction by multiplying the depreciable basis of the asset by the applicable bonus percentage. For property placed in service starting September 28, 2017 through December 31, 2022, the bonus percentage is 100%. You get the full 100% deduction no matter what month during the year you place the property into service. This differs from regular depreciation rules, where property bought later in the year may be subject to a smaller deduction for the first year.

> EXAMPLE: Stan, a printer, purchased and placed into service a new printing press for his business in December of 2018. The press cost $10,000 plus $1,000 in shipping costs and $2,000 in installation costs. He deducts the equipment with 100% bonus depreciation, which allows him to deduct the full $13,000 cost for 2018.

The amount you can deduct is initially based on the property's cost. The cost includes the amount you paid for the property, plus sales tax, delivery, and installation charges. It doesn't matter if you pay cash or finance the purchase with a credit card or bank loan. But if you pay for property with both cash and a trade-in, the value of the trade-in is not deductible with bonus depreciation. You must depreciate the amount of the trade-in.

If you use property solely for business as in the above example, you can deduct 100% of the cost (subject to the other limitations discussed below). But if you use property for both business and personal purposes, you must reduce your deduction by the percentage of the time that you use the property for personal purposes.

> EXAMPLE: Max buys a $4,000 computer. The year he buys it, he uses it for his consulting business 75% of the time, and for personal purposes 25% of the time. He may currently deduct 75% of the computer's cost (or $3,000) using bonus depreciation. The remaining $1,000 is not deductible because the 25% personal use of the computer is not a business expense.

Class-Wide Requirement

If you use bonus depreciation, you must use it for all assets that fall within the same class. You cannot pick and choose the assets you want to apply it to within a class. For example, if you buy a car and take bonus depreciation, you must take bonus depreciation for any other property you buy that year within the same class. Cars are five-year property, so you must take bonus depreciation that year for any other five-year property—for example, computers and office equipment. (See the "Depreciation Periods" chart, below, for a list of the various classes of property.)

The bonus depreciation deduction is applied automatically to all taxpayers who qualify for it. However, the deduction is optional. You need not take it if you don't want to. You can elect not to take the deduction by attaching a note to your tax return. It might be advantageous to do this if you expect your income to go up substantially in future years, placing you in a higher tax bracket.

> CAUTION
> **When you opt out, you do so for the entire class of assets.** It's very important to understand that if you opt out of the bonus, you must do so for the entire class of assets, not just one asset within a class. This is the same rule that applies when you decide to take the bonus.

Bonus Depreciation Percentages

As the following chart shows, the bonus depreciation percentages vary over the years. The 100% bonus depreciation amount is scheduled to remain in effect for property placed into service through December 31, 2022. The bonus amount will then phase down each year in 20% increments.

Year Property Placed In Service	Bonus Depreciation Percentage
1/1/2015 through 9/27/2017 (new property only)	50%
9/28/2017 through 2022	100%
2023	80%
2024	60%
2025	40%
2026	20%
2027 and later	0%

Section 179 Deduction

Section 179 of the tax code is similar to bonus depreciation in that it allows you to deduct in one year the entire cost of personal property you use in your business (as well as certain real property improvements—see below). This is called first-year expensing or Section 179 expensing. (Expensing is an accounting term that means currently deducting a long-term asset.)

Section 179 may be used to deduct much the same property as bonus depreciation. However, during 2018 through 2022, Section 179 will likely not be used much by businesses because they can deduct 100% of the cost of the same property using bonus depreciation. Section 179 has several disadvantages that make it less desirable than bonus depreciation.

First, you can only use Section 179 for property you use over 50% of the time for business; but this isn't the case with bonus depreciation, except for listed property. If your use of the property falls below 50% you have to give back your Section 179 deduction through recapture (see below). There is no such recapture with bonus depreciation except for listed property.

In addition, you can't use Section 179 to deduct in one year more than your net taxable business income for that year—not counting the Section 179 deduction but including your spouse's salary and business income. Amounts that are not deductible are carried forward and can be deducted in future years. Thus, Section 179 may never result in a loss, whereas there is no such limitation on bonus depreciation.

There is also an annual limit on the amount of property that can be deducted with Section 179. For 2018, the limit is $1 million. The $1 million limit is phased out if the amount of qualifying property you place into service during the year exceeds $2.5 million. The annual deduction limit applies to all of your businesses combined, not to each business you own and run. If you're a partner in a partnership, member of a limited liability company (LLC), or shareholder in an S corporation, the limit applies both to the business entity and to each owner personally.

Unlike bonus depreciation, Section 179 expensing doesn't apply class-wide. So, you may pick and choose which assets you wish to deduct using Section 179 within the same asset class, which is a potential advantage. Section 179 deductions are not automatic. You must claim a Section 179 deduction on your tax return by completing IRS Form 4562, Part I, and checking a specific box. If you neglect to do this, you might lose your deduction.

Regular Depreciation

Because it provides a big tax deduction immediately, most small business owners look first to the de minimis safe harbor, bonus depreciation, or Section 179 to deduct asset costs.

However, you must use regular depreciation for:
- personal property items that you convert to business use
- intangible assets, such as patent, copyright, trademark, or business goodwill
- items purchased from a relative, or
- property inherited or received as a gift or inheritance.

Depreciation involves deducting the cost of a business asset a little at a time over a period of years. This means it will take you much longer to get your full deduction.

The depreciation period—called the "recovery period" by the IRS— begins when you start using the asset and lasts for the entire estimated useful life of the asset. The tax code has assigned an estimated useful life for all types of business assets, ranging from three to 39 years. Most of the assets you buy for your business will probably have an estimated useful life of five to seven years.

Asset Depreciation Periods	
Type of Property	**Recovery Period**
Computer software (software that comes with your computer is not separately depreciable unless you're separately billed for it)	3 years
Office machinery (computers and peripherals, copiers)	5 years
Cars and light trucks	5 years
Construction and research equipment	5 years
Office furniture	7 years
Residential buildings	27.5 years
Nonresidential buildings purchased before 5/12/93	31.5 years
Nonresidential buildings purchased after 5/12/93	39 years

You are free to continue using property after its estimated useful life expires, but you can't deduct any more depreciation.

RESOURCE
Need to know the depreciation period for an asset not included in the table "Asset Depreciation Periods" above? See IRS Publication 946, *How to Depreciate Property*. You can obtain this and all other IRS publications from the IRS website at www.irs.gov.

Calculating Depreciation

There are several different systems you can use to calculate depreciation. Most tangible property, however, is depreciated using the Modified

Accelerated Cost Recovery System (MACRS). A slightly different system, the Alternative Depreciation System, or ADS, applies to depreciation of specified "listed property," property used outside the United States, and certain farm and imported property.

Under MACRS, there are three different methods you can use to calculate your depreciation deduction: the straight-line (SL) method or one of two accelerated-depreciation methods. Once you choose your method, you're stuck with it for the entire life of the asset.

In addition, you must use the same method for all property of the same kind purchased during the year. For example, if you use the straight-line method to depreciate a computer, you must use that method to depreciate all other computers you purchase for your business during that year.

The straight-line method requires you to deduct an equal amount each year over the useful life of an asset. However, you ordinarily deduct only a half-year's worth of depreciation in the first year. You make up for this by adding an extra half-year of depreciation at the end.

Most small businesses use one of two types of accelerated depreciation: the "double declining-balance" method or the "150% declining-balance" method. The advantage to these methods is that they provide larger depreciation deductions in the earlier years and smaller ones later on. The double declining-balance method starts out by giving you double the deduction you'd get for the first full year with the straight-line method. The 150% declining-balance method gives you one and one-half times the straight-line deduction.

Determining which depreciation method is best for you and calculating how much depreciation you can deduct is a complex task. If you want to do it yourself, you should probably get and use tax preparation software that can help you do the calculations. (See Chapter 8.)

Car Expenses

Most self-employed people do at least some driving related to business. For example, you might drive to visit clients or customers, to pick up or deliver work, to obtain business supplies, or to attend seminars. Of course, driving costs money, and you are allowed to deduct your driving expenses when you use your car, van, pickup, or panel truck for business.

There are two ways to calculate the car expense deduction. You can:
- use the standard mileage rate, which requires relatively little record keeping, or
- deduct your actual expenses, which requires more record keeping, but can give you a larger deduction.

You can figure your deduction both ways the first year before deciding which method to use on your tax return.

Either way, you'll need to keep records showing how many miles you drive your car for business during the year, called "business miles." You can use a paper logbook for this purpose; but there are also numerous apps that work with your smartphone to automatically track your mileage using GPS.

CAUTION
Commuting expenses are not deductible. You usually cannot deduct commuting expenses (the cost involved in getting to and from work). However, if your main office is at home, you may deduct the cost of driving to meet clients. This is one of the advantages of having a home office. (See Chapter 4.)

Standard Mileage Rate

The easiest way to deduct car expenses is to take the standard mileage rate. When you use this method, you need only keep track of how many business miles you drive, not the actual expenses for your car (such as gas or repairs).

You can use the standard mileage rate for a car that you own or lease. You must use the standard mileage rate in the first year you use a car for business or you are forever foreclosed from using that method for that car. If you use the standard mileage rate the first year, you can switch to the actual expense method in a later year. For this reason, if you're not sure which method you want to use, it's a good idea to use the standard mileage rate the first year you use the car for business. This leaves all your options open for later years. However, this rule does not apply to leased cars. If you lease your car, you must use the standard mileage rate for the entire lease period if you use it in the first year.

There are some restrictions on switching back to the standard mileage rate after you have used the actual expense method. You can't switch back to the standard mileage rate after using the actual expense method if you took accelerated depreciation, a Section 179 deduction, or bonus depreciation on the car. You can switch back to the standard mileage rate only if you used the straight-line method of depreciation during the years you used the actual expense method. This depreciation method gives you equal depreciation deductions every year, rather than the larger deductions you get in the early years using accelerated depreciation methods. As a practical matter, once you switch from the standard rate to the actual expense method, it's nearly impossible to switch back to the standard rate.

Each year, the IRS sets the standard mileage rate: a specified amount of money you can deduct for each business mile you drive during the year. In 2018, the rate was 54.5 cents per mile. The rates are the same whether you own or lease your car.

To figure out your deduction, simply multiply your business miles by the standard mileage rate.

> **EXAMPLE:** Ed, a salesman, drove his car a total of 10,000 miles for business in 2018. His deduction is $5,450 (54.5¢ × 10,000 = $5,450).

If you choose to take the standard mileage rate, you cannot deduct actual operating expenses, such as depreciation or Section 179 deduction, maintenance, repairs, gasoline and its taxes, oil, insurance, and vehicle registration fees. These costs are already factored into the standard mileage rate.

The only expenses you can deduct (because these costs aren't included in the standard mileage rate) are:
- interest on a car loan
- parking fees and tolls for business trips (but you can't deduct parking ticket fines or the cost of parking your car at your place of work), and
- personal property tax that you paid when you bought the vehicle based on its value (often included as part of your auto registration fee).

Auto loan interest is usually the largest of these expenses. Unfortunately, many people fail to deduct it because of confusion about the tax law. Taxpayers are not allowed to deduct interest on a loan for a car that is for personal use, so many people believe they also can't deduct interest on a business car. This is not the case. You may deduct interest on a loan for a car you use in your business.

If you use your car for both business and personal trips, you can deduct only the business use percentage of interest and taxes.

Actual Expenses

Instead of taking the standard mileage rate, you can elect to deduct the actual expenses of using your car for business. To do this, deduct the actual cost of depreciation for your car (subject to limitations), interest payments on a car loan, lease fees, rental fees, license fees, garage rent, repairs, gas, oil, tires, and insurance. The total deductible amount is based on the percentage of time you use your car for business. You can also deduct the full amount of any business-related parking fees and tolls.

Deducting all these items will take more time and effort than using the standard mileage rate because you'll need to keep records of all your expenses. However, it may provide you with a larger deduction than the standard rate. It all depends on the cost of your vehicle and how much you drive for business. As a result of the Tax Cuts and Jobs Act, the actual expense method can result in larger deductions than the standard mileage rate during the first several years you own a car.

> **EXAMPLE:** In January 2018, Vicky bought a $20,000 car. During the year, she drove it 10,000 miles for her consulting practice and 5,000 miles for personal purposes. If she used the standard mileage rate, she would be entitled to a $5,450 deduction: 54.5¢ × 10,000 miles = $5,450. Instead, however, she takes the actual expense deduction. She keeps careful records of all of her costs for gas, oil, repairs, insurance, and depreciation. These amount to $6,200 for the year. She gets an extra $750 deduction by using the actual expense method.

Mixed Uses

If you use your car for both business and personal purposes, you must also divide your expenses between business and personal use.

> **EXAMPLE:** In one recent year, Laura, a salesperson, drove her car 10,000 miles for her business and 10,000 miles for personal purposes. She can deduct 50% of the actual costs of operating her car.

If you own only one car, you normally can't claim to use it only for business. An IRS auditor is not likely to believe that you walk or take public transportation everywhere except when you're on business.

Expense Records Required

When you deduct actual car expenses, you must keep records of the costs of operating your car. This includes not only the number of business miles and total miles you drive, but also gas, repair, parking, insurance, and similar costs. (See Chapter 14.) If this seems to be too much trouble, use the standard mileage rate. That way, you'll have to keep track only of how many business miles you drive, not what you spend for gas and similar expenses.

Limits on Depreciation Deductions

When you use the actual expense method, you get to deduct an amount for depreciation of your vehicle each year until you deduct the entire cost of the car. Although the general concept of depreciation is the same for every type of property, special rules apply to depreciation deductions for cars. These rules can give you a lower annual deduction for cars than you'd be entitled to using the normal depreciation rules.

The Tax Cuts and Jobs Act greatly increased the annual maximum depreciation deductions for vehicles starting in 2018. As a result, using the actual expense method can result in a much larger annual deduction for business mileage than the standard mileage rate, which doesn't allow a separate deduction for depreciation because it's included in the standard rate. This is especially likely if you purchase an expensive car and use it over 50% of the time for business.

The chart below shows the maximum annual depreciation deduction allowed for passenger automobiles, trucks, vans, and minivans with a gross loaded vehicle weight under 6,000 pounds. The chart shows that if you place a passenger vehicle into service in your business in 2018, you may take a maximum depreciation deduction of $10,000. The second year, you may deduct up to a whopping $16,000. That's $26,000 in depreciation deductions in the first two years—$34,000 if bonus depreciation is also claimed. These are by far the highest annual limits for passenger vehicle depreciation that have ever been allowed. The annual limits are now so high that only vehicles placed into service during 2018 that cost $50,000 or more are impacted.

Depreciation Limits for Passenger Automobiles	
(must be reduced by percentage of personal use)	
Year placed in service	2018
1st tax year	$10,000 ($18,000 if $8,000 bonus depreciation used)
2nd tax year	$16,000
3rd tax year	$9,600
4th and later years	$5,760

The deduction limits in the above chart are based on 100% business use of the automobile. If you don't use your car solely for business, the deduction limits are reduced based on your percentage of personal use. Moreover, your actual depreciation deduction, up to the annual limit, depends on the cost of your car and how much you drive for business.

> **EXAMPLE:** Jean purchases a $50,000 passenger automobile in 2018 that she uses 60% of the time for her real estate brokerage business. Her depreciable basis is $30,000 ($50,000 cost x 60% business use = $30,000 basis). Because she uses the vehicle more than 50% for business, she may use accelerated depreciation. Her depreciation deduction for 2018 is 20% x $30,000 = $6,000, well within the $10,000 annual limit. Jean may also take bonus depreciation in 2018, which is an additional $4,000 deduction (50% of the $8,000 maximum bonus depreciation deduction). Her total 2018 depreciation deduction is $10,000. In 2019, she may deduct 32% x $30,000 = $9,600. In 2020, she may deduct 11.92% x $30,000 = $3,576. Thus, in the first three years she deducts $23,176 of her $30,000 basis.

The depreciation limits are not reduced if a car is in service for less than a full year. This means that the limit is not reduced when the automobile is either placed in service or disposed of during the year.

100% Bonus Depreciation for SUVs and Other Weighty Vehicles

The depreciation limits discussed above apply only to passenger automobiles: vehicles with a gross loaded weight of less than 6,000 pounds. However, in the case of trucks and vans, the 6,000-pound weight limit is based on gross loaded weight and vehicles that weigh more than this amount are not subject to the limits. If a more than 6,000-pound vehicle is placed in service during 2018 through 2022, it will qualify for 100% first-year bonus depreciation. This means you can deduct 100% of the cost in one year if you use the vehicle 100% for business. If you use the vehicle less than 100% for business, you must reduce your deduction accordingly. But you must use the vehicle at least 51% of the time for business to use bonus depreciation.

> EXAMPLE: Bill purchases a 6,500 lb. SUV for $50,000 in 2018. He uses the vehicle 60% of the time for his nursery business, so his depreciable basis is $30,000 (60% x $50,000 = $30,000). He may deduct his entire $30,000 basis in 2018 with 100% bonus depreciation.

Leasing a Car

If you lease a car that you use in your business, you can deduct the part of each lease payment that goes toward the business use of the car. However, you cannot deduct any part of a lease payment that is for commuting or personal use of the car.

Leasing companies typically require you to make an advance or down payment to lease a car. You must spread such payments over the entire lease period for purposes of deducting their cost. You cannot deduct any payments you make to buy a car, even if the payments are called lease payments.

RESOURCE
Want more information about the rules for claiming car expenses?
See IRS Publication 463, *Travel, Entertainment, Gift, and Car Expenses.* You can obtain this and all other IRS publications from the IRS website at www.irs.gov.

Travel Expenses

If you travel for your business, you can deduct your airfare, hotel bills, meals, and other expenses. If you plan your trip right, you can even mix business with pleasure and still get a deduction for your airfare. However, IRS auditors scrutinize these deductions closely. Many taxpayers claim them without complying with the copious rules the IRS imposes. To avoid unwanted attention, you need to understand the limitations on this deduction and keep proper records.

Travel Within the United States

Some businesspeople seem to think they have the right to deduct the cost of any trip they take. This is not the case. You can deduct a trip within the United States only if all of the following apply:
- It's primarily for business.
- You travel outside your city limits.
- You're away at least overnight or long enough to require a stop for sleep or rest.

Business Purpose of Trip

For your trip to be deductible, you must spend more than half of your time on activities that can reasonably be expected to help advance your business.
   Acceptable activities include:
- visiting or working with clients or customers
- attending trade shows, or
- attending professional seminars or business conventions where the agenda is clearly connected to your business.

Business does not include sightseeing or recreation that you attend by yourself or with family or friends, nor does it include personal investment seminars or political events.

Use common sense before claiming that a trip is for business. The IRS will likely question any trip that doesn't have some logical connection to your business. For example, if you build houses in Alaska, an IRS auditor would probably be skeptical about a deduction for a trip you took to Florida to learn about new home air-conditioning techniques.

Again, if your trip within the United States is not primarily for business, none of your travel expenses are deductible. But you can still deduct expenses you incur on your trip that are directly related to your business, such as the cost of attending a professional educational seminar.

Travel Outside City Limits

You don't have to travel any set distance to get a travel expense deduction. However, you can't take this deduction if you just spend the night in a motel across town. You must travel outside your city limits. If you don't live in a city, you must go outside the general area in which your business is located.

Sleep or Rest

Finally, you must stay away overnight or at least long enough to require a stop for sleep or rest. You cannot satisfy the rest requirement by merely napping in your car.

> **EXAMPLE 1:** Phyllis, a self-employed salesperson based in Los Angeles, flies to San Francisco to meet potential clients, spends the night in a hotel, and returns home the following day. Her trip is a deductible travel expense.

> **EXAMPLE 2:** Andre, a self-employed truck driver, leaves his workplace on a regularly scheduled round-trip between San Francisco and Los Angeles and returns home 18 hours later. During the run, he has six hours off at a turnaround point where he eats two meals and rents a hotel room to get some sleep before starting the return trip. Andre can deduct his meal and hotel expenses as travel expenses.

Combining Business With Pleasure

Provided that your trip is primarily for business, you can tack on a vacation to the end of the trip, make a side trip purely for fun, or go to the theater and still deduct your entire airfare. What you spend while having fun is not deductible, but you can deduct your expenses while on business.

> **EXAMPLE:** Bill flies to Miami for a four-day business meeting. He then stays an extra three days in Miami swimming and enjoying the sights. Because Bill spent over half his time on business—four days out of seven—the cost of his flight is entirely deductible, as are his hotel and meal costs during the business meeting. He may not deduct his hotel, meal, or other expenses during his vacation days.

Foreign Travel

The rules differ if you travel outside the United States and are more lenient in some ways. However, you must have a legitimate business reason for your foreign trip. A sudden desire to investigate a foreign business won't qualify: You can't deduct business expenses for a business unless you're already involved in it.

Trips Lasting No More Than Seven Days

If you're away no more than seven days and you spend the majority of your time on business, you can deduct all of your travel costs.

However, even if your trip was primarily a vacation, you can deduct your airfare and other transportation costs as long as at least part of the trip was for business. You can also deduct your expenses while on business. For this reason, it's often best to limit business-related foreign travel to seven days.

> **EXAMPLE:** Jennifer flies to London for a two-day business meeting. She then spends five days sightseeing. She can deduct the entire cost of her airfare and the portion of her hotel and meals she spent while attending the meeting.

Trips Lasting More Than Seven Days

More stringent rules apply if your foreign trip lasts more than one week. To get a full deduction for your expenses, you must spend at least 75% of your time away on business.

If you spend less than 75% of your time on business, you must determine the percentage of your time spent on business by counting the number of business days and the number of personal days. You can deduct only the percentage of your travel costs that relates to business days. A business day is any day you have to spend at a particular place on business or in which you spend four or more hours on business matters. Days spent traveling to and from your destination also count as business days.

> **EXAMPLE:** Sam flies to London and stays 14 days. He spends seven days on business and seven days sightseeing. He therefore spent 50% of his time on business. He can deduct half of his travel costs.

Taking Your Family With You

Generally, you cannot deduct the expense of taking your spouse, children, or others along with you on a business trip or to a business convention. The only deductions allowed are for expenses of a spouse or another person who is your employee and has a genuine business reason for going on a trip with you. Typing notes or assisting in entertaining customers are not enough to warrant a deduction; the work must be essential. For example, if you hire your adult child as a salesperson for your product or service and he or she calls on prospective customers during the trip, both of your expenses are deductible.

When you travel with your family, you deduct your business expenses as if you were traveling alone. However, the fact that your family is with you doesn't mean you have to reduce your deductions. For example, if you drive to your destination, you can deduct the entire cost of the drive, even if your family rides along with you. Similarly, you can deduct the full cost of a single hotel room even if you obtain a larger, more expensive room for your whole family.

Deductible Expenses

You can deduct virtually all of your expenses when you travel on business, including:

- airfare to and from your destination
- hotel or other lodging expenses
- taxi, public transportation, and car rental expenses
- telephone and Internet expenses
- the cost of shipping your personal luggage or samples, displays, or other things you need for your business
- computer rental fees
- laundry and dry cleaning expenses, and
- tips you pay on any of the other costs.

However, only 50% of the cost of meals is deductible. The IRS reasons that you would have eaten at home and spent less had you stayed home. You cannot deduct expenses for personal sightseeing or recreation.

You must keep good records of your expenses. (See Chapter 14.)

Entertainment and Meals

The Tax Cuts and Jobs Act made major changes to the longstanding deductions for business-related entertainment and meals. Starting in 2018, most business-related entertainment is not deductible. For example, you may not deduct country club or skiing outings; theater or sporting event tickets; entertainment at nightclubs; hunting, fishing, or similar trips; or other vacations. This is true even if the expenses result in a specific business benefit like landing a new client. Nondeductible entertainment expenses also include membership fees and dues for any club organized for business, pleasure, recreation, or other social purposes, and any entertainment facility fees.

Meals at restaurants and other facilities away from the workplace with clients, prospects, employees, business associates, and others have long been deductible provided that the meal was either "directly related to" or "associated with" the active conduct of the taxpayer's trade or business. These tests could be satisfied if you had a bona fide business discussion, negotiation, meeting, or other business transaction before, during, or after the meal. If the discussion occurred during the meal, however, you had to have a reasonable expectation that you would get some specific business benefit—for example, obtaining a new client. If either test was met, and you properly documented the cost and purpose of the meal, you could deduct 50% of the cost.

When the Tax Cuts and Jobs Act eliminated the deduction for business-related entertainment, it also appeared to eliminate deductions for client and prospect meals because such meals were deducted as an entertainment expense. However, IRS and Congressional officials have indicated that this result was not intended. So, it appears likely that action will be taken to retain deductions for client and prospect meals. The best course is to continue to keep track of expenses for such meals in the expectation that the deduction will be restored; 50% of the cost of meals consumed while traveling for business remains deductible.

Pass-Through Tax Deduction

The Tax Cuts and Jobs Act established a brand-new tax deduction for pass-through businesses. If you qualify, you can deduct from your income taxes up to 20% of your business income, effectively reducing the income tax you pay on your business income by 20%. This deduction went into effect in 2018 and is scheduled to last through 2025. Unfortunately, it's a very complex tax deduction and all of the kinks have yet to be worked out by the IRS. Here are the basics you need to understand.

You Must Have a Pass-Through Business

First, to benefit from the pass-through deduction, you must have a pass-through business. A pass-through business is any business that is a:

- sole proprietorship (a one-owner business in which the owner personally owns all the business assets)
- partnership
- S corporation
- limited liability company (LLC), or
- limited liability partnership (LLP).

The vast majority of self-employed people are sole proprietors. Those who aren't usually form LLCs or S corporations. So, most self-employed taxpayers will qualify for this deduction. However, you won't qualify for the pass-through deduction if you've formed a regular C corporation.

Employees do not qualify for the pass-through deduction, which is another reason to avoid being classified as an employee. (See Chapter 15.)

Your Pass-Through Deduction Is Based on Your Qualified Business Income

The pass-through deduction is based on your "qualified business income" (QBI). This is the net income (profit) your pass-through business earns, not including:

- short-term or long-term capital gain or loss—for example, a landlord would not include capital gain earned from selling a rental property
- dividend income
- interest income
- wages paid to S corporation shareholders
- guaranteed payments to partners in partnerships or LLC members, or
- business income earned outside the United States.

QBI is determined separately for each separate business you own. Your business must earn a profit to qualify for the deduction.

20% Deduction for Taxable Income Below $157,500 ($315,000 for Marrieds)

To calculate your deduction, you need to determine your taxable income—total income from all sources minus all your deductions. Your pass-through deduction can never exceed 20% of your taxable income.

If your taxable income is below $157,500 if single, or $315,000 if married filing jointly, your pass-through deduction is equal to 20% of your QBI, which is the maximum possible pass-through deduction.

> **EXAMPLE:** Tom is single and operates his business as a sole proprietorship. His business earns $100,000 in QBI during the year. His total taxable income for the year is $120,000. His pass-through deduction is 20% x $100,000 QBI = $20,000. He may deduct $20,000 from his income taxes.

If your taxable income is within the $157,500/$315,000 thresholds, that's all there is to the pass-through deduction.

Deduction for Income Above $157,500 ($315,000 for Marrieds)

Calculating the pass-through deduction is much more complicated if you're single and your taxable income is over $157,500, or if your taxable income exceeds $315,000, you're married, and you file a joint tax return with your spouse (as the vast majority of married people do).

First, a limitation based on how much you pay your employees or how much property you use in your business is phased in. Once your taxable income reaches $207,500 (single) or $415,000 (married), your pass-through deduction can't exceed the greater of (1) 50% of the W-2 employee wages paid by your business, or (2) 25% of W-2 wages, plus 2.5% of the original purchase price of the long-term property used in the production of income—for example, the real property or equipment used in the business. So, if you have neither employees nor business property, you get no deduction. This is intended to encourage pass-through owners to hire employees and/or buy property for their business.

> **EXAMPLE:** Hal and Wanda are married and file jointly. Their taxable income this year is $500,000, including $400,000 in QBI they earned in profit from their pass-through business. They have one part-time employee who they paid $25,000 in wages and no business property. Because their taxable income was over $415,000, their pass-through deduction is limited to the greater of (1) 50% of the W-2 wages they pay their employee, or (2) 25% of W-2 wages plus 2.5% of their business property. In this scenario, (1) is $12,500 (50% x $25,000 = $12,500) and (2) is $6,250 (25% x $25,000) + (2.5% x 0) = $6,250. (1) is greater so their pass-through deduction is $12,500.

In addition, if your taxable income is over $157,500 (single) or $315,000 (married), the deduction is phased out if your business involves providing services in the fields of:

- health (doctors, dentists, nurses, and other health professionals)
- law
- accounting (includes the preparation of and financial statements and preparing tax returns)
- actuarial science
- performing arts
- consulting (providing advice and counsel to clients)
- athletics
- financial services
- brokerage services
- trading or dealing in securities, partnership interests, or commodities
- investing and investment management, or
- any business where the principal asset is the reputation or skill of one or more of its owners.

If you're such a service provider, you get no pass-through deduction at all if your taxable income exceeds $207,500 (single) or $415,000 (married).

> **EXAMPLE:** Assume that Hal and Wanda from the above example are lawyers. Because this is a service business and their taxable income is over $415,000, they are entitled to no pass-through deduction at all.

Taking the Pass-Through Deduction

The pass-through deduction is a personal deduction you may take on your Form 1040 whether or not you itemize. There will likely be a separate tax form to be completed to claim the deduction, which the IRS has yet to devise. You'll then transfer the amount of the deduction to a line on your Form 1040.

The pass-through deduction is not an "above the line" deduction on the first page of Form 1040 that reduces your adjusted gross income (AGI). So, for example, it doesn't reduce your income for purposes of qualifying for Obamacare health insurance credits. Moreover, the deduction only reduces income taxes, not Social Security or Medicare taxes.

Health Insurance

Self-employed people must pay for their own health insurance. If you don't make a lot of money, this can be tough. Fortunately, there are some specific tax deductions designed to help you.

In addition, if you have employees, including your spouse, you may qualify for additional tax breaks, including a special tax credit for health insurance costs and medical reimbursement plans (discussed in Chapter 6). It's important that you learn about these deductions and take advantage of them. They can save you thousands of dollars in taxes every year and make health insurance far more affordable.

Personal Income Tax Deduction for the Self-Employed

Self-employed people are allowed to deduct from their income 100% of the cost of health insurance premiums (including dental and long-term care coverage) for themselves, their spouses, and their dependents (up to age 27). Sole proprietors, partners in partnerships, LLC members, and S corporation shareholders who own more than 2% of the company stock can all use this deduction. And you get the deduction whether you purchase your health insurance policy as an individual or have your business obtain it for you.

Self-employed people who have Medicare coverage may deduct their Medicare premiums as part of the self-employed health insurance deduction. This includes all Medicare Parts (not just Part B).

This is not a business deduction. It is a special personal deduction for the self-employed. The deduction applies to your federal, state, and local income taxes, but not to self-employment taxes.

> EXAMPLE: Kim is a sole proprietor who pays $10,000 each year for health insurance for herself, her husband, and her three children. Her business earned a $70,000 profit for the year. She may deduct her $10,000 annual health insurance expense from her gross income for federal and state income tax purposes. Her combined federal and state income tax rate is 30%, so she saves $3,000 in income taxes (30% × $10,000 = $3,000).

However, there is a significant limit: You may deduct only as much as you earn from your business. If your business earns no money or incurs a loss, you get no deduction. Thus, if Kim from the above example earned only $3,000 in profit from her business, her self-employed deduction would be limited to that amount; she wouldn't be able to deduct the remaining $7,000 in premiums she paid for the year.

You may not take the self-employed health insurance deduction if you are eligible to participate in a subsidized health insurance plan maintained by your employer or your spouse's employer. This is so even if the plan requires co-payments, or you have to pay additional premiums to obtain all the coverage you need.

Other Ways to Deduct Health Insurance Expenses

The self-employed personal health insurance deduction is not the only way to deduct your health insurance expenses. Some of the other methods available can give you a larger overall deduction because they'll reduce your Social Security and Medicare taxes as well as your income taxes.

Hire Your Spouse

If you're a sole proprietor, you can hire your spouse as an employee and provide him or her with health insurance. The insurance should be purchased in the name of the spouse-employee, not in the employer's name. The policy can cover your spouse, you, your children, and other dependents as well.

You can deduct the entire cost of providing health insurance as a business expense on your Schedule C. This reduces both your income and Social Security and Medicare taxes. If you do this and you're self-employed, you should not take the health insurance deduction for self-employed people discussed above.

However, there is a catch: Your spouse must be a bona fide employee. In other words, he or she must do real work in your business, you must pay applicable payroll taxes, provide workers compensation coverage (if required by your state law), and otherwise treat your spouse like any other employee.

But, if your spouse does work as your sole employee, you can not only pay for health insurance for your spouse (and family), but provide a health reimbursement plan as well. Under such a plan, you reimburse your spouse-employee for uninsured health expenses incurred by your spouse and the rest of the family (including you). You get to deduct the reimbursed amounts as a business expense. And, you need not include the reimbursements in your or your spouse's taxable income. For details, and a sample plan, refer to *Deduct It! Lower Your Small Business Taxes*, by Stephen Fishman (Nolo).

Work as an Employee of Your Incorporated Business

If your business is organized as a C corporation, you ordinarily will work as its employee and will be entitled to a full menu of tax-free employee fringe benefits, including health insurance (see Chapter 2). This means the corporation can purchase health insurance for you, deduct the cost as a business expense, and not have to include the cost in your employee compensation. Your health insurance is completely tax-free.

If you want to convert your health insurance premiums to a tax-free fringe benefit and you don't have a C corporation, you must form one to run your business and have the corporation hire you as its employee. You can do this even if you're running a one-person business. As an employee of a C corporation, you must receive a salary, and your corporation must pay your Social Security and Medicare taxes. Your corporation deducts your health insurance premiums from its taxes; you don't deduct them from your personal taxes. Because you own the corporation, you get the benefit of the deduction.

There are disadvantages to incorporating, however. Incorporating costs money, you'll have to comply with more burdensome bookkeeping requirements, and you will have a more complex tax return. You'll also have to pay state and federal unemployment taxes for yourself, which you don't need to pay if you're not an employee of your business. And, depending on your state's requirements, you may have to provide yourself with workers' compensation coverage.

Personal Itemized Deduction for Medical Expenses

All taxpayers—whether or not they own a business—are entitled to a personal income tax deduction for medical and dental expenses for themselves and their dependents. Eligible expenses include both health insurance premiums and out-of-pocket expenses not covered by insurance. However, there are two significant limitations on the deduction, which make it virtually unusable for most taxpayers.

First, to take the personal deduction, you must itemize your deductions on IRS Schedule A. You can itemize deductions only if all of your itemized deductions exceed the standard deduction for the year. The Tax Cuts and Jobs Act greatly increased the standard deduction to $24,000 for joint returns and $12,000 for single returns in 2018. Itemized deductions include medical expenses, home mortgage interest, state and local taxes (up to a $10,000 annual limit), charitable contributions, and a few others. As a result, far fewer taxpayers will be able to itemize than ever before.

Even if you do itemize, you can deduct only the amount by which your medical and dental expenses exceed 7.5% of your adjusted gross income (AGI) for 2018. The percentage threshold is scheduled to increase to 10% of AGI for 2019 and later. This limitation eats up most or all of your deduction. The more money you make, the less you can deduct. For this reason, most business owners need to look elsewhere for meaningful medical expense deductions.

Health Savings Accounts

Starting in 2004, self-employed people were allowed to establish health savings accounts (HSAs). These are designed to be used in conjunction with high-deductible health insurance plans and provide important tax benefits. For detailed information on HSAs, see Chapter 6.

Retirement Accounts

When you're self-employed, you don't have an employer to provide you with a retirement or pension plan. It's up to you to establish and fund your own plan to supplement any Social Security benefits you'll receive when you retire. Luckily, when it comes to saving for retirement, the self-employed are actually better off than most workers. This is because the federal government allows you to set up retirement accounts specifically designed for small business people that provide terrific income tax benefits.

These include simple IRAs, SEP-IRAs, Keogh plans, and solo 401(k)s. You can establish such accounts through a bank, savings and loan, or credit union; an insurance company, a brokerage house; a mutual fund company; or another financial institution.

These accounts provide you with two enormous tax benefits:

- You pay no taxes on the income your retirement investments earn until you withdraw the funds upon retirement.
- You can deduct the amount you contribute to your retirement account from your income taxes for the year, subject to certain limits.

 RESOURCE
Want detailed information on the tax aspects of retirement accounts?
Pick up these IRS titles:
- IRS Publication 560, *Retirement Plans for the Small Business,* and
- IRS Publication 590-A, *Contributions to Individual Retirement Arrangements.*

Start-Up Costs

The IRS refers to expenses you incur before you actually start your business as "business start-up costs." Such costs include, for example, license fees, fictitious business name registration fees, advertising costs, attorney and accounting fees, travel expenses, market research, and office supplies expenses. Business start-up costs are capital expenses because you incur them to acquire an asset (a business) that will benefit you for more than one year. Normally, you can't deduct these types of capital expenses until you sell or otherwise dispose of the business. However, a special tax rule allows you to deduct a portion of your start-up expenses the first year you are in business, and then deduct the remainder in equal amounts over 15 years. You can deduct up to $5,000 the first year. Without this special rule for business start-up costs, these expenses (capital expenses) would not be deductible until you sold or otherwise disposed of your business.

EXAMPLE: Diana decides to start a freelance public relations business. Her office opens for business on July 1. Before that date, however, Diana incurs various expenses, including travel expenses to obtain office space, office rent and utilities, lease expenses for office furniture and computer equipment, and advertising expenses. She spent $10,000 of her life savings to get her business up and running. Because these are start-up expenses, she cannot deduct them all in her first year of business. But she can deduct up to $5,000 the first year she is in business and the remainder in equal amounts over the next 15 years. (I.R.C. § 195.)

If you have more than $50,000 in start-up expenses, however, you are not entitled to the full $5,000 deduction. You must reduce the $5,000 deduction by the amount that your start-up expenditures exceed $50,000. For example, if you have $53,000 in start-up expenses, you may deduct only $2,000 the first year, instead of $5,000. If you have $55,000 or more in start-up expenses, you get no current deduction for start-up expenses. Instead, the whole amount must be deducted over 180 months. Likewise, if you have more than $5,000 in start-up expenses, you must deduct the excess over 180 months. To do so, you must complete and attach IRS Form 4562, *Depreciation and Amortization*, to your return for the first tax year you are in business.

 RESOURCE
Want more information on business start-up costs?
See IRS Publication 535, *Business Expenses*, available from www.irs.gov.

The Bane of Self-Employment Taxes

All Americans who work in the private sector are required to pay taxes to help support the Social Security and Medicare systems. Although these taxes are paid to the IRS, they are entirely separate from federal income taxes.

Employees have their Social Security and Medicare taxes directly deducted from their paychecks by their employers, who must make matching contributions. Such taxes are usually referred to as "FICA" taxes.

But if you're self-employed, your clients or customers will not pay or withhold your Social Security and Medicare taxes. You must pay them to the IRS yourself. When self-employed workers pay these taxes, they are called "self-employment" taxes or SE taxes. This chapter shows you how to determine how much you must pay in SE taxes.

 SKIP AHEAD
If your net income from your business for the year is less than $400, you don't have to pay any self-employment taxes. You can skip this chapter.

Who Must Pay

Sole proprietors, partners in partnerships, and members of limited liability companies must all pay self-employment taxes if their net earnings from self-employment are $400 or more for the year.

Corporations do not pay SE taxes. However, if you're incorporated and work as an employee of your corporation, you will ordinarily be paid a salary on which you must pay FICA taxes, just like any other employee. You do not pay SE taxes. Your corporation, however, must withhold half of your Social Security and Medicare taxes from your salary and pay the other half. (See Chapter 6.)

Self-Employment Taxes

Self-employment taxes consist of two separate taxes: the Social Security tax and the Medicare tax.

The Social Security tax is a flat 12.4% tax on net self-employment income up to an annual ceiling, which is adjusted for inflation each year. In 2018, the ceiling is $128,400 in net self-employment income. A person who earns that much (or more) in net SE income will pay $15,922 in Social Security taxes.

There are two Medicare tax rates. Everyone must pay a 2.9% tax on income up to an annual ceiling: $200,000 for single taxpayers and $250,000 for married couples filing jointly. Those who earn more must pay a 3.8% tax on income that exceeds the ceiling. In other words, such income is subject to an extra 0.9% of Medicare tax.

> EXAMPLE: Mona, a single self-employed consultant, earned $250,000 in net self-employment income in 2018. She must pay both Social Security and Medicare taxes on the first $128,400 of her income—a 15.3% tax. She must also pay the 2.9% Medicare tax on $128,401 through $200,000. She must then pay a 3.8% Medicare tax on the remaining $50,000 of her income. Her total Social Security and Medicare tax bill: $23,621.

Of course, employees pay Social Security and Medicare taxes as well. These are often called "payroll" taxes because employers withhold them from their employees' pay and send them to the IRS. The tax rates and annual ceilings for employee payroll taxes are the same as for self-employment taxes.

However, employers are required to pay half of their employees' payroll taxes themselves, while withholding the other half from employees. (Employers need not pay half of the extra 0.9% Medicare tax for employees who earn more than $200,000 (for individuals) or $250,000 (for married couples filing jointly), nor must they withhold this amount from their pay.) As a result, most employees pay only half as much in Social Security and Medicare tax as do the self-employed.

To help ameliorate this unfairness, self-employed taxpayers are allowed to deduct 50% of their SE taxes from their income for federal self-employment and income tax purposes. As a result, the "real" self-employment tax rate is somewhat lower than the official rate; how much lower depends on your income.

Earnings Subject to SE Taxes

You pay self-employment taxes on your net self-employment income, not your entire income. To determine your net self-employment income, you must first figure out the net income you've earned from your business. Your net business income includes all income from your business, minus all business deductions allowed for income tax purposes. Deducting your business expenses from your SE income makes them doubly valuable: They will reduce not only your income taxes, but your SE taxes as well.

However, you can't deduct retirement contributions you make for yourself to a self-employed SEP, SIMPLE, or qualified retirement plan or the self-employed health insurance deduction. If you're a sole proprietor (like most self-employed people) use IRS Schedule C, *Profit or Loss From Business*, to determine your net business income.

If you have more than one business, combine the net income or loss from them all. If you have a job in addition to your business, your employee income is not included in your self-employment income. Nor must you include investment income, such as interest you earn on your savings.

You then get one more valuable deduction before determining your net self-employment income: You get to subtract half of the SE tax to come up with your net SE income. This is intended to help ease the tax burden on the self-employed. To do this, multiply your net business income by 92.35%, or 0.9235.

> **EXAMPLE:** Billie, a self-employed consultant, earned $70,000 from her business and had $20,000 in business expenses, leaving a net business income of $50,000. She multiplies this amount by 0.9235 to determine her net self-employment income, which is $46,175. This is the amount on which Billie must pay SE and income tax.

You may also claim 50% of what you pay in SE tax as an adjustment to income on your tax return (Form 1040). (Taxpayers who earn more than the $200,000 and $250,000 thresholds can't deduct any of the extra 0.9% increase in Medicare tax they must pay on income that exceeds the threshold.) For example, if you owe $10,000 in SE tax, you can deduct

$5,000 as an adjustment to income on line 27 of your Form 1040, reducing your taxable income by that amount. If you're in the 24% income tax bracket, this will save you $1,200 in income tax. This adjustment to income is available whether or not you itemize deductions.

S Corporation Status: A Way Around the SE Tax Thicket

As a person in business for yourself, you may be able to take advantage of an important wrinkle in the SE tax rules: Distributions from S corporations to their owners are not subject to SE taxes. This is so even though such distributions are included in your income for income tax purposes.

If you incorporate your business and elect to become an S corporation, you may distribute part of your corporation's earnings to yourself without paying SE taxes on them. You can't distribute all your earnings to yourself this way, however, because your S corporation must pay you a reasonable salary on which FICA taxes must be paid.

Paying and Reporting SE Taxes

You must pay SE taxes directly to the IRS during the year as part of your estimated taxes. You have the option of either:

- paying the same amount in tax as you paid the previous year, or
- estimating what your income will be this year and basing your estimated tax payments on that. (See Chapter 11.)

When you file your annual tax return, you must include IRS Form SE, *Self-Employment Tax*, along with your income tax return. This form shows the IRS how much SE tax you were required to pay for the year. You file only one Form SE no matter how many unincorporated businesses you own. Add the SE tax to your income taxes on your personal income tax return (Form 1040) to determine your total tax.

Even if you do not owe any income tax, if you owe $400 or more in SE taxes, you must still complete Form 1040 and Schedule SE.

Outside Employment

If you also have an outside job in which you're classified as an employee for which Social Security and Medicare taxes are withheld from your wages, you must pay the Social Security tax on your wages (rather than your SE income) first. If your wages are at least equal to the Social Security tax income ceiling, you won't have to pay the 12.4% Social Security tax on your SE income. But no matter how much you earn from your job, you'll have to pay Medicare tax on all your SE income over the Social Security tax ceiling ($128,400 in 2018). This is a 2.9% tax up to $200,000 in net SE income for single people and $250,000 for married couples filing jointly; the tax goes up to 3.8% for net SE income over these thresholds.

However, if your employee wages are lower than the Social Security tax income ceiling, you'll have to pay Social Security taxes on your SE income until your wages and SE income combined exceed the ceiling amount.

Paying Estimated Taxes

What many self-employed people like best about their employ-ment status is that it gives them the freedom to plan and handle their own finances. Unlike employees, they don't have taxes withheld from their compensation by their clients or customers. As a result, many self-employed people have higher take-home pay than employees earning similar amounts.

Unfortunately, however, self-employed workers do not have the luxury of waiting until April 15 to pay all their taxes for the previous year. The IRS wants to get its money a lot faster than that, so the self-employed are required to pay taxes on their estimated annual incomes in four payments spread out over each year. These are called "estimated taxes" and include both income taxes (see Chapter 9) and self-employment taxes (see Chapter 10).

Because the self-employed have to pay estimated taxes, self-employed people need to budget their money carefully. If you fail to set aside enough of your earnings to pay your estimated taxes, you could face a huge tax bill on April 15, and have a tough time coming up with the money to cover it.

CAUTION
Most states have estimated taxes, too. If your state has income taxes, it probably requires the self-employed to pay estimated taxes. The due dates are generally the same as for federal estimated taxes. Contact your state tax office for information and the required forms. You can find your state tax agency on the IRS website at www.irs.gov/businesses/small-businesses-self-employed/state-links-1.

Who Must Pay Estimated Taxes

You must pay estimated taxes if you are a sole proprietor, partner in a partnership, or member of a limited liability company and you expect to owe at least $1,000 in federal tax for the year. If you've formed a C corporation, the corporation may also have to pay estimated taxes.

However, if you paid no taxes last year—for example, because your business made no profit or you weren't working—you don't have to pay any estimated tax this year, no matter how much tax you expect to owe. But this is true only if you were a U.S. citizen or resident for the year and your tax return for the previous year covered the whole 12 months.

You also don't have to pay estimated tax if you have a job and the amount withheld from your pay by your employer will amount to at least 90% of the total tax you'll have to pay for the year.

> CAUTION
> **Don't forget self-employment taxes.** Your estimated tax payments must cover not only your income taxes for the year, but your self-employment taxes as well (Social Security and Medicare taxes). See Chapter 10 for more information on self-employment taxes. If you earn just $7,500 in net income from being self-employed, you'll owe $1,039 in self-employment tax alone ($859 Social Security tax and $201 Medicare tax) which will trigger the need to make quarterly estimated tax payments.

Sole Proprietors

A sole proprietor and his or her business are one and the same for tax purposes, so you simply pay your estimated taxes out of your own pocket. You, not your business, pay the taxes.

Partners and Limited Liability Companies

Partnerships and limited liability companies (LLCs) are similar to sole proprietorships. They don't pay any taxes; instead, all partnership and LLC income passes through to the partners or LLC members. The partners or LLC members must pay individual estimated tax on their shares of the partnership or LLC income. This is so whether the income is actually paid to them or not. The partnership or LLC itself pays no tax. The only exception is if the owners of an LLC elect to be taxed as a C corporation, which is very unusual.

Corporations

A corporation is separate from you for tax purposes. Both you and your corporation might have to pay estimated taxes.

Ordinarily, you will be an employee of your corporation and receive a salary from it. The corporation must withhold income and employment taxes from your salary just as for any employee. (See Chapter 13.) You won't need to pay any estimated tax on your salary. But if you receive dividends or distributions from your corporation, you'll need to pay tax on them during the year unless the total tax due on the amounts you received is less than $500. You can either pay estimated tax or increase the tax withheld from your salary; it doesn't make much practical difference which you choose.

If you've formed a C corporation, it must pay quarterly estimated taxes if it will owe $500 or more in corporate tax on its profits for the year. These taxes are paid to the IRS using the Electronic Federal Tax Payment System (EFTPS), discussed below, or a financial institution, payroll tax service, or tax pro pays them electronically. However, most small C corporations don't have to pay any income taxes or estimated taxes because all the profits are taken out of the corporation by the owners in the form of salaries, bonuses, and benefits. (See Chapter 2.)

Usually, S corporations don't have to pay estimated taxes because all profits are passed through to the shareholders, as in a partnership or an LLC. (See Chapter 2.)

RESOURCE
Want detailed guidance on estimated taxes for your C corporation?
See IRS Publication 542, *Corporations*. You can obtain this and all other IRS publications from the IRS website at www.irs.gov.

How Much You Must Pay

You should determine how much estimated tax to pay after completing your tax return for the previous year. Most people want to pay as little estimated tax as possible during the year so they can earn interest on their money instead of handing it over to the IRS. However, the IRS imposes penalties if you don't pay enough estimated tax. There's no need to be overly concerned about these penalties: They aren't terribly large and it's easy to avoid them. All you have to do is pay at least the lesser of:

- 90% of your total tax due for the current year, or
- 100% of the tax you paid the previous year (110% if you're a high-income taxpayer, as described in "High-Income Taxpayers," below).

Generally, you make four estimated tax payments each year. As described in this section, there are three different ways you can calculate your payments. You can use any one of the three methods without paying a penalty as long as you pay the minimum total the IRS requires, as explained above. One of the methods—basing your payments on last year's tax—is extremely easy to use. The other two are more complex to figure out but might permit you to make smaller payments.

Payments Based on Last Year's Taxes

The easiest and safest way to calculate your estimated tax is to pay 100% of the total federal taxes you paid last year. You can base your estimated tax on the amount you paid last year, even if you weren't in business that year, as long as your return covered a full 12-month period.

You should determine how much estimated tax to pay for the current year when you file your tax return for the previous year, no later than April 15. Take the total amount of tax you had to pay for the year and divide by four. If this comes out to an odd number, round up to get an even number. These are the amounts you'll have to pay in estimated tax. You'll make four equal payments throughout the year and the following year. (See the chart "Estimated Tax Due," below, to learn when you must make your payments.)

> EXAMPLE: Gary, a self-employed consultant, earned $70,000 last year. He figures his taxes for the prior year on April 1 of this year and determines he owes $9,989.32 in taxes for the year. To determine his estimated tax for the current year he divides this amount by four: $9,989.32 divided by four equals $2,497.33. He rounds this up to $2,500. He'll make four $2,500 estimated tax payments to the IRS throughout the current year. As long as he pays this much, Gary won't have to pay a penalty, even if he ends up owing more than $10,000 in taxes for the current year (due to increased income or decreased deductions).

High-Income Taxpayers

To avoid penalties for paying too little estimated taxes, high-income taxpayers—those with adjusted gross incomes of more than $150,000 (or $75,000 for married couples filing separate returns)—must pay more. They must pay 110% of the prior year's income tax.

Your adjusted gross income, or AGI, is your total income minus deductions for:

- IRA, Keogh, solo 401(k), and SEP-IRA contributions
- health insurance
- one-half of your self-employment tax, and
- alimony, deductible moving expenses, and penalties you pay for early withdrawals from a savings account before maturity or early redemption of certificates of deposit.

To determine your AGI, look at line 37 on your last year's tax return, Form 1040.

> **EXAMPLE:** Mary, a self-employed consultant, earned $250,000 in gross income in 2018. Her adjusted gross income was $200,000 after subtracting the value of her solo 401(k) contributions, her health insurance deduction, and half of her self-employment taxes. Mary paid $50,000 in income and self-employment taxes in 2017. In 2018, Mary must pay 110% of the tax she paid in 2017—$55,000 in estimated tax. As long as she pays this amount she won't have to pay a penalty to the IRS, even if she ends up owing more in taxes than she did in 2017.

Midcourse Correction

Your third estimated tax payment is due on September 15. By this time, you should have a pretty good idea of what your income for the year will be. If you're reasonably sure that your income for the year will be at least 25% less than what you earned last year, you can forgo the last estimated tax payment due on January 15 of the next year. You have already paid enough estimated tax for the year.

If it looks as if your income will be greater than last year, you don't have to pay more estimated tax. The IRS cannot penalize you so long as you pay 100% of what you paid last year, or 110% if you're a high-income taxpayer.

You May Owe Tax on April 15

Basing your estimated tax on last year's income is generally the best method to use if you expect your income to be higher this year than last year. You'll be paying the minimum possible without incurring a penalty.

Medicare Tax on Investment Income for Higher-Income Taxpayers

If you have investment income in addition to business income, you may be subject to the 3.8% net investment income tax ("NII tax" for short; it's also called the Medicare Contribution Tax) that took effect in 2013. You must pay this tax only if (1) your adjusted gross income (AGI) exceeds specified threshold amounts ($200,000 for single people and $250,000 for married couples filing jointly), and (2) you have net investment income.

Investment income consists of:

- income from investment assets, including interest, dividends, rents (less expenses), and annuities
- income from any business in which you don't materially participate (aren't active in running), and
- net capital gains (gains less capital losses) you earn from the sale of property that is not part of an active business, including rental property, stocks and bonds, and mutual funds.

The NII tax is a flat 3.8% tax. However, it is not imposed on your total AGI or investment income. Instead, it is assessed only on the lesser of (1) your net investment income, or (2) the amount by which your AGI exceeds the applicable $200,000 or $250,000 threshold.

> **EXAMPLE:** Burt, a single taxpayer, earns $300,000 in net self-employment income. He also earned $50,000 in net investment income during the year. His AGI is $350,000. Burt must pay the 3.8% NII tax on the lesser of (1) his $50,000 of net investment income, or (2) the amount by which his $350,000 AGI exceeds the $200,000 threshold for single taxpayers: $150,000. Because $50,000 is less than $150,000, he must pay the 3.8% tax on $50,000. His NII tax for the year is $1,900 (3.8% x $50,000).

The NII tax is not withheld or paid to the IRS by the financial institutions with which you have accounts. Instead, you must pay it yourself as an addition to your regular income taxes when you file your Form 1040. However, the tax is also subject to the IRS's estimated tax rules. If you expect to owe NII tax, you'll need to adjust your estimated tax payments to account for the tax increase in order to avoid underpayment penalties. Alternatively, if you have an employer, you could have your employee tax withholding increased.

Form 1040: U.S. Individual Income Tax Return

Form **1040**	Department of the Treasury—Internal Revenue Service (99) **U.S. Individual Income Tax Return**	2017	OMB No. 1545-0074	IRS Use Only—Do not write or staple in this space.

For the year Jan. 1–Dec. 31, 2017, or other tax year beginning , 2017, ending , 20   **See separate instructions.**

Your first name and initial	Last name		Your social security number
If a joint return, spouse's first name and initial	Last name		Spouse's social security number

Home address (number and street). If you have a P.O. box, see instructions.   Apt. no.   ▲ Make sure the SSN(s) above and on line 6c are correct.

City, town or post office, state, and ZIP code. If you have a foreign address, also complete spaces below (see instructions).

Presidential Election Campaign
Check here if you, or your spouse if filing jointly, want $3 to go to this fund. Checking a box below will not change your tax or refund. ☐ You ☐ Spouse

Foreign country name	Foreign province/state/county	Foreign postal code

Filing Status
Check only one box.

1. ☐ Single
2. ☐ Married filing jointly (even if only one had income)
3. ☐ Married filing separately. Enter spouse's SSN above and full name here. ▶
4. ☐ Head of household (with qualifying person). (See instructions.) If the qualifying person is a child but not your dependent, enter this child's name here. ▶
5. ☐ Qualifying widow(er) (see instructions)

Exemptions

6a ☐ Yourself. If someone can claim you as a dependent, **do not** check box 6a . . . . .
 b ☐ Spouse . . . .

c Dependents: (1) First name Last name	(2) Dependent's social security number	(3) Dependent's relationship to you	(4) ✓ if child under age 17 qualifying for child tax credit (see instructions)
			☐
			☐
			☐
			☐

If more than four dependents, see instructions and check here ▶ ☐

d Total number of exemptions claimed . . . .

Boxes checked on 6a and 6b
No. of children on 6c who:
• lived with you
• did not live with you due to divorce or separation (see instructions)
Dependents on 6c not entered above
Add numbers on lines above ▶

Income

Attach Form(s) W-2 here. Also attach Forms W-2G and 1099-R if tax was withheld.

If you did not get a W-2, see instructions.

7	Wages, salaries, tips, etc. Attach Form(s) W-2	7	
8a	**Taxable** interest. Attach Schedule B if required	8a	
b	Tax-exempt interest. **Do not** include on line 8a . . .	8b	
9a	Ordinary dividends. Attach Schedule B if required	9a	
b	Qualified dividends	9b	
10	Taxable refunds, credits, or offsets of state and local income taxes	10	
11	Alimony received	11	
12	Business income or (loss). Attach Schedule C or C-EZ	12	
13	Capital gain or (loss). Attach Schedule D if required. If not required, check here ▶ ☐	13	
14	Other gains or (losses). Attach Form 4797	14	
15a	IRA distributions . 15a	b Taxable amount . . .	15b	
16a	Pensions and annuities 16a	b Taxable amount . . .	16b	
17	Rental real estate, royalties, partnerships, S corporations, trusts, etc. Attach Schedule E	17	
18	Farm income or (loss). Attach Schedule F	18	
19	Unemployment compensation	19	
20a	Social security benefits 20a	b Taxable amount . . .	20b	
21	Other income. List type and amount	21	
22	Combine the amounts in the far right column for lines 7 through 21. This is your **total income** ▶	22	

Adjusted Gross Income

23	Educator expenses	23		
24	Certain business expenses of reservists, performing artists, and fee-basis government officials. Attach Form 2106 or 2106-EZ	24		
25	Health savings account deduction. Attach Form 8889 .	25		
26	Moving expenses. Attach Form 3903	26		
27	Deductible part of self-employment tax. Attach Schedule SE .	27		
28	Self-employed SEP, SIMPLE, and qualified plans . .	28		
29	Self-employed health insurance deduction . . .	29		
30	Penalty on early withdrawal of savings	30		
31a	Alimony paid b Recipient's SSN ▶	31a		
32	IRA deduction	32		
33	Student loan interest deduction	33		
34	Tuition and fees. Attach Form 8917	34		
35	Domestic production activities deduction. Attach Form 8903	35		
36	Add lines 23 through 35		36	
37	Subtract line 36 from line 22. This is your **adjusted gross income** . . . . ▶		37	

For Disclosure, Privacy Act, and Paperwork Reduction Act Notice, see separate instructions.   Cat. No. 11320B   Form **1040** (2017)

Form 1040: U.S. Individual Income Tax Return (page 2)

Form 1040 (2017)   Page **2**

Tax and Credits	38	Amount from line 37 (adjusted gross income)	38	
	39a	Check if: ☐ **You** were born before January 2, 1953, ☐ Blind. ☐ **Spouse** was born before January 2, 1953, ☐ Blind. } Total boxes checked ▶ 39a		
	b	If your spouse itemizes on a separate return or you were a dual-status alien, check here▶ 39b☐		
Standard Deduction for—	40	**Itemized deductions** (from Schedule A) **or** your **standard deduction** (see left margin) . .	40	
• People who check any box on line 39a or 39b **or** who can be claimed as a dependent, see instructions.	41	Subtract line 40 from line 38	41	
	42	**Exemptions.** If line 38 is $156,900 or less, multiply $4,050 by the number on line 6d. Otherwise, see instructions	42	
	43	**Taxable income.** Subtract line 42 from line 41. If line 42 is more than line 41, enter -0- . .	43	
	44	**Tax** (see instructions). Check if any from: **a** ☐ Form(s) 8814 **b** ☐ Form 4972 **c** ☐ _____	44	
	45	**Alternative minimum tax** (see instructions). Attach Form 6251	45	
	46	Excess advance premium tax credit repayment. Attach Form 8962	46	
• All others: Single or Married filing separately, $6,350	47	Add lines 44, 45, and 46 . . . . ▶	47	
	48	Foreign tax credit. Attach Form 1116 if required	48		
	49	Credit for child and dependent care expenses. Attach Form 2441	49		
	50	Education credits from Form 8863, line 19	50		
Married filing jointly or Qualifying widow(er), $12,700	51	Retirement savings contributions credit. Attach Form 8880	51		
	52	Child tax credit. Attach Schedule 8812, if required . . .	52		
	53	Residential energy credits. Attach Form 5695	53		
Head of household, $9,350	54	Other credits from Form: **a** ☐ 3800 **b** ☐ 8801 **c** ☐	54		
	55	Add lines 48 through 54. These are your **total credits**	55	
	56	Subtract line 55 from line 47. If line 55 is more than line 47, enter -0- . . . . ▶	56	
Other Taxes	57	Self-employment tax. Attach Schedule SE	57	
	58	Unreported social security and Medicare tax from Form: **a** ☐ 4137 **b** ☐ 8919 . .	58	
	59	Additional tax on IRAs, other qualified retirement plans, etc. Attach Form 5329 if required . .	59	
	60a	Household employment taxes from Schedule H	60a	
	b	First-time homebuyer credit repayment. Attach Form 5405 if required	60b	
	61	Health care: individual responsibility (see instructions) Full-year coverage ☐	61	
	62	Taxes from: **a** ☐ Form 8959 **b** ☐ Form 8960 **c** ☐ Instructions; enter code(s) _____	62	
	63	Add lines 56 through 62. This is your **total tax** . . . . ▶	63	
Payments	64	Federal income tax withheld from Forms W-2 and 1099 . .	64		
	65	2017 estimated tax payments and amount applied from 2016 return	65		
If you have a qualifying child, attach Schedule EIC.	66a	**Earned income credit (EIC)**	66a		
	b	Nontaxable combat pay election	66b			
	67	Additional child tax credit. Attach Schedule 8812	67		
	68	American opportunity credit from Form 8863, line 8 . . .	68		
	69	Net premium tax credit. Attach Form 8962	69		
	70	Amount paid with request for extension to file	70		
	71	Excess social security and tier 1 RRTA tax withheld	71		
	72	Credit for federal tax on fuels. Attach Form 4136	72		
	73	Credits from Form: **a** ☐ 2439 **b** ☐ Reserved **c** ☐ 8885 **d** ☐	73		
	74	Add lines 64, 65, 66a, and 67 through 73. These are your **total payments** . . . . ▶	74	
Refund	75	If line 74 is more than line 63, subtract line 63 from line 74. This is the amount you **overpaid**	75	
	76a	Amount of line 75 you want **refunded to you.** If Form 8888 is attached, check here . . ▶☐	76a	
Direct deposit? See instructions.	▶ b	Routing number |_|_|_|_|_|_|_|_|_| ▶ **c** Type: ☐ Checking ☐ Savings		
	▶ d	Account number |_|_|_|_|_|_|_|_|_|_|_|_|_|_|_|_|		
	77	Amount of line 75 you want **applied to your 2018 estimated tax** ▶	77		
Amount You Owe	78	**Amount you owe.** Subtract line 74 from line 63. For details on how to pay, see instructions ▶	78	
	79	Estimated tax penalty (see instructions)	79		

Third Party Designee — Do you want to allow another person to discuss this return with the IRS (see instructions)? ☐ **Yes.** Complete below.   ☐ **No**

Designee's name ▶	Phone no. ▶	Personal identification number (PIN) ▶ |_|_|_|_|_|

Sign Here
Joint return? See instructions.
Keep a copy for your records.

Under penalties of perjury, I declare that I have examined this return and accompanying schedules and statements, and to the best of my knowledge and belief, they are true, correct, and accurately list all amounts and sources of income I received during the tax year. Declaration of preparer (other than taxpayer) is based on all information of which preparer has any knowledge.

Your signature	Date	Your occupation	Daytime phone number
Spouse's signature. If a joint return, **both** must sign.	Date	Spouse's occupation	If the IRS sent you an Identity Protection PIN, enter it here (see inst.) |_|_|_|_|_|_|

Paid Preparer Use Only

Print/Type preparer's name	Preparer's signature	Date	Check ☐ if self-employed	PTIN
Firm's name ▶			Firm's EIN ▶	
Firm's address ▶			Phone no.	

Go to *www.irs.gov/Form1040* for instructions and the latest information.   Form **1040** (2017)

Of course, if you do end up earning more than last year, you will have to make up the underpayment when you file your tax return for the year. To make sure you have enough money for this, it's a good idea to sock away a portion of your income in a separate bank account just for taxes.

Payments Based on Estimated Taxable Income

As a result of the Tax Cuts and Jobs Act (TCJA), income tax rates for most taxpayers are somewhat lower in 2018 and later than they were in 2017 and earlier. So, if you base your 2018 estimated tax on 100% (or 110%) of what you paid in 2017, you could end up paying more than you need to. You can avoid this by basing your estimated tax on what you think your net income will be in 2018 or later. You should also use this method if you think your net income will be less this year than last year.

The problem with using this method is that you must estimate your total income and deductions for the year before they happen to figure out how much to pay. Obviously, this can be difficult or impossible to compute accurately. And there are no magic formulas to look to for guidance. The best way to proceed is to sit down with your tax return for the previous year.

Try to figure out whether your income this year will be more or less than last year. You'll find all your income for last year listed on your Form 1040. Also, determine whether your deductions will be greater than last year.

Pay special attention to your business income and expense figures in Parts I and II of your Schedule C, *Profit or Loss From Business*. Decide whether it's likely that you'll earn more, less, or about the same business income this year than last. You'll probably earn more, for example, if you plan to work more hours than last year. Also, determine whether your deductible business expenses will be greater this year than last. For example, if you plan to purchase expensive business equipment and deduct the cost, your net profit could decline. In addition, you could qualify for the pass-through tax deduction, which can give you an income tax deduction equal to as much as 20% of your net business income. (See Chapter 9.)

Take comfort in knowing that you need not make an exact estimate of your taxable income. You won't have to pay a penalty if you pay at least 90% of your tax due for the year.

> EXAMPLE: Larry, a self-employed consultant, earned $100,000 last year and paid $25,000 in income and self-employment taxes. As a result of the TCJA tax cuts and the 20% pass-through deduction, Larry expects to owe only $20,000 in tax in 2018. He pays 90% of this amount, or $18,000, in four estimated tax payments during the year.

IRS Form 1040-ES contains a worksheet to use to calculate your estimated tax. You can obtain the form from the IRS website at www.irs.gov.

Tax preparation software (discussed in Chapter 8) can help you with the calculations. You can also find estimated tax calculators online.

If you have your taxes prepared by an accountant, he or she should determine what estimated tax to pay. If your income changes greatly during the year, ask your accountant to help you prepare a revised estimated tax payment schedule.

Payments Based on Quarterly Income

A much more complicated way to calculate your estimated taxes is to use the "annualized income installment method." It requires that you separately calculate your tax liability at four points during the year—March 31, May 31, August 31, and December 31—prorating your deductions and personal exemptions. You base your estimated tax payments on your actual tax liability for each quarter. (See the table "Estimated Tax Due," below.)

This method is often the best choice for people who receive income very unevenly throughout the year, including those who work in seasonal businesses. Using this method, they can pay little or no estimated tax for the quarters in which they earned little or no income.

> EXAMPLE: Ernie's income from his air-conditioning repair business is much higher in the summer than it is during the rest of the year. By using the annualized income installment method, he makes one large estimated tax payment on September 15, after the quarter in which he earns most of his income. His other three annual payments are quite small.

If you use this method, you must file IRS Form 2210 (*Underpayment of Estimated Tax by Individuals, Estates, and Trusts*) with your tax return to show your calculations.

> **SEE AN EXPERT**
>
> **You'll need help with the math.** You really need a good grasp of tax law and mathematics to use the annualized income installment method. The IRS worksheet used to calculate your payments using this method contains 43 separate steps. If you want to use this method, give yourself a break and hire an accountant or at least use tax preparation software to help with the calculations.

> **RESOURCE**
>
> **Want more information on the annualized income method?** See IRS Publication 505, *Tax Withholding and Estimated Tax,* for a detailed explanation. You can obtain the form from the IRS website at www.irs.gov.

When to Pay

You must ordinarily pay your estimated taxes in four installments, with the first one due on April 15. However, you don't have to start making payments until you actually earn income. If you don't receive any income by March 31, you can skip the April 15 payment. In this event, you'd ordinarily make three payments for the year, starting on June 15. If you don't receive any income by May 31, you can skip the June 15 payment as well and so on.

Estimated Tax Due	
Income received for the period	**Estimated tax due**
January 1 through March 31	April 15
April 1 through May 31	June 15
June 1 through August 31	September 15
September 1 through December 31	January 15 of the next year

Special Rule for Farmers and Fishermen

If at least two-thirds of your annual income comes from farming or fishing, you need make only one estimated tax payment on January 15. The first three payment periods in the chart above don't apply.

You can also skip the January 15 payment if you file your tax return and pay all taxes due for the previous year by January 31 of the current year. This is a little reward the IRS gives you for filing your tax return early. However, it's rarely advantageous to file early because you'll have to pay any tax due on January 15 instead of waiting until April 15. In other words, you'll lose three months of interest on your hard-earned money.

CAUTION

The year may not begin in January. Don't get confused by the fact that the January 15 payment is the fourth estimated tax payment for the previous year, not the first payment for the current year. The April 15 payment is the first payment for the current year.

Your estimated tax payment must be postmarked by the dates noted above, but the IRS need not actually receive them then. If any of these days falls on a weekend or legal holiday, the due date is the next business day.

CAUTION

Beware the ides of April. April 15 can be a financial killer for the self-employed because you not only have to pay any income and self-employment taxes that are due for the previous year, you also have to make your first estimated tax payment for the current year. If you've underpaid your estimated taxes by a substantial amount, you could have a whopping tax bill.

Many self-employed people establish separate bank accounts to save up for taxes into which they deposit a portion of each payment they receive from clients. This gives them some assurance that they'll have enough money to pay their taxes. The amount you should deposit depends on your federal and state income tax brackets and the amount of your tax deductions. Depending on your income, you'll probably need to deposit 25% to 50% of your pay. If you deposit too much, of course, you can always spend the money later on other things.

> **EXAMPLE:** Wilma, a self-employed worker who lives in Massachusetts, is in the 24% federal income tax bracket and must pay a 6% state income tax. She must also pay a 15.3% self-employment tax. All these taxes amount to 45.3% of her pay. But she doesn't have to set aside this much because her deductions will reduce her actual tax liability. Using the amount of her deductions from last year as a guide, Wilma determines she needs to set aside 35% to 40% of her income for estimated taxes.

Tell the IRS If You Move

If you make estimated tax payments and you change your address during the year, use IRS Form 8822, *Change of Address*, to notify the IRS (file Form 8822-B, *Change of Address or Responsible Party Business*, if you have a separate business address you change and don't change your home address). Or send a signed letter to the IRS Center where you filed your last return stating:

- your full name and your spouse's full name
- your old address and spouse's old address (if different)
- your new address, and
- Social Security numbers for you and your spouse.

How to Pay

The IRS wants to make it easy for you to send in your money, so the mechanics of paying estimated taxes are very simple. You have four choices of how to pay:

- by mail
- electronically, using the government's EFTP system
- by electronic withdrawal from your bank account, or
- by credit or debit card.

Paying by Mail

To pay by mail, you file federal estimated taxes using IRS Form 1040-ES. This form contains instructions and four numbered payment vouchers for you to send in with your payments. You must provide your name, address, Social Security number (or EIN if you have one), and amount of the payment on each voucher. You file only one payment voucher with each payment, no matter how many unincorporated businesses you have. If you're married and file a joint return, the names on your estimated tax vouchers should be exactly the same as those on your income tax return even if your spouse isn't self-employed, so that the money gets credited to the right account.

If you made estimated tax payments last year, you should receive a copy of the current year's Form 1040-ES in the mail. It will have payment vouchers preprinted with your name, address, and Social Security number. If you did not pay estimated taxes last year, get a copy of Form 1040-ES from the IRS website at www.irs.gov. After you make your first payment, the IRS should mail you a Form 1040-ES package with the preprinted vouchers.

Use the preaddressed return envelopes that come with your Form 1040-ES package. If you use your own envelopes, make sure you mail your payment vouchers to the address shown in the Form 1040-ES instructions for the region in which you live. Do not mail your estimated tax payments to the same place you sent your Form 1040.

Paying by EFTPS

The IRS has created the Electronic Federal Tax Payment System (EFTPS) to enable taxpayers to pay their taxes. The system allows taxpayers to use the phone, personal computer software, or the Internet to initiate tax payments to EFTPS directly. The system is free to use. The payments are debited from your bank account. This is a great way to pay estimated tax.

You must enroll with EFTPS before you can use it. You can enroll online at the EFTPS website. Within 15 calendar days your personal identification number (PIN) will be mailed to your IRS address of record. You will also receive confirmation materials including instructions on how to obtain your Internet password for secure use of EFTPS. For more information or details on how to enroll, visit www.EFTPS.gov or call EFTPS Customer Service at 800-555-4477.

Paying by Electronic Funds Withdrawal

You may pay your estimated tax through an electronic funds withdrawal from your bank account or by using the IRS's Direct Pay option. This is a free and secure way to have your estimated taxes paid directly from your checking or savings account. You'll receive instant confirmation that your payment has been submitted to the IRS. Your bank account information is not retained in IRS systems after payments are made. For more information, visit www.irs.gov/payments/direct-pay.

Paying by Credit Card

You may pay your estimated taxes by credit card or debit card through a private company that provides this service. You'll have to pay the company a fee based on the amount of your payment (the fee does not go to the IRS). You can arrange to make your payment by phone or through the Internet. For details and cost information, go to the IRS website's page on credit or debit payments, www.irs.gov/uac/pay-taxes-by-credit-or-debit-card.

Unless you pay off your credit card balance immediately, paying your estimated tax this way is a bad idea. The interest your credit card company charges will likely far exceed the interest penalty you'd have to pay the IRS for paying late.

Paying the Wrong Amount

If you pay too little estimated tax, the IRS will make you pay a penalty. If you pay too much, you can get the money refunded or apply it to the following year's estimated taxes.

Paying Too Little

The IRS imposes an interest penalty if you underpay your estimated taxes. The interest is assessed on the difference between the amount you should have paid for each installment and the amount you actually paid, for as long as the underpayment remains outstanding. The interest rate is set by the IRS each year. Currently, it's only about 3%. This means that it would be cheaper to pay the penalty to the IRS than to borrow money to pay your estimated taxes on time.

However, if you underpay your state estimated taxes, the penalties could be larger. For example, Connecticut charges a penalty of 1% per month up to 12% a year; in Kansas, the penalty can go as high as 24%. If you live in a state with such high underpayment penalties, make sure you don't trigger them by paying less than you owe.

Many self-employed people decide to pay the penalty at the end of the tax year rather than take money out of their businesses during the year to pay estimated taxes. If you do this, though, make sure you pay all the taxes you owe for the year by April 15 of the following year. If you don't, the IRS will tack on additional interest and penalties. The IRS usually adds a penalty of 0.5% to 1% per month to a tax bill that's not paid when due.

To avoid these charges, you can pay your estimated taxes by credit card. But if you don't pay off your balance quickly, the interest you pay on your credit card balance may exceed the IRS penalty.

Because the penalty is figured separately for each payment period, you can't avoid having to pay it by increasing the amount of a later payment. For example, you can't avoid a penalty by doubling your June 15 payment to make up for failing to make your April 15 payment. If you miss a payment, the IRS suggests that you divide the amount equally among your remaining payments for the year. But this won't avoid a penalty on payments you missed or underpaid.

Because the penalty must be paid for each day your estimated taxes remain unpaid, you'll have to pay more if you miss a payment early in the tax year rather than later. For this reason, you should try to pay your first three estimated tax payments on time. You can let the fourth payment (due on January 15) go. The penalty you'll have to pay for missing this payment will likely be very small.

The IRS will assume you've underpaid your estimated taxes if you file a tax return showing that you owe $500 or more in additional tax, and the amount due is more than 10% of your total tax bill for the year.

If you have underpaid, you can determine the amount of the underpayment penalty by completing IRS Form 2210, *Underpayment of Estimated Tax by Individuals*, and pay the penalty when you send in your return. Figuring the amount of the penalty can be complicated, so you might want to use tax preparation software to do this calculation for you. However, it is not necessary for you to calculate the penalty you owe. You can leave it to the IRS to determine the penalty and send you a bill. If you receive a bill, you may wish to complete Form 2210 anyway to make sure you aren't overcharged.

Paying Too Much

If you pay too much estimated tax, you have two options: You may have the IRS refund the overpayment to you, or you can credit all or part of the overpayment to the following year's estimated taxes. Unfortunately, you can't get back the interest your overpayment earned while sitting in the IRS coffers; that belongs to the government.

To take the credit, write in the amount you want credited instead of refunded to you on Line 77 of your Form 1040. The payment is considered to have been made on April 15. You can use all the credited amount toward your first estimated tax payment for the following year, or you can spread it out any way you choose among your payments. Be sure to take the amount you have credited into account when figuring your estimated tax payments.

It doesn't make much practical difference which option you choose. Most people take the credit so they don't have to wait for the IRS to send them a refund check.

Rules for Salespeople, Drivers, and Clothing Producers

This chapter covers statutory employee and statutory independent contractor rules—specific rules for people who work in certain industries.

 SKIP AHEAD

Who needs this chapter? Read this chapter only if you work as a:

- business-to-business salesperson
- full-time life insurance salesperson
- clothing or needlecraft producer who works at home
- driver who distributes food products, beverages, or laundry (see Chapter 16 if you are driver for a service such as Uber or Lyft)
- direct seller, or
- licensed real estate agent.

If you fall within the first four categories, you may be a statutory employee; read the next section. If you fall within the last two categories, you may be a statutory independent contractor (IC); skip directly to "Statutory Independent Contractors." If none of these apply to you, skip this chapter.

Statutory Employees

If you are a business-to-business or life insurance salesperson; clothing producer who works at home; or driver who distributes food products, beverages, or laundry; and if you also meet several other primary requirements described below, you are a "statutory employee." For certain purposes, Congress has passed statutes (laws) that govern your employment status.

Practically speaking, being a statutory employee has only two consequences for you, but neither of them is particularly good. The first and worst consequence of statutory employee status is that the hiring firms for which you work must pay half of your Social Security and Medicare taxes themselves and withhold the other half from your pay for the IRS, just as for any other employee. (See Chapter 13.) As a result, you'll receive less take-home pay. This is not only because 7.65% of your earnings must be deducted from your paychecks, but also because hiring firms will probably insist on paying you less than they would if you were an IC to make up for the fact that they have to pay the other 7.65% of your Social Security and Medicare tax for you. The upside is that you won't need to include these Social Security and Medicare taxes in your own estimated tax payments. (See Chapter 11.)

The second consequence of being a statutory employee is that you'll receive a Form W-2, *Wage and Tax Statement*, from the hiring firms for which you work instead of a Form 1099-MISC, the form used to report ICs' income to the IRS. (See Chapter 13.) The W-2 will show the Social Security and Medicare tax withheld from your pay and your Social Security and Medicare income. You'll have to file your W-2s with your tax returns, so the IRS will know exactly how much income you've earned as a statutory employee. The hiring firms will also file a copy with the Social Security Administration.

As a statutory employee, you report income and earnings on Schedule C, *Profit or Loss From Business*, the same form used by self-employed people who are sole proprietors. Unlike regular employees whose business deductions are strictly limited, you can deduct the full amount of your business expenses. (See Chapter 9.)

If You Have Multiple Businesses

If you have another business in which you are not classified as a statutory employee, you must file a separate Schedule C for that business. You aren't allowed to use expenses from your statutory employment to offset earnings from your self-employment.

EXAMPLE: Margaret works as a business-to-business salesperson in which she qualifies as a statutory employee. She also works part time as a self-employed marketing consultant. This year she had $5,000 in travel expenses from her selling job. She can't deduct any of this expense from her earnings as a consultant. She can deduct it only from her income as a salesperson. When Margaret does her taxes, she must file a separate Schedule C for each of her occupations.

Fortunately, it's easy to avoid being classified as a statutory employee and to be an independent contractor instead. You are an IC for income tax purposes as long as you qualify under the regular IRS rules. (See Chapter 15.) If you qualify, no income tax need be withheld from your compensation, so you'll have higher take-home pay. But you will need to pay your income taxes four times during the year in the form of estimated taxes. (See Chapter 11.)

Most hiring firms would prefer that you be classified as an IC for employment tax purposes instead of as a statutory employee. That would allow them to avoid the burden of paying half of your FICA (Social Security and Medicare) taxes themselves and withholding your share from your pay. This chapter describes some simple ways you can avoid this status. Doing so may help you get work you might be denied as a statutory employee.

Requirements for Statutory Employee Status

You're a statutory employee only if you satisfy all of these requirements:
- You perform services personally for the hiring firm.
- You make no substantial investment in the equipment or facilities you use to work.
- You have a continuing relationship with the hiring firm.

Personal Service

You're a statutory employee only if your oral or written agreement with the hiring firm requires you to do substantially all the work yourself. In other words, you can't hire helpers or subcontract the work out to others.

No Substantial Investment

Statutory employees must not have a substantial investment in equipment or premises used to perform their work, such as office space, machinery, or office furniture. An investment is substantial if it is more than an employee would be expected to provide (for example, paying office rent or buying expensive computer equipment). Vehicles you use on the job do not count as substantial investments.

Avoiding Statutory Employee Status

Even if you do the type of work normally performed by a statutory employee, you can avoid being classified as one. To do this, set up your work relationship so that it does not satisfy one or more of the three requirements discussed above. For example, you can:

- Sign a written agreement with the person or firm that hires you stating that you have the right to subcontract or delegate the work out to others. This way, you make clear that you don't have to do the work personally.
- Avoid having a continuing relationship with any one hiring firm by working on single projects, not ongoing tasks.
- Invest in outside facilities, such as your own office.

However, even if you do these things, some hiring firms may want to classify you as a statutory employee because they don't understand the law. You may have to educate the people or firms you work for about these rules.

Continuing Relationship

A continuing relationship means you work for the hiring firm on a regular or recurring basis. A single job is not considered a continuing relationship. But regular part-time or seasonal employment qualifies.

Types of Statutory Employees

You won't be a statutory employee just because you satisfy the three threshold requirements explained above. You must also satisfy additional requirements for each type of statutory employee occupation. These rules present you with yet more ways to avoid statutory employee status. If the type of work you do and the way you do it don't fall squarely within the additional rules below, you won't be classified as a statutory employee.

Business-to-Business Salespeople

If you're a business-to-business salesperson (that is, you sell products or services on behalf of a business to other businesses, not consumers), you're

a statutory employee only if you satisfy the three threshold requirements discussed above and you also:
- work at least 80% of the time for one person or company
- sell on behalf of, or turn your orders over to, the hiring firm
- sell merchandise for resale or supplies for use in the buyer's business operations, as opposed to goods purchased for personal consumption at home, and
- sell only to wholesalers, retailers, contractors, or those who operate hotels, restaurants, or similar establishments (but this does not include manufacturers, schools, hospitals, churches, municipalities, or state and federal governments).

EXAMPLE: Linda sells books to retail bookstores for Scrivener & Sons Publishing Company. Her territory covers the entire Midwest. She works only for Scrivener and is paid a commission based on the amount of each sale. She turns her orders over to Scrivener's, which ships the books to each bookstore customer. Linda is a statutory employee of Scrivener's.

Life Insurance Salespeople

If your full-time occupation is soliciting life insurance applications or annuity contracts, you're a statutory employee only if you satisfy the threshold requirements explained above and:
- You work primarily for one life insurance company, and
- the company provides you with work necessities such as office space, secretarial help, forms, rate books, and advertising material.

EXAMPLE: Walter works full time selling life insurance for the Old Reliable Life Insurance Company. He works out of Old Reliable's Omaha office, where he is provided with a desk, clerical help, rate books, and insurance applications. Walter is Old Reliable's statutory employee.

Clothing or Needlecraft Producers

If you make or sew buttons, quilts, gloves, bedspreads, clothing, needle-craft, or similar products, you're a statutory employee only if you satisfy the threshold requirements explained above and you:

- work away from the hiring firm's place of business (usually in your own home or workshop or in another person's home)
- work only on goods or materials the hiring firm furnishes
- work according to the hiring firm's specifications (generally, such specifications are simple and consist of patterns or samples), and
- are required to return the processed material to the hiring firm or person designated by it.

If your work setup meets all these requirements, the hiring firm must pay the employer's share of FICA on your compensation and withhold your share of FICA taxes from your pay. However, no FICA tax is imposed if the hiring firm pays you less than $100 for a calendar year.

EXAMPLE: Rosa works at home, sewing buttons on shirts and dresses. She does work for various companies, including Upscale Fashions, Inc. Upscale provides Rosa with all the clothing and the buttons she must sew. The only equipment Rosa provides is a needle. Upscale gives Rosa a sample of each outfit showing where to put the buttons. When Rosa finishes each batch of clothing, she returns it to Upscale. Rosa is a statutory employee.

Food, Beverage, and Laundry Distributors

You're also a statutory employee if you work as a driver and distribute meat or meat products, vegetables or vegetable products, fruits or fruit products, bakery products, beverages other than milk, or laundry or dry cleaning to customers designated by the hiring firm as well as those you solicit. It makes no difference whether you operate from your own truck or trucks that belong to the person or firm that hired you.

EXAMPLE: Alder Laundry and Dry Cleaning enters into an agreement with Sharon to pick up and deliver clothing for its customers. Sharon is a statutory employee because she meets all three threshold requirements: Her agreement with Alder acknowledges that she will do the work personally, she has no substantial investment in facilities (her truck doesn't count because it's used to deliver the product), and she has a continuing relationship with Alder.

Statutory Independent Contractors

If you're a direct seller or licensed real estate agent, you are automatically considered an independent contractor for Social Security, Medicare, and federal unemployment tax purposes, provided that:

- Your pay is based on sales commissions, not on the number of hours you work.
- You have a written contract with the hiring firm providing that you will not be treated as an employee for federal tax purposes.

Consider yourself lucky, and be thankful that your industry lobbyists were able to get these special rules adopted by Congress. Because your worker status is automatically determined by law, hiring firms need not worry about the IRS. This should make it very easy for you to get work as an independent contractor in your chosen field.

You undoubtedly know whether or not you're a licensed real estate agent whom the IRS will automatically classify as a statutory independent contractor.

You're a direct seller for IRS purposes if you sell consumer products to people in their homes or at a place other than an established retail store, such as at swap meets. Consumer products include tangible personal property that is used for personal, family, or household purposes, including vacuum cleaners, cosmetics, encyclopedias, and gardening equipment. It also includes intangible products, such as cable services and home study educational courses.

> **EXAMPLE:** Larry is a Mavon Guy, selling men's toiletries door to door. Mavon pays him a 20% commission on all his sales, and nothing else. He has a written contract with Mavon that provides that he will not be treated as an employee for federal tax purposes. Larry is a statutory nonemployee—that is, an independent contractor—for federal employment tax purposes.

If they also satisfy the requirements outlined above, people who sell or distribute newspapers or shopping news are also considered to be direct sellers. This is true whether they are paid based on the number of papers they deliver or whether they purchase newspapers, sell them, and keep the money they earn from the sales.

Taxes for Workers You Hire

f, like many self-employed people, you hire others to assist you, it's wise to learn a little about federal and state tax requirements that apply to you and your workers. This chapter covers these requirements.

 SKIP AHEAD

If you do all the work in your unincorporated business yourself, you don't need to read this chapter.

Hiring People to Help You

Sooner or later, most self-employed people need to hire people to help them:

- A freelance graphic designer might hire a part-time assistant to help meet a pressing deadline for a large client.
- An architect might hire a computer consultant to help choose and install a new computer system and explain how to use new design software.
- an author may hire a public relations professional to help publicize the launch of a new book.

Whenever you hire a helper, you need to be concerned about obeying federal and state tax laws.

Independent Contractors Versus Employees

The tax rules you have to follow when you hire helpers differ depending upon whether your helpers qualify as employees or as self-employed independent contractors (ICs) by the IRS and other government agencies.

If you hire an employee, you must withhold taxes from the person's pay, and you must pay other taxes for the employee yourself. You must also comply with complex and burdensome bookkeeping and reporting requirements.

If you hire an IC, you need not comply with these requirements. All you have to do is report the amount you pay the IC to the IRS and your state tax department.

However, hiring an IC is not necessarily cheaper than hiring an employee. Some ICs charge far more than what you'd pay an employee to do similar work. Nevertheless, many self-employed people still prefer to hire ICs instead of employees because of the smaller tax and bookkeeping burdens.

Determining Worker Status

Initially, it's up to you to determine whether any person you hire is an employee or an IC. If you decide that a worker is an employee, you must comply with the federal and state tax requirements discussed in the next section. If you decide the worker is an IC, you need only comply with simpler income reporting and tax identification number requirements, also discussed below.

However, your decision about how to classify a worker is subject to review by various government agencies, including:

- the IRS
- the Department of Labor
- your state's tax department
- your state's labor department
- your state's unemployment compensation insurance agency, and
- your state's workers' compensation insurance agency.

Any agency that determines that you misclassified an employee as an IC may impose back taxes, fines, and penalties.

Scrutinizing agencies use various tests to determine whether a worker is an IC or an employee. The determining factor is usually whether you have the right to control the worker. If you have the right to control the way a worker does his or her work—both as to the final results and the details of when, where, and how the work is done—then the worker is your employee. On the other hand, if your control over the worker's work is limited to accepting or rejecting the final results the worker achieves, he or she is an IC. (See Chapter 15 for a detailed discussion of how to determine whether a worker is an IC or an employee.)

CAUTION

Part-timers and temps can be employees. Don't think that a person you hire to work part time or for a short period must be an IC. People who work for you only temporarily or part time are your employees if you have the right to control the way they work.

Safe Harbor Makes It Easier to Win Audits

A part of the Tax Code known as the "safe harbor," or Section 530, enables firms that hire ICs to win IRS employment tax audits. To qualify for safe harbor protection, you must satisfy three requirements. You must have:
- filed all required 1099 forms for the workers in question
- consistently treated the workers involved and others doing substantially similar work as ICs, and
- had a reasonable basis for treating the workers as ICs. For example, treating such workers as ICs may be a common practice in your industry, or perhaps an attorney or accountant told you that the workers qualified as ICs.

If you're audited for employment tax purposes, the auditor must first determine whether you qualify for safe harbor protection. If you do, no assessments or penalties may be imposed. You may continue treating the workers involved as ICs for these purposes, and the IRS will not question their status.

This means you need not pay the employer's share of the workers' Social Security and Medicare taxes or withhold income or Social Security taxes from their pay. However, the workers could still be considered employees for other purposes, such as pension plan rules and state unemployment compensation taxes.

RESOURCE

Want a detailed discussion of the practical and legal issues employers face when hiring ICs? See *Working With Independent Contractors*, by Stephen Fishman (Nolo).

Tax Concerns When Hiring Employees

Any time you hire an employee, you become an unpaid tax collector for the federal government. You are required to withhold and pay both federal and state taxes for the worker. These taxes are called "payroll taxes" or "employment taxes."

Pros and Cons of Hiring Employees Versus ICs

There are advantages and disadvantages to hiring both employees and ICs.

Hiring Employees

Pros	Cons
You don't need to worry about government auditors claiming you misclassified employees.	You must pay federal and state payroll taxes for employees.
You can closely supervise employees.	You must provide employees with office space and equipment.
You can give employees extensive training.	You are liable for your employees' actions.
Employees can't sue you for damages if they are injured on the job, provided you have workers' compensation insurance.	You must usually provide employees with workers' compensation coverage.
You automatically own any intellectual property employees create on the job.	You ordinarily provide employees benefits such as vacations and sick leave.
Employees can generally be fired at any time.	You can be sued for labor law violations.

Hiring ICs

Pros	Cons
You don't have to pay federal and state payroll taxes for ICs.	You risk exposure to audits by the IRS and other agencies.
You don't have to provide office space or equipment for ICs.	You can't closely supervise or train ICs.
You are generally not liable for ICs' actions.	You may lose copyright ownership if you don't obtain an assignment of rights.
You don't have to provide workers' compensation insurance for ICs.	ICs can sue you for damages if they are injured on the job.
You don't have to provide employee benefits to ICs.	ICs may usually work for your competitors as well as you.
Your exposure to lawsuits for labor law violations is reduced with ICs.	ICs usually can't be terminated unless they violate their contracts.

You must also satisfy these requirements if you incorporate your business and continue to actively work in it. In this event, you will be an employee of your corporation.

Federal Payroll Taxes

The IRS regulates federal payroll taxes, which include:

- Social Security and Medicare taxes (also known as FICA)
- unemployment taxes (also known as FUTA), and
- income taxes (also known as FITW).

Hiring Temporary Help

If you need extra help, one option is to hire a "temp" from a temporary help agency. When you hire a temp, you do not hire an individual worker yourself. Instead, you contract with the temp agency to provide you with a service: a person who will perform specified tasks for your business. The temp is an employee of the temp agency. The temp agency pays the temp's salary and payroll taxes, and provides workers' compensation coverage.

It may cost more per hour to hire a temp, but you will save on paperwork and won't need to worry about whether the worker is your employee or an IC. However, make sure to deal with a reputable agency that satisfies all employer tax and insurance requirements. If the agency fails to pay the temp's payroll taxes or provide workers' compensation coverage, you could end up having to foot the bill.

CAUTION
Don't forget yourself. If you incorporate your business and work as an employee of your corporation, your corporation—not you personally—must pay these payroll taxes for you.

RESOURCE

Want detailed information on federal payroll taxes? Pick up a copy of IRS Publication 15 (Circular E), *Employer's Tax Guide*. It is an outstanding resource that you should have if you hire employees. You can get a free copy from the IRS website at www.irs.gov.

FICA

FICA is an acronym for Federal Income Contributions Act, the law requiring employers and employees to pay Social Security and Medicare taxes. The IRS imposes FICA taxes on both employers and employees. If you hire an employee, you must collect and remit his or her part of the taxes by withholding it from paycheck amounts and sending it to the IRS. You must also pay a matching amount yourself for each employee.

The IRS determines the amounts you must withhold and pay each year. For 2018, for example, employers and employees are each required to pay 7.65% on the first $128,400 of an employee's annual wages. The 7.65% figure is the sum of the 6.2% Social Security tax and the 1.45% Medicare tax.

There is no Social Security tax on the portion of an employee's annual wages that exceed the $128,400 income ceiling. However, there is no such limit on the Medicare tax: Both you and the employee must pay the 1.45% Medicare tax on any wages that exceed the ceiling. The ceiling for the Social Security tax changes annually. You can find the Social Security tax income ceiling as well as the Social Security and Medicare tax rates for the current year in IRS Publication 15 (Circular E), *Employer's Tax Guide*.

Starting in 2013, Medicare taxes went up by 0.9% on employee wages that exceed a second annual ceiling—$200,000 for single taxpayers or $250,000 for married couples filing jointly. Employees must pay the entire increase out of their own pockets. Thus, employees pay 1.45% until their wages reach $200,000 (for single taxpayers) or $250,000 (for married taxpayers filing jointly). Then they pay 2.35%. The employer must withhold this amount and pay 1.45% itself.

FUTA

FUTA is an acronym for the Federal Unemployment Tax Act, the law that establishes federal unemployment insurance taxes. Most employers must pay both state and federal unemployment taxes. But even if you're exempt from the state tax, you may still have to pay the federal tax. Employers alone are responsible for FUTA; you may not collect or deduct it from employees' wages.

You must pay FUTA taxes if:

• You pay $1,500 or more to employees during any calendar quarter (that is, any three-month period beginning with January, April, July, or October).

• You had at least one employee for some part of a day in any 20 or more different weeks during the year. The weeks don't have to be consecutive, nor does it have to be the same employee each week.

Technically, the FUTA tax rate is 6%, but in practice, you rarely pay this much. You are given a credit of 5.4% if you pay the applicable state unemployment tax in full and on time. This means that the actual FUTA tax rate is usually 0.6%. The FUTA tax is assessed on only the first $7,000 of an employee's annual wage—which means that the FUTA tax is usually $42 per year per employee. However, employers in several states must pay more than $42 in FUTA tax because their states failed to repay unemployment insurance loans from the federal government.

FITW

FITW is an acronym for federal income tax withholding. When you hire an employee you're not only a tax collector for the government, but you are also a manager of your employee's income. The IRS fears that employees will not save enough from their wages to pay their tax bill on April 15. It also wants to speed up tax collections. So the IRS tells you, the employer, not to pay your employees their entire wages but to send the money to the IRS. This practice is the employee version of the estimated taxes that ICs must pay. (See Chapter 11.)

As an employer, you must calculate and withhold federal income taxes from all your employees' paychecks. Employees are solely responsible for paying federal income taxes; the employer's only responsibility is to withhold the funds and remit them to the government.

You must ask each employee you hire to fill out IRS Form W-4, *Employee's Withholding Allowance Certificate*. The information on this form determines how much tax you must withhold from the employee's pay. By January 31 of each year, you must give each employee you hired or employed the previous year a copy of IRS Form W-2, *Wage and Tax Statement*, showing how much he or she was paid and how much tax was withheld for the year. You must also send copies to the Social Security Administration.

You can obtain copies of these forms from the IRS website at www.irs.gov.

RESOURCE
Want detailed information on FITW? See IRS Publication 505, *Tax Withholding and Estimated Tax.*

Get Some Help (and Deduct the Cost)

Figuring out how much to withhold, doing the necessary record keeping, and filling out the required forms can be complicated. Software such as *QuickBooks* or *QuickPay* can help with all the calculations and prepare your employees' checks and IRS forms. You can also hire a bookkeeper or payroll tax service to do the work; your bank may also provide payroll tax services. Amounts you pay a bookkeeper or payroll tax service are deductible business operating expenses. The cost will be quite small if you only have a few employees.

Be aware, however, that even if you use a payroll tax service, you remain personally liable if your taxes are not paid on time. The IRS recommends that an employer: (1) keep its company address on file with the IRS, rather than the address of the payroll service provider, so that the company will be contacted by the IRS if there are any problems; and (2) contact the IRS about any bills or notices you receive as soon as possible. This is especially important if it involves a payment you thought your payroll service already made. Call the number on the bill, write to the IRS office that sent the bill, contact the IRS business tax hotline (800-829-4933), or visit a local IRS office. If you suspect that your payroll service provider is not properly depositing your taxes or filing your tax returns, or is otherwise engaged in fraud, you can file a complaint with the IRS using IRS Form 14157, *Complaint: Tax Return Preparer.* Such complaints receive expedited handling and investigation by the IRS.

Paying Payroll Taxes

You must periodically deposit federal income tax withheld, and both the employer and employee portion of Social Security and Medicare taxes. There are two deposit schedules, monthly and semiweekly; smaller employers generally pay monthly. To determine your payment schedule, review IRS Publication 15, *Employer's Tax Guide*. If you fail to make a timely deposit, you may be subject to a 10% failure-to-deposit penalty.

Deposits for FUTA Tax (Form 940) are required for the quarter within which the tax due exceeds $500. The tax must be deposited by the end of the month following the end of the quarter.

If you have employees, you must also report these payments to the IRS on Form 941, *Employer's Quarterly Federal Tax Return*, after each calendar quarter in which you have employees. Form 941 shows how many employees you had, how much they were paid, and the amount of FICA and income tax withheld.

Employers with total employment tax liability of $1,000 or less may file employment tax returns once a year instead of quarterly. Those employers can use Form 944, *Employer's Annual Federal Tax Return*. The IRS should notify you if you're eligible to file Form 944. If you believe you are eligible but have not been notified, call the IRS at 800-829-4933.

If you are a new employer, you must call the IRS at the number listed above, on or before the first day of the month that the first required Form 941 for the current year is due, to request to file Form 944 rather than Form 941.

Once each year, you must also file IRS Form 940, *Employer's Annual Federal Unemployment Tax Return* (or the simpler Form 940-EZ). This form shows the IRS how much federal unemployment tax you owe.

You must make all federal tax deposits directly to the IRS electronically using the IRS Electronic Federal Tax Payment System (EFTPS). For information on EFTPS or to get an enrollment form, call EFTPS Customer Service at 800-555-4477 or visit its website, www.eftps.gov.

Penalties for Failing to Pay FICA and FITW

As far as the IRS is concerned, an employer's most important duty is to withhold and pay Social Security and income taxes. Employee FICA and FITW are also known as "trust fund taxes" because the employer is deemed to hold the withheld funds in trust for the U.S. government.

If you fail to pay trust fund taxes, you can get into the worst tax trouble there is. The IRS can—and often does—seize a business's assets and force it to close down if it owes back payroll taxes. Although very rare, you can also get thrown in jail.

At the very least, you'll have to pay all the taxes due plus interest. The IRS may also impose a penalty known as the trust fund recovery penalty if it determines that you willfully failed to pay the taxes. The agency can claim you willfully failed to pay taxes if you knew the taxes were due and didn't pay them. If you paid such taxes in the past and then stopped paying them, that constitutes pretty good evidence that you knew the taxes were due.

The trust fund recovery penalty is also known as the 100% penalty because the amount of the penalty is equal to 100% of the total amount of employee FICA and FITW taxes the employer failed to withhold and pay to the IRS. This can be a staggering sum. As a business owner, you'll be personally liable for the 100% penalty: You will have to pay it out of your own pocket, even if you've incorporated your business.

Their Dogs Ate Their Homework

You are responsible for making sure that your FICA and FITW taxes are paid, even if you hire someone else to deal with it for you. For example, the IRS assessed a $40,000 penalty against two brothers in the floor covering business when their company failed to pay FITW and FICA for its employees for over two years. The brothers had the money to pay the taxes and had entrusted the task to an office manager. The manager failed to make the payments. The brothers pleaded ignorance, claiming that the manager intercepted and screened the mail and altered check descriptions and quarterly reports.

Both the IRS and the court were unmoved. Although the court stated that it was not unreasonable for the brothers to entrust the payments to their office manager, the brothers were still ultimately responsible to make sure the taxes were paid and were therefore liable for the penalty. (*Conklin Bros. v. United States*, 986 F.2d 315 (9th Cir. 1993).)

RESOURCE

Want more information on IRS matters? For guidance on how to deal with the IRS if you are having trouble meeting your payroll tax obligations, see *Tax Savvy for Small Business*, by Fred Daily and Jeffrey A. Quinn (Nolo).

Rules for Family Members

Self-employed people often hire family members. A tax rule helps promote this family togetherness: If you hire your child, spouse, or parent as an employee, you may not have to pay FICA and FUTA taxes.

Employing your child. You need not pay FUTA taxes for services performed by your child who is under 21 years old. You need not pay FICA taxes for your child who is under 18 and works in your trade or business or a partnership owned solely by you and your spouse.

> **EXAMPLE:** Lisa, a 16-year-old, makes deliveries for her mother's mail order business, which is operated as a sole proprietorship. Although Lisa is her mother's employee, her mother need not pay FUTA taxes until Lisa reaches 21 and need not pay FICA taxes until Lisa reaches 18.

However, these rules do not apply—and you must pay both FICA and FUTA—if you hire your child to work for:

- your corporation, or
- your partnership, unless all the partners are parents of the child.

> **EXAMPLE:** Ron, a 17-year-old, works in a computer repair business that is half owned by his mother and half owned by her partner, Ralph, who is no relation to the family. The business must pay FICA and FUTA taxes for Ron because he is working for a partnership, and not all of the partners are his parents.

In addition, if your child has no unearned income (for example, interest or dividend income), you have to withhold income taxes from your child's pay only if it exceeds the standard deduction for the year. The standard deduction was $12,000 in 2018 and is adjusted every year for inflation. Children who are paid less than this amount need not pay any income taxes on their earnings. However, you must withhold income taxes if your child has more than $350 in unearned income for the year and his or her total income exceeds $1,050.

EXAMPLE 1: Connie, a 15-year-old girl, is paid $4,000 a year to help out in her parent's home business. She has no income from interest or any other source. Her parents need not withhold income taxes from Connie's salary.

EXAMPLE 2: Connie is paid $4,000 in salary and has $500 in interest income on a savings account. Her parents must withhold income taxes from her salary because she has more than $350 in unearned income (the interest) and her total income for the year was more than $1,050.

Income Tax Break for Child Employees

You must withhold income taxes from your child's pay only if it exceeds the standard deduction for the year. The Tax Cuts and Jobs Act almost doubled the standard deduction to $12,000 in 2018 and it is adjusted every year for inflation. A child who is paid less than this amount need not pay any income taxes on his or her salary.

You might consider getting your child to do some work around the office instead of paying him or her an allowance for doing nothing. If your child's pay is below the standard deduction amount, it is not only tax free, but you can also deduct the amount from your own taxes as a business expense if the child's work is business related (for example, cleaning your office, answering the phone, or making deliveries). However, you can deduct your child's wages only if they are reasonable. In other words, you must pay your child about what you'd pay a stranger for the same work. Don't try paying your child $100 per hour for office cleaning so you can get a big tax deduction.

If you pay your child $600 or more during the year, you must file Form W-2 reporting the earnings to the IRS. No matter how much you pay your child, each year you should fill out and have your child sign IRS Form W-4, *Employee's Withholding Allowance Certificate.* If you pay your child less than $200 per week, keep the form in your records. If you pay your child more than $200 per week, keep a copy of the form for your records and file a copy of the form with the IRS.

Employing your spouse. If you pay your spouse to work in your trade or business, the payments are subject to FICA taxes and federal income tax withholding, but not FUTA taxes.

EXAMPLE: Kay's husband, Simon, is a sole proprietor computer programmer. Kay works as his assistant, for which she is paid $1,500 per month. Simon must pay the employer's share of FICA taxes for Kay and withhold employee FICA and federal income taxes from her pay. Simon need not pay FUTA taxes for Kay.

But this rule does not apply—and FUTA must be paid—if your spouse works for:

- a corporation, even if you control it, or
- a partnership, even if your spouse is a partner along with you.

EXAMPLE: Laura's husband, Rob, works as a draftsperson in Laura's architectural consulting firm, a corporation of which she is the sole owner. The corporation must pay FICA, FUTA, and FITW for Rob.

State Payroll Taxes

Employers in all states are required to pay and withhold state payroll taxes for employees. These taxes include:

- state unemployment compensation taxes in all states
- state income tax withholding in most states, and
- state disability taxes in a few states.

Unemployment Compensation

Federal law requires that all states provide most types of employees with unemployment compensation, also called UC or unemployment insurance. Employers are required to contribute to a state unemployment insurance fund. Employees make no contributions, except in Alaska, New Jersey, and Pennsylvania, where employers must withhold small employee contributions from employees' paychecks. Employees who are laid off or fired for reasons other than serious misconduct are entitled to receive unemployment benefits from the state fund. You need not provide unemployment for independent contractors.

If your payroll is very small—less than $1,500 per calendar quarter—you probably won't have to pay UC taxes. In most states, you must pay state UC taxes for employees if you're paying FUTA taxes. However, some states have more strict requirements. Contact your state labor department for details on your state's law. You can find links to state unemployment tax agencies at www.careeronestop.org, a website sponsored by the U.S. Department of Labor (search under the "Find Local Help" tab).

State Income Tax Withholding

All states except Alaska, Florida, Nevada, South Dakota, Texas, Washington, and Wyoming have state income taxation. New Hampshire and Tennessee impose state income taxes on dividend and interest income only. If you do business in a state that imposes state income taxes, you must withhold the applicable tax from your employees' paychecks and pay it to the state taxing authority. No state income tax withholding is required for workers who qualify as independent contractors.

It's easy to determine whether you need to withhold state income taxes for a worker: If your state has state income taxes and you are withholding federal income taxes for a worker, you must withhold state income taxes as well. Each state has its own income tax withholding forms and procedures. Contact your state tax department for information (find a link to each state's agency at the IRS website at www.irs.gov/businesses/small-businesses-self-employed/state-links-1).

State Disability Insurance

Five states have state disability insurance that provides employees with coverage for injuries or illnesses that are not related to work. Injuries that are job related are covered by workers' compensation. The states with disability insurance are: California, Hawaii, New Jersey, New York, and Rhode Island. Puerto Rico also has a disability insurance program.

In these states, employees contribute to disability insurance in amounts their employers withhold from their paychecks. Employers must also make contributions in Hawaii, New Jersey, New York, and Puerto Rico.

Except in New York, the disability insurance coverage requirements are the same as for unemployment (UC) insurance. If you pay UC for a worker, you must withhold and pay disability insurance premiums as well. You need not provide disability for independent contractors.

Workers' Compensation Insurance

Subject to some important exceptions, employers in all states must provide their employees with workers' compensation insurance to cover work-related injuries or illnesses. Workers' compensation is not a payroll tax. You must purchase a workers' compensation policy from a private insurer or state workers' compensation fund. (See Chapter 6.)

Employers in California Must Withhold for Paid Leave

In 2004, California became the first state in the nation to provide its workers with paid family and medical leave, including parental leave. The program is funded by employees, through an increase in the withholdings employers take from their paychecks and pay into the state's disability insurance (SDI) fund. To fund the paid leave program, California employers must withhold a slightly larger amount from their employees' paychecks for SDI; there is no separate line item withholding required specifically for the paid leave program. For more information on the program, go to www.edd.ca.gov/Disability/Paid_Family_Leave.htm.

Tax Concerns When Hiring Independent Contractors

If you hire an independent contractor, or IC, you don't have to worry about withholding and paying state or federal payroll taxes or filling out lots of government forms. This is one reason self-employed people generally prefer to hire other ICs rather than employees.

However, depending on how, and how much, you pay an IC during the year, you may have to (1) file IRS Form 1099-MISC telling the IRS how much you paid the worker, and (2) obtain the IC's taxpayer identification number (or Social Security number).

The IRS imposes these requirements because it is very concerned that many ICs don't report all the income they earn to avoid paying taxes. To help prevent this, the IRS wants to find out how much you pay any ICs you hire and make sure it has their correct taxpayer ID numbers.

Exception for Electronic Payments

The 1099-MISC reporting and taxpayer ID requirements apply only when you pay an IC directly by check, cash, or direct deposit to the IC's bank. They do not apply if you pay an IC by credit card, debit card, or by using a third-party settlement organization (TPSO) like PayPal or Payable. This is so even if you pay an IC more than $600 during the year.

In this event, the electronic payments may have to be reported to the IRS by the payment processor on IRS Form 1099-K, *Payment Card and Third Party Network Transactions*. But this has nothing to do with you, the hirer of the IC. This is one of the main advantages of paying an IC electronically, since the IRS uses 1099-MISC filings as an audit lead.

Exception for Payments to Corporations

The filing and ID requirements apply whenever you hire, and pay by check or cash, ICs who are sole proprietors, LLC members, or partners in partnerships. This includes the majority of all ICs. However, the reporting requirements don't apply to corporations.

This means that if you hire an incorporated IC, you don't have to file anything with the IRS. However, it's wise to make sure you have the corporation's full legal name and federal employer identification number. Without this information, you may not be able to prove to the IRS that the payee was incorporated. An easy way to do this is to have the IC fill out IRS Form W-9, *Request for Taxpayer Identification Number and Certificate*, and keep it in your files. This simple form merely requires the corporation to provide its name, address, and EIN. (You can obtain this form from the IRS website at www.irs.gov.)

CAUTION
When in doubt, file a Form 1099. The IRS may impose a $250 fine if you fail to file a Form 1099 when required. But, far more serious, you'll be subject to severe penalties if the IRS later audits you and determines that you misclassified the worker. For a detailed discussion of the consequences of not filing a 1099 form, see *Working With Independent Contractors*, by Stephen Fishman (Nolo).

There is one exception to the rule that you don't have to file 1099 forms for check or cash payments to corporations. You must report all payments of $600 or more you make to a doctor or lawyer who is incorporated, if the payments are for your business. You need not report payments you make to incorporated doctors or lawyers for personal services (for example, if you hire a doctor to take care of a personal health problem or hire a lawyer to write your will).

Threshold for Income Reporting

You need to obtain an unincorporated IC's taxpayer ID number and file a 1099 form with the IRS only if you pay the IC $600 or more by check or cash during a year for business-related services. It makes no difference whether the sum was one payment for a single job or the total of many small payments for multiple jobs.

In calculating whether the payments made to an IC total $600 or more during a year, you must include payments for parts or materials the IC used in performing the services. For example, if you hire a painter to paint your home office, the cost of the paint would be included in the tally.

However, not all payments you make to ICs are counted toward the $600 threshold.

You don't need to count payments solely for merchandise or inventory. This includes raw materials and supplies that will become a part of merchandise you intend to sell.

You need only count payments you make to ICs for services they perform in the course of your trade or business. A trade or business is an activity carried on for gain or profit. You don't count payments for services that are not related to your business, including payments you make to ICs for personal or household services or repairs, including payments to babysitters, gardeners, and housekeepers. Running your home is not a profit-making activity.

Obtaining Taxpayer Identification Numbers

Some ICs work in the underground economy: They are paid in cash and never pay any taxes or file tax returns. The IRS may not even know they exist. The IRS wants help to find these people. If you pay an IC $600 or more directly by check, cash, or direct deposit to the IC's bank, you must obtain the IC's taxpayer ID number.

If an IC won't give you his or her number or the IRS informs you that the number the IC gave you is incorrect, the IRS assumes the person isn't going to voluntarily pay taxes. So it requires you to withhold taxes from the compensation you pay the IC and remit them to the IRS. This is called "backup withholding." If you fail to backup withhold where required, the IRS will impose an assessment against you equal to 24% of what you paid the IC.

If you pay an IC electronically by credit card, debit card, or by using a third-party settlement organization (TPSO) like PayPal or Payable, you need not obtain the IC's taxpayer ID information, or backup withhold from the IC's pay if you fail to do so. It's the third-party payment processor's duty to obtain this information. If the IC fails to provide it, the processor must backup withhold from the IC's payments. You make your full payment to the payment processor, and it handles the backup withholding.

Avoiding Backup Withholding

Backup withholding can be a bookkeeping burden for you. Fortunately, it's very easy to avoid. Have the IC fill out and sign IRS Form W-9, *Request for Taxpayer Identification Number*, and retain it in your files. You don't have to file the W-9 with the IRS. This simple form merely requires the IC to list his or her name, address, and taxpayer ID number Multimember LLCs, partnerships, and sole proprietors with employees must have a federal employer identification number (EIN), which they obtain from the IRS. In the case of sole proprietors without employees, the taxpayer ID number is the IC's Social Security number.

If the IC doesn't already have an EIN but promises to obtain one, you don't have to backup withhold for 60 days after he or she applies for one. Have the IC fill out and sign the W-9 form, stating "Applied For" in the space where the ID number is supposed to be listed. If you don't receive the IC's ID number within 60 days, start backup withholding.

Backup Withholding Procedure

If you are unable to obtain an IC's taxpayer ID number or the IRS informs you that the number the IC gave you is incorrect, you'll have to begin backup withholding as soon as you pay an IC $600 or more during the year by check, cash, or direct deposit to the IC's bank. You need not backup withhold on payments totaling less than $600.

To backup withhold, deposit with your bank 28% of the IC's compensation every quarter. You must make these deposits separately from the payroll tax deposits you make for employees. Report the amounts withheld on IRS Form 945, *Annual Return of Withheld Federal Income Tax*. This is an annual return you must file by January 31 of the following year. See the instructions to Form 945 for details.

Filling Out Your Form 1099

You must file a 1099-MISC form for each IC to whom you paid $600 or more during the year by check, cash, or direct deposit to the IC's bank. All your 1099 forms must be submitted together along with one copy of Form 1096, which is a transmittal form (the IRS equivalent of a cover letter).

You must file your 1099-MISC forms by January 31 each year to report payments for the prior year. You can complete your 1099-MISC forms yourself. One way is to order the official IRS 1099-MISC forms (which are scannable) from the IRS (you can't photocopy or download this multi-part form from the IRS website). Go to www.irs.gov/businesses/online-ordering-for-information-returns-and-employer-returns. You can also use tax preparation or accounting software to prepare your 1099-MISCs. Alternatively, there are inexpensive online services that will complete and file the forms for you, such as efilemyforms.com, efile4biz.com, and efile1099now.com.

State New Hire Reporting Requirements

Several states require a business that hires independent contractors to file a report with a state agency providing the contractors' contact information and how much the contractors are paid. The purpose of this requirement is to aid in the enforcement of child support orders issued against independent contractors.

Filing 1099s Electronically

If you wish, you may file your 1099s with the IRS electronically instead of by mail. You must get permission from the IRS to do this by filing IRS Form 4419, *Application for Filing Information Returns Electronically.* For more information, you can visit the IRS website at www.irs.gov or call the IRS Information Reporting Program at 886-455-7438. The IRS does not have a 1099-MISC form you can fill out online and file electronically. However, there are many online payroll tax services you can use to do so.

You may also send 1099 forms to your ICs by email. But you may do this only if the contractor agrees. If he or she doesn't agree, you must deliver the 1099 by mail or in person.

The following states impose reporting requirements for those hiring independent contractors: Alabama, Arizona, California (if paid over $600 per year), Connecticut (if paid over $5,000 per year), Iowa, Maine (if paid over $2,500 per year), Massachusetts, Minnesota (only where a contractor works for the state), Nebraska, New Hampshire, New Jersey, Ohio (if paid $2,500 per year), Texas, and West Virginia (if paid over $2,500 per year). Find the state agency to contact at: www.acf.hhs.gov/css/resource/state-new-hire-reporting-websites.

Record Keeping and Accounting Made Easy

U nless it is your chosen trade, you probably didn't become self-employed so you could be a bookkeeper or accountant. But even though it can be a pain, all self-employed people need to keep records of their income and expenses. Among other things, keeping good records will enable you to reap a rich harvest in tax deductions. Time spent on record keeping is usually time well spent.

Simple Bookkeeping

Except in a few cases, the IRS does not require that you keep any special kind of records. You may choose any system suited to your business that clearly shows your income and expenses. If you are in more than one business, keep a separate set of books for each business.

If, like most self-employed people, you run a one-person service business and are a sole proprietor, you don't need a fancy or complex set of books. You can get along very nicely with just a few items. They include:
- a business checking account
- income and expense records, and
- supporting documents for your income and expenses, such as receipts and canceled checks.

Hiring a Bookkeeper

If you really hate record keeping, you always have the option of hiring someone to keep your records for you. You should have no problem finding a bookkeeper through referrals from friends or colleagues or online sources (such as Craigslist). Even if you decide to use a bookkeeper, you should still continue to write all your business checks and make deposits yourself. Giving such authority to a bookkeeper can lead to embezzlement.

Business Checking Account

One of the first things you should do when you become self-employed is set up a separate checking account for your business. Your business checkbook will serve as your basic source of information for recording your business expenses and income. Deposit all your self-employment compensation, such as the checks you receive from clients, into the account and make all business-related payments by writing checks from the account. If you accept payment through PayPal or other payment processors, have the money deposited to your business checking account. Likewise, if you pay business expenses through PayPal, have the money deducted from your business checking account. Don't use your business account for personal expenses or your personal account for business expenses.

Keeping a separate business account is not required by law if you're a sole proprietor, but it will provide many important benefits:

- It will be much easier for you to keep track of your business income and expenses.
- It will prove helpful if you're audited by the IRS.
- It will help convince the IRS that you are running a business and not engaged in a hobby. Hobbyists don't generally have separate bank accounts for their hobbies. (See Chapter 9.)
- It will help to establish that you're an independent contractor, not an employee. Employees don't have separate business accounts.

Setting Up Your Bank Account

At a minimum, you'll need to open a separate checking account in which you will deposit all your self-employment income and from which you will pay all your business expenses. There is no need to open your business checking account at the same bank where you have your personal checking account. Shop around and open your account with the bank that offers you the best services at the lowest price.

Benefits of Keeping Records

Keeping good records will help you with these important tasks:

- **Monitor the progress of your business.** Without records, you'll never have an accurate idea of how your business is doing. You may think you're making money when you're really not. Records can show whether your business is improving or you need to make changes to increase the likelihood of success.
- **Prepare financial statements.** You need good records to prepare accurate financial statements. These include income (profit and loss) statements and balance sheets. These statements can be essential in dealing with your bank or creditors.
- **Keep track of deductible expenses.** You may forget expenses when you prepare your tax return unless you record them when they occur. Every $100 in expenses you forget to deduct will cost you about $42 in additional income and self-employment taxes if you earn a midlevel income (in the 24% marginal tax bracket).
- **Prepare your tax returns.** You need good records to prepare your tax return or to enable an accountant to prepare your return for you in a reasonable amount of time. These records should show the income, expenses, and credits you report on your tax returns. Generally, these can be the same records you use to monitor your business and prepare your financial statements.
- **Win IRS audits.** If you're audited by the IRS, it will be up to you to prove that you have accurately reported your income and expenses on your tax returns. An IRS auditor will not simply take your word that your return is accurate. You need accurate records and receipts to back up your returns.

If you're doing business under your own name, consider opening up a second individual account in your name and using it solely for your business instead of opening a business account. You'll usually pay less for a personal account than for a business account.

If you do open a business account, make sure it is in your business name. If you're a sole proprietor, this can be your personal name. (If you're doing business under an assumed name, you'll likely have to give your bank a copy of your fictitious business name statement.) If you've formed a corporation or limited liability company, the account should be in your corporate or company name.

Use a Separate Credit Card for Business

Use a separate credit card for business expenses instead of using one card for both personal and business items. Credit card interest for business purchases is 100% deductible while interest for personal purchases is not. Using a separate card for business purchases will help you keep track of how much interest you've paid for business purchases. The card doesn't have to be in your business name; it can just be one of your personal credit cards.

If you've incorporated, check with your bank to find out what documentation is required to open the account. You will probably need to show the bank a corporate resolution authorizing the opening of a bank account and showing the names of the people authorized to sign checks.

Typically, you will also have to fill out a separate bank account authorization form provided by your bank. You will also need to have a federal employer identification number. (See Chapter 5.) Similarly, if you've established a limited liability company (see Chapter 2), you'll likely have to show the bank a company resolution authorizing the account.

You may also want to establish interest-bearing accounts for your business, in which you can deposit cash you don't need immediately. For example, you may want to set up a business savings account or a money market mutual fund in your business name.

Paying Yourself

To pay yourself when you're a sole proprietor, write a business check to yourself and deposit the money in your personal account. Alternatively, you can set up periodic electronic bank transfers between your personal and business accounts. This is known as an "owner's draw" or a "personal draw." Use your personal account to pay your nonbusiness or personal expenses.

Personal draws are not deductible business expenses and should not be listed as such on your Schedule C. You need not report personal draws to the IRS, but you should keep track of them and keep them separate from the total net self-employment income you report on your Schedule C. You pay taxes only on your net self-employment income, not on your draws. Your net self-employment income is your total business income minus business expenses (which don't include draws).

Paying Others

All your business expenses should ultimately be paid through your business checking account. This way you'll have a single account showing all the money you spent on your business during the year. You can do this by paying business expenses by checks drawn on your business account, by using a debit card linked to your business checking account, or by making electronic fund transfers from this account. If you pay with an old fashioned paper check, and it's not clear from the name of the payee what the check is for, describe the business reason for the check, such as the equipment or service you purchased.

However, you don't have to pay all your expenses by check or electronic funds transfer. You can also use electronic payment services like PayPal, debit cards, or credit cards. This is fine. But you should fund these payments from your business checking account—for example, you should pay your business credit card bill each month with funds from your business checking account; PayPal payments should also be funded from this account.

When you pay a bill electronically, you'll always have an electronic record of the payment. But, if the business purpose for the payment is not clear, make a note of it, whether online or elsewhere.

Income and Expense Records

In addition to a business checkbook, you should maintain income and expense records.

These records, which should be updated at least monthly, will show you how much you're spending and for what and how much money you're making. They will also make it easier for you or a tax pro to prepare your tax returns. Instead of having to locate, categorize, and add up the amount of each bill or canceled check at tax time, you can simply use the figures in your records.

The first choice you need to make is whether to keep paper records you create by hand or to use computerized electronic record keeping. Either method is acceptable to the IRS.

Manual Record Keeping

Although it may seem old-fashioned, some small business owners keep their records by hand on paper, especially when they are first starting out. You can use a columnar pad, notebook paper, or blank ledger books. There are also "one-write systems" that allow you to write checks and keep track of expenses simultaneously.

Manual bookkeeping may take a bit more time than using a computer, but has the advantage of simplicity. You'll always be better off using handwritten ledger sheets, which are easy to create and understand and simple to keep up to date, instead of complicated computer software that you don't understand or use properly.

RESOURCE

Want to know more about manual records? For an excellent guide to small business bookkeeping by hand, refer to *Small Time Operator*, by Bernard B. Kamoroff (Taylor Trade Publishing).

Create Your Own Spreadsheet

You can create your own spreadsheet to keep track of your expenses and income with a program such as *Excel*. Many templates are available to help you do this; you can also customize your own spreadsheet. See the discussion of how to track business expenses, below, to see what you should include in your spreadsheet.

Personal Finance Software

A personal finance program such as *Quicken* may be perfectly adequate for a one-owner service business. Such programs are easy to use because they work off of a computerized checkbook. When you buy something for your business, you write a check using the program. It automatically inputs the data into a computerized check register, and you print out the check using your computer (payments can also be made online). You'll have to input credit card and cash payments separately.

You create a list of expense categories just like you do when you create a ledger sheet or spreadsheet. Software like *Quicken* comes with preselected categories, but these are not adequate for many businesses, so you'll probably have to create your own. The expense category is automatically noted in your register when you write a check.

The software can then take this information and automatically create income and expense reports, showing you how much you've spent or earned for each category. This serves the same purpose as the expense journal. It can also create profit and loss statements. *Quicken* provides all the tools many small service businesses need. However, if your business involves selling goods or maintaining an inventory, or if you have employees, you'll need more sophisticated software.

Small Business Accounting Software

Small business accounting programs such as *QuickBooks*, *QuickBooks Self-Employed*, *AccountEdge*, and *Sage 50* can do everything personal financial software can do and much more, including pay and generate bills, download credit card and bank transactions, reconcile bank accounts, generate sophisticated reports, create budgets, track inventory, track employee time, calculate payroll withholding, generate invoices, keep track of accounts receivable, and maintain fixed asset records.

These software packages are more expensive than personal finance software and are harder to learn to use. If you don't need their advanced features, there is no reason to use them.

Online Bookkeeping

Online bookkeeping relies on a Web-based computer application rather than desktop bookkeeping software. Your data is stored online in the "cloud" by the online bookkeeping service. This means you won't lose your data if your home computer is stolen or destroyed. Popular online account services that charge a monthly fee include *FreshBooks*, *QuickBooks Online*, *Sage One*, *Outright*, *Xero*, *FreeAgent*, *Cheqbook*, *Intaaact*, *Clear Books*, *Wave*, and *Kashflow*.

Before You Purchase or Subscribe to Software

You don't want to spend your hard-earned money on software only to discover that you don't like it. Take these steps before you purchase accounting software or subscribe to an online bookkeeping service:

- Talk to others in similar businesses to find out what they use. If they don't like a software package, ask them why.
- Think carefully about how many features you need. The more complex the software, the harder it will be to learn and use it.
- Obtain a demo or "light" version you can try out for free to see if you like it. You can usually download one from the software company's website.

A list and comparison of most available accounting software packages and online subscription services can be found at http://en.wikipedia.org/wiki/Comparison_of_accounting_software.

Simple Business Income and Expenses Tracking

Most self-employed service providers don't need a fancy system to keep track of their income and expenses. You can create easy-to-use income and expense journals by using an electronic spreadsheet, or do so manually with paper ledger sheets.

Expense Journal

Your expense journal will show what you buy for your business. You need to create what accountants call a "chart of accounts": a listing of all your expenses by category. To decide what your expense categories should be, sit down with your first month's bills and receipts and divide them up into categorized piles. Some common expense categories many self-employed people have include:

- business meals
- travel
- telephone
- supplies and postage
- office rent
- utilities for an outside office
- professional dues, publications, and books
- business insurance
- payments to other self-employed people
- advertising costs
- equipment
- license fees
- website maintenance fees, and
- Internet connection fees.

You should always include a final category called "Miscellaneous" for various expenses that are not easily categorized.

Depending on the nature of your business, you may not need all these categories, or you might need additional or different headings. For example, a graphic designer might have categories for printing and typesetting expenses or a writer might have a category for agent fees.

Entertainment Expenses Are No Longer Deductible

As a result of the Tax Cuts and Jobs Act, most business-related entertainment expenses are no longer deductible starting in 2018. For example, you may not deduct athletic or theater tickets for clients. So, you don't need to document these nondeductible expenses. (See Chapter 9 for more details.)

You can add or delete expense categories as you go along. For example, if you find your miscellaneous category contains many items for a particular type of expense, add it as an expense category.

You don't need a category for automobile expenses, because these expenses require a different kind of documentation for tax purposes.

In separate columns, list the check number (or identifying number for electronic payments) for each payment, the date, and the name of the person or company paid. Once a month, go through your check register, credit card slips, records of electronic payments through PayPal or similar payment processors, receipts, and other expense records and record the required information for each transaction. Also, total the amounts for each category when you come to the end of the page so you can keep a running total of what you've spent for each category for the year to date.

Income Journal

The income journal shows you how much money you're earning and the source of each payment. At a minimum, your income ledger should have columns for the source of the funds (for example, the client's name), your invoice number if there is one, the amount of the payment, and the date you received it. If you have lots of different sources of income, you can create different categories for each source and devote separate columns to them in your journal.

Automobile Mileage and Expense Records

If you use a car or another vehicle for business purposes other than just commuting to and from work, you're entitled to take a deduction for gas and other auto expenses. You can either deduct the actual cost of your gas and other expenses or take the standard rate deduction based on the number of business miles you drive. In 2018, the standard rate was 54.5¢ per mile.

Either way, you must keep a record of the total miles you drive during the year. And if you use your car for both business and personal use, you must record your business and personal mileage.

To keep track of your business driving, you can use either a paper mileage logbook that you keep in your car or an electronic application. Logbooks are available in stores; there are dozens of apps that you can use to record your mileage with a smart phone.

If you record your mileage with an electronic app, check the manual to see how to implement this system. If you use a paper mileage logbook, here's what to do: Obtain a mileage logbook from a stationery or office supply store; you can get one for a few dollars. Keep it in your car with a pen attached. Note your odometer reading in the logbook on the day you start using your car for business. Record your mileage every time you use your car for business and note the business purpose for the trip. Add up your business mileage when you get to the end of each page in the logbook. This way you'll only have to add the page totals at the end of the year instead of slogging through all the individual entries.

If you think you may want to take the deduction for your actual auto expenses instead of the standard rate, keep receipts for all your auto-related expenses, including gasoline, oil, tires, repairs, and insurance. At tax time, add them up to determine how big a deduction you'll get using the actual expense method. Also add in the amount you're entitled to deduct for depreciation of your auto. (See "Car Expenses" in Chapter 9 for more information on depreciating your vehicle.) Your total deduction using your actual auto expenses may or may not be larger than the deduction you'll get using the standard rate.

CAUTION

Use a credit card for gas. If you use the actual expense method for car expenses, use a credit card when you buy gas. It's best that this be a separate card, either a gas company card or a separate bank card. The monthly statements you receive will serve as your gas receipts. If you pay cash for gas, you must either get a receipt or make a note of the amount in your mileage logbook.

Costs for business-related parking (other than at your office) and for tolls are separately deductible, whether you use the standard rate or the actual expense method. Get and keep receipts for these expenses.

Supporting Documents

The IRS knows very well that you can claim anything in your books, because you create them yourself. For this reason, the IRS requires that you have documents to support the entries in your books and on your tax returns. You don't have to file any of these documents with your tax returns, but you must have them available to back up your returns if you're audited.

Income Documents

When the IRS audits a small business, it usually asks for both your business and your personal bank statements. If you don't have them, the IRS may subpoena them from your bank. If your bank deposits are greater than the income you report on your tax return, the IRS auditor will assume you've underreported your income and impose additional tax, interest, and penalties.

To avoid this, you need to be able to prove the source(s) of all your income. Keep supporting documents showing the source(s) and amounts of all the income you receive as an independent contractor. This includes bank deposit slips, payments records from PayPal and other payment processors, invoices, and the 1099-MISC forms your clients give you. Keep your bank statements as well.

Expense Documents

You also need documents that support your business expenses. In the absence of a supporting document, an IRS auditor will likely conclude that an item you claim as a business expense is really a personal expense and refuse to allow the deduction. If you're in the midlevel income, 24% tax bracket, every $100 in disallowed deductions will cost you $24 in federal taxes, plus interest and penalties. And your income subject to Social Security tax for the year will go up, costing you about $12 for every $100 in disallowed deductions.

Proving Payment With Bank Statements

Sometimes, you'll need to use a bank account statement to prove an expense. Some banks no longer return canceled checks, or you may pay for something with an ATM card or electronic funds transfer. Moreover, you may not always have a credit card slip when you pay by credit card (for example, when you buy an item online). In these situations, the IRS will accept an account statement as proof that you purchased the item. The chart below shows what type of information you need to include on such an account statement.

If payment is made by:	The statement must show:
Check	Check number Amount Payee's name Date the check amount was posted to the account by the bank
Electronic funds transfer	Amount transferred Payee's name Date the amount transferred was posted to the account by the bank
Credit card	Amount charged Payee's name Transaction date

Some people believe the only documentation they need to prove that an expense was for their business is a sales receipt. This is not the case. A sales receipt only proves that somebody purchased the item listed in the receipt. It does not show who purchased it. You could write a note on the receipt stating that you bought the item, but you could easily lie. Indeed, for all the IRS knows, you could hang around stores picking up receipts people throw away to create tax deductions for yourself.

Likewise, a cancelled check is not adequate documentation for a business expense. All a canceled check proves is that you spent money for something. It does not show what you bought. Of course, you can write a note on your check stating what you purchased, but why should the IRS believe what you write on your checks yourself?

However, when you put a canceled check together with a sales receipt (or an invoice, a cash register tape, or a similar document), you have concrete proof that you purchased the item listed in the receipt. The check proves that you bought something, and the receipt proves what that something was.

Using a credit card is a great way to pay business expenses. The credit card slip will prove that you bought the item listed on the slip. You'll also have a monthly statement to back up your credit card slips. You should use a separate credit card for your business.

Save supporting documents to prove to the IRS that an expense was related to your business. Sometimes it will be clear from the face of a receipt, sales slip, or the payee's name on your canceled check that the item you purchased was for your business. But if it's not clear, note what the purchase was for on the document.

Travel, Meal, and Gift Expenses

Deductions for business-related meals, travel (including meals while traveling), and gifts are hot-button items for the IRS because they have been greatly abused by many taxpayers. You need to have more records for these expenses than for almost any others, and they will be closely scrutinized if you're audited.

Whenever you incur an expense for business-related meals, travel, or gifts you must document the following four things:

- **The amount.** How much you spent, including tax and tip for meals. Document the amount of each separate travel expense, such as airfare and lodging. However, the cost of meals and incidental expenses may be combined on a daily basis by category—for example, daily meal, gas, taxi, or Uber expenses.
- **The time and place.** The dates of departure and return for travel, or the date and description of the gift.

- **The business purpose.** The business reason for travel or the business benefit derived (or expected to be derived) from it. The business benefit derived (or expected to be derived) as a result of a gift.
- **The business relationship.** If gifts are involved, show the business relationship of the people receiving the gift—for example, list their names and occupations and any other information needed to establish their business relationship to you.

The IRS does not require that you keep receipts, canceled checks, credit card slips, or any other supporting documents for travel expenses (including meals while traveling) or gifts that cost less than $75. But you must still document the information listed above. This exception does not apply to lodging—that is, hotel or similar costs—when you travel for business. You do need receipts for these expenses, even if they are less than $75.

CAUTION

The unclear status of business meal deductions. The Tax Cuts and Jobs Act appeared to eliminate deductions for most business meals (except those while traveling) starting in 2018. (See Chapter 9.) The Act also eliminated the special requirements for documenting such expenses—requirements that remain applicable to travel and gift expenses. But it is expected that action will be taken to restore the deduction for business meals. So, the prudent course is to continue to document them and follow the rules for travel and gift expenses covered above.

Record keeping is not as hard as it sounds. You can record the information in a variety of ways, and it doesn't have to be all in one place. Information shown on a receipt, canceled check, or other item doesn't have to be duplicated in a log, appointment book, calendar, or account book. So, for example, you can record the information with:

- a receipt, credit card slip, or similar document alone
- a receipt combined with an appointment book entry, or
- an appointment book entry alone (for expenses less than $75).

However you document your expense, you are supposed to do it in a timely manner. You don't need to record the details of every expense on the day you incur it. It's sufficient to record them on a weekly basis. But if you're prone to forget details, it's best to get everything you need in writing within a day or two.

Asset Records

When you purchase property such as computers, office furniture, copiers, or cellular telephones to use in your business, you must keep records to verify:

- when and how you acquired the asset
- the purchase price
- the cost of any improvements (for example, a major upgrade for your computer)
- the Section 179 deduction you took (see Chapter 9)
- the deductions you took for regular or bonus depreciation (see Chapter 9)
- how you used the asset
- when and how you disposed of the asset
- the selling price, and
- the expenses of the sale.

Use an Asset Log

Set up an asset log showing this information for each item you purchase.

You can purchase asset logs from stationery or office supply stores, or set one up yourself using ledger paper or a spreadsheet program.

You can also use accounting software such as *Quicken Home & Business* or *QuickBooks* instead. If you have an accountant prepare your tax returns, he or she can create an asset log for you.

Be sure to keep your receipts for each asset you purchase because they'll usually verify what you purchased, when you bought the asset, and how much you paid.

Listed Property

"Listed property" is a term the IRS uses to refer to a certain type of business asset that can easily be used for personal as well as business purposes. Listed property includes cars, boats, airplanes, and other vehicles; and any other property generally used for entertainment, recreation, or amusement (for example, DVD players or cameras).

Because all listed property is long-term business property, it cannot be deducted like a business expense. Instead, you must depreciate it over several years unless you can deduct it in one year with the de minimis safe harbor, Section 179 expensing, or using bonus depreciation. (See Chapter 9 for more on deducting listed property.) The IRS imposes special record-keeping requirements to depreciate or take a Section 179 deduction for listed property.

If you use listed property for both business and personal uses, you must document your usage, both business and personal. Keep a logbook, business diary, or calendar showing the dates, times, and reasons for which the property is used.

If you use the property about the same amount throughout the year, you keep your usage record for a representative part of the year instead of the whole year—for example, the first week of each month or three months of the year.

How Long to Keep Records

You need to keep copies of your tax returns and supporting documents available in case you are audited by the IRS or another tax agency. You might also need them for other purposes (for example, to get a loan, mortgage, or insurance).

You should keep your records for as long as the IRS has to audit you after you file your returns for the year. These statutes of limitation range from three years to forever, as listed in the table below.

IRS Statute of Limitations	
If:	The limitation period is:
You failed to pay all the tax due	3 years
You underreported your gross income for the year by more than 25%	6 years
You filed a fraudulent return	No limit
You did not file a return	No limit

To be on the safe side, you should keep your tax returns indefinitely. They usually don't take up much space, so this shouldn't be a big hardship. Your supporting documents probably take up more space. You should keep these for at least six years after you file your return. If you file a fraudulent return, keep your supporting documents indefinitely (if you have any). If you're audited, they will show that at least some of your deductions were legitimate.

Keep your long-term asset records for three years after the depreciable life of the asset ends. For example, keep records for five-year property (such as computers) for eight years. You should keep your ledger sheets for as long as you're in business, because a potential buyer of your business might want to see them.

If You Don't Have Proper Tax Records

Because you're human, you may not have kept all the records required to back up your tax deductions. Don't despair, for all is not lost: You may be able to fall back on what is known as the "*Cohan* rule." This rule (named after the Broadway entertainer George M. Cohan, who was involved in a tax case in the 1930s) is the taxpayer's best friend. The *Cohan* rule recognizes that all businesspeople must spend at least some money to stay in business, so they must have had at least some deductible expenses, even if they don't have adequate records to back them up.

Reconstructing Tax Records

If you can show that you possessed adequate records at one time, but now lack them due to circumstances beyond your control, you may reconstruct your records for an IRS audit. Circumstances beyond your control include acts of nature, such as floods, fires, or earthquakes, or theft. (Treas. Reg. 1.275.5(c)(5).) Losing your tax records while moving does not constitute a circumstance beyond your control. Reconstructing records means you either create brand-new records specifically for your audit or you obtain other evidence to corroborate your deductions. This might include statements from people or companies from whom you purchased items for your business.

If you're audited and lack adequate records for a claimed deduction, the IRS can use the *Cohan* rule to make an estimate of how much you must have spent and allow you to deduct that amount. However, you must provide at least some credible evidence on which to base this estimate, such as receipts, canceled checks, notes in your appointment book, or other records. Moreover, the IRS will allow you to deduct only the smallest amount you must have spent, based on the records you provide. In addition, the *Cohan* rule cannot be used for travel, meal, entertainment, or gift expenses, or for listed property.

If an auditor claims you lack sufficient records to back up a deduction, you should always bring up the *Cohan* rule and argue that you should still get the deduction based on the records you do have. At best, you'll probably get only part of your claimed deductions. If the IRS auditor disallows your deductions entirely or doesn't give you as much as you think you deserve, you can appeal in court and bring the *Cohan* rule up again there; you might have more success making this argument to a judge. However, you can't compel an IRS auditor or a court to apply the *Cohan* rule in your favor. They have discretion to decide whether to apply the rule and how large a deduction to give you.

> EXAMPLE: Ajuba Gaylord had a part-time business as a home-based salesperson. One year, she took a $474 deduction for postage and more than $1,100 for meals and entertainment. The IRS disallowed both deductions because she had no documentary evidence showing that the expenses were for her business. However, the tax court applied the *Cohan* rule and allowed her a $75 deduction for postage. It reasoned that this was the least that she must have spent, given the nature of her business. However, the court would not use the *Cohan* rule to grant her a deduction for meal and entertainment expenses. (*Gaylord v. Comm'r.*, T.C. Memo 2003-273.)

Accounting Methods

An accounting method is a set of rules used to determine when and how your income and expenses are reported. Accounting methods might sound like a rather dry subject, but your choice about how to account for your business expenses and income will have a huge impact on your tax deductions. You don't have to become an expert on the subject, but you should understand the basics.

You choose an accounting method when you file your first tax return for your business. If you want to change your accounting method later, you must get IRS approval. If you operate two or more separate businesses, you can use a different accounting method for each. For example, a dentist who also operates a separate laboratory business may use separate accounting methods for each business. (A business is separate for tax purposes only if you keep a separate set of books and records for it.)

There are two basic methods of accounting: cash basis and accrual basis. Most professionals use the cash basis method.

Cash Method

The cash basis method is by far the simpler method of accounting. Individuals who are not in business use this method, as do most small businesses that provide services.

The cash method is based on the commonsense idea that you haven't earned income for tax purposes until you actually receive the money, and you haven't incurred an expense until you actually pay the money. Using the cash basis method, then, is like maintaining a checkbook. You record income only when the money is received and expenses only when they are actually paid. If you borrow money to pay business expenses, you incur an expense under the cash method only when you make payments on the loan.

The cash method is by far the most popular because it is the simplest and easiest to understand and apply. It can also save on taxes because taxable income can be deferred by postponing billings to the following year. Deductions can be speeded up by buying things before year end. For these reasons, the IRS has not been in favor of the cash method. Before 2018, there were restrictions on the ability to use the cash method by C corporations and businesses that produced, bought, or sold merchandise and were required to maintain an inventory. However, the Tax Cuts and Jobs Act greatly expanded the number of businesses that may use the cash method. Starting in 2018, any business with no more than $25 million in average gross receipts during the prior three tax years can use the cash method. Businesses other than regular C corporations can use the cash method even if their gross receipts exceed $25 million, provided that the method clearly reflects their income.

> EXAMPLE 1: Helen, a marketing consultant, completes a market research report on September 1, 2018, but isn't paid by the client until February 1, 2019. Using the cash method, Helen records the payment when she receives it, in February 2019.

> EXAMPLE 2: On December 1, 2018, Helen goes to the Acme electronics store and buys a laser printer for her consulting business. She buys the item on credit from Acme. She's not required to make any payments until March 1, 2019. Helen does not record the expense until 2019, when she actually pays for the printer.

When Is an Expense Paid?

Although it's called the cash method, a business expense is paid when you pay for it by check, credit card, or electronic funds transfer, as well as by cash. If you pay by check, the amount is deemed paid during the year in which the check is drawn and mailed. For example, a check dated December 31, 2018 is considered paid during 2018 only if it has a December 31, 2018 postmark. If you're using a check to pay a substantial expense, you may wish to send it by certified mail so you'll have proof of when it was mailed.

No Postponing Income

You cannot hold checks or other payments from one tax year to another to avoid paying tax on the income. You must report the income in the year the payment is received or made available to you without restriction.

> **EXAMPLE:** On December 1, 2018, Helen receives a $5,000 check from a client. She holds the check and doesn't cash it until January 10, 2019. She must still report the $5,000 as income for 2018 because she constructively received it that year.

Prepayment of Expenses

The general rule is that you cannot prepay expenses when you use the cash method. You can't hurry up the payment of expenses by paying them in advance. An expense you pay in advance can be deducted only in the year to which it applies.

However, there is an important exception to the general rule, called the 12-month rule. Under the 12-month rule, you may deduct a prepaid expense in the current year if the expense is for a right or benefit that extends no longer than the earlier of:

- 12 months, or
- until the end of the tax year after the tax year in which you made the payment.

> **EXAMPLE:** You are a calendar year taxpayer and you pay $10,000 on July 1, 2018, for a small business insurance policy that is effective for one year beginning July 1, 2018. The 12-month rule applies because the benefit you've paid for—a business insurance policy—extends only 12 months into the future. Therefore, the full $10,000 is deductible in 2017.

To use the 12-month rule, you must apply it when you first start using the cash method for your business. If you haven't been using the rule and want to start doing so, you must get IRS approval. You must file IRS Form 3115, *Application for Change in Accounting Method*, but IRS approval is granted automatically. (See "Obtaining IRS Permission to Change Your Accounting Method," below.)

Accrual Method

In the accrual basis method of accounting, you report income or expenses as they are earned or incurred, rather than when they are actually collected or paid. Many self-employed people do not favor the accrual method because it can be complicated to use and can require them to pay tax on income they haven't actually received.

When Income Is Received

With the accrual method, transactions are counted as income when a service is provided, an order is made, or an item is delivered, regardless of when the money for it (the receivable) is actually received or paid. As a result, you can end up owing taxes on income you haven't been paid. This is particularly bad news for self-employed people, who often have to wait a while before they are paid by their clients or customers. As a result, few self-employed people use this accounting method.

Obtaining IRS Permission to Change Your Accounting Method

You choose your accounting method by checking a box on your tax form when you file your tax return for the first year you are in business. Once you choose a method, you cannot change it without getting permission from the IRS. Permission is granted automatically for many types of changes, including using the 12-month rule to deduct prepaid expenses. You must file IRS Form 3115, *Application for Change in Accounting Method*, with your tax return for the year you want to make the change (if the change is granted automatically).

Tax Year

You are required to pay taxes for a 12-month period, also known as the "tax year." Sole proprietors, partnerships, limited liability companies, S corporations, and personal service corporations (see Chapter 2) are required to use the calendar year as their tax years (that is, January 1 through December 31).

However, there are exceptions that permit some small businesses to use a tax year that does not end in December, also known as a "fiscal year." You need to get IRS permission to use a fiscal year. The IRS doesn't like businesses to use fiscal years, but it might grant you permission if you can show a good business reason for it.

One good reason to use a fiscal year is that your business is seasonal. For example, if you earn most of your income in the spring and incur most of your expenses in the fall, a tax year ending in July or August might be better than a calendar tax year ending in December, because the income and expenses on each tax return will be more closely related. To get permission, you must file IRS Form 8716, *Election to Have a Tax Year Other Than a Required Tax Year.*

Safeguarding Your Self-Employed Status

The IRS and other government agencies that rely on employee withholdings and taxes would prefer you to be an employee rather than a self-employed person. This chapter shows you how to avoid being viewed as an employee when you work for yourself.

The terms generally used to describe self-employed people for tax purposes are "independent contractor" or "IC." These terms are, therefore, used throughout this chapter.

Who Decides Your Work Status?

Initially, it's up to you and each hiring firm you deal with to decide whether you should be classified as an independent contractor or an employee. But the decision about how you should be classified is subject to review by various government agencies, including:

- the IRS
- your state's tax department
- your state's unemployment compensation insurance agency
- your state's workers' compensation insurance agency, and
- the U.S. Department of Labor and the National Labor Relations Board.

Because independent contractors often cost less than employees, some employers classify their workers as contractors even though they are really employees. One federal study found that employers misclassified 3.4 million workers as independent contractors, while the Labor Department estimates that up to 30% of companies misclassify employees.

And, starting in 2015, the incentive for larger companies to misclassify workers as ICs became even greater. Obamacare now requires employers with 50 or more full-time equivalent employees to provide minimally adequate health insurance coverage or pay a penalty to the IRS. ICs aren't included in the count. Employers with less than 50 full-time employees need not provide such coverage (see Chapter 6).

The IRS considers worker misclassification to be a serious problem that costs the U.S. government billions of dollars in taxes that would otherwise be paid if the workers were classified as employees and taxes were automatically withheld from their paychecks. Most state agencies live by the same theory.

The IRS or your state tax department might question your status in a routine audit of your tax returns. More commonly, however, you'll come to the government's attention if it investigates the classification practices of a firm that hired you. Government auditors may question you and examine your and your hiring firm's records. Because the rules for determining whether you're an independent contractor or employee are rather vague and subjective, it's often easy for the government to claim that you're an employee even though both you and the hiring firm sincerely believed you qualified as an independent contractor.

What Happens If the Government Reclassifies You?

If you're like most independent contractors, you probably think that a government agency determination that one or more of the firms that hire you should classify you as an employee is solely the hiring firm's problem. Unfortunately, this is not the case.

It is true that if the IRS or another government agency audits you or a hiring firm you've worked for and determines that you should have been classified as an employee instead of an independent contractor, it can and probably will impose assessments and penalties on the firm. Some companies have gone bankrupt because of such assessments.

Rest assured that the government will not penalize or fine *you* if you've been misclassified as an independent contractor. However, you can be affected adversely in other ways. For example, the hiring firm may end the working relationship because it doesn't want to pay the additional expenses involved in treating you as an employee. It is not unusual for IRS settlement agreements with hiring firms to require that the firms terminate contracts with independent contractors even if the independent contractors would prefer that those agreements continue. Or, the hiring firm may insist on reducing your compensation to make up for the extra employee expenses. And even if none of these things happen, you'll likely be treated differently on the job. For example, the hiring firm—now your employer—will probably expect you to follow its orders and may attempt to restrict you from working for other companies.

Worker Gets the Ax When the IRS Calls

Dave, a financial analyst, was hired by a large New York bank and classified as an independent contractor for IRS purposes. He signed an independent contractor agreement and submitted invoices to the bank's accounting department to be paid. The bank withheld no taxes from his pay, paid no Social Security or Medicare taxes for him, and provided him with no employee benefits.

Otherwise, however, Dave was treated largely as an employee. He worked on a team along with regular bank employees and shared their supervisor. He performed the same functions as the employees and worked the same core hours. Because the bank required him to work at its headquarters, he received an admittance card key, office equipment, and supplies from the bank.

Dave's happy worklife changed abruptly when the IRS notified the bank that it wanted to examine its employment records to determine whether the company was complying with tax laws. Fearing that it should have classified Dave as an employee instead of an independent contractor, the bank summarily fired him in the hope this would lessen potential problems with IRS auditors. It didn't work. The bank was required to reclassify Dave as an employee for the two years he had worked for the bank. Dave was entitled to a refund of half of his SE Social Security and Medicare taxes for those years, and he was able to collect unemployment benefits, but he was still out of a job.

Tax Consequences

An IRS determination that you should be classified as an employee can also have adverse tax consequences for you. If you haven't filed a federal tax return for the year(s) involved yet, you must file Form 1040 for the affected tax year(s), reporting the Form 1099-MISC income reported to you by your employer as wages. No Social Security or Medicare tax (FICA tax) was withheld from these wages, so you must also calculate and pay the employee portion of these taxes with your return.

If you've already filed a tax return for the year(s) involved, you'll have to file an amended return with the IRS to reflect the correct amount of tax under your status as an employee. On the plus side, you'll be entitled to a refund of part of the self-employment tax you paid.

However, now that you are an employee, you'll lose any deductions you took because you treated yourself as self-employed, including all the business expenses you deducted in Schedule C, such as mileage, business travel, equipment, and office expenses. You'll also lose the self-employed health insurance deduction, the deduction for one-half of your self-employment tax, and the deduction for contributions to a Keogh-type retirement plan or SEP-IRA.

As a result of the Tax Cuts and Jobs Act, during 2018 through 2025, employees are not allowed to deduct any of their unreimbursed job-related expenses, like mileage. (Before 2018, these expenses could be deducted as miscellaneous itemized deductions on Schedule A if, and to the extent that, they exceeded 2% of your adjusted gross income.) So, you'll get no deduction for any of your work-related expenses. You should seek to have your employer reimburse you for these expenses. (Reimbursement might be required under state law.) The change to employee status may also increase your tax bill because you must now compute FICA tax on your gross wages instead of computing self-employment tax on your net income. Your employer will also have to start withholding your income tax and FICA tax from your pay.

Finally, employees don't qualify for the new pass-through tax deduction that the Tax Cuts and Jobs Act established. This deduction, which took effect in 2018, enables self-employed business owners to deduct up to 20% of their net business income from their income taxes. (See Chapter 9.)

From a tax perspective, however, by far the worst thing that can happen to you if you're reclassified as an employee by the IRS is that any Keogh retirement plan you have will lose its tax-qualified status. Generally, in a Keogh plan, your contributions are tax deductible, and you don't pay any tax on the interest your investment earns until you retire. But if your Keogh is disqualified, you'll have to pay tax on your contributions and on the interest you've earned from your investments. If you have a substantial amount invested in a Keogh plan, you could face a staggering tax bill.

Review IRS Notice 989, *Commonly Asked Questions When IRS Determines Your Work Status is "Employee,"* for an excellent and thorough discussion of all the tax steps you may have to take if you've been misclassified. You can download it from the IRS website at www.irs.gov.

IRS Audit Silences Independent Contractor's Voice

John, a New Hampshire–based voice actor who narrated corporate videos and TV commercials, thought he was an independent contractor. He was characterized as one by hundreds of clients, for whom he usually worked for only a few hours or days.

However, when the IRS audited him, it determined that he was really his clients' temporary employee because he worked on the clients' premises and some of his clients paid his union dues. When John told his clients that they had to classify him as an employee, issue a W-2, and pay payroll taxes, some of them told him they couldn't afford to hire him anymore because of the added expense.

In addition, John had to refile his tax returns for the years in question and recharacterize the compensation he received as wages instead of self-employment income. John was entitled to a refund for half of the self-employment taxes he paid on this compensation. But he lost some substantial business deductions, including a $10,000 deduction he took in one year for mileage and auto expenses. The loss of these deductions more than outweighed the refund of self-employment taxes. As a result, John lost work for future years and had to pay more taxes for past years.

Qualifying for Employee Benefits

One good thing that can happen if you're reclassified as an employee is that you may qualify for benefits your employer gives to its other employees, such as health insurance, pension benefits, and unemployment insurance.

If you've incurred out-of-pocket expenses for medical care, you may be entitled to reimbursement. However, these benefits may be short-lived if the hiring firm decides it can't afford to keep you on as an employee.

Determining Worker Status

Various government agencies and courts use slightly different tests to determine how workers should be classified. Unfortunately, these tests are confusing, subjective, and often don't lead to a conclusive answer about whether you're an independent contractor or employee. This is why some hiring firms are afraid to hire independent contractors.

This section provides an overview of the most important test for independent contractor status. However, it's practically impossible for anyone to learn and follow all the different tests various government agencies use to determine worker status. You'll be better off simply following the guidelines later in this chapter for preserving your independent contractor status.

Most, but not all, government agencies use the "right of control" test to determine whether you're an employee or independent contractor. You're an employee under this test if a hiring firm has the right to direct and control how you work, both as to the final results and as to the details of when, where, and how you perform the work.

The employer may not always exercise this right. For example, if you're experienced and well trained, your employer may not feel the need to closely supervise you. But if the employer has the right to do so, you're still considered an employee.

> EXAMPLE: Mary takes a job as a hamburger cook at the local AcmeBurger. AcmeBurger personnel carefully train her in how to make an AcmeBurger burger, including the type and amount of ingredients to use, the temperature at which the burger should be cooked, and so on.
>
> Once Mary starts work, AcmeBurger managers closely supervise how she does her job. Virtually every aspect of Mary's behavior on the job is under AcmeBurger control, including what time she arrives at and leaves work, when she takes her lunch break, what she wears, and the sequence of the tasks she must perform. If Mary proves to be an able and conscientious worker, her supervisors may not look over her shoulder very often. But they have the right to do so at any time. Mary is AcmeBurger's employee.

In contrast, you're an independent contractor if the hiring firm does not have the right to control how you do the job. Because you're an independent businessperson not solely dependent on the firm for your livelihood, its control is limited to accepting or rejecting the final results you achieve. Or if a project is broken down into stages or phases, the firm's input is limited to approving the work you perform at each stage. Unlike an employee, you are not supervised daily.

> EXAMPLE: AcmeBurger develops a serious plumbing problem. AcmeBurger does not have any plumbers on its staff, so it hires Plumbing by Jake, an independent plumbing repair business owned by Jake. Jake looks at the problem and gives an estimate of how much it will cost to fix. The manager agrees to hire him, and Jake and his assistant commence work.
>
> Because Jake is clearly running his own business, it's virtually certain that AcmeBurger does not have the right to control the way Jake performs his plumbing services. Its control is limited to accepting or rejecting the final result. If AcmeBurger doesn't like the work Jake has done, it can refuse to pay him. Jake is an independent contractor.

It can be difficult to figure out whether a hiring firm has the right to control you. Government auditors can't look into your mind to see if you are controlled by a hiring firm. They have to rely instead on indirect or circumstantial evidence indicating control or lack of it, such as whether a hiring firm provides you with tools and equipment, where you do the work, how you're paid, and whether you can be fired.

The factors each agency relies upon to measure control vary. Some agencies look at 14 factors to see if you're an employee or independent contractor; some look at 11; some consider only three. Which of these factors is of the greatest or least importance is anyone's guess. This can make it very difficult to know whether you pass muster to be an independent contractor.

The IRS Approach to Worker Status

The IRS uses the right of control test to determine whether you're an independent contractor or employee for tax purposes. IRS auditors look at three areas to determine whether a hiring firm has the right to control a worker. These are:

- your behavior on the job
- your finances, and
- your relationship with the hiring firm.

The chart on the following page shows the primary factors the IRS looks at in each area.

The IRS test is not a model of clarity. There is no guidance on how important each factor is and how many factors must weigh in favor of independent contractor status for you to be classified as an independent contractor. The IRS says there is no magic number of factors. Rather, the factors that show lack of control must outweigh those that indicate control. No one factor alone is enough to make you an employee or an independent contractor.

To make your life easier, this chapter offers a list of eight guidelines for you to follow when doing your work. (See "Tips for Preserving Your IC Status," below.) If you do, it's likely that you will be viewed as an independent contractor by the IRS and any other government agency.

Payment by the Hour

If you want to be classified as an independent contractor, it's better not to be paid an hourly wage unless it's a common practice in your line of business. (The IRS recognizes that some independent contractors—lawyers, for example—are usually paid by the hour.) Instead, get paid by the job or project where feasible.

Expenses

Paying business expenses yourself rather than getting reimbursed by your client will help establish your IC status. It really makes no difference what the expense is, as long as it's for your business. It can be office rent, equipment, salaries, travel expenses, telephone bills, photocopying charges, or anything else.

Although not fatal, any expense that your client reimburses you for will not help establish your IC status. In fact, it could actually impair your effort (and your client's efforts) to prove that you are not an employee of the client.

Advertising

Failure to offer your services to the public is a sign of employee status. In the past, the IRS usually considered only advertising in telephone books and newspapers as evidence that an independent contractor offered services to the public. Of course, many independent contractors don't get business this way; they rely primarily on word of mouth. The IRS now recognizes this fact of life and doesn't consider advertising essential for proving independent contractor status.

Form of Direction

The IRS makes a distinction between receiving instructions on how to work—a very strong indicator of employee status—and being given suggestions. A suggestion about how work is to be performed does not constitute the right to control. However, if you must comply with suggestions or suffer adverse consequences (such as being fired or not assigned more work), then the suggestions are, in fact, instructions.

Training

Periodic or ongoing training about how to do your work is strong evidence of an employment relationship. However, a client may provide you with a short orientation or information session about the company's policies, new product line, or new government regulations without jeopardizing your independent contractor status. Training programs that are voluntary and that you attend without receiving pay do not disqualify you from being classified as an independent contractor.

IRS Test for Worker Status		
Behavioral Control Factors showing whether a hiring firm has the right to control how you perform the specific tasks you've been hired to do	**You will more likely be considered self-employed if you:** • are not given instructions by the hiring firm • provide your own training	**You will more likely be considered an employee if you:** • receive instructions you must follow about how to do your work • receive training from the hiring firm
Financial Control Factors showing whether a firm has a right to control your financial life	**You will more likely be considered self-employed if you:** • have a significant investment in equipment and facilities • pay business or travel expenses yourself • make your services available to the public • are paid by the job • have opportunity for profit or loss	**You will more likely be considered an employee if you:** • use equipment and facilities provided by the hiring firm free of charge • are reimbursed for your business or traveling expenses • make no effort to market your services to the public • are paid by the hour or other unit of time • have no opportunity for profit or loss (for example, because you're paid by the hour and have all expenses reimbursed)
Relationship Between Worker and Hiring Firm Factors showing whether you and the hiring firm believe that you are self-employed or an employee	**You will more likely be considered self-employed if you:** • don't receive employee benefits such as health insurance • sign a client agreement with the hiring firm • can't quit or be fired at will • are performing services that are not a part of the hiring firm's regular business activities	**You will more likely be considered an employee if you:** • receive employee benefits • have no written client agreement • can quit at any time without incurring any liability to the hiring firm • can be fired at any time • are performing services that are part of the hiring firm's core business

Investment

A significant investment in equipment and facilities is not necessary for independent contractor status. The manual notes that some types of work simply do not require expensive equipment, including writing and certain types of consulting. But even if expensive equipment is needed to do a particular type of work, an independent contractor can always rent it.

Performing Key Services

One of the most important factors IRS auditors look at is whether the services performed by a worker are key to the hiring firm's regular business. The IRS figures that if the services you perform are vital to a company's regular business, the company will be more likely to control how you perform them. For example, a law firm is less likely to supervise and control a painter it hires to paint its offices than a paralegal it hires to work on its regular legal business.

However, IRS auditors are required to examine all the facts and circumstances. For example, a paralegal hired by a law firm could very well be an independent contractor if he or she was a specialist hired to help with especially difficult or unusual legal work.

 CAUTION

Written agreements are more important than ever. A written independent contractor agreement can never make you an independent contractor by itself. However, if the evidence is so evenly balanced that it is difficult or impossible for an IRS auditor to decide whether you're an independent contractor or employee, the existence of a written independent contractor agreement can tip the balance in favor of independent contractor status. This makes using written independent contractor agreements especially important. (See Chapter 18.)

Full-Time Work

Working full time for a single client should not by itself make you an employee in the eyes of the IRS. Nevertheless, it is never helpful to your IC status to work for just one client at a time. There may be many situations where it can't be avoided; for example, if you can't get any other work at the time or if the nature of the work you are doing for the client demands your full time and attention. Still, you should attempt to keep the period of exclusivity to a minimum (six months to a year). Performing the same services full time for the same client year after year inevitably makes you look like an employee of that client.

Long-Term Work for a Single Client

Performing services for the same client year after year used to be a sign that you were an employee. The IRS now recognizes that independent contractors may work for a client on a long-term basis, either because they sign long-term contracts or because their contracts are regularly renewed by the client because they do a good job, price their services reasonably, or no one else is readily available to do the work.

Time and Place of Work

It is not important to the IRS where or when you work. For example, the fact that you work at a client's offices during regular business hours is not considered evidence of employee status. On the other hand, the fact that you work at home at hours of your own choosing is not strong evidence that you're an independent contractor either, because many employees now work at home as well.

Rules for Technical Services Workers

If you're a computer programmer, systems analyst, engineer, or provide similar technical services and obtain work through brokers, special tax rules may make it very difficult for you to work as an independent contractor, even if you qualify under the IRS test.

Most hiring firms can rely on a defense, found in Section 530 of the Tax Code, if the IRS claims they misclassified workers. By using Section 530, an employer who misclassifies a worker as an independent contractor can avoid paying any fines or penalties for failing to pay employment taxes if it can show it had a reasonable basis for treating the worker as an independent contractor. Section 530 has made hiring firms' lives a little easier by giving them an additional defense against the IRS.

However, another part of the Tax Code, Section 1706, provides that the Section 530 defense may not be used by brokers that contract to provide their clients with:

- engineers
- designers
- drafters
- computer programmers
- systems analysts, or
- other skilled workers in similar technical occupations.

Section 1706 doesn't make anyone an employee. But it does make it harder for brokers to avoid paying assessments and penalties if the IRS claims they've misclassified technical services workers as independent contractors. Because of Section 1706, brokers who contract to provide companies with technical services workers usually classify the workers as their employees and issue them W-2s. One result of this is that you'll likely receive less pay from the broker than if you were classified as an independent contractor because it has to pay payroll taxes for you and provide workers' compensation coverage.

Some brokers may make an exception and treat you as an independent contractor if you are clearly running an independent business (for example, because you deal directly with many clients and are incorporated). For example, one Silicon Valley software tester occasionally obtains work through brokers and is never classified as an employee of a broker. Brokers feel safe treating her as an independent contractor because she has incorporated her business, has employees, and has many clients, including several Fortune 500 companies. The brokers sign a contract with the tester's corporation, not with her personally.

Section 1706 has no application at all if you contract directly with a client instead of going through a broker. But many high-tech firms are still wary of hiring independent contractors.

Tips for Preserving Your IC Status

If you consistently follow the guidelines discussed in this section, it's likely that any government agency or court would determine that you qualify as an independent contractor. However, there are no guarantees.

Some of these guidelines may be a bit stricter than those now followed by the IRS. This is because not all government agencies follow the IRS standards. Various state agencies, such as state tax departments and unemployment compensation and workers' compensation agencies, may have tougher classification standards than the IRS. This means you can't rely solely on the IRS rules.

> EXAMPLE: Debbi, an independent contractor accountant based in Rhode Island, clearly qualifies as an independent contractor under the IRS test. However, very restrictive Rhode Island employment laws require that she be classified as an employee for state purposes if she performs services for other accounting firms. This means they must withhold state income taxes from her pay, pay unemployment taxes, and provide her with workers' compensation insurance. In addition, if Debbi has employees of her own, they may become the firm's employees as well under Rhode Island law.

Some hiring firms are terrified of government audits and nervous about hiring independent contractors. Employer reluctance to hire ICs may increase because the IRS, federal Labor Department, and many state agencies have vowed in recent years to step up enforcement against hiring firms that, in their view, misclassify employees as ICs. Companies that have had problems with government audits in the past or are in industries that are targeted by government auditors are likely to be especially skittish. Recent targets include trucking firms, courier services, securities dealers, high-technology firms, nurse registries, building contractors, and manufacturer representatives. Such hiring firms may be more willing to hire you as an independent contractor if you can show that you follow the guidelines. Document your efforts and be ready to show the documentation to nervous clients.

Many other companies don't give government audits a second thought and are more than happy to classify you as an independent contractor to save the money and effort involved in treating you as an employee. These companies may not worry about whether you qualify as an independent contractor, but you should. You could still end up getting fired, taking a pay cut, or having to pay extra taxes if some government bureaucrat decides you're really an employee. So, even though your client may not appreciate your efforts, continue to follow the guidelines discussed here; both you and your client will be glad you did if the government comes calling.

Retain Control of Your Work

The most fundamental difference between employees and independent contractors is that employers have the right to tell their employees what to do. Never permit a hiring firm to supervise or control you as it does its employees. It's perfectly all right for the hiring firm to give you detailed guidelines or specifications for the results you're to achieve. But how you go about achieving those results should be entirely up to you.

A few guidelines will help emphasize that you are the one who is responsible:

- Do not ask for or accept instructions or orders from the hiring firm about how to do your job. For example, you should decide what equipment or tools to use, where to purchase supplies or services, who will perform what tasks, and what routines or work patterns must be used. It's fine for a hiring firm to give you suggestions about these things, but you must always preserve your right to accept or reject such suggestions.

- Do not ask for or receive training on how to do your work from a hiring firm. If you need additional training, seek it elsewhere.

- A hiring firm may give you a deadline for when your work should be completed, but you should generally establish your own working hours. For example, if you want, you could work 20 hours two days a week and take the rest of the week off. In some cases, however, it may be necessary to coordinate your working hours with the client's schedule (for example, if you must perform work on the client's premises or work with its employees).

- Decide on your own where to perform the work. A client should not require you to work at a particular location. Of course, some services must be performed at a client's premises or another particular place.
- Decide whether to hire assistants to help you and, if you do, pay and supervise them yourself. Only you should have the right to hire and fire your assistants.
- Do not attend regular employee meetings or functions such as employee picnics.
- Avoid providing frequent formal reports about the progress of your work, such as daily emails or phone calls to the client. It is permissible, however, to give reports when you complete various stages of a project.
- Do not obtain, read, or pay any attention to a hiring firm's employee manuals or other rules for employees. The rules governing your relationship with the hiring firm are contained solely in your independent contractor agreement, whether written or oral. (See Chapter 18.)

If you work outside the client's premises, it's usually not difficult to avoid being controlled. Neither the client nor its employees will have much opportunity to try to supervise you. For example, Katherine, a freelance legal writer, never has any problems being controlled by a large legal publisher for whom she performs freelance assignments. She says anonymity on the job helps with this: "I get my freelance assignments by email, do all the work at home and in the local law library, and then transmit my projects to the publisher via email. I've hardly ever been in the publisher's office."

On the other hand, you could have problems if you work in a client's workplace. The client's supervisors or managers may try to treat you like an employee. Before you start work, make clear to the client that you do not fall within its regular personnel hierarchy; you are an outsider. You might ask the client to designate one person with whom you will deal. If anyone in the company gives you a problem, you can explain that you deal only with your contact person and refer the problem person to your contact.

Note, however, that it's fine for a client to require you to comply with government regulations about how to perform your services. For example, a client may require a construction contractor to comply with municipal building codes that impose detailed rules on how a building is constructed. The IRS and other government agencies would not likely consider this to be an exercise of control over the contractor by the client.

Show Opportunities for Profit or Loss

Because they are in business for themselves, independent contractors have the opportunity to earn profits or suffer losses. If you have absolutely no risk of loss, you're probably not an independent contractor.

Business Expenses

The best way to show an opportunity to realize profit or loss is to have recurring business expenses. If receipts do not match expenses, you lose money and may go into debt. If receipts exceed expenses, you earn a profit.

Good examples of independent contractor expenses include:
- salaries for assistants
- travel and other similar expenses incurred in performing your services
- substantial investment in equipment and materials
- rent for an office or workplace
- training and educational expenses
- advertising
- licensing, certification, and professional dues
- insurance
- leasing of equipment
- supplies, and
- repairs and maintenance of business equipment.

Don't go out and buy things you don't really need. But if you've been thinking about buying equipment or supplies to use in your business, go ahead and take the plunge. You'll not only solidify your independent contractor status, you'll get a tax deduction as well. (See Chapter 9.)

In addition, it's best that you don't ask clients to reimburse you for expenses such as travel, photocopying, and postage. It's a better practice to bill clients enough for your services to pay for these items yourself. Setting your compensation at a level that covers your expenses also frees you from having to keep records of your expenses. Keeping track of the cost of every phone call or photocopy you make for a client can be a real chore and may be more trouble than it's worth.

Get Paid by the Project

Another excellent way to show opportunity for profit or loss is to be paid an agreed price for a specific project, rather than to bill by unit of time, such as by the hour. If the project price is higher than the expenses, you'll make money; if not, you'll lose money.

However, this form of billing may be too risky for many independent contractors. And some professions—for example, attorneys and accountants —are typically paid by the hour. If hourly payment is customary in your field, this factor should not affect your independent contractor status.

Look Like an Independent Business

Take steps to make yourself look like an independent businessperson. There are several things you can do to cultivate this image:
- Don't obtain employee-type benefits from your clients, such as health insurance, paid vacation, sick days, pension benefits, or life or disability insurance; instead, charge your clients enough to purchase these items yourself.
- Incorporate your business instead of operating as a sole proprietor. (See Chapter 2.)
- Obtain a fictitious business name instead of using your own name for your business. (See Chapter 3.)
- Obtain all necessary business licenses and permits. (See Chapter 5.)
- Obtain business insurance. (See Chapter 6.)
- Maintain a separate bank account for your business. (See Chapter 14.)

You may have an easier time getting work if you do these things. For example, a large corporation that regularly used the services of one independent contractor asked her to incorporate or at least obtain a business license because it was worried she might otherwise be viewed as the company's employee.

Work Outside Hiring Firms' Premises

The IRS no longer considers working at a hiring firm's place of business to be an important factor in determining whether a worker is an independent contractor or employee, but many state agencies still do. For example, in about half the states you may be considered an employee for unemployment compensation purposes if you work at the hiring firm's place of business or another place it designates.

Working at a location specified by a hiring firm implies that the firm has control, especially if the work could be done elsewhere. If you work at a hiring firm's place of business, you're physically within the firm's direction and supervision. If you can choose to work off the premises, the firm obviously has less control.

Unless the nature of the services you're performing requires it, don't work at the hiring firm's office or other business premises. An independent contractor hired to lay a carpet or paint an office must obviously work at the hiring firm's premises. But if your work can be done anywhere, do it outside the client's premises.

Working at a home office will not, alone, show that you're an independent contractor as far as the IRS is concerned because many employees are now doing so. Renting an office outside your home, however, will show independent contractor status. It shows that you're operating your own business and gives you a recurring business expense to help establish risk of loss.

Make Your Services Widely Available

Independent contractors normally offer their services to the general public, not just to one person or entity. The IRS recognizes that many independent contractors rely on word of mouth to get clients and don't do any active marketing. However, nervous clients and other government auditors will be impressed if you market your services to the public.

There are many relatively inexpensive ways to market yourself. For example, you can:

- obtain business cards and stationery
- set up a website for your business

- hang a shingle in front of your home or office, advertising your services (unless this might cause problems with neighbors or local zoning authorities)
- maintain listings in business and telephone directories (both print and online)
- attend trade shows and similar events
- join professional organizations
- market your services via social media, such as Twitter or Facebook
- advertise in newspapers, trade journals, and magazines, and on the Web
- mail or email brochures or other promotional materials to prospective clients, and
- phone potential clients to drum up business.

Keep copies of advertisements, promotional materials, and similar items to show to prospective clients and government auditors.

Have Multiple Clients

IRS guidelines provide that you can work full time for a single client on a long-term basis and still be an independent contractor. Nevertheless, having multiple clients shows that you're running an independent business because you are not dependent on any one firm for your livelihood. Government auditors will rarely question the status of an independent contractor who works for three or four clients simultaneously.

However, the nature of your work may require that you work full time for one client at a time. In this event, at least try to work for more than one client over the course of a year. For example, work full time for one client for six months and full time for another client for the other six months.

Having multiple clients also increases your economic security. One independent contractor thinks of herself as an eight-legged spider, with each client a separate leg. If she loses one client, things are still economically stable because she has her other legs to stand on.

If you seem to be locked into having just one client, you may be able to drum up new business by offering special rates for small jobs that you would otherwise lose.

CAUTION

Don't sign noncompete agreements. Some clients may ask or require you to sign noncompete agreements restricting your ability to work for the client's competitors while working for the client, afterwards, or both. You should avoid such restrictions. Not only will they make you look like an employee, they may also make it impossible for you to earn a living.

Use Written Agreements

Use written independent contractor agreements for all but the briefest, smallest projects. Among other things, the agreement should make clear that you are an independent contractor and the hiring firm does not have the right to control the way you work. A written agreement by itself won't make you an independent contractor but it is helpful, particularly if you draft it rather than the hiring firm.

Also, don't accept new projects after the original project is completed without signing a new independent contractor agreement. You can easily be converted from an independent contractor to an employee if you perform assignment after assignment for a client without negotiating new contracts. (See Chapters 18 and 19 for more about written agreements.)

Avoid Accepting Employee Status

Some clients will refuse to hire you as an independent contractor and insist on classifying you as an employee. Some companies may hire you as their own employee. Others may insist that you contract with a broker or an employment agency that treats you as its employee. The firm then hires you through the broker.

It's best to avoid performing the exact same services while classified as both an independent contractor and employee for the following reasons:

- Being classified as both an independent contractor and an employee on your tax returns may make an IRS audit more likely and lead government auditors to conclude that you're an employee for all purposes.

- You'll often be paid less as an employee than if you were an independent contractor because the hiring firm or broker will have to provide you with workers' compensation and unemployment insurance. (However, you may be able to collect unemployment when your services end.)
- You may not be able to deduct unreimbursed expenses incurred while you were an employee or the deductions may be limited. (See Chapter 9.)
- You can't apply your employee income to your independent contractor business to help it show a profit. If your business keeps showing losses, the IRS might conclude that it is a hobby and disallow your business deductions. (See Chapter 9.)

If you run into a client that is paranoid about classifying you as an independent contractor, explain that you ordinarily do business as an independent contractor and that other clients who have classified you as an independent contractor haven't had any problems. Let the client know about the steps you have taken to make sure that you qualify as an independent contractor, such as working for multiple clients, having your own office, having a fictitious business name and business bank account, marketing your services widely, and possibly getting paid by the project instead of by the hour.

Can You Work as an Employee and IC for the Same Firm?

The IRS says that you can be both an employee and independent contractor for the same hiring firm. The IRS Chief Counsel advised that a professional consultant working on two projects at the same time for the same company could be classified as an employee on one project and an IC on the other. In such cases, the IRS examines the work relationship separately for each service provided. If the worker qualifies as an IC for one project, the fact that he or she is an employee for the other project is not controlling. (IRS Info. Ltr. 01-0069.) In these situations, everyone needs to carefully document that the worker is being properly treated as an IC on the IC project.

Special Concerns for Gig Workers

A growing number of self-employed people obtain work through online hiring platforms like Uber, Lyft, Upwork, and Freelancer. Participating in the new "gig economy" can help you get work while continuing to enjoy the benefits of being self-employed, such as independence, flexibility, and control over your work schedule. All the legal and tax issues covered in other chapters of this book apply to gig workers, just as they do to other self-employed workers—for example, you have to take the necessary legal steps to start up your business, pay taxes on your profits, and keep good records. However, the gig economy presents some unique challenges: dealing with often impersonal hiring portals, low pay, and cutthroat competition. This chapter covers the special legal and tax concerns faced by gig workers, such as the often one-sided contracts you're required to enter into with hiring platforms, your status as an independent contractor, and tax reporting.

Introduction to the Gig Economy

The gig economy (also referred to as the on-demand economy, sharing economy, peer-to-peer economy, matching economy, and various other names) enables self-employed people to sell their services to the public through online hiring platforms. Prospective clients or customers use such platforms' websites and smartphone apps to search for providers or specify jobs they need done. Service providers (whom we'll call gig workers) contract with the hiring platform to be listed on the platform and provide services to its clients. The gig worker and client may enter into a separate agreement through the platform setting forth the terms of the project. The client pays the worker through the platform, which charges the worker a fee for its service. Gig workers usually work for their clients or customers on a short-term or temporary basis—for example, a gig worker may help design an app or pick up a client's laundry.

Gig workers provide many different types of services; the best known are driver services provided through Uber and Lyft. However, gig workers provide many different types of services, including:

- household services, such as household moving and cleaning (for example, through TaskRabbit and Handy)

- a variety of business services, such as accounting, marketing, and design services (for example, through Freelancer and Upwork)
- design work (for example, through 99designs and Visual.ly)
- coding and other types of hi-tech services (for example, though GetACoder)
- food and grocery delivery services (for example, through Instacart and Postmates), and
- health and medical care (for example, through Heal and Pager).

No one knows exactly how many people work in the gig economy: Estimates range from 600,000 to 2.5 million workers, with around 400,000 people driving for Uber alone; but the number is growing rapidly, and is expected to double by the year 2020.

Some self-employed people obtain all or most of their work through one or more online hiring platforms. However, most people use such platforms only to supplement the work they obtain through more traditional means, or only when they are first starting out. Few gig workers are getting rich. One survey found that 74% earned $5,000 or less in 2015 from on-demand platform work (*Shortchanged: The Tax Compliance Challenges of Small Business Operators Driving the On-Demand Platform Economy*, Kogod Tax Policy Center, Washington, DC (2016).)

Your Contract With the Hiring Platform

To obtain work through a hiring platform, you must first enter into a contract with the platform. This contract may be called "terms and conditions," "terms of service," "platform terms for vendors," or something else. You'll need to agree to the contract before you can register for work and be listed on the platform. Ordinarily, you agree to the terms by clicking on an "I agree" or submit button. This creates a binding legal contract between you and the hiring platform in which you agree to provide services to the platform's clients.

These contracts are usually written with the platform's best interests in mind, not yours. Moreover, you ordinarily have no ability to change or negotiate any of the contract terms. It's take it or leave it. Obviously, you should read any such agreement carefully before accepting work through any online platform. The agreement will largely govern your relationship with the platform and the clients you work with through the platform. These contracts are not all the same. Some are more favorable to the gig worker than others.

Here are some issues you should pay particular attention to.

Fees

Hiring platforms make money by collecting fees from providers who obtain work through the platform; clients who list jobs are charged a fee as well by some platforms. Typically, the fee is a percentage of what you earn, but some platforms charge a flat-fee or combine flat-fees with percentage commissions. The fees that platforms take can be quite substantial—as high as 20% or more—and may vary according to how much money you earn from the platform. For example, Upwork charges a 20% fee on the first $500 earned from a client, 10% on the next $9,500, and a 5% fee on billings over $10,000. Some platforms also charge a monthly or annual membership fee. Such fees and commissions are all tax deductible by you, but they will reduce your take-home earnings, so you should plan accordingly.

Pricing Your Services

Some platforms allow providers to set their own prices—for example, Upwork and TaskRabbit permit providers to set their own hourly rates. Others won't give you this freedom—for example, Uber and Lyft set the fee for each ride through their apps; drivers cannot negotiate the price with their customers. Some platforms use an auction model in which providers bid on jobs listed by clients or customers. This can lead to a race to the bottom. Prices may be set by the hour, by the project, or some other basis.

Intellectual Property Ownership

If your services involve creation of intellectual property for clients—for example, software, graphics, or writing—you should pay particular attention to the intellectual property ownership provisions of the hiring platform's contract and any separate agreement you enter into with your clients. Typically, gig workers are required to give up all rights in the work they create for their clients. Often, such work is classified as a work made for hire. In this event, you aren't even considered the author of the work for copyright ownership purposes. (See "Copyright Ownership" in Chapter 17 for a detailed discussion.) This means you won't be able to reuse the work. However, in some cases you may be able to retain ownership of your work product and license it to the client; or at least obtain ownership of your "background technology"—materials you use over and over again. One reason to work for a platform when you're first starting out is to develop a portfolio of work you can show to future prospective clients outside the platform. Make sure the contract permits you to include copies of your work in your personal off-platform portfolio.

Payment and Resolving Disputes

When you obtain work through a hiring platform, your clients pay the platform, not you directly. The platform pays you after it deducts its fee. For longer projects, a client may be required to put money into an escrow account maintained by the platform, with the money released to you as you complete project milestones and the client signs off on them. If you have a payment dispute with a client, you are usually required to seek resolution through the platform's support or help center. If this doesn't work to your satisfaction, you may be required to submit the dispute to mandatory arbitration rather than sue a client in court. This system can avoid payment disputes; or help you resolve disputes when they develop. However, gig workers' experiences with hiring platforms' support vary widely.

Noncircumvention

"Circumvention" means you accept additional work from a client you initially identify through a hiring platform by dealing with him or her directly instead of going through the platform. When you do this the client pays you directly, instead of paying through the platform. Circumvention enables you to avoid having to pay a fee to the platform, thus it's deeply frowned upon by the platform. To avoid this, hiring platform contracts usually have a noncircumvention provision. For example, if you obtain work for a client through a hiring platform, you may be barred from doing any future work for that client outside the platform for a specified time period—one or two years is common; or, you may be allowed to do so only if you (or the client) pay a substantial fee to the platform. Violation of the noncircumvention provision can lead to you being kicked off the platform. For example, the Upwork user agreement provides that you must use Upwork as your exclusive method of working with any client you identify through the site for 24 months; or, you can pay an "opt-out" fee equal to 15% of what the client pays you during the 24-month period, but not less than $2,500. This is one big difference between gig work and working as a traditional independent contractor. It can make it difficult for you to operate outside the platform.

Your Worker Status

Almost all gig workers are classified as independent contractors for tax and other purposes—that is, they are not the employees of the hiring platform or the clients they work for through the platform. The hiring platform's contract will usually contain a provision providing that you are an independent contractor and that you agree to such status. As explained in Chapter 1, when you're an independent contractor you are not entitled to receive from the hiring platform or your clients any employee-type benefits such as health insurance, paid vacation, sick leave, retirement benefits, or unemployment benefits. Nor do most labor law protections apply. This means you are not entitled to the minimum wage, overtime pay, or the right to form a union.

Gig workers perform a wide variety of services requiring many different skill and education levels—everything from dog walking to software development. In many cases, the independent contractor classification seems fully justified. This is especially true for workers who have a large measure of control over their work—for example, where the hiring platform allows providers to select or refuse jobs, set their own hours and pay, and control other aspects of their work.

However, some hiring platforms exercise more control over price-setting and assignment decisions than is typical in an independent contractor-client relationship. This is particularly true for platforms that offer driving services, such as Uber and Lyft. Indeed, several lawsuits and administrative complaints have been filed by Uber and Lyft drivers claiming that they should be classified as employees of Uber or Lyft, not independent contractors. This litigation is ongoing and no one can predict what the outcome will be. It's possible that Uber and/or Lyft drivers will end up having to be classified as employees in some states for some purposes, and not for others. For example, they may have to be classified as employees in California for purposes of California's labor laws, but not for IRS purposes (this has already happened to FedEx drivers). It will take years for all this to shake out. In the meantime, you should assume you are what Uber and Lyft adamantly say you are: an independent contractor.

Beware the Arbitration Clause

Hiring platform agreements often contain an "arbitration clause." This is a provision that says that any disputes with the company must be resolved through private mandatory arbitration, meaning you can't take the dispute to court. Moreover, you are not allowed to bring or join any class action suit against the company. Since suing a hiring platform for worker misclassification is difficult and expensive, the only way it usually can be done is via a class action suit where the claims of an entire class of claimants are joined—for example, a class action lawsuit has been brought against Uber on behalf of all Uber drivers in California claiming they should have been classified as Uber employees, not independent contractors (see http://uberlawsuit.com).

The legal validity of such arbitration clauses has been upheld by the United States Supreme Court, so they are here to stay. Usually, you are given the opportunity to opt out of such an arbitration clause when you agree to the contract with the hiring platform—this means the clause won't apply to you. If you want to preserve your right to challenge your classification as an independent contractor in court, you should opt out. To do so, you must notify the platform of your decision to opt out within a specified time— within 30 days after you sign the agreement is typical.

Your Taxes

Unfortunately, most hiring platforms provide little or no information about, or help with, the taxes gig workers must pay. Many gig workers are woefully ignorant about taxes. One recent survey of gig workers found that:

- one-third did not know they were required to file quarterly estimated payments with the IRS
- 36% did not understand what kind of records they needed to keep for tax purposes
- 43% did not know how much tax they would owe on their gig income or set aside any money to pay such taxes, and
- almost half did not know about the deductions they could claim to reduce the tax they had to pay on their gig income. (Source: *Shortchanged: The Tax Compliance Challenges of Small Business Operators Driving the On-Demand Platform Economy,* Kogod Tax Policy Center, Washington, DC (2016).)

Such ignorance can be very costly—every dollar in deductions you fail to claim to could cost you over 40 cents in extra taxes. Commonly overlooked deductions include mileage and other local travel expenses, and the home office deduction for gig workers who work at home. It's important to understand that when you perform gig work as an independent contractor you're running a business and must act accordingly. For tax purposes, it makes no difference that you obtain work through an online hiring platform; you're treated the same as any other small business and are subject to the full array of taxes covered in Chapter 8, including federal and state income taxes, self-employment taxes (Social Security and Medicare taxes), and local taxes in some areas. An online hiring platform will not pay these taxes for you.

RESOURCE

IRS tax resource for gig workers. The IRS has created a Sharing Economy Tax Center webpage at: www.irs.gov/businesses/small-businesses-self-employed/sharing-economy-tax-center. It contains links to IRS publications and forms useful for gig workers.

Filing Your Taxes

If, like most gig workers, you're a sole proprietor (See Chapter 2), you report the income you earn on your own personal tax return, IRS Form 1040. To show whether you have a profit or loss from your sole proprietorship, you file IRS Schedule C, *Profit or Loss From Business,* with your return. On this form you list all your business income and deductible expenses. If your net earnings from self-employment are over $400, you must file a federal tax return with Schedule C and Schedule SE, *Self-Employment Tax.*

You'll also have to pay state income tax on your earnings and include them on your state income tax return. The only exception is if you live in one of the nine states without income taxes: Alaska, Florida, Nevada, New Hampshire, South Dakota, Tennessee, Texas, Washington, and Wyoming. If you provide services in more than one state, the income you earn in each state will usually be taxable in that state, as well as the state where you live (if it has income taxes). In most states, you will receive a state tax credit on your home state tax return for the amount of income taxes you paid to other states.

Tax Deductions

You only pay tax on the profit you have left after you subtract all your expenses from your business income. The more deductions you have, the less tax you'll pay. Virtually everything you spend on your business is deductible. The deductions you have depend on the type of work you do. For example, an Uber driver will have substantial mileage deductions, but likely few or no office expenses; while a graphic artist who works at home will likely qualify for a home office deduction. You might also qualify for the new pass-through tax deduction established by the Tax Cuts and Jobs Act; if so, starting in 2018, you might be able to deduct from your income tax up to 20% of your net gig income. Tax deductions are covered in detail in Chapter 9. Also, see Chapter 4, which discusses tax deductions available for home offices (as well as outside offices).

Tax Deductions for Uber Drivers

Uber drivers are the most numerous gig workers. Tax deductions for an Uber driver would typically include:

- car expenses—these can be deducted using the standard mileage rate (54.5 cents per mile during 2018), or by deducting actual expenses (gas, repairs, depreciation, insurance, registration, car lease expenses, etc.)
- the cost of a smartphone (100% deductible if used just for business, otherwise the business use percentage is deductible), or the cost of an Uber-provided mobile device subscription
- water, candies, gum and other items provided to passengers (but you can't deduct food you eat while you drive)
- Uber fee
- other fees, such as Uber fuel card fees, airport fees, split fare fees, safe rides fees, city fees, and black car fund fees (fees to fund workers' compensation coverage for drivers in New York state)
- parking and tolls, and
- interest on a car loan (if the car is used for both personal and business use, the business use percentage is deductible on Schedule C).

Paying Estimated Taxes

When you work through an online hiring platform as an independent contractor ordinarily no taxes will be withheld from your pay by the platform or your clients. Be aware, however, that when you register with an online hiring platform, you must provide a completed IRS W-9, *Request for Taxpayer Identification Number and Certification*. This verifies your identity and address for tax purposes. If you don't complete a W-9, the company is required to withhold 24% of your income and pay it to the IRS. This is called backup withholding.

As a self-employed gig worker, you have to pay all your taxes yourself. Self-employed people are not allowed to wait until April 15 to pay all the income and self-employment (Social Security and Medicare) taxes they owe for the prior year. Instead, they are required to prepay their taxes by making estimated tax payments to the IRS during the year. You must pay estimated taxes if you expect to owe at least $1,000 in federal tax for the year from your gig business. You'll probably need to earn a profit of at least $5,000 or $6,000 from your business to owe this much tax. The IRS imposes modest interest penalties if you don't pay enough estimated tax. Fortunately, you'll avoid having to pay any penalties if you pay at least 90% of your total tax due for the year, or as least as much as you paid the prior year.

Estimated tax must ordinarily be paid in four installments: April 15, June 15, September 15, and January 15 (of the following year). However, you don't have to start making payments until you actually earn income. If you don't receive any income by March 31, you can skip the April 15 payment. In this event, you'd ordinarily make three payments for the year starting on June 15. If you don't receive any income by May 31, you can skip the June 15 payment as well, and so on.

If you don't pay enough estimated tax, or you don't pay any, you could have a huge tax bill due on April 15. It's wise to save some money from your earnings to pay your taxes. See Chapter 11 for a detailed discussion of paying estimated taxes.

Tax Reporting by Hiring Platforms

All independent contractors, including gig workers, may have the amount of payments they receive during the year reported (by the hiring platform) to the IRS and state tax departments. The IRS uses this information to double-check that you report all your income on your tax return. These reporting rules are covered in detail in Chapter 9. There are two main IRS forms used for this purpose: Form 1099-MISC, *Miscellaneous Income*, which is used for check and cash payments, and Form 1099-K, *Payment Card and Third Party Network Transactions*, which is used for electronic and credit card payments.

Ordinarily, gig workers are paid electronically via the hiring platform, which processes the payments. Payment services like PayPal are typically used, or payment may be made directly to your bank account. Since you are paid electronically, neither your clients nor the hiring platform are required to file a 1099-MISC form reporting your payments to the IRS.

However, some hiring platforms will file a 1099-MISC if you are paid more than $600 during the year, even though it is not required.

The electronic payments you receive have to be reported to the IRS by the payment processor (such as PayPal) or hiring platform on IRS Form 1099-K if you are paid over $20,000 and have more than 200 transactions during the calendar year. Copies of the 1099-K form are sent to the IRS, you, and your state tax department. The deadline for filing is January 31 of the year following the year the payments were made. If you are paid less than $20,000 or have fewer than 200 transactions, a 1099-K need not be filed (but some platforms file one anyway).

Many gig workers don't earn enough or have enough transactions that require that a 1099-K be filed. A recent survey found that 60% of gig workers did not receive a Form 1099-K (or Form 1099-MISC) from their platform or payment processor. However, whether or not the IRS receives a 1099-K or any other form reporting your income to the IRS, you're supposed to report all of your income in your annual tax return. Thus, you should keep careful track of how much you're paid throughout the year.

If you are issued a 1099-K, it will list the total (gross) amount of money processed by the platform or payment processor for you during the year, not the net amount you actually received. For example, there will be no deductions for the platform's fees, processing fees, or refunds. You must list the total amount shown on the 1099-K as business income on Schedule C and then deduct platform fees and other expenses to arrive at your net taxable business income.

When you sign up with a hiring platform, pay special attention to its policies on tax reporting. These may be set forth in the platform's terms and condition, an FAQ, or a help page.

The Importance of Good Records

It's very important for you to keep track of all the deductible expenses you incur throughout the year, since they will decrease the amount of profit you'll have to pay tax on. The online platforms you work with will usually have a record of your payments; but they will likely not otherwise help you with record keeping. There are many accounting and tax preparation apps and software you can use to keep track of your expenses and even prepare your tax return yourself. See Chapter 14 for a detailed discussion of record keeping.

Your Insurance

If, as is usually the case, you are classified as an independent contractor, you will not be provided with health insurance coverage by the hiring platform, nor will you be covered by unemployment insurance or workers' compensation. Many hiring platforms provide their clients with a certain amount of liability insurance coverage in the event of wrongdoing or damages caused by gig workers. For example, TaskRabbit provides up to $1 million in liability insurance coverage to clients to cover property damage, bodily injuries, or thefts caused by "Taskers" while performing tasks for clients (see www.taskrabbit.com/guarantee). However, such coverage typically doesn't cover losses or injuries suffered by the gig workers themselves; also, it doesn't prevent a client from suing you in addition to the hiring platform. Thus, you may wish to obtain your own liability insurance coverage.

If you're a gig worker who drives for Uber or Lyft or other ridesharing company, you need to pay special attention to your auto insurance coverage. Your personal auto insurance policy likely does not provide coverage for ridesharing—you should check with your insurer to make sure. Both Uber and Lyft provide auto insurance coverage with up to $1 million in liability protection, but this insurance is only in effect when you're signed in to the app. Full coverage is provided when you are carrying passengers or on your way to a fare. Limited liability-only coverage is provided if you are waiting for a fare. You should supplement this coverage with insurance to cover you when you're not signed into the app or waiting for a fare. Several insurers offer low-cost ridesharing insurance to supplement the coverage provided by Uber and Lyft. If you can't obtain such coverage, you may need to obtain more expensive commercial auto insurance.

See Chapter 6 for a detailed discussion of insurance.

Other Legal Requirements for Gig Workers

Depending on the type of services you provide and where you provide them, there may be other legal requirements you need to comply with. For example:

- in some states, you may need to collect sales taxes from your clients or customers—for example, Uber drivers are required to collect sales taxes in nine states (see Chapter 8 for more information on sales taxes)
- you may need a business license from your city or county (see Chapter 5 for a detailed discussion of business licenses and permits)
- if you want to use a company name instead of your own name, you'll need to comply with fictitious business name rules; you may even want to trademark your name (see Chapter 3 for legal requirements for business names)
- you'll need an employer identification number (EIN) from the IRS if you form a business entity such as an LLC or corporation, or have employees (see Chapter 5), and
- if you hire other people to help you perform your services, you'll need to determine whether they should be classified as your employees or independent contractors and comply with the applicable legal requirements (see Chapter 13).

Where to Find Gigs

There are hundreds of online hiring platforms through which clients contract for all types of services. You can find a list of the top 100 platforms at https://hurdlr.com/blog/on-demand/on-demand-economy-gigs. Research online or talk to others who offer services like yours to find out which platforms they use. You are free to work for more than one hiring platform at a time. If one doesn't work out, try another.

The competition for new clients on hiring platforms can be fierce. In addition to pricing your services competitively, creating a compelling profile on the platform can help you get business. The best profiles are complete, well-written, error-free, and feature a professional, friendly looking photo. Depending on the type of services you provide, you may need to put together a portfolio or samples of your work that potential clients can review. For example, a graphic artist who sells her services through Upwork should have a portfolio of past work available at her profile page. Some platforms also offer skills testing—for example, Web, mobile, and software developers can take standardized tests establishing their technical proficiency in programming languages.

RESOURCE

For more guidance on how to succeed in the gig economy, refer to *The Gig Economy: The Complete Guide to Getting Better Work, Taking More Time Off, and Financing the Life You Want,* by Diane Mulcahy (AMACOM).

Copyrights, Patents, and Trade Secrets

S elf-employed people are often hired to create or contribute to the creation of copyrights, patents, or trade secrets by producing writings, photos, graphics, music, software, designs, or inventions. This chapter explains the legalities surrounding these creative works: who owns them and how those who create them can protect their rights.

RESOURCE

Gig Workers: If you're a gig worker who obtains work through online hiring platforms, ownership of any intellectual property you create on a client's behalf will be governed by the contract you enter into with the hiring platform. Typically, you'll be required to transfer all your rights to the client. See Chapter 16 for a detailed discussion.

Intellectual Property

Products of the human intellect that have economic value—that is, ideas or creations that are worth money—are tagged with the lofty name of "intellectual property." This includes works of which you are the author, such as writings, computer software, films, music, and inventions, as well as techniques, processes, or other information not generally known.

A body of federal and state law creates intellectual property ownership rights similar to those for tangible personal property, such as automobiles. Intellectual property may be owned, bought, and sold just like other property.

There are four separate bodies of law that protect intellectual property: copyrights and patents (which are governed solely by federal law) and trademarks and trade secrets (which are protected under both state and federal laws).

Copyrights

Federal copyright law (17 U.S.C. §§ 101 and following) protects all original works of authorship. A work of authorship is any work created by a person that other people can understand or perceive, either by themselves or with the help of a machine such as a computer or television. Authorship can include all kinds of written works, plays, music, artwork, graphics, photos, films and videos, computer software, architectural blueprints and designs, choreography, and pantomimes.

The owner of a copyright has a bundle of rights that enable him or her to control how the work may be used. These include the exclusive right to copy and distribute the protected work, to create works derived from it (updated editions of a book, for example), and to display and perform the work. These rights come into existence automatically the moment a work is created. The owner need not take any additional steps or file legal documents to secure a copyright.

Copyright owners typically profit from their works by selling or licensing all or some of these rights to others, such as publishers. (See "Copyright Ownership," below, for more on establishing and transferring copyrights.)

 RESOURCE
Want a detailed discussion of copyrights and copyright law?
See *The Copyright Handbook: What Every Writer Needs to Know,* by Thomas J. Tuytschaevers and Stephen Fishman (Nolo).

Patents

Federal patent law (35 U.S.C. §§ 100 and following) protects inventions that are new, useful, and not obvious to someone versed in the relevant technology. To obtain a patent, an inventor must file an application with the U.S. Patent and Trademark Office (USPTO) in Washington, DC, and pay a fee. If the USPTO determines that the invention is sufficiently new, useful, and unobvious, it will issue the inventor a patent.

A patent gives an inventor a monopoly on the use and commercial exploitation of the invention. A patent lasts 20 years from the application date. Anyone who wants to use or sell a patented invention during a patent's term must obtain the patent owner's permission. A patent may protect articles (for example, machines, chemical manufactures, and biological creations) and processes (methods of accomplishing things).

RESOURCE

Need more information on patents? For a detailed discussion of patents and patent law, see *Patent It Yourself,* by Thomas J. Tuytschaevers and David Pressman (Nolo).

Trade Secrets

A trade secret is information that other people do not generally know and that provides its owner with a competitive advantage in the marketplace. The information can be an idea, a writing, formula, process or procedure, technical design, customer list, marketing plan, or any other secret that gives the owner an economic advantage.

To establish a trade secret, you must take reasonable steps to keep the information or know-how a secret. For example, you should not publish it or otherwise make it freely available to the public. The laws of most states will protect the owner from disclosures of the secret by:

- the owner's employees
- people who agree not to disclose it, such as independent contractors the owner hires
- industrial spies, and
- competitors who wrongfully acquire the information.

In the course of your work, you may be exposed to your client's most valuable trade secrets, including highly confidential marketing plans, new products under development, manufacturing techniques, or customer lists. Understandably, your client doesn't want you blabbing its trade secrets to others, particularly its competitors.

To make sure you'll keep such information confidential, many clients will ask you to sign a nondisclosure agreement stating that you may not reveal the client's trade secrets to others without permission. A nondisclosure provision can be included in a client agreement or can be a separate document. Carefully review any nondisclosure provision a client asks you to sign.

On the other hand, you may have your own trade secrets you don't want others you deal with to disclose. In this event, you should ask them to sign your own nondisclosure agreement. (See "Using Nondisclosure Agreements," below, for a detailed discussion of nondisclosure agreements and a sample form.)

Types of Intellectual Property

	What Is Protected?	Examples	Length of Protection
Trade Secret	Formula, method, device, machine, compilation of facts, or any information that is confidential and gives a business an advantage	Coca-Cola formula; special method for assembling a patented invention; new invention for which a patent application has not been filed	As long as information remains confidential and functions as a trade secret
Utility Patent	Machines, compositions, plants, processes, or articles of manufacture	Cellular telephone; the drug known as Vicodin; a hybrid daffodil; the Amazon one-click process; a rake	17 years from date of issue for patents filed before or on June 17, 1995; 20 years from date of filing for patent applications filed after June 17, 1995
Copyright	Books, photos, music, recordings, fine art, graphics, videos, film, architecture, or computer programs	*The Firm* (book and movie); Andy Warhol prints; *Roy Orbison's Greatest Hits* (music recording, compact disc, artwork, and video); architectural plans for design of apartment building; Macromedia *Dreamweaver* program	Life of the author plus 70 years for works created by a single author; 120 years from date of creation or 95 years from first publication for other works, such as works made for hire
Trademark	Word, symbol, logo, design, slogan, trade dress, or product configuration	*Nike* name and distinctive swoosh logo; "What Do You Want To Do Today" slogan; Mr. Clean character; Absolut vodka bottle	As long as business continuously uses the trademark in connection with goods, but federal registrations must be renewed every ten years

Trademarks

State and federal trademark laws protect the right to exclusively use a name, logo, or another device that identifies and distinguishes a product or service. In addition to names and logos, trademark law can be used to protect product packaging designs and the shape or design of a product, like a Coca-Cola bottle. If a competitor uses a protected trademark, the trademark holder can go to court to stop the use and obtain money damages.

 RESOURCE
Want additional information on trademarks? See *Trademark: Legal Care for Your Business & Product Name,* by Stephen Fishman (Nolo).

Copyright Ownership

Any work of authorship you produce for a client is automatically protected by a copyright the moment it is created. At that same moment, somebody becomes the owner of the copyright. Who owns the copyright in a work you create is important because the owner alone has the right to copy, distribute, or otherwise commercially exploit (earn money from) the work. Unfortunately, self-employed people and hiring firms can get into disputes about who owns the copyright in the work the self-employed person creates.

To avoid disputes over ownership, you need to understand some of the basics of copyright law, which this section provides.

Works Created by Independent Contractors

Self-employed workers ordinarily qualify as independent contractors for copyright purposes. The fundamental rule is that as an independent contractor, you own the copyright in works of authorship you create for a client unless you sign a document transferring those rights to the client. Without your signature on such a document, the client—the person who paid you to create the work—may have no copyright rights at all or, at most, may share copyright ownership with you.

As the owner of the copyright, you have the right to resell your work to others or to copy, distribute, and create new works based on the work.

> EXAMPLE: Tom hires Jane, an independent contractor app developer to create an app. Tom and Jane have an oral work agreement. Jane creates the app. Because Jane never signed an agreement transferring any of them to Tom, Jane still owns all the copyright rights in the app. Jane has the exclusive right to sell the app to others or permit them to use it. Even though Tom paid Jane to create the app, he doesn't own it and can't sell or license it to others.

You Don't Need a C in a Circle to Have a Copyright

Many self-employed people don't know that a work need not contain a copyright notice—the familiar © symbol followed by the publication date and copyright owner's name—to be protected by copyright laws. Likewise, you are not required to register your copyright.

Giving others notice of the copyright and registering it are both optional. However, both are highly desirable if the work is published. They enable the copyright owner to receive the maximum money damages possible if someone copies and uses the work without permission and the owner files and wins a copyright infringement suit.

You can register your copyright by filling out a short registration form online at the U.S. Copyright Office website (www.copyright.gov). You must also provide the Copyright Office one or two copies of the work and pay a registration fee.

For more information on copyrights, see *The Copyright Handbook: What Every Writer Needs to Know*, by Stephen Fishman (Nolo).

In the real world, copyrights are rarely left to fate. Independent contractors are normally asked to sign written agreements transferring all or some of their copyright rights to the clients who hire them. But if you find yourself working with an inexperienced client who doesn't understand the ownership rules, be sure to take the initiative and set forth in writing who will own the copyright in your work.

Copyright transfers can take one of three forms, which we'll discuss further below. You can:
- transfer some of your rights
- transfer all of your rights, or
- sign a work-for-hire agreement, which transfers all of your copyright rights and then some.

Which rights you transfer to clients and which you keep for yourself is a matter for negotiation. If you give up your copyright, you may be able to negotiate a higher fee for your services, but you may lose future income on the copyright. (See "Dividing Up Your Copyright Bundle," below.)

After you and the client reach an agreement on copyright ownership, one of you must write a copyright transfer agreement, and you both must sign it to make it legally valid. You may include the understanding as a clause in a client agreement or negotiate it as a separate freestanding agreement.

!   CAUTION
Beware of conflicting copyright transfers. If you're performing similar work for two or more clients simultaneously and agree to assign the intellectual property rights in your work to both clients, you could end up transferring the same rights twice. Before you agree to sell a client anything you create, review your existing agreements to make sure you haven't already sold it.

Transferring Some Rights

You are not legally required to give a client all your copyright rights. You can transfer some rights and retain others. When you do this, you may sell the rights you retain to people other than the client.

As discussed above, a copyright is really a bundle of rights, including the exclusive rights to copy, distribute, perform, and display a work and create derivative works (such as adaptations or new editions) from a work. Each of these rights can be transferred together or separately. They can also be divided and subdivided by media, geography, time, market segment, or any other way you and a client can think up. You can often make more money by dividing up your copyright rights and selling them piecemeal to several different purchasers than you could selling them all to a single client.

Exactly how you can most profitably divide your copyright rights depends on the nature of the work and the market for it. For example, the copyright in computer software is often divided by geography or type of computer system.

> **EXAMPLE:** Bill, a famous freelance video game designer, is hired by Fun & Sun Gameware to create a new video game. He signs an agreement transferring to Gameware the right to distribute the game for the Nintendo video game system in the United States only. Bill retains all his other copyright rights. He sells the right to publish the game in Japan to Nippon Games and sells the right to create a film based on the game to Repulsive Pictures.

Photographer Wins Pyrrhic Victory Against Magazine

Resolving copyright ownership disputes can take a great deal of time, angst, and money if you have to go to court. Even if you eventually win your case, you may feel like a loser. Consider the case of Marco, a professional photographer who took photographs for several issues of *Accent Magazine*, a trade journal for the jewelry industry, over a six-month period. Marco had an oral agreement with the magazine and was paid a fee of about $150 per photograph. *Accent*, claiming it owned the copyright in the photos, wanted to reuse them without paying Marco an additional fee. Marco claimed that he owned the photos and that *Accent* had to pay him for permission to use them again. Marco and the magazine were never able to resolve the issue of who owned the photos.

When the magazine tried to use the photos without Marco's permission, he asked a court to block publication. The court refused, and Marco filed an appeal with the federal appeals court in Philadelphia. After about two years, Marco won his appeal. But he probably ended up spending far more on attorneys' fees than the photos were worth. (*Marco v. Accent Publishing Co., Inc.*, 969 F.2d 1547 (3d Cir. 1992).)

The copyright in a freelance article may be divided by priority of publication. For example, a writer may grant a website the right to publish an article for the first time and then retain the rights to sell it to others later. Similarly, graphic artists often grant a client the right to use an image or design only in a certain publishing category and keep the right to resell their work for use in other categories.

EXAMPLE: Sally, a self-employed graphic designer, creates and sells 25 spot illustrations for use in a school textbook. She grants the textbook publisher the exclusive right to use the images in textbooks but retains the right to sell them to others to use for different purposes (for example, in online articles).

When you divide up your copyright rights this way, the transfer is often called a "license." Licenses fall into two broad categories: exclusive and nonexclusive.

Exclusive Licenses

When a copyright owner grants someone an exclusive license, he or she gives that person, called the "licensee," the exclusive right to one or more, but not all, of the copyright rights. An exclusive license is a transfer of copyright ownership. It must be in writing to be valid.

EXAMPLE: Jane writes an article on economics and grants *The Economist's Journal* the exclusive right to publish it for the first time in the United States and Canada. Jane has granted the *Journal* an exclusive license. Only the *Journal* may publish the article for the first time in the United States and Canada; the magazine owns this right. But Jane retains all her other copyright rights. This means that she has the right to republish her article after it appears in the *Journal* and to include it in a book. She also retains the right to create derivative works from it, such as expanding it into a book-length work.

Nonexclusive Licenses

In contrast, a nonexclusive license gives a person the right to exercise one or more of a copyright owner's rights but does not prevent the copyright owner from giving other people permission to exercise the same right or rights at the same time. A nonexclusive license is the most limited form of copyright transfer you can grant to a client.

As with exclusive licenses, nonexclusive licenses may be limited as to time, geography, media, or in any other way. They can be granted orally or in writing. The much better practice, however, is to put it in writing; this can avoid possible misunderstandings.

> **EXAMPLE:** Lawrence, a freelance computer programmer, agrees to create an accounting program for AcmePool, a swimming pool company. Lawrence thinks that other swimming pool companies might be interested in buying the program as well, so he grants AcmePool only a nonexclusive right to use the program. This means he can sell it to others, not just AcmePool. AcmePool has no right to sell the program. AcmePool agreed to the deal because Lawrence charged much less than he would have charged had AcmePool acquired ownership of the program.

Dividing Up Your Copyright Bundle

It's often wise to keep as many rights for yourself as possible because you may be able to sell them to others and make additional money from your work.

However, you may not be able to keep many copyright rights. Many clients want to own all of the copyright rights in works they pay self-employed people to create. Other clients will pay you substantially less for some rights than they would for all your rights. If the market for your work is limited, it may make more economic sense to sell all your rights and get as much money as possible from the client instead of taking less and then trying to sell your work to others.

The normal practices in your particular field will usually have a big impact on the negotiations. These traditions and the terminology used to describe various types of copyright transfers vary widely. If you're not familiar with them, ask others in your field or contact professional organizations or trade groups for information.

Transferring All Rights

When people transfer all the copyright rights they own in a work of authorship, the transaction is called an "assignment" or an "all rights transfer." When such a transaction is completed, the original copyright owner no longer has any ownership rights at all. The new owner—the "assignee"—has all the copyright rights the transferor formerly held. The new owner is then free to sell licenses or to assign the copyright to someone else.

An assignment can be made either before or after a work is created, but it must be in writing to be valid. An assignment can be a separate document or it can be included in a client agreement.

> EXAMPLE: Tom hires Jane, a self-employed programmer, to create a computer program. Before Jane starts work, Tom has her sign an independent contractor agreement providing, among other things, that she transfers all her copyright rights in the program to Tom. Jane completes her work and delivers the program, and Tom pays her. Tom owns all the copyright rights in the program.

Works Made for Hire

When employees create works of authorship as part of their jobs, their employers automatically own all the copyright rights in the work. Works created on the job are called "works made for hire." Certain types of works created by independent contractors can also qualify as works made for hire. When a work is made for hire, the person who ordered or commissioned it and paid for it is considered to be the author for copyright purposes, not the person who created it. This commissioning party—not the actual creator—automatically owns all the copyright rights.

Types of Works Made for Hire

Nine categories of works created by independent contractors can be works made for hire:

- a contribution to a collective work (for example, a work created by more than one author, such as a newspaper magazine, or an anthology or encyclopedia)
- a part of an audiovisual work (for example, a motion picture screenplay)

Assignments Can Be Revoked ... Eventually

There are many sad stories about authors and artists who were paid a pittance when they were young or unknown, only to have their work become extremely valuable later in their lives or after their deaths. For example, the creators of *Superman* sold all their copyright rights in *Superman* to a comic book company for a mere $10,000 when they were young. They saw the company earn millions from their creation, but they shared in none of this money.

To protect copyright owners and their families from unfair exploitation, the Copyright Act gives authors or their heirs the right to get back full copyright rights 35 years after they were assigned. Authors don't have to pay anything to reclaim their rights: They simply need to file the appropriate documentation with the Copyright Office and the copyright owner to whom they assigned their rights.

> EXAMPLE: Art, a teenage video game enthusiast, is hired as an independent contractor in 1984 to create a new computer arcade game by Fun & Sun Gameware. He assigns all his copyright rights in the game to Fun & Sun Gameware for $1,500. The game becomes a best seller and earns Fun & Sun Gameware millions. Art is entitled to none of this money, but he or his heirs can terminate the transfer of copyright rights to Fun & Sun Gameware in the year 2019 and get back all rights in the game without paying Fun & Sun Gameware anything.

This termination right may be exercised only by individual authors or their heirs, and only as to copyright transfers after 1977. However, the creator of a work made for hire has no such termination rights.

One of the first artists to successfully exercise his copyright termination rights was the lyricist and performer Victor Willis. He reclaimed his share of the copyright to 33 songs he cowrote when he was lead singer for the 1970s disco group Village People, including the hits "Y.M.C.A." and "In the Navy." To do so, he was forced to file suit against the companies that controlled the Village People song catalog; overcoming—among other things—the specious claim that he was an employee of the Village People's record company, not an independent contractor.

- a translation
- supplementary works (for example, forewords, afterwords, supplemental pictorial illustrations, maps, charts, editorial notes, bibliographies, appendixes, and indexes)
- a compilation (for example, an electronic database)
- an instructional text
- a test
- answer material for a test, and
- an atlas.

Written Agreement Requirement

It's not enough that your work falls into one of these categories. You and the client must sign a written agreement stating that the work you create shall be a work made for hire. The agreement must be signed before you begin work to be effective. The client cannot wait until after your work is completed and delivered and then decide that it should be a work made for hire.

Think of a work-for-hire agreement as the hydrogen bomb of copyright transfers: When you sign such an agreement, you not only give up all your ownership rights in the work until the end of time, you're not even considered the work's author. You won't be legally entitled to any credit for your work, such as having your name attached if the work is published, unless your agreement with the client requires it.

> **EXAMPLE:** The editor of *The Egoist Magazine* asks Gloria, a freelance writer, if she would be interested in writing an article for the magazine on nightlife in Palm Beach. Gloria agrees, and the editor sends her a letter agreement setting forth such terms as compensation, article length, and due date. The letter also specifies that the article "shall be a work made for hire."
>
> Gloria signs the agreement, writes the article, and is paid by the magazine. Because the article qualifies as a work made for hire, the magazine is the initial owner of all the copyright rights in the article. The magazine is free to sell reprint rights in the article, film and TV rights, translation rights, and any other rights anyone wants to buy. Gloria is not entitled to license or sell any rights in the article because she doesn't own any.

Many writer and artist organizations strongly advise their members to refuse to sign work-for-hire agreements. However, an increasing number of clients insist on such agreements. In some cases, signing a work-for-hire agreement is a take-it-or-leave-it proposition: If you don't agree to sign, the client will find someone else who will. For example, *The New York Times* requires freelance contributors to sign work-for-hire agreements; the paper will simply refuse to publish a freelance article unless the author signs on the dotted line.

On the other hand, you can often get a client to agree to something less than a work-for-hire agreement if you ask. If the client refuses, you can still sign the work-for-hire agreement, but you lose nothing by asking.

Sharing Ownership With Clients

If a client does not obtain a copyright transfer from you, you will own the work you create for the client. However, a client who qualifies as a coauthor might be considered a joint owner of the work along with you. For this to occur, the client must actually help you create the work. Giving suggestions or supervision is not enough.

A client who qualifies as a coauthor will jointly share copyright ownership in the work with you. As coauthors, you're each entitled to use or let other people use the work without obtaining approval of the other coauthor. But any profits you make must be shared with the other coauthors. This could cause problems. For example, if coauthors sold the same work to competing publishers, the value of the work could be diluted. It's usually in coauthors' interests to work together to avoid this.

> EXAMPLE: Marlon, a legendary actor, hires Tom, a freelance writer, to ghostwrite his autobiography. Tom is an independent contractor, not Marlon's employee. Marlon fails to have Tom sign a written agreement transferring to Marlon his copyright rights in the work. However, Marlon worked closely with Tom in writing the autobiography, contributing not only ideas but also writing portions of the book.
>
> As a result, Marlon and Tom would probably be considered coauthors and joint owners of the autobiography. Both would have the right to sell the autobiography to a publisher, serialize it in magazines, sell it to movie producers, or otherwise commercially exploit the work. However, Marlon and Tom would have to share any profits earned.

If a client doesn't qualify as a coauthor, at most it will have a non-exclusive right to use the work. But it wouldn't be allowed to sell or license any copyright rights in the work because it wouldn't own any. The independent contractor would own all the rights and be able to sell or license them without the client's permission, and without sharing the profits with the client.

> **EXAMPLE:** Mark pays Sally, a freelance photographer, to take some pictures of toxic waste dumps to supplement his treatise on toxic waste management. Sally didn't sign an agreement transferring her copyright rights in the photos to Mark. Mark does not qualify as a coauthor of the photos because he didn't help take them. As a result, Sally owns the copyright in the photos. Mark has a nonexclusive license to use the photos in his treatise, but this doesn't prevent Sally from selling the photos to others or otherwise exploiting her copyright rights.

Patent Ownership

Patent rights initially belong to the person who develops an invention. However, patent rights can be assigned—that is, transferred—to others just as copyrights can. Firms that hire independent contractors to help create new technology or anything else that might qualify for a patent normally have the independent contractors assign to them in advance all patent rights in the work. Such an assignment may be included in an independent contractor agreement or in a separate document.

If you have no signed assignment, it's far from clear who will own inventions you develop. Unlike copyrights, where silence indicates independent contractor ownership, there is no such presumption in the world of patents. The law regarding ownership of inventions by employees is very clear: An employer owns any inventions an employee was hired to create. But courts have just begun to address who owns inventions made by independent contractors in the absence of a written ownership agreement.

You can assert ownership over your invention or other work, but be prepared for a costly legal dispute if you do. The client could claim you had a duty to assign your patent rights to it even though there was no written assignment agreement. You would probably have a good chance of winning such a case, but it would not be a sure thing. It's best to avoid such disputes in advance by clearly defining in writing who will own the work.

Trade Secret Ownership

Trade secret ownership rules are similar to those for patents. You are the initial owner of any trade secrets you develop while working for a client. But ownership rights in trade secrets can be assigned to others just as patents can be. Hiring firms typically require independent contractors to sign written agreements assigning their trade secret ownership rights to the client in advance.

In the absence of such an agreement, you probably own your trade secrets and can sell them to others, including the client's competitors. However, if you used the client's resources to develop the trade secret information, the client might have a nonexclusive license to use it without your permission. This is called a "shop right."

Using Nondisclosure Agreements

It is relatively simple to protect tangible valuables, like jewelry, computers, and luxury cars that you can lock up in vaults, drawers, or garages. But it is not so easy to protect knowledge and ideas, even though such intellectual property may be the key to building your creative dream. Many self-employed entrepreneurs are fearful of sharing their intellectual property with others, which they almost always have to do to gain financial backing on other essential deals or partnerships. Fortunately, the informed and consistent use of well-drafted nondisclosure agreements can help you protect these assets if you have to disclose them to potential backers, partners, clients, and others.

What Is a Nondisclosure Agreement?

Nondisclosure agreements—also known as NDAs or confidentiality agreements—are frequently used in the business world before confidential information is disclosed. Nondisclosure agreements have just one purpose: to protect your trade secrets. Trade secrets include any information that is not generally known that has economic value or gives you a competitive edge. It includes—but is not limited to—such things as:

- unpublished computer code
- product development (and other related) agreements
- business plans
- financial projections
- marketing plans
- sales data
- cost and pricing information
- customer lists, and
- patent pending applications.

By using a nondisclosure agreement, you agree to share such information only after the other party agrees, in writing, to keep the information secret.

Using a nondisclosure agreement accomplishes several basic purposes:

- It conclusively establishes that the person to whom you disclose the information has a legal duty not to disclose your trade secrets without your permission.
- It makes clear to the person who receives a trade secret that it must be kept in confidence. This will impress upon him or her that you are serious about maintaining your trade secrets.
- If you ever file a lawsuit, a signed nondisclosure agreement will help you prove that you treated the information you disclosed as a trade secret and that the person to whom you disclosed the information knew that he or she should keep it confidential.

When to Use a Nondisclosure Agreement

Before you give any person access to information that gives you a competitive advantage, you should have him or her sign a nondisclosure agreement. You may need to ask any or all of the following people to sign:

- clients and potential clients
- employees and potential employees
- consultants or independent contractors
- business partners and investors
- licensees or customers, and
- suppliers.

Nondisclosure Agreements Can Be a Touchy Issue

In high-tech industries, nondisclosure agreements are as common as relatives at weddings. However, many people refuse to sign them. Often, venture capitalists, securities analysts, and top consultants refuse to sign NDAs because they review lots of ideas, many of which are similar. They think that signing NDAs will make it impossible for them to do business and may expose them to the potential for expensive lawsuits. Instead, such people follow the honor system.

Refusal to sign nondisclosure agreements is also common in the publishing industry and in Hollywood, where editors and executives review large numbers of ideas for books and scripts that are often similar in content or focus. Occasionally, companies outside the United States, where business is sometimes less legalistic, may also balk at signing NDAs.

Possibly the best way to deal with this problem is to take the time to develop a relationship of trust with the people with whom you are considering working before telling them all your best ideas. This might involve dealing with lower-level information and ideas to see how they are treated before revealing your most important information.

However, some people and companies will never sign an NDA. In that event, you must decide whether to go ahead and disclose the information or walk away. If the person or company has an impeccable reputation for integrity, you may conclude that it is worthwhile to go ahead and make the disclosure anyway.

Keep in mind that you may be able to successfully sue such people for trade secret violations even if they haven't signed an NDA. You'll need to consult with a lawyer if you find yourself in this situation.

Clients

It will often be necessary for you to disclose your trade secrets to people and companies for whom you perform your services or sell your ideas. For example, a self-employed computer programmer may have to make trade secret computer code available to a client, or an inventor may have to disclose the idea for a new invention to a manufacturer. Always try to have the client sign a nondisclosure agreement before you disclose such information. (Some clients may refuse to do so; see "Nondisclosure Agreements Can Be a Touchy Issue," above.)

Employees

It is advisable to have all employees who may come into contact with your trade secrets sign nondisclosure agreements. Employees should sign such agreements before they begin work or on their very first day of work. If you have employees who have not signed nondisclosure agreements, you should ask them to do so before they are given access to any trade secrets.

If your business is a partnership, all partners should sign a partnership agreement containing a nondisclosure provision.

Consultants or Independent Contractors

The consultant you hire today may end up working for a competitor tomorrow. Never expose a consultant to trade secrets without having a signed nondisclosure agreement on file. It's best to include such an agreement within an overall consulting or independent contractor agreement that covers all aspects of the parties' relationship, including the services to be performed, who will own the consultant's or independent contractor's work product, and payment. Several consultant and independent contractor agreements are included in *Working With Independent Contractors*, by Stephen Fishman (Nolo).

Business Partners and Investors

Trade secrets must frequently be disclosed during negotiations with prospective business partners, investors, licensees, suppliers, or customers. It's advisable to have the other party sign a nondisclosure agreement before you disclose any trade secrets. This way, you will be protected if the negotiations do not result in a final agreement.

Other Means of Protecting Trade Secrets

Using nondisclosure agreements is the single most important thing you can do to protect your trade secrets. But it's not your only strategy. You don't have to turn your office into an armed camp to protect your trade secrets, but you must take reasonable precautions to keep them confidential.

Such precautions may include:

- marking documents containing trade secrets "Confidential"
- locking away trade secret materials after business hours
- maintaining computer security
- limiting the number of people who know about your confidential information, and
- destroying documents containing trade secrets as soon as the documents are no longer needed.

Drafting a Nondisclosure Agreement

This section describes a sample nondisclosure agreement that you can use with any outside individual or company to whom you grant access to your trade secrets.

 FORM ON NOLO.COM

You can download a copy of the full Nondisclosure Statement from this book's companion page on Nolo.com. For details on finding this and other forms on Nolo.com, which you can tailor to your own use, see "List of Forms Available on the Nolo Website" at the end of Appendix A of this book.

Introductory Paragraph

Fill in the date the agreement will take effect. This can be the date it is signed or a date in the future. Next, fill in the name you use for your business. You are referred to as the "Discloser" throughout the rest of the agreement. Finally, fill in the name of the individual or company you are granting access to your trade secrets, referred to as the "Recipient."

Suggested Language: Introduction

This is an agreement, effective _____ , between _____
_____ (the "Discloser") and _____
_____ (the "Recipient"), in which Discloser agrees to disclose, and
Recipient agrees to receive, certain trade secrets of Discloser on the following
terms and conditions: _____
_____ .

Trade Secrets

Select either alternative clause by checking the appropriate box. Here's how
to choose:

Alternative 1. It's best to specifically identify the trade secrets covered by
the agreement, so use this clause if you can individually list the material
you are providing. However, be careful that your description is not so
narrowly worded that it may leave out important information you wish
to have covered by the agreement. If you later discover that you want
to disclose confidential information not included in the agreement, you
and the other person or company can complete and sign an addendum
identifying the additional protected information. Alternatively, you could
complete a whole new NDA.

Suggested Language: Trade Secrets (Alternative 1)

Recipient understands and acknowledges that the following information
constitutes trade secrets belonging to Discloser: _____
_____ .

Alternative 2. Use this clause if it's not possible to specifically identify
the trade secrets you are providing. This clause is appropriate if the
information you will disclose does not exist when you sign the agreement,

if you're not sure what you will be disclosing, or if it's simply too much trouble to identify everything that you could disclose. This clause contains a general description of the types of information covered. It includes virtually everything that could be a trade secret.

Suggested Language: Trade Secrets (Alternative 2)

Recipient understands and acknowledges that Discloser's trade secrets consist of information and materials that are valuable and not generally known by Discloser's competitors. Discloser's trade secrets include:

(a) any and all information concerning Discloser's current, future, or proposed products, including, but not limited to, formulas, designs, devices, computer code, drawings, specifications, notebook entries, technical notes and graphs, computer printouts, technical memoranda and correspondence, product development agreements, and related agreements

(b) information and materials relating to Discloser's purchasing, accounting, and marketing, including, but not limited to, marketing plans, sales data, business methods, unpublished promotional material, cost and pricing information, and customer lists

(c) information of the type described above that Discloser obtained from another party and that Discloser treats as confidential, whether or not owned or developed by Discloser, and

(d) [other:] _____

_____ .

Purpose of Disclosure

The Purpose of Disclosure section of the Nondisclosure Agreement is in two parts. In the first part, you'll describe the reason for disclosing trade secrets. For example, this may be for you to perform consulting services for the recipient or to further the parties' business relationship.

Suggested Language: Purpose of Disclosure

Recipient shall make use of Discloser's trade secrets only for the purpose of:

_____

_____.

In consideration of Discloser's disclosure of its trade secrets to Recipient, Recipient agrees that it will treat Discloser's trade secrets with the same degree of care and safeguards that it takes with its own trade secrets, but in no event less than a reasonable degree of care. Recipient agrees that, without Discloser's prior written consent, Recipient will not:

(a) disclose Discloser's trade secrets to any third party

(b) make or permit to be made copies or other reproductions of Discloser's trade secrets, or

(c) make any commercial use of the trade secrets.

Recipient represents that it has, and agrees to maintain, an appropriate agreement with each of its employees and independent contractors who may have access to any of Discloser's trade secrets sufficient to enable Recipient to comply with all the terms of this Agreement.

Nondisclosure

The second part, covering nondisclosure, is the heart of the agreement. The Recipient promises to treat the Discloser's trade secrets with a reasonable degree of care and not to disclose them to third parties without the Discloser's consent. Recipient also promises not to make commercial use of the information without Discloser's permission.

Finally, the Recipient may not disclose the information to its employees or consultants unless they have signed confidentiality agreements protecting the trade secret rights of third parties, such as the Discloser. If an employee or a consultant has signed such an agreement, it's not necessary for him or her to sign a separate agreement promising to keep the Discloser's information confidential.

If the Recipient breaks these promises, the Discloser can sue in court to obtain monetary damages and possibly a court order to prevent the Recipient from using the information.

Return of Materials

In this clause, the Recipient promises to return original materials you've provided, as well as copies, notes, and documents pertaining to the trade secrets. This agreement gives Recipient 30 days to return the materials, but you can change this time period if you wish.

Suggested Language: Return of Materials

Upon Discloser's request, Recipient shall promptly (within 30 days) return all original materials provided by Discloser and any copies, notes, or other documents in Recipient's possession pertaining to Discloser's trade secrets.

Exclusions

This provision describes all the types of information that are not covered by the agreement. These exclusions are based on court decisions and state trade secret laws that say these types of information do not qualify for trade secret protection.

Suggested Language: Exclusions

This agreement does not apply to any information that:

(a) was in Recipient's possession or was known to Recipient, without an obligation to keep it confidential, before such information was disclosed to Recipient by Discloser

(b) is or becomes public knowledge through a source other than Recipient and through no fault of Recipient

(c) is or becomes lawfully available to Recipient from a source other than Discloser, or

(d) is disclosed by Recipient with Discloser's prior written approval.

Term of Agreement

There are two alternative provisions dealing with the agreement's "term," which is the length of time the agreement remains in effect. Select the clause that best suits your needs by checking the appropriate box.

Alternative 1. This provision has no definite time limit. In other words, the Recipient's obligation of confidentiality lasts until the trade secret information ceases to be a trade secret. This may occur when the information becomes generally known, is disclosed to the public by the Discloser, or ceases being a trade secret for some other reason. This gives the Discloser the broadest protection possible. Disclosers ordinarily prefer to use this provision.

Suggested Language: Term (Alternative 1—No Time Limit)

This Agreement and Recipient's duty to hold Discloser's trade secrets in confidence shall remain in effect until the above-described trade secrets are no longer trade secrets or until Discloser sends Recipient written notice releasing Recipient from this Agreement, whichever occurs first.

Alternative 2. Some recipients don't want to be subject to open-ended confidentiality obligations. Use this clause if the Recipient requires that the agreement state a definite date by which the agreement—and the Recipient's confidentiality obligations—expires. Five years is a common time period, but the time limit can be much shorter, even as little as six months. In Internet and technology businesses, the time period may need to be shorter because of the fast pace of innovation. But the Discloser should attempt to make sure the time period lasts as long as the confidential information is likely to remain valuable.

Suggested Language: Term (Alternative 2—Specific Expiration Date)

This Agreement and Recipient's duty to hold Discloser's trade secrets in confidence shall remain in effect until _____ or until whichever of the following occurs first:

- Discloser sends Recipient written notice releasing Recipient from this Agreement.
- The above-described trade secrets are no longer trade secrets.

No Rights Granted

This provision makes clear that the Recipient is acquiring absolutely no ownership rights in or to the information. This means the Recipient cannot sell or license the information to others.

Suggested Language: No Rights Granted

Recipient understands and agrees that this Agreement does not constitute a grant or an intention or commitment to grant any right, title, or interest in Discloser's trade secrets to Recipient.

Warranty

A warranty is a promise. In this provision, the Discloser promises to the Recipient that it has the right to disclose the information. This is intended to assure the Recipient that it won't be sued by some third party who claims the trade secrets belonged to it and that the Discloser had no right to reveal them to the Recipient.

Suggested Language: Warranty

Discloser warrants that it has the right to make the disclosures under this Agreement.

Injunctive Relief

If the Recipient violates a nondisclosure agreement, one of the most important legal remedies a trade secret owner can obtain is an "injunction": a court order preventing the violator from using or profiting from the Discloser's trade secrets.

This provision is intended to make such a court order easier for the Discloser to obtain. Some Recipients may object to including this provision because they want to make it as hard as possible for the Discloser to obtain an injunction.

Suggested Language: Injunctive Relief

Recipient acknowledges and agrees that in the event of a breach or threatened breach of this Agreement, money damages would be an inadequate remedy and extremely difficult to measure. Recipient agrees, therefore, that Discloser shall be entitled to an injunction to restrain Recipient from such breach or threatened breach. Nothing in this Agreement shall be construed as preventing Discloser from pursuing any remedy at law or in equity for any breach or threatened breach.

Attorneys' Fees

This agreement says that if a lawsuit is brought to enforce the agreement, the loser pays the winner's attorneys' fees. Without such a provision, attorneys' fees are usually not recoverable.

Suggested Language: Attorneys' Fees

If any legal action arises relating to this Agreement, the prevailing party shall be entitled to recover all court costs, expenses, and reasonable attorneys' fees.

Modifications

This provision requires that any changes to the agreement be made in writing and signed by both parties to be legally effective. This means, for example, that a change agreed to over the telephone won't be legally enforceable. To be enforceable, one of the parties must write down the change and both parties must sign it.

Suggested Language: Modifications

This Agreement represents the entire agreement between the parties regarding the subject matter and supersedes all prior agreements or understandings between them. All additions or modifications to this Agreement must be made in writing and signed by both parties to be effective.

No Agency

This clause is intended to make clear to both parties that the nondisclosure agreement does not make the two parties partners or allow either party to act as an agent for the other. This prevents either party from entering into contracts or incurring debts on behalf of the other party.

Suggested Language: No Agency

This Agreement does not create any agency or partnership relationship between the parties.

Applicable Law

Every state has its own laws regarding contract interpretation. These laws differ from state to state. The parties can choose any state's laws to govern the agreement, regardless of where they are located or where the agreement is signed. It's usually advantageous to have the law of your home state govern the agreement, because this is the law both you and your attorney are probably most familiar with. However, state laws on trade secrecy don't differ enough to make this a make-or-break issue.

Suggested Language: Applicable Law

This Agreement is made under, and shall be construed according to, the laws of the state of _____ .

Notice of Immunity From Liability

The federal Defend Trade Secrets Act (DTSA), which went into effect in 2016, extends federal civil protection to trade secrets and allows companies and individuals to sue under federal law when their secrets are wrongfully misappropriated. The DTSA requires that the following notice of immunity from liability be included in nondisclosure agreements with employees and independent contractors. The notice makes it clear that an individual may disclose a trade secret to report a suspected legal violation or during litigation. If you fail to include such notice in a nondisclosure agreement, you'll be prohibited from recovering exemplary (double) damages and attorneys' fees from an employee or IC you successfully sue for trade secret violations. However, failure to include the provision does not prevent filing a lawsuit in federal court under the DTSA.

Suggested Language: Notice of Immunity From Liability

Pursuant to 18 U.S.C. § 1833(b), an individual may not be held criminally or civilly liable under any federal or state trade secret law for disclosure of a trade secret: (i) made in confidence to a government official, either directly or indirectly, or to an attorney, solely for the purpose of reporting or investigating a suspected violation of law; and/or (ii) in a complaint or other document filed in a lawsuit or other proceeding, if such filing is made under seal. Additionally, an individual suing an employer for retaliation based on the reporting of a suspected violation of law may disclose a trade secret to his or her attorney and use the trade secret information in the court proceeding, so long as any document containing the trade secret is filed under seal and the individual does not disclose the trade secret except pursuant to court order.

Signatures

The parties don't have to be in the same room when they sign the agreement. It's even fine if the dates are a few days apart. But the NDA is not valid until both parties have signed it. So don't start revealing your secrets until then. Each party should sign at least two copies and keep at least one. This way, both parties have an original signed agreement. (See "Putting Your Agreement Together," in Chapter 18, for detailed information on how to sign a legal agreement.)

Using Written Client Agreements

A contract—also called an agreement—is a legally binding promise. Whenever you agree to perform services for a client, you enter into a contract: You promise to do work, and the client promises to pay you for it.

The word "contract" often intimidates people who conjure up visions of voluminous legal documents laden with legalese. However, a contract need not be long or complex. Many contracts consist of only a few simple paragraphs. Indeed, most contracts don't even have to be in writing. Even so, it's never a good idea to rely on an oral agreement with a client.

Client Agreements Don't Have to Be Intimidating

Some self-employed workers shy away from using written agreements. You might be afraid of intimidating your clients or making them think you don't trust them. This could happen if you're not careful. For example, a prospective client might think twice about hiring you if you present a 20-page contract for a simple one-day project. The client might conclude that you're either paranoid, hard to deal with, or both.

You can avoid this problem, however, if you calibrate your agreements to your assignments. Use simple contracts or short letter agreements for simple projects and save the longer, more complex agreements for bigger jobs.

RESOURCE

Want to know more about contracts? For detailed guidance on contract law and practices, including explanations of common contract terms and "boilerplate" provisions, refer to *Contracts: The Essential Business Desk Reference,* by Richard Stim (Nolo).

CROSS-REFERENCE

Gig Workers: If you're a gig worker who obtains work through online platforms like Upwork or Uber, you'll likely have no choice but to agree to use the contract provided by the platform. See Chapter 16 for special issues regarding gig workers.

Reasons to Use Written Agreements

Most contracts don't have to be in writing to be legally binding. For example, you and a client can enter into a contract over the phone or during a lunch meeting at a restaurant; no magic words need be spoken. You just have to agree to perform services for the client in exchange for something of value, usually money. Theoretically, an oral agreement is as valid as a 50-page contract drafted by a high-powered law firm.

> EXAMPLE: Gary, a freelance translator, receives an email from a vice president of Acme Oil Co. The VP asks Gary to translate some Russian oil industry documents for $2,000. Gary says he'll do the work for the price. Gary and Acme have a valid oral contract.

Some Agreements Must Be in Writing

Some types of agreements must be in writing to be legally enforceable. Each state has a law, usually called the "statute of frauds," listing the types of contracts that must be in writing to be valid.

A typical list includes:

- any contract that cannot possibly be performed in less than one year; for example, if John agrees to perform consulting services for Acme Corp. for the next two years for $2,000 per month, the agreement cannot be performed in less than one year and it must be in writing to be legally enforceable.
- contracts for the sales of goods—that is, tangible personal property, such as a computer or car—worth $500 or more
- a promise to pay someone else's debt; for example, if the president of a corporation personally guarantees to pay for the services you sell to the corporation, the guarantee must be in writing to be legally enforceable
- contracts involving the sale of real estate or real estate leases lasting more than one year, or
- contracts transferring ownership of a copyright.

In the real world, however, using oral agreements is like driving without a seatbelt. Things will work out fine as long as you don't have an accident; but if you do have an accident, you'll wish you had buckled up. An oral agreement can work if you and your client agree completely about its terms and both obey them. Unfortunately, things don't always work this way.

Below are some of the most important reasons why you should always sign a written agreement with a client before starting work.

Written Agreements Preempt Talk

When you put your agreement in writing, it is usually treated as the final word on the areas it covers. That is, it takes precedence over anything that you and the client said to each other but did not include in your written agreement.

However, if you and the client end up in court or arbitration because you disagree over the terms or meaning of your contract, the things you and the client said to each other during the negotiating process but didn't write down can be used to explain unclear terms in the written contract or to prove additional terms where the writing is incomplete. Because you and the client may disagree about what was said during negotiations, it's best to make the written contract as clear and complete as possible.

Avoiding Misunderstandings

Courts are crowded with lawsuits filed by people who enter into oral agreements with one another and later disagree over what was said. Costly misunderstandings can develop if you perform services for a client without a document clearly stating what you're supposed to do. Such misunderstandings may be innocent. For example, you and the client may have simply misinterpreted one another. Or they may be purposeful: Without a writing to contradict him or her, a client can claim that you orally agreed to anything.

Consider a good written client agreement to be your legal lifeline. If disputes develop, the agreement will provide ways to solve them. If you and the client end up in court, a written agreement will establish your legal duties to each other.

For these same reasons, your clients should be happy to sign a well-drafted contract. Be wary of any client who refuses to put your agreement in writing. Such a client might be a bad credit risk. If a prospective client balks at signing an agreement, you may wish to obtain a credit report on the client or talk with others who have worked for that client to see if they had any problems. If you think the client might pose a problem when it comes to paying you, ask for a substantial down payment up front and for periodic payments if the project is lengthy.

Assuring That You Get Paid

A written agreement clearly setting out your fees will help ward off disputes about how much the client agreed to pay you. If a client fails to pay and you have to negotiate or eventually even sue for your money, the written agreement will be proof of how much you're owed. Relying on an oral agreement with a client can make it very difficult for you to get paid, in full or at all.

Oral Agreement Costs IC $600

One self-employed worker learned the hard way that an oral agreement isn't worth the paper on which it's not printed. Jane, a commercial illustrator who worked as a freelancer, orally agreed to do a series of drawings for a dress designer. Jane did the drawings and submitted her bill for $2,000. The designer refused to pay, alternately claiming that payment was conditional on the drawings' being published in a fashion magazine and that Jane was charging too much.

Jane filed a lawsuit against the designer in small claims court to collect her $2,000. The judge had no trouble finding that Jane had an enforceable oral contract with the designer, who admitted that he had asked Jane to do the work. However, the judge awarded Jane only $1,400 because she could not document her claim that she was to be paid $100 per hour, and the designer made a convincing presentation that illustrators usually charge no more than $70 per hour.

Defining Projects

The process of deciding what to include in an agreement helps both you and the client. It forces you both to think carefully, perhaps for the first time, about exactly what you're supposed to do. Hazy and ill-defined ideas get reduced to a concrete contract specification or description of the work that you will perform. This gives you and the client a yardstick by which to measure your performance, the best way to avoid later disputes that you haven't performed adequately.

Establishing Independent Contractor Status

A well-drafted client agreement will also help establish that you are an independent contractor, not the client's employee. You can suffer severe consequences if the IRS or another government agency decides you're an employee instead of an independent contractor. (See Chapter 15.)

Reviewing a Client's Agreement

Many clients have their own agreements they'll ask you to sign. This may be a copy of an agreement they've used in the past with other people they've hired, a standard agreement prepared by an attorney, or a letter summarizing the terms to which you've agreed. You'll almost always be better off using your own agreement, not one provided by your client, because it gives you the greatest control over the contract terms. Take the initiative and send the client an agreement to sign immediately after you accept an assignment: Do not wait for the client to provide you with an agreement of its own.

If a client insists on using its own agreement, read that document carefully (see Chapter 20 for advice). It may contain provisions that are unfair to you, such as language requiring you to repay the client if an IRS auditor determines that you're an employee and imposes fines and penalties against the client. Pay special attention to noncompetition provisions that restrict your right to work for other companies and nondisclosure provisions that prevent you from using information you learn while working for the client.

Remember that any contract can be rewritten, even if the client claims it's a standard agreement that all outside workers sign. This is a matter for negotiation. Seek to delete or rewrite unfair provisions. There may also be provisions you want to add. (See "Provisions to Consider Adding" in Chapter 20.)

RESOURCE

For practical guidance on how to conduct contract negotiations, see:
- *Getting to Yes: Negotiating Agreement Without Giving In*, by Roger Fisher, et al. (Penguin Books).
- *Negotiating Rationally*, by Max H. Bazerman and Margaret A. Neale (Free Press), and
- *Negotiation* (Harvard Business Essentials), by Richard Luecke (Harvard Business School Press).

Creating Your Own Client Agreement

You don't need to hire a lawyer to draft an independent contractor agreement. All you need is a brain and a little common sense. This book contains a number of sample forms you can use, along with guidance on how to tailor them to fit your particular needs. This may take a little work, but when you're done, you'll have an agreement you can use over and over again with minor alterations.

Types of Agreements

There are two main types of client agreements. Use the type of agreement that best suits your needs and the needs of your clients.

Letter Agreements

A letter agreement is usually a short contract written in the form of a letter. After you and the client reach a tentative agreement—over the phone, in a meeting, or by email—you set forth the contract terms in a letter written on your stationery, sign two copies, and send them to the client. If the client agrees to the terms in the letter, he or she signs both copies at the bottom and returns one signed copy to you. At that point, you and the client have a fully enforceable, valid contract. Many self-employed people use letter agreements because they seem less intimidating to clients than more formal-looking contracts. Others use them because of business custom. See Chapter 19 for a sample letter agreement.

Standard Contracts

A standard contract usually contains a number of paragraphs and captions. It is usually longer and more comprehensive than a letter agreement. It's a good idea to use a standard contract in these cases:

- The project is long and complex or involves a substantial amount of money.
- You're dealing with a client you don't trust, either because the client is new or because your past dealings indicate the client is untrustworthy.

See Chapter 19 for a sample standard contract (independent contractor agreement) that almost any self-employed person who sells services can adapt to meet his or her needs.

Proposals Are Not Client Agreements

Clients often hire through a competitive bidding process by asking a number of people to submit written proposals describing how they'll perform the work and the prices they'll charge. The client chooses the IC who submits the best proposal.

Some self-employed people write quite lengthy and detailed proposals and depend on them instead of standard contracts. This is a mistake. Proposals do not normally address many important issues that should be covered in a contract, such as the term (length) of the agreement, how it can be terminated, and how disputes will be resolved. If a problem arises that is not covered by the proposal, you and the client will have to negotiate a solution in the middle of the project. If you can't reach a solution, either you or the client may end up taking the other to court to resolve the matter.

The best course is to have a signed contract in hand before starting work. If you submit a proposal to a client, it should state that if the client agrees to proceed, you will forward a contract for signature within a specified number of days.

The Drafting Process

Draft contract forms you can use over again with various clients. You can use the forms as the basis for your agreement and make alterations you need to suit the particular situation. If you perform the same type of work for every client, you might need just one or two form agreements. This might include a brief letter agreement for small jobs and a longer standard contract for larger projects. However, if your work varies, you may need several different agreements. If you hire self-employed people to work for you, you'll need an agreement for them as well. (See Chapter 19.)

> **EXAMPLE:** Ellen, a freelance publicist, usually uses a letter agreement with her clients. However, when she is hired to do a particularly long project, she prefers to use a longer standard contract because it affords her added protection if something goes wrong. She also occasionally hires other freelance publicists to work for her as ICs when she gets very busy. Ellen uses a lengthy subcontractor agreement with them because it helps to establish that they're ICs instead of her employees and makes their duties as clear as possible.
>
> Ellen uses the forms in this book to draft three different IC agreements she keeps on her computer and uses over and over again: a letter agreement, a standard IC agreement, and a subcontractor agreement.

Electronic Contracts

Traditionally, contracts have taken the form of paper documents, signed by hand in ink. However, this is not legally required. Electronic agreements with no paper or other hard copies are perfectly legal.

Using electronic agreements can be much faster and easier than dealing with paper. For example, you draft a contract on your computer and email a digital copy to a client, and the client emails it back with a digital signature indicating acceptance. There is no need to deal with the post office or a courier service to deliver a copy. Your electronic agreement can be a full-blown standard contract or a shorter letter-type agreement.

The validity of electronic agreements is secured by the federal Electronic Signatures in Global and International Commerce Act (the E-Sign Act). In addition, all states have adopted the Uniform Electronic Transactions

Act (UETA), which establishes the legal validity of electronic signatures and contracts in a way similar to the federal law. If a state has adopted the UETA or a similar law, the federal electronic signature law won't override the state law. But if a state has no law or state law doesn't recognize electronic signatures, the federal law will trump it. This ensures that electronic contracts and electronic or digital signatures will be valid in all states, regardless of where the parties live or where the contract is executed.

Contracts by Email

Instead of drafting a formal contract, you can create a legally binding contract through a simple exchange of emails even where the parties don't both print and physically sign a document. A binding contract can come into existence whenever one party promises to provide goods or services, and the other side promises to pay for it.

So, be careful. If a client sends you an email asking if you'll perform certain services for a set amount of money and you email back "OK," you may have created a legally binding contract. If you later decide that the original price is too low, you could be out of luck. To avoid this trap, say in your reply email something like "Sounds good, let's draft an agreement to hammer out the details."

Putting Your Agreement Together

Whether you use a simple letter agreement or formal standard contract, make sure it's properly signed and put together. This is not difficult if you know what to do.

Signatures

A written contract should be signed by the parties to ensure that it is legally enforceable. Paper contracts are ordinarily signed in ink (although ink is not legally required; pencil or even a typewritten signature will do). However, because a traditional ink signature isn't possible on an electronic contract, it is necessary to use a digital or electronic signature, which can be done in a variety of ways.

You need not be together when you sign, nor do you have to sign at the same time. There's no legal requirement that the signatures be located in any specific place in a business contract, but they are customarily placed at the end of the agreement (before any attachments or exhibits); that helps signify that you both have read and agreed to the entire document.

It's very important that both you and the client sign the agreement properly. Failure to do so can have drastic consequences. How to sign depends on the legal form of your business and the client's business.

Sole Proprietors

If you and the client are sole proprietors, you can simply sign your own names because a sole proprietorship is not a separate legal entity.

However, if you use a fictitious business name (see Chapter 2), it's best for you to sign on behalf of your business. This will help show that you're an IC, not an employee.

> **EXAMPLE:** Chris Kraft is a sole proprietor who runs a marketing research business. Instead of using his own name for the business, he calls it AAA Marketing Research. He should sign his contracts like this:

AAA Marketing Research

By: _____
        Chris Kraft

Partnerships

If either you or the client is a partnership, a general partner should sign on the partnership's behalf. Only one partner needs to sign. The signature block for the partnership should state the partnership's name and the name and title of the person signing on the partnership's behalf. If a partner signs only his or her name without mentioning the partnership, the partnership is not bound by the agreement.

> **EXAMPLE:** Chris, a self-employed marketing consultant, contracts to perform marketing research for a Michigan partnership called The Argus Partnership. Randy Argus is one of the general partners. He signs the contract on the partnership's behalf like this:

The Argus Partnership

A Michigan Partnership

By: _____

     Randy Argus, a General Partner

If the client is a partnership and the person who signs the agreement is not a partner, the signature should be accompanied by a partnership resolution stating that the person signing the agreement has the authority to do so. A partnership resolution is a document signed by one or more of the general partners stating that the person named has the authority to sign contracts on the partnership's behalf.

Electronic vs. Digital Signatures

Electronic and digital signatures are not the same. Digital signatures are created via cryptographic "scrambling" technology to ensure that the e-signature really belongs to the person who was supposed to sign the contract. Various software packages—both free and commercially distributed—are available to make using digital signatures easy.

Electronic signatures refers to any means of creating a signature other than using sophisticated cryptography. It includes, for example, using computer or mobile applications to upload a scanned version of the signer's signature, typing the signer's name into a signature area, or signing with a computer mouse or finger. Many applications are available for this purpose.

Corporations

If either you or the client is a corporation, the agreement must be signed by someone who has authority to sign contracts on the corporation's behalf. The corporation's president or chief executive officer (CEO) is presumed to have this authority.

If someone other than the president of an incorporated client signs—for example, the vice president, treasurer, or other corporate officer—ask to see a board of directors resolution or corporate bylaws authorizing him or her to sign. If the person signing doesn't have authority, the corporation won't be legally bound by the contract.

Keep in mind that if you sign personally instead of on your corporation's behalf, you'll be personally liable for the contract.

The signature block for a corporation should state the name of the corporation and indicate by name and title the person signing on the corporation's behalf.

> EXAMPLE: Chris, a self-employed marketing consultant, contracts to perform marketing research with a corporation called Kiddie Krafts, Inc. The contract is signed by Susan Ericson. Because she is the president of the corporation, Chris doesn't need a corporate resolution showing she has authority to bind the corporation. The signature block should appear in the contract like this:

Kiddie Krafts, Inc.

A California Partnership

By: _____

    Susan Ericson, President

Limited Liability Companies

The owners of a limited liability company (LLC) are called "members." Members may hire others to run their LLC for them. These people are called "managers." If either you or your client is an LLC, the agreement should be signed by a member or manager on the LLC's behalf.

> EXAMPLE: Amy Smart, a California-based self-employed graphic artist, has formed an LLC to run her business called Great Graphics, LLC. She should sign all her agreements like this:

Great Graphics, LLC

A California Limited Liability Company

By: _____

    Amy Smart, Member

Dates

A contract must have a date. This can be in the first paragraph, or you can simply put a date line next to the place where each person signs, like this:

Date: _____ , 20xx

You and the client don't have to sign on the same day. Indeed, you can sign weeks apart.

The date the contract is signed does not have to be the same date that it becomes effective or when performance must begin. This can be a later date set out in the contract.

Addendums

An easy way to keep a letter agreement or standard contract as short as possible is to use addendums, also called attachments, exhibits, riders, or schedules. An addendum is simply any document attached to—and made part of—a contract. You can use one to list lengthy details, such as performance specifications. This makes the main body of the agreement shorter and easier to read.

Because an addendum is attached *after* the signature page, parties often initial each page of the addendum to guarantee that it will be considered part of the agreement. Another (or complementary) approach is to include the words "incorporated by reference" the first time an addendum is mentioned in a contract (for example, "The parties shall abide by the delivery specifications in attached Addendum, incorporated by reference"). You can also use a special clause within the main body of the contract to make this point, as shown below.

> EXAMPLE: "Any attached Addendums and any other attachments or exhibits to this Agreement are incorporated in this Agreement by reference."

Altering the Contract

Sometimes it's necessary to make last-minute changes to a contract just before it's signed. If you use a computer to prepare the agreement, it's usually easy to make the changes and print out a new agreement.

However, it's not necessary to prepare a new contract. Instead, the changes may be handwritten or typed onto all existing copies of the agreement. If you use this approach, be sure that all those signing the agreement also sign their initials as close as possible to the place where the change is made. If both people who sign don't initial each change, questions might arise as to whether the change was part of the agreement.

Copies of the Contract

Prepare at least two copies of your letter agreement or standard contract. Make sure that each copy contains all the needed exhibits and attachments. Both you and the client should sign both copies. That way, each of you can keep one copy of the complete agreement signed by both parties.

Changing the Agreement After It's Signed

No contract is engraved in stone. You and the client can always modify or amend your contract if circumstances change. You can even agree to call the whole thing off and cancel your agreement.

> EXAMPLE: Barbara, a self-employed well digger, agrees to dig a 50-foot-deep well on property owned by Kate for $2,000. After digging ten feet, Barbara hits solid rock that no one knew was there. To complete the well, she'll have to lease expensive heavy equipment. To defray the added expense, she asks Kate to pay her $4,000 instead of $2,000 for the work. Kate agrees. Barbara and Kate have amended their original agreement.

Neither you nor the client is ever obligated to accept a proposed modification to your contract. Either of you can always say no and accept the consequences. At its most dire, this may mean a court battle over breaking the original contract. However, you're usually better off reaching some sort of agreement with the client, unless he or she is totally unreasonable.

Unless your contract is one that must be in writing to be legally valid— for example, an agreement that can't be performed in less than one year— it can usually be modified by an oral agreement. In other words, you need not write down the changes.

EXAMPLE: Art signs a contract with Zeno to build an addition to his house. Halfway through the project, Art decides that he wants Zeno to do some extra work not covered by their original agreement. Art and Zeno have a telephone conversation in which Zeno agrees to do the extra work for extra money. Although nothing is put in writing, their change to their original agreement is legally enforceable.

Many self-employed workers and their clients change their contracts often and never write down the changes. The flexibility afforded by such an informal approach to contract amendments might be just what you want. However, misunderstandings and disputes can arise from this approach. It's always best to have some sort of writing showing what you've agreed to do. You can do this informally. For example, you can simply send a confirming letter following a telephone call with the client summarizing the changes you both agreed to make. Be sure to keep a copy for your files.

However, if the amendment involves a contract provision that is very important—your payment, for example—insist on a written amendment and insist that you and the client sign it. The amendment should set forth all the changes and state that the amendment takes precedence over the original contract.

FORM ON NOLO.COM
You can download a copy of the Contract Amendment form from this book's companion page on Nolo.com. For details on finding these and other forms on Nolo.com, which you can tailor to your own use, see "List of Forms Available on the Nolo Website" at the end of Appendix A of this book.

Contracts may undergo multiple amendments, so it's usually a good idea to number each amendment (for example "Amendment No. 1" or "First Amendment"). In addition, amendments should be filed and maintained with the original agreement so that anyone viewing the file will know that the agreement has been amended.

EXAMPLE: David Dawson contracts with Acme, Inc. to perform consulting services and complete his work by July 1, 2018. Dawson discovers he will need more time to complete the project. He and Acme agree to extend the deadline for completion to November 1, 2018. They sign a formal contract amendment as follows:

Sample Contract Amendment

Contract Amendment

This Amendment is made between David Dawson and Acme Inc. to amend the Original Agreement titled Consulting Agreement signed by them on April 1, 2018.

The Original Agreement is amended as follows: Section 2 of the Agreement is replaced in its entirety by the following:

2. Deadline. Consultant's work must be completed by November 1, 2018.

All provisions of the Original Agreement, except as modified by this Amendment, remain in full force and effect, and are reaffirmed. If there is any conflict between this Amendment and any provision of the Original Agreement, the provisions of this Amendment will control.

Signatures

Acme, Inc.

By: ___/s/ *Yolanda Allende*_____

Yolanda Allende [ ]
President
September 1, 2018

Consultant/Contractor: David Dawson

By: ___/s/_____

David Dawson
Taxpayer ID Number: 987-65-4321
September 1, 2018

Drafting Your Own Client Agreement

This chapter guides you in creating a client agreement that you can use for almost any type of service you provide your clients. This is a full-blown formal contract that covers the major issues you'll want to address with clients in writing.

Some self-employed people prefer not to use formal contracts because they're afraid they will intimidate clients. If you prefer something a little less formal, this book also provides a short, simple letter agreement that will meet your needs. (See "Using Letter Agreements," below.)

However, it's a good idea to use a more comprehensive formal contract if:

- You are hired to do a project that is long and complex or involves a substantial amount of money.
- You're dealing with a new client or a client who has been untrustworthy in the past.

FORM ON NOLO.COM

You can download copies of the full contract (Independent Contractor Agreement) and the more informal Letter Agreement from this book's companion page on Nolo.com. For details on finding these and other forms on Nolo.com, which you can tailor to your own use, see "List of Forms Available on the Nolo Website" at the end of Appendix A of this book.

RESOURCE

Want agreements for specific services? The agreement provided here can be modified for use by almost any self-employed person. If you prefer a ready-made contract, you can find client agreements tailored to specific occupations in *Consultant & Independent Contractor Agreements*, by Stephen Fishman (Nolo), including agreements for use by consultants, household service providers, salespeople, accountants and bookkeepers, artists, writers, and construction contractors.

CROSS-REFERENCE

Gig Workers: If you're a gig worker who obtains work through online hiring platforms, you'll be required to agree to a contract created by the hiring platform. Ordinarily, there is no ability to negotiate the terms of such agreements. See Chapter 16 for a detailed discussion of contracts.

Essential Provisions

There are a number of provisions that should be included in most client agreements. All of these sample clauses are included in the sample agreement provided here. Later in the chapter, we'll also show you how an entire agreement looks when assembled.

The provisions here may be all you need for a basic agreement. Or you may need to combine them with some of your own clauses or one or more of the optional clauses discussed in "Optional Provisions," below.

Title of agreement. You don't need a title for a client agreement, but if you want one, call it "Independent Contractor Agreement," "Client Agreement," "Agreement for Professional Services," or "Consulting Agreement." Consulting agreement may sound a little more high-toned than independent contractor agreement; it is most often used by highly skilled professionals. Because you are not your client's employee, do not use "Employment Agreement" as a title.

Suggested Language

INDEPENDENT CONTRACTOR AGREEMENT

Names of parties. Here, at the beginning of your contract, it's best to refer to yourself by your full business name. Later on in the contract, you can use an obvious abbreviation.

If you're a sole proprietor, use the full name you use for your business. This can be your own name or a fictitious business name or an assumed name you use to identify your business. (See Chapter 3.) For example, if consultant Al Brodsky calls his one-person marketing research business "ABC Marketing Research," he would use that name on the contract. Using a fictitious business name helps show that you're a business, not an employee.

If your business is incorporated, use your corporate name, not your own name. For example, use "John Smith, Incorporated" instead of "John Smith." Similarly, if you've formed a limited liability company (see Chapter 2), use the name of the LLC, not your personal name. For example, "Jane Brown, a Limited Liability Company" instead of "Jane Brown."

For the sake of brevity, identify yourself and the client by shorter names in the rest of the agreement. You can use an abbreviated version of your full name (for example, "ABC" for ABC Marketing Research). Or you can refer to yourself simply as "Contractor" or "Consultant." Refer to the client initially by its company name and subsequently by a short version of the name or as "Client" or "Firm." Do not refer to yourself as an employee or to the client as an employer.

Include the addresses of the principal place of business of both the client and yourself. If you or the client have more than one office or workplace, the principal place of business is the main office or workplace.

Suggested Language: Names and Addresses of Parties

This Agreement is made between [*client's name*] (Client) with a principal place of business at [*client's business address*] and [*your name*] (Contractor), with a principal place of business at [*your business address*].

Services to Be Performed

The agreement should describe in as much detail as possible what you are expected to accomplish. Word the description carefully to emphasize the results you're expected to achieve. Don't describe the method by which you will achieve the results. As an independent contractor, it should be up to you to decide how to do the work. The client's control should be limited to accepting or rejecting your final results. The more control the client exercises over how you work, the more you'll look like an employee. (See Chapter 15.)

> EXAMPLE: Jack hires Jill to prepare an index for his multivolume history of ancient Sparta. Jill should describe the results she is expected to achieve as: "Contractor agrees to prepare an index of Client's *History of Sparta* of at least 100 single-spaced pages.

The agreement should *not* tell Jill how to create the index. Here's an example not to follow: "Contractor will prepare an alphabetical three-level index of Client's *History of Sparta*. Contractor will first prepare 3-by-5-inch index cards listing every index entry beginning with Chapter One. After each chapter is completed, Contractor will deliver the index cards to Client for Client's approval. When index cards have been created for all 50 chapters, Contractor will create a computer version of the index using *Complex Software* Version 7.6. Contractor will then print out and edit the index and deliver it to Client for approval."

It's perfectly okay for the agreement to establish very detailed specifications for your finished work product. But the specs should describe only the end results you must achieve, not how to obtain those results. You can include the description in the main body of the agreement. Or if it's a lengthy explanation, put it on a separate document and attach it to the agreement.

Suggested Language: Services to Be Performed
(Alternative A—If Services Are Listed)

Contractor agrees to perform the following services: [*Describe services you will perform.*]

Suggested Language: Services to Be Performed
(Alternative B—If Exhibit Is Attached)

Contractor agrees to perform the services described in Exhibit A, which is attached to and made part of this Agreement.

Payment

Self-employed people who provide services to others can be paid in many different ways. The two most common payment methods are:

- a fixed fee, or
- payment by unit of time.

Whatever method you choose, you can encourage the client to pay you on time by charging a late payment fee; see "Late Fees" (under "Optional Provisions"), below.

Fixed Fee

In a fixed-fee agreement, you charge an agreed amount for the entire project.

Suggested Language: Payment (Alternative A—Fixed Fee)

In consideration for the services to be performed by Contractor, Client agrees to pay Contractor $ [*amount*].

Unit of Time

Many self-employed people—for example, lawyers, accountants, and plumbers—customarily charge by the hour, day, or other unit of time. Charging by the hour does not support your independent contractor status, but you can get away with it if it's a common practice in the field in which you work.

Suggested Language: Payment (Alternative B—Unit of Time)

In consideration for the services to be performed by Contractor, Client agrees to pay Contractor at the rate of $ [*amount*] per [*hour, day, week, month, or other unit of time*].

Whatever unit of time you use, make sure your meaning is clear. For example, does monthly payment mean you'll be paid every 30 days or at the end of every calendar monthly? There's a difference.

Capping Your Payment

Clients often wish to place a cap on the total amount they'll spend on the project when you're paid by the hour because they're afraid you might work slowly to earn a larger fee. If the client insists on a cap, make sure it allows you to work enough hours to get the project done.

Suggested Optional Language: Payment (Cap on Payment)

[*OPTIONAL*: Contractor's total compensation will not exceed $ [*amount*] without Client's written consent.]

Revisions

You may have to revise your work once or more before satisfying the client. For example, a freelance designer may have to revise a logo three or four times to make a client happy. If you and the client anticipate that revisions to your work product may be required before it is finally approved by the client, the contact should provide how many revisions are included in the payment amount set forth above. You can also specify what you will charge for each additional revision, often called a "round."

Suggested Optional Language: Revisions

The contract price set forth above includes up to _____ rounds of revisions, provided that such revisions do not require work exceeding the scope of the services Contractor agreed to perform under this Agreement. Additional revisions will be billed at the rate of _____ .

Terms of Payment

Terms of payment means how you will bill the client and be paid. Generally, you will have to submit an invoice to the client setting out the amount due before you can get paid. An invoice doesn't have to be fancy or filled with legalese. It should include an invoice number, the dates covered by the invoice, the hours expended if you're being paid by the hour, and a summary of the work performed. (See Chapter 7 for a detailed discussion and sample invoice form. You can find a blank electronic copy at this book's online companion page; see the appendix for information.)

Payment Upon Completing Work

The following provision requires you to send an invoice after you complete work. The client is required to pay your fixed or hourly fee within a set number of days after you send the invoice. The time period of 30 days is a typical payment term, but it can be shorter or longer if you wish. You can even require payment upon the client's receipt of your invoice When economic conditions are poor, clients may insist on a longer term, such as 60 or 90 days.

Note that the time for payment starts to run as soon as you send your invoice, not when the client receives it. This will help you get paid more quickly.

**Suggested Language: Terms of Payment
(Alternative A—Payment on Completion)**

Upon completing Contractor's services under this Agreement, Contractor will submit an invoice. Client will pay Contractor within [*10, 15, 30, 45, or 60*] days from the date of Contractor's invoice.

Divided Payments

You can also opt to be paid part of your fee when the agreement is signed and the remainder when the work is finished. The amount of the up-front payment is subject to negotiation. Many self-employed people like to receive at least one-third to one-half of a fee before they start work. If the client is new or might have problems paying you, it's wise to get as much money in advance as you can.

The following provision requires that you be paid a specific amount when the client signs the agreement and the rest when the work is finished.

**Suggested Language: Terms of Payment:
(Alternative B—Divided Payments)**

Contractor will be paid $ [*amount*] upon signing this Agreement and the remaining amount due when Contractor completes the services and submits an invoice. Client will pay Contractor within [*10, 15, 30, 45, or 60*] days from the date of Contractor's invoice.

Fixed-Fee Installment Payments

If the project is long and complex, you may prefer to be paid in installments rather than waiting until the project is finished to receive the bulk of your payment. One way to do this is to break the job into phases or milestones and be paid a fixed fee when each phase is completed. Clients often like this pay-as-you-go arrangement too.

To do this, draw up a schedule of installment payments, tying each payment to your completion of specific services. It's usually easier to set forth the schedule in a separate document and attach it to the agreement as an exhibit. The main body of the agreement should simply refer to the attached payment schedule.

Suggested Language: Terms of Payment (Alternative C—Installment Payments)

Contractor will be paid according to the Schedule of Payments set forth in Exhibit [*A or B*] attached to and made part of this agreement.

The following is a form of a schedule of payments you can complete and attach to your agreement. This schedule requires four payments: a down payment when the contract is signed and three installment payments. However, you and your client can schedule as many payments as you like.

Suggested Language: Payment Schedule Exhibit—Schedule of Payments

Client will pay Contractor according to the following schedule of payments:

1. $ [*sum*] when this Agreement is signed.
2. $ [*sum*] when an invoice is submitted and the following services are completed: [*Describe first stage of services.*]
3. $ [*sum*] when an invoice is submitted and the following services are completed: [*Describe second stage of services.*]
4. $ [*sum*] when an invoice is submitted and the following services are completed: [*Describe third stage of services.*]

[*LIST ANY ADDITIONAL PAYMENTS*]

All payments will be due within [*10, 15, 30, 45, or 60*] days from the date of Contractor's invoice.

Hourly Payment for Lengthy Projects

Use the following clause if you're being paid by the hour or another unit of time and the project will last more than one month. Under this provision, you submit an invoice to the client each month setting forth how many hours you've worked, and the client is required to pay you within a specific number of days from the date of each invoice.

**Suggested Language: Terms of Payment
(Alternative D—Payments After Invoice)**

Contractor will send Client an invoice monthly. Client will pay Contractor within [*10, 15, 30, 45, or 60*] days from the date of each invoice.

Expenses

Expenses are the costs you incur that you can attribute directly to your work for a client, such as traveling done on the client's behalf. Expenses do not include your normal fixed overhead costs, such as your office rent or the cost of commuting to and from your office; nor do they include materials the client provides you to do your work.

In the past, the IRS viewed the payment of a worker's expenses by a client as a sign of employee status. However, the agency now views this factor as less important. IRS auditors will focus instead on whether a worker has any expenses that were not reimbursed, particularly fixed ongoing costs such as office rent or employee salaries. (See Chapter 15.)

Even though the IRS has changed its stance, other government agencies may consider payment of a worker's business or travel expenses to be a strong indication of an employment relationship. For this reason, it is usually best that your compensation be high enough to cover your expenses; you should not be reimbursed separately for them.

Setting your compensation at a level high enough to cover your expenses has another advantage: It frees you from having to keep records of your expenses. Keeping track of the cost of every phone call or photocopy you make for a client can be a real chore and may be more trouble than it's worth.

However, if a project will require expensive travel, you may wish to bill the client separately for these costs. The following provision contains an optional clause that covers this.

Suggested Language: Expenses
(Alternative A—If IC Is Responsible for Expenses)

Contractor will be responsible for all expenses incurred while performing services under this Agreement.

[*OPTIONAL:* However, Client will reimburse Contractor for all reasonable travel and living expenses necessarily incurred by Contractor while away from Contractor's regular place of business to perform services under this Agreement. Contractor will submit an itemized statement of such expenses. Client will pay Contractor within 30 days from the date of each statement.]

In some professions, however, clients customarily pay expenses. For example, attorneys, accountants, and many self-employed consultants typically charge their clients separately for photocopying charges, deposition fees, and travel. Where there is an otherwise clear independent contractor relationship and payment of expenses is customary in your trade or business, you can probably get away with doing it.

Suggested Language: Expenses
(Alternative B—If Client Is Responsible for Expenses)

Client will reimburse Contractor for the following expenses that are directly attributable to work performed under this Agreement:

- travel expenses other than normal commuting, including airfares, rental *vehicles*, and highway mileage in company or personal vehicles at $ [*amount*] per mile
- postage and courier services
- printing and reproduction
- computer services, and
- other expenses resulting from the work performed under this Agreement.

Contractor will submit an itemized statement of Contractor's expenses. Client will pay Contractor within 30 days from the date of each statement.

Materials

Generally, you should provide all the materials and equipment necessary to complete a project. However, this might not always be possible. For example:

- A computer consultant may have to perform work on the client's computers.
- A marketing consultant may need research materials from the client.
- A freelance copywriter may need copies of the client's old sales literature.

Specify any materials you need from the client in your agreement.

You Provide All Materials

If you furnish all the materials and equipment, use the following clause.

Suggested Language: Materials (Alternative A—If IC Provides Materials)

Contractor will furnish all materials and equipment used to provide the services required by this Agreement.

Client Provides Materials or Equipment

List the materials or equipment the client will provide. If you need these items by a specific date, specify the deadline as well.

Suggested Language: Materials (Alternative B—If Client Provides Materials)

Client will make available to Contractor, at Client's expense, the following materials, facilities, and equipment: _____[List]_____ .

These items will be provided to Contractor by [date].

Term of Agreement

The term of the agreement refers to when the agreement begins and ends. Unless the agreement provides a specific starting date, it begins on the date it is signed. If you and the client sign on different dates, the agreement begins on the date the last person signs. Normally, you shouldn't begin work until the client signs the agreement, so it's best not to provide a specific start date that might be before the client signs.

The agreement should have a definite ending date. Ordinarily, this date marks the final deadline for you to complete your services. However, even if the project is lengthy, the end date should not be too far in the future. A good outside time limit is 12 months: A longer term makes the agreement look like an employment agreement, not an independent contractor agreement. If you have not completed the work at the end of 12 months, you can negotiate and sign a new agreement.

Suggested Language: Term of Agreement

This Agreement will become effective when signed by both parties and will end no later than _____ , 20xx.

Terminating the Agreement

Signing a contract doesn't make you bound by it permanently: You and the client can agree to call off your agreement at any time. In addition, contracts typically contain provisions that allow either party to terminate the agreement under certain circumstances. Termination means either party can end the contract without the other side's agreement.

When a contract is terminated, both you and the client stop performing: You discontinue your work, and the client has no obligation to pay you for any work you may do after the effective date of termination. However, the client is legally obligated to pay you for any work you did prior to the termination date.

EXAMPLE: Murray, a self-employed website developer, agrees to design a website for Mary. They sign a client agreement. About halfway through the project, Murray decides to terminate the agreement because Mary refuses to pay him the advance required by the contract. When the termination becomes effective, Murray has no obligation to do any further work for Mary, but he is still entitled to be compensated for the work he already did.

On the downside, however, you remain liable to the client for any damages it may have suffered due to your failure to perform as agreed before the termination date.

EXAMPLE: Jill, a self-employed graphic artist, contracts with Aaron to design the cover for a book Aaron plans to publish. Aaron terminates the agreement when Jill fails to deliver the cover by the contract deadline. Jill has no duty to create the cover, and Aaron is not required to pay Jill even if she does produce a cover. However, Jill is liable for any damages Aaron suffered by her failure to live up to the agreement. The delay in providing a cover cost Aaron an extra $1,000 in printing bills. Jill is liable for this amount.

It's important to clearly define the circumstances under which you or the client may end the agreement.

In the past, the IRS viewed a termination provision giving either you, the client, or both of you the right to terminate the agreement at any time to be strong evidence of an employment relationship. However, the agency no longer considers this to be such an important factor. Even so, it's wise to place some limits on the client's right to terminate the contract. It's usually not in your best interest to give a client the right to terminate you for any reason or no reason at all, because the client may abuse that right.

Instead, both you and the client should be able to terminate the agreement without legal repercussions only if there is reasonable cause to do so; or, at the very least, only by giving written notice to the other.

Termination With Reasonable Cause

Termination with reasonable cause means either you or the client must have a good reason to end the agreement. A serious violation of the agreement is reasonable cause to terminate the agreement. However, what is considered serious depends on the particular facts and circumstances.

A minor or technical contract violation is not serious enough to justify ending the contract for cause. For example, if a client promises to let you use its office space a few hours a week but fails to do so, this would be a minor transgression and wouldn't justify terminating the agreement. However, if a self-employed programmer agrees to perform programming services for an especially low price because the client promises to let her use its mainframe computer, and the client then reneges and tells the programmer to lease her own mainframe, the programmer would likely be justified in terminating the agreement.

Unless your contract provides otherwise, a client's failure to pay you on time may not necessarily constitute reasonable cause for you to terminate the agreement. You may, however, add a clause to your contract providing that late payments are always reasonable cause for terminating the contract.

The following suggested clause provides that you may terminate the agreement if the client doesn't pay you what you're owed within 20 days after you make a written demand for payment. For example, if you send a client an invoice due within 30 days and the client fails to pay within that time, you may terminate the agreement 20 days after you send the client a written demand to be paid what you're owed. This may give clients an incentive to pay you.

The suggested clause also makes clear that the client must pay you for the services you performed before the contract was terminated.

Suggested Language: Terminating the Agreement
(Alternative A—Reasonable Cause)

With reasonable cause, either party may terminate this Agreement effective immediately by giving written notice of termination for cause. Reasonable cause includes:

- a material violation of this agreement, or
- nonpayment of Contractor's compensation 20 days after written demand for payment.

Contractor will be entitled to full payment for services performed prior to the effective date of termination. This obligation and any payment obligations pending at termination, survive termination.

Termination Without Cause

Sometimes you or the client do not want to agree to a limited right to terminate. Instead, you want to be able to get out of the agreement at any time without incurring liability. For example, a client's business plans may change so that it no longer needs your services. Or you may have too much work and need to lighten your load.

If you want a broader right to end the work relationship, add a provision to the contract that gives either of you the right to terminate the agreement for any reason upon written notice. You must provide a minimum amount of notice before the termination takes effect. A contract that can be freely terminated without notice is not legally valid. What's more, being able to terminate without notice tends to make you look like an employee. A period of 30 days is a common notice period, but shorter notice may be appropriate if the project is of short duration.

If the client terminates the agreement after you've begun work, it's only fair that you should get paid for your efforts. Your contract should provide how you will be paid for your partially completed work. There are a couple of ways to do this. First, you and the client can agree that you will be paid a specific sum of money if the client terminates the agreement early. (This is often called a "kill fee.") Or, the contract could require the client to pay you for the work you've completed as of the termination date, an amount that will have to be determined in the future.

Suggested Language: Terminating the Agreement
(Alternative B—Without Cause)

Either party may terminate this Agreement at any time by giving [*5, 10, 15, 30, 45, or 60*] days written notice of termination. Contractor will be entitled to full payment for services performed prior to the date of termination.

This obligation, and any payment obligations pending at termination, survive termination.

Independent Contractor Status

One of the most important functions of an independent contractor agreement is to help establish that you are an independent contractor, not your client's employee. The key to doing this is to make clear that you, not the client, have the right to control how the work will be performed.

You will need to emphasize the factors the IRS and other agencies consider in determining whether a client controls how the work is done. Of course, if you merely recite what you think the IRS wants to hear but fail to adhere to these understandings, agency auditors won't be fooled. Think of this clause as a reminder to you and your client about how to conduct your business relationship. (See Chapter 15.)

Suggested Language: Independent Contractor Status

Contractor is an independent contractor, not Client's employee. Contractor's employees or contract personnel are not Client's employees. Contractor and Client agree to the following rights consistent with an independent contractor relationship:

- Contractor has the right to perform services for others during the term of this Agreement.
- Contractor has the sole right to control and direct the means, manner, and method by which the services required by this Agreement will be performed.
- Contractor has the right to hire assistants as subcontractors or to use employees to provide the services required by this Agreement.
- Contractor or Contractor's employees or contract personnel will perform the services required by this Agreement; Client will not hire, supervise, or pay any assistants to help Contractor.
- Neither Contractor nor Contractor's employees or contract personnel will receive any training from Client in the skills necessary to perform the services required by this Agreement.
- Client will not require Contractor or Contractor's employees or subcontractors to devote full time to performing the services required by this Agreement.
- Neither Contractor nor Contractor's employees or contract personnel are eligible to participate in any employee retirement, health, vacation pay, sick pay, or other fringe benefit plan of Client.

Local, State, and Federal Taxes

The agreement should address federal and state income taxes, Social Security taxes, and sales taxes.

Income and Other Taxes

Your client should not pay or withhold any income or Social Security taxes on your behalf: Doing so is a very strong indicator that you are an employee, not an independent contractor. Indeed, some courts have classified workers as employees based upon this factor alone. Keep in mind that one of the best things about being self-employed is that you don't have taxes withheld from your paychecks. (See Chapter 8.)

Include a straightforward provision, such as the one suggested below, to help make sure the client understands that you'll pay all applicable taxes due on your compensation so the client should not withhold taxes from your payments.

Suggested Language: Income Taxes

Contractor will pay all income taxes and FICA (Social Security and Medicare taxes) incurred while performing services under this Agreement. Client will not:

- withhold FICA from Contractor's payments or make FICA payments on Contractor's behalf
- make state or federal unemployment compensation contributions on Contractor's behalf, or
- withhold state or federal income tax from Contractor's payments.

Sales Taxes

A few states require self-employed people to pay sales taxes, even if they only provide their clients with services. These states include Hawaii, New Mexico, South Dakota, and West Virginia. Other states require you to pay sales taxes on specified services.

Whether or not you're required to collect sales taxes, include the following provision in your agreement to make it clear that the client will have to pay these and similar taxes. States change sales tax laws frequently, and more are beginning to view services as a good source of sales tax revenue. This provision could come in handy in the future even if you don't need it now.

Suggested Language: Sales Taxes

The charges included here do not include taxes. If Contractor is required to pay any federal, state, or local sales, use, property, or value-added taxes based on the services provided under this Agreement, the taxes will be billed to Client separately. Contractor will not pay any interest or penalties incurred due to late payment or nonpayment of any taxes by Client.

Notices

When you want to do something important regarding the agreement, you must tell the client about it. This is called giving notice. For example, you need to give the client notice if you want to modify or terminate the agreement.

The following suggested provision gives you several options for providing the client with notice: by personal delivery, mail, fax, or email followed by a confirming letter.

This provision states that if notice is given by email, it must be followed up by notice by postal mail. Relying solely on notice by email can be dangerous: Email can be easily overlooked or accidentally deleted by the recipient.

If the notice procedure set forth in the clause is followed, notice is "deemed given." This means that, for legal purposes, the recipient has received notice, whether he or she actually got it or not. This prevents the recipient from avoiding the notice in order to claim he or she never got it.

If you give notice by mail, it is not effective until three days after you send it. For example, if you want to end the agreement on 30 days' notice and you mail your notice of termination to the client, the agreement will not end until 33 days after you mail the notice.

Suggested Language: Notices

All notices and other communications in connection with this Agreement will be in writing and will be deemed given as follows:
- when delivered personally to the recipient's address as stated on this Agreement
- three days after being deposited in the United States mail, with postage prepaid to the recipient's address as stated in this Agreement, or
- when sent by fax or email to the last fax number or email address of the recipient known to the person giving notice. Notice is effective upon receipt, provided that a duplicate copy of the notice is promptly given by first-class mail or the recipient delivers a written confirmation of receipt.

No Partnership

You want to make sure that the client and you are considered separate legal entities, not partners. If a client is viewed as your partner, you'll be liable for its debts, and the client will have the power to make contracts that obligate you to others without your consent.

Suggested Language: No Partnership

This Agreement does not create a partnership relationship. Neither party has authority to enter into contracts on the other's behalf.

Applicable Law and Jurisdiction

It's a good idea for your agreement to indicate which state's law will govern if you have a dispute with the client. This is particularly helpful if you and the client are in different states. There is some advantage to having the law of your own state control, because local attorneys will likely be more familiar with that law.

The agreement should also contain a jurisdiction provision (also called a "forum selection" clause). This requires the parties to agree in advance as to where a legal case can be filed if there is a dispute under the contract. This can be important, especially if the parties are located far apart. If you're in Oregon and your client is in Florida, do you want to have to go to Florida to file a lawsuit if the client fails to pay you? Probably not.

Often, the applicable law and jurisdiction provisions are combined.

Suggested Language: Applicable Law and Jurisdiction

This Agreement will be governed by the laws of the state of [*state in which you have your main office*]. Any disputes arising from this Agreement must be handled exclusively in the federal and state courts located in [*insert county and state in which parties agree to litigate*].

Exclusive Agreement

When you put your agreement in writing, it is treated as the last word on the areas it covers, if you and the client intend it to be the final and complete expression of your agreement. The written agreement takes precedence over any written or oral agreements or promises made previously. This means that neither you nor the client can rely on letters or oral statements either of you may have made or other material not covered by the contract.

Business contracts normally contain a provision stating that the written agreement is the complete and exclusive agreement between those involved. This is to help make it clear to a court or a mediator or arbitrator that the parties intended the contract to be their final agreement. Such a clause helps avoid claims that promises not contained in the written contract were made and broken.

Make sure that all documents containing any of the client's representations upon which you are relying are attached to the agreement as exhibits. If they aren't attached, they likely won't be considered to be part of the agreement.

Suggested Language: Exclusive Agreement

This Agreement (including any attached exhibits) is the entire Agreement between Contractor and Client.

Signatures

The end of the main body of the agreement should contain spaces for you to sign, write in your title, and date. Make sure the person signing the agreement has the authority to do so. (See "Putting Your Agreement Together" in Chapter 18.)

Suggested Language: Signatures

Client: _____ [*name of client*] _____

By: _____
(Signature)

_____
(Typed or Printed Name)

Title: _____

Date: _____

Contractor: ___ [*name of contractor*] _____

By: _____
(Signature)

_____
(Typed or Printed Name)

Title: _____

Taxpayer ID Number: _____

Date: _____

It is common, and perfectly legal, to use electronic or digital signatures in a contract instead of handwritten signatures. If you do so, include a provision at the end of the agreement making it clear that such signatures are valid.

Optional Language: Signatures (Electronic or Digital Signatures)

This agreement may be signed by an electronic or digital signature.

Optional Provisions

There are several optional provisions you may wish to include in your agreement. They are not necessary for every client agreement, but they can be extremely helpful. You should carefully consider including them in your contracts. Pay especially close attention to the provisions regarding:

- resolving disputes
- contract changes, and
- attorneys' fees.

It's usually to your advantage to include all of these provisions in your agreement.

Resolving Disputes

As you probably know, court litigation can be very expensive. To avoid this cost, people have developed alternative forms of dispute resolution that don't involve going to court, including mediation and arbitration.

The suggested clause below requires the client and you to take advantage of these alternate forms of dispute resolution. You're first required to submit the dispute to mediation. You agree on a neutral third person to serve as a mediator to try to help you settle your dispute. The mediator has no power to impose a decision, only to try to help you arrive at one.

If mediation doesn't work, the clause provides that you must submit the dispute to binding arbitration. Arbitration is like an informal court trial without a jury, in which an arbitrator makes the decisions instead of a judge. It is usually much faster and cheaper than a lawsuit. You may, but are not required to, be represented by a lawyer.

You should indicate where the mediation or arbitration would occur. You'll usually want this to be in the city or county where your office is located. You don't want to have to travel a long distance to attend a mediation or arbitration.

However, every state has an alternative to mediation or arbitration that can be even cheaper and quicker than either of these approaches: small claims court. Small claims courts are designed to help resolve disputes involving a relatively small amount of money. The amount ranges from about $5,000 to $15,000, depending on the state in which you live. If your dispute involves more money than the small claims limit, you can waive the excess (that is, give up your right to sue for anything over the limit) and still bring a small claims suit. You don't need a lawyer to sue in small claims court; indeed, lawyers are barred from small claims court in several states. Small claims court is particularly useful when a client owes you a relatively small amount of money. (See Chapter 7.)

The following clause also provides that you or the client can elect to skip mediation and arbitration and instead take your dispute to small claims court.

Suggested Language: Resolving Disputes

If a dispute arises under this Agreement, the parties agree to first try to resolve the dispute with the help of a mutually agreed-upon mediator in [*city or county where mediation will occur*]. Any costs and fees other than attorneys' fees associated with the mediation will be shared equally by the parties.

If it proves impossible to arrive at a mutually satisfactory solution through mediation, the parties agree to submit the dispute to binding arbitration in [*city or county where arbitration will occur*] under the rules of the American Arbitration Association. Judgment upon the award rendered by the arbitrator may be entered in any court having jurisdiction to do so.

However, the complaining party may refuse to submit the dispute to mediation or arbitration and instead bring an action in an appropriate small claims court.

Modifying the Agreement

It's very common for either you or your client to want to change the terms of an agreement after you have started work. For example, the client might want to make a change in the contract specifications that could require you to do more work. Or you might discover that you underestimated how much time the project will take and need to charge more to complete it.

When you modify your agreement in this way, you should write down the changes on a separate document, have both parties sign it, and attach it to your original agreement. See "Changing the Agreement After It's Signed" in Chapter 18 for a detailed discussion and a sample contract amendment form.

FORM ON NOLO.COM
You can download a copy of the Contract Amendment form from this book's companion page on Nolo.com. For details on finding these and other forms on Nolo.com, which you can tailor to your own use, see "List of Forms Available on the Nolo Website" at the end of Appendix A of this book.

The following provision recognizes that the original agreement you enter into with the client may have to be changed. This provision states that you and the client must write down your changes and both sign the writing. Such a contract provision may be overkill; both you and the client can still make changes without agreeing to in advance. However, making this requirement explicit stresses the importance of documenting changes in writing.

Neither you nor the client must accept a proposed change to a contract. Because you are obligated to deal with each other fairly and in good faith, however, you cannot simply refuse all modifications without attempting to reach a resolution.

! CAUTION
Resolve disputes over modification with alternative dispute resolution (ADR). If you use this clause, check to be sure you have also included the optional provision on resolving disputes. That way, if you and the client can't agree on the changes, the agreement will require that you submit your dispute to mediation; and, if that doesn't work, to binding arbitration. This avoids expensive lawsuits in court.

Suggested Language: Modifying the Agreement

Client and Contractor recognize that:
- Contractor's original cost and time estimates may be too low due to unforeseen events or to factors unknown to Contractor when this Agreement was made.
- Client may desire a midproject change in Contractor's services that would add time and cost to the project and possibly inconvenience Contractor.
- Other provisions of this Agreement may be difficult to carry out due to unforeseen circumstances.

If any intended changes or any other events beyond the parties' control require adjustments to this Agreement, the parties will make a good-faith effort to agree on all necessary particulars. Such agreements will be put in writing, signed by the parties, and added to this Agreement.

Attorneys' Fees

Contrary to the rule in most other countries, American law requires each party to a lawsuit to pay its own attorney fees, unless a legal statute provides otherwise. For example, the federal copyright law allows a person who successfully sues someone for infringement to be awarded attorneys' fees by the court. However, parties can change this default rule by signing a contract that requires the losing side in a legal dispute to pay the winning (or "prevailing") side's attorney fees and costs.

Under the following provision, if either party has to sue the other in court to enforce the agreement and wins—that is, becomes the prevailing party—the loser is required to pay the other party's attorneys' fees and expenses.

If you have to sue the client in court to enforce the agreement and you win, this provision can make filing a lawsuit economically feasible. It might help you to convince a lawyer to file a case against your client without your having to provide an up-front cash retainer. It will also give the client a strong incentive to negotiate with you if you have a good case.

Sometimes, however, an attorneys' fees provision can work against you. It may help your client find an attorney to sue you and make you more eager to settle. And it can make litigation more stressful for you, because if you lose—for example, because you don't have enough evidence to support your case—you could be stuck with a very big bill. Particularly if you think you're more likely to violate the agreement than your client is, an attorneys' fees provision is probably not a good idea.

Suggested Language: Attorneys' Fees

If any legal action is necessary to enforce this Agreement, the prevailing party will be entitled to reasonable attorneys' fees, costs, and expenses in addition to any other relief to which he or she may be entitled.

Late Fees

Many self-employed people charge a late fee if the client doesn't pay within the time specified in the IC agreement or invoice. Charging late fees for overdue payments can get clients to pay on time. The late fee is normally expressed as a monthly interest charge; 1.5% per month (18% per year) is common. If you wish to charge a late fee, make sure it's mentioned in your agreement. You should also clearly state your late fee on all your invoices.

> CAUTION
> **Some states restrict late fees.** Your state might restrict how much you can charge as a late fee. Charging extensive interest is called "usury," and it's illegal. (See "Charge Late Fees" in Chapter 7 to learn more.)

Suggested Language: Late Fees

Time is of the essence with respect to all payments to be made by Client under this Agreement. If Client is late in any payment provided for in this Agreement, Client will pay interest on the payment from the date due until paid at a rate of _____% per month, or the maximum rate permitted by law, whichever is less.

Liability to the Client

If something goes wrong with your work, you might end up getting sued by the client and having to pay damages.

> EXAMPLE: Julie, a self-employed computer programmer, designs an inventory accounting program for a cosmetics company. A bug in the program causes the program to crash, and the company is unable to conduct normal business for several days, losing tens of thousands of dollars. The company sues Julie, claiming that her program design was deficient.

Such lawsuits could easily cost more than you were paid for your work and could even bankrupt you. To avoid this, many self-employed people include provisions in their agreements limiting their liability. This is particularly wise if problems with your work or services could cause the client substantial injuries or economic losses.

The following optional clause limits your total liability for any damages to the client to a set dollar amount or to no more than you were paid, whichever is less. It also relieves you of liability for lost profits or other special damages to the client.

Such damages are also called "incidental" or "consequential" damages. These are damages that can far exceed the amount the client actually paid you for your work. They arise out of circumstances you knew about or should have foreseen when the contract was made. This type of damages often involves lost profits that logically result from your failure to live up to your agreement. For example, if you knew that your failure to deliver your work on time could cost the client a valuable business opportunity, you could be required to make up the lost profits the client would have earned had you delivered the work on time. The optional clause below states that you will not be responsible for these types of damages.

Suggested Language: Limited Liability (Cap on Liability)

Contractor's total liability to Client under this Agreement for damages, costs, and expenses, regardless of cause, will not exceed $_____ or the compensation received by Contractor under this Agreement, whichever is less.

UNLESS A RESULT OF GROSS NEGLIGENCE OR WILLFUL MISCONDUCT, CONTRACTOR WILL NOT BE LIABLE FOR CLIENT'S LOST PROFITS OR SPECIAL, INCIDENTAL, OR CONSEQUENTIAL DAMAGES, WHETHER IN AN ACTION IN CONTRACT OR TORT, EVEN IF CONTRACTOR HAS BEEN ADVISED BY CLIENT OF THE POSSIBILITY OF SUCH DAMAGES.

Liability to Others

The work that you do can affect people other than the client. Such people are called third parties. You need to be particularly concerned about your liability to third parties if you're engaged in a hazardous or risky project that could result in injuries to others if something goes wrong.

Third parties typically enter the picture when they are directly or indirectly injured by the work you've performed for a client. The injuries can be physical, economic, or both. For example, if an elevator crashes due to faulty software a self-employed programmer designed for the elevator manufacturer, the injured elevator passengers would be third parties to the programmer. Even though the programmer never met or contracted with them, the programmer might be legally responsible for their injuries.

If third parties are damaged as a result of the work you perform for a client, they'll likely sue everyone involved, including you. Both you and the client may be liable for the full amount of such claims. Legal clauses called "indemnification provisions" require one party to pay the other's attorneys' fees and damages arising from such claims. Such provisions don't affect third parties who sue you, nor do they absolve you from liability to third parties for your actions. An indemnification clause requires only one party (for example, your client) to pay any amounts due from the other (for example, you) as a result of such liability.

> **EXAMPLE:** Bart, a self-employed software engineer, creates an experimental software program designed to automate a chemical factory for BigCorp. The program fails, which results in a chemical spill, damaging nearby property.
>
> The property owners affected by the chemical spill could sue not only BigCorp but Bart as well, claiming that he negligently designed the software. Bart could be forced to defend himself against the lawsuit filed by total strangers to him.

You may wish to include the following provision in your agreement requiring the client to indemnify you against third-party claims. This means the client will be responsible for defending any lawsuits and for all damages and injuries that third parties suffer if something goes wrong with your work.

To accomplish this, the provision uses a standard legal phrase that is a bit convoluted. It states that the client shall "indemnify, defend, and hold harmless" the contractor against third-party claims. This means the client is required to assume responsibility for dealing with third-party claims and must repay you if they end up costing you anything.

Many clients will balk at including an indemnification provision in your agreement. Moreover, as a practical matter, such a provision is useless if the client doesn't have the money or insurance to pay the amount due. You may be better off charging the client enough to obtain your own liability insurance protecting you against third-party claims. (See Chapter 6.)

Suggested Language: Liability to Others

Client will indemnify, defend, and hold harmless Contractor against all liabilities, damages, and expenses, including reasonable attorneys' fees, resulting from any third-party claim or lawsuit arising from Contractor's performance under this Agreement.

CAUTION

Don't agree to indemnify the client. Some clients will not only refuse to indemnify you against third-party claims, they'll want you to indemnify them. In that case, you'll have to repay the client if a third party sues. For obvious reasons, you should say no to such provisions. (See Chapter 20.)

Intellectual Property Ownership

If you're hired to create or contribute to the creation of intellectual property—for example, important business documents, marketing plans, software programs, graphics, designs, photos, music, inventions, or trademarks—the agreement should specify who owns your work.

There are many options regarding ownership of intellectual property that self-employed people create, explained in detail in Chapter 17. Typically, your client will want to own all the intellectual property rights in your work, but this doesn't have to be the case. For example, you could retain sole ownership and grant the client a license to use your work. The only limit on how you deal with ownership of your work is your imagination, as well as the agreement of your client.

You Retain Ownership

Under the following clause, you keep ownership of your work and merely give the client a nonexclusive license to use it. This means that the client may use your work but does not own it and may not sell it to others. The license is royalty free: The sole payment you receive for it is the sum the client paid you for your services. The client will make no additional payments for the license.

Suggested Language: Intellectual Property Ownership
(Alternative A—Nonexclusive Transfer)

Contractor grants to Client a royalty-free nonexclusive license to use anything created or developed by Contractor for Client under this Agreement ("Contract Property"). The license will have a perpetual term, and the Client may not transfer it. Contractor will retain all copyrights, patent rights, and other intellectual property rights to the Contract Property. This license is conditioned upon full payment of all compensation due Contractor under this Agreement.

You Transfer Ownership to Client

Under the following clause you transfer all your ownership rights to the client. But you must first receive all your compensation from the client.

You also agree to help prepare any documents necessary to help the client obtain any copyright, patent, or other intellectual property rights at no charge to the client. This would probably amount to no more than signing a patent or copyright registration application. However, the client is required to reimburse you for the expense of getting and assigning the rights.

Suggested Language: Intellectual Property Ownership
(Alternative B—Transfer All Rights)

Contractor assigns to Client all patent, copyright, and trade secret rights in anything created or developed by Contractor for Client under this Agreement. This assignment is conditioned upon full payment of the compensation due Contractor under this Agreement.

Contractor will help prepare any documents Client considers necessary to secure any copyright, patent, or other intellectual property rights at no charge to Client. However, Client will reimburse Contractor for reasonable out-of-pocket expenses.

Reusable Materials

Many self-employed people who create intellectual property for clients have certain materials they use over and over again for different clients. For example, computer programmers may have certain utilities or program tools they incorporate into the software they create for many different clients.

You may lose the legal right to reuse such materials if you transfer all your ownership rights in your work to the client. To avoid this, include a provision like the one below in your agreement. It provides that you retain ownership of such materials and only gives the client a nonexclusive license to use them. The license is royalty free, which means that the sole payment you receive for it is the sum the client paid you for your services. The client will make no additional payments for the license. The license also has a perpetual term, meaning it will last as long as your copyright, patent, or other intellectual property rights do.

If you know what such materials consist of in advance, it's a good idea to list them in an exhibit attached to the agreement. This isn't required, however.

Optional Language: Reusable Materials (Right to Reuse)

Contractor owns or holds a license to use and sublicense various materials in existence before the start date of this Agreement (Contractor's Materials).

[OPTIONAL: Contractor's Materials include, but are not limited to, those items identified in Exhibit ___ , attached to and made part of this Agreement.]

Contractor may, at its option, include Contractor's Materials in the work performed under this Agreement. Contractor retains all right, title, and interest, including all copyrights, patent rights, and trade secret rights in Contractor's Materials. Contractor grants Client a royalty-free nonexclusive license to use any Contractor's Materials incorporated into the work performed by Contractor under this Agreement. The license will have a perpetual term and may not be transferred by Client.

Assignment and Delegation

An assignment is the process by which rights or benefits under a contract are transferred to someone else. For example, a client might assign the right to receive the benefit of your services to someone else. Such a person is called an assignee. When this occurs, the assignee steps into the original client's shoes. You must now work for the assignee, not the client with whom you contracted. If you fail to perform, the assignee may sue you for breach of contract.

> **EXAMPLE:** Terri, a self-employed designer, agrees to design a cover and chapter headings for several books published by Scrivener & Sons. Scrivener assigns this right to Pop's Books. This means that Terri must perform the work for Pop's instead of Scrivener. If Terri fails to do so, Pop's can sue her for breach of contract.

You may also assign the benefits you receive under an IC agreement to someone else.

> **EXAMPLE:** Jimmy agrees to provide Fastsoft with 20 hours of computer pro-gramming service for $1,000. Jimmy assigns, or transfers, his right to payment to his friend Kate. This means that Fastsoft must pay Kate the $1,000.

Delegation is the flipside of assignment. Instead of transferring benefits under a contract, you transfer the duties. As long as the new person does the job correctly, all will be well. However, the person delegating duties under a contract usually remains responsible if the person to whom the delegation was made fails to perform competently.

> **EXAMPLE:** Jimmy finds he is too busy to do the work by the deadline, so he assigns or transfers to Mindy his duty to perform 20 hours of programming services for Fastsoft. This means that Mindy, not Jimmy, will now do the work. But Jimmy remains liable if Mindy doesn't perform adequately.

You assign your rights and/or delegate duties under your contract by entering into an agreement—preferably in writing—with the person who is stepping into your shoes, called the assignee. You should also provide written notice of the assignment and/or delegation to the client.

Legal Restrictions

Unless a contract provides otherwise, you can ordinarily assign and delegate freely, subject to some important legal limitations. For example, a client can't assign the benefit of your services to someone else without your consent if it would increase the work you must do or otherwise magnify your burden under the contract. Similarly, you can't delegate your duties without the client's consent if it would decrease the benefits the client would receive.

One of the most important limitations for self-employed people is that contracts for personal services are ordinarily not assignable or delegable without the client's consent. This type of contract involves services that are personal in nature. Examples include contracts for the services of lawyers, physicians, architects, writers, and artists. In such cases, courts consider it unfair for either a client or a self-employed person to change horses midstream.

> **EXAMPLE:** Arthur contracts with Betty, a freelance artist, to paint his portrait. She later attempts to delegate her duties to her friend Carla, leaving Carla to paint Arthur's portrait instead of her. Arthur does not have to agree to this change because Betty's contract with Arthur was a contract for personal services.

Contract Restrictions

Your contract may also place limits on assignment and delegation. Contractual limits on your right to delegate your duties to others are not supportive of your independent contractor status because they allow the client to control who will do the work. Moreover, it is often advantageous for you to have the right to delegate your contractual obligations to others. This gives you flexibility, for example, to hire someone else to do the work if you don't have time to do it.

However, some clients may balk at allowing you to delegate your contractual duties without the client's consent. This is usually because the client has hired you because of your special expertise, reputation for performance, or financial stability, and the client doesn't want some other person performing the services. Also, there may be cases in which you do not want the client to have the right to assign the benefit of your services to someone else, who may turn out to be incompetent.

In this event, you may include the following provision in your agreement. It bars both you and the client from assigning your rights or delegating your duties without the other party's consent.

Suggested Language: Assignment and Delegation

Neither party may assign any rights nor delegate any duties under this Agreement without the other party's prior written approval. Any assignment or delegation in violation of this section is void

Sample Client Agreement

The following sample agreement is a fixed-fee agreement calling for mediation and arbitration of disputes and payment of attorneys' fees. If you don't understand any of the provisions, refer back to the relevant discussion in this chapter.

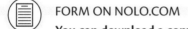 FORM ON NOLO.COM

You can download a copy of the full contract (Independent Contractor Agreement) from this book's companion page on Nolo.com. For details on finding this and other forms on Nolo.com, which you can tailor to your own use, see "List of Forms Available on the Nolo Website" at the end of Appendix A of this book.

Using Letter Agreements

Many self-employed people and their clients use letter agreements instead of more formal standard contracts. A letter agreement is usually a short contract written in the form of a letter. Although letter agreements may lack the appearance of gravitas of standard agreements, they are perfectly valid, binding contracts.

Typically, when you use a letter agreement, you and a client will first reach a tentative agreement in a meeting, over the phone, or by email, or through some combination of these. Then, one of you drafts a letter documenting the important terms, signs it, and sends it to the other person to sign.

Sample Independent Contractor Agreement

Independent Contractor Agreement

This Agreement is made between Acme Widget Co. (Client), with a principal place of business at 123 Main Street, Marred Vista, CA 90000, and ABC Consulting, Inc. (Contractor), with a principal place of business at 456 Grub Street, Santa Longo, CA 90001.

Services to Be Performed

Contractor agrees to perform the following services: Install and test Client's DX9-105 widget manufacturing press so that it performs according to the manufacturer's specifications.

Payment

In consideration for the services to be performed by Contractor, Client agrees to pay Contractor $20,000.

Terms of Payment

Upon completing Contractor's services under this Agreement, Contractor will submit an invoice. Client will pay Contractor within 30 days from the date of Contractor's invoice.

Expenses

Contractor will be responsible for all expenses incurred while performing services under this Agreement.

Materials

Contractor will furnish all materials and equipment used to provide the services required by this Agreement.

Term of Agreement

This Agreement will become effective when signed by both parties and will end no later than May 1, 20xx.

Terminating the Agreement

With reasonable cause, either party may terminate this Agreement effective immediately by giving written notice of termination for cause. Reasonable cause includes:

- a material violation of this agreement, or

Sample Independent Contractor Agreement (continued)

- nonpayment of Contractor's compensation 20 days after written demand for payment.

Contractor will be entitled to full payment for services performed prior to the effective date of termination. This obligation, and any payment obligations pending at termination, survive termination.

Independent Contractor Status

Contractor is an independent contractor, not Client's employee. Contractor's employees or contract personnel are not Client's employees. Contractor and Client agree to the following rights consistent with an independent contractor relationship:

- Contractor has the right to perform services for others during the term of this Agreement.
- Contractor has the sole right to control and direct the means, manner, and method by which the services required by this Agreement will be performed.
- Contractor has the right to hire assistants as subcontractors, or to use employees to provide the services required by this Agreement.
- Contractor or Contractor's employees or contract personnel will perform the services required by this Agreement; Client will not hire, supervise, or pay any assistants to help Contractor.
- Neither Contractor nor Contractor's employees or contract personnel will receive any training from Client in the skills necessary to perform the services required by this Agreement.
- Client will not require Contractor or Contractor's employees or contract personnel to devote full time to performing the services required by this Agreement.
- Neither Contractor nor Contractor's employees or contract personnel are eligible to participate in any employee retirement, health, vacation pay, sick pay, or other fringe benefit plan of Client.

Local, State, and Federal Taxes

Contractor will pay all income taxes and FICA (Social Security and Medicare taxes) incurred while performing services under this Agreement. Client will not:

Sample Independent Contractor Agreement (continued)

- withhold FICA from Contractor's payments or make FICA payments on Contractor's behalf
- make state or federal unemployment compensation contributions on Contractor's behalf, or
- withhold state or federal income tax from Contractor's payments.

Sales Taxes

The charges included here do not include taxes. If Contractor is required to pay any federal, state, or local sales, use, property, or value-added taxes based on the services provided under this Agreement, the taxes will be billed to Client separately. Contractor will not pay any interest or penalties incurred due to late payment or nonpayment of any taxes by Client.

Notices

All notices and other communications in connection with this Agreement will be in writing and will be deemed given as follows:

- when delivered personally to the recipient's address as stated on this Agreement
- three days after being deposited in the United States mail, with postage prepaid to the recipient's address as stated in this Agreement, or
- when sent by fax or email to the last fax number or email address of the recipient known to the person giving notice. Notice is effective upon receipt provided that a duplicate copy of the notice is promptly given by first-class mail, or the recipient delivers a written confirmation of receipt.

No Partnership

This Agreement does not create a partnership relationship. Neither party has authority to enter into contracts on the other's behalf.

Applicable Law and Jurisdiction

This Agreement will be governed by the laws of the state of California. Any disputes arising from it must be handled exclusively in the federal and state courts located in Mariposa County, California.

Exclusive Agreement

This Agreement (including any attached exhibits) is the entire Agreement between Contractor and Client.

Sample Independent Contractor Agreement (continued)

Resolving Disputes

If a dispute arises under this Agreement, the parties agree to first try to resolve the dispute with the help of a mutually agreed-upon mediator in Mariposa County. Any costs and fees other than attorneys' fees associated with the mediation will be shared equally by the parties.

If it proves impossible to arrive at a mutually satisfactory solution through mediation, the parties agree to submit the dispute to binding arbitration in Mariposa County under the rules of the American Arbitration Association. Judgment upon the award rendered by the arbitrator may be entered in any court having jurisdiction to do so.

However, the complaining party may refuse to submit the dispute to mediation or arbitration and instead bring an action in an appropriate small claims court.

Modifying the Agreement

Client and Contractor recognize that:

- Contractor's original cost and time estimates may be too low due to unforeseen events or to factors unknown to Contractor when this Agreement was made.
- Client may desire a midproject change in Contractor's services that would add time and cost to the project and possibly inconvenience Contractor.
- Other provisions of this Agreement may be difficult to carry out due to unforeseen circumstances.

If any intended changes or any other events beyond the parties' control require adjustments to this Agreement, the parties will make a good-faith effort to agree on all necessary particulars. Such agreements will be put in writing, signed by the parties, and added to this Agreement.

Attorneys' Fees

If any legal action is necessary to enforce this Agreement, the prevailing party will be entitled to reasonable attorneys' fees, costs, and expenses in addition to any other relief to which he or she may be entitled.

Sample Independent Contractor Agreement (continued)

Signatures

Client: ___Acme Widget Co._____

By: ___Basilio Chew_____
                          (Signature)

___Basilio Chew_____
                          (Typed or Printed Name)

Title: ___President_____

Date: ___April 30, 20xx_____

Contractor: ___ABC Consulting, Inc._____

By: ___George Bailey_____
                          (Signature)

___George Bailey_____
                          (Typed or Printed Name)

Title: ___President_____

Taxpayer ID Number: ___123-45-6789_____

Date: ___April 30, 20xx_____

Some clients have their own form letter agreements they use with all self-employed people they hire and will insist on using them. Review such a letter carefully to make sure it meshes with the client's and your own oral statements and does not contain unfair provisions. (See Chapter 20.)

However, many clients will be happy for you to take on the work of drafting the agreement. You'll almost always be better off if you draft the agreement yourself because you can:

- avoid including any terms that are unduly favorable to the client, and
- make sure the agreement is completed and sent out quickly.

Take the initiative and offer to draw up the letter agreement. Explain that this is part of your service and that using an agreement you've drafted helps establish that you're not the client's employee.

Use the information in this chapter to draft one or more appropriate form letters you can use over and over again with minor alterations.

> CAUTION
>
> **Don't begin work until the client signs on the bottom line.** No matter who drafts a letter agreement, don't begin work until you have a copy signed by the client. You don't want to begin work only to discover that the client wants to cancel the project or make major changes in your agreement.

Pros and Cons of Letter Agreements

Letter agreements are usually shorter and easier to draft than regular contracts. They are also less formal looking. As a result, they often seem less intimidating to clients. Many clients who are fearful of signing a formal contract without having a lawyer review it will not hesitate to sign a letter agreement.

In some fields, using letter agreements is the commonly accepted practice for doing business. For example, letter agreements are commonly used when freelance writers accept short assignments from magazines or other publications. If this is the case in your field of work, you may have to use letter agreements as a matter of course.

Because letter agreements are usually much shorter than standard client agreements, they are particularly useful for brief projects where relatively little money is involved. A potential client could well think you're crazy if you insist on a lengthy formal contract for a simple one-day project.

However, in the interests of brevity, letter agreements typically make no mention of many provisions contained in longer standard agreements that could prove useful if a problem arises, such as provisions concerning dispute resolution, how the agreement may be terminated, or cementing your status as an independent contractor.

Both your client and you may be better off using a standard client agreement if:

- The project is a large and complex one that involves a substantial amount of money.
- You're dealing with a new client you're not sure you can trust.
- You are otherwise worried that problems or disputes may occur.

What to Include

A letter agreement can be as short as one paragraph. At a minimum, however, it should contain:

- a description of the services you will perform
- the deadline by which you must complete your services
- the fees you will charge, and
- when you will be paid.

Your agreement doesn't have to end here, however. Depending on the nature of your services and the client, you may want to include any of several other provisions.

Services to Be Performed

The single most important part of the agreement is the description of the services you'll perform for the client. This description will set out the specifics of the work you're required to do and will serve as the yardstick to measure whether your performance was satisfactory.

Describe the work you're expected to accomplish in as much detail as possible. However, word the description carefully to emphasize the results you're expected to achieve. Don't describe the method by which you will achieve the results. It should be up to you to decide how to do the work. The client's control should be limited to accepting or rejecting your final results.

It's fine for the agreement to establish detailed specifications for your finished work product, but it should describe only the end results you must achieve, not how to obtain those results.

You can include the description in the main body of the agreement. Or, if it's a lengthy explanation, you can put it on a separate document and attach it to the letter agreement.

Suggested Language: Services to Be Performed
(Alternative A—Description in Agreement)

I will perform the following services on your behalf: [*Describe services you will perform.*]

Suggested Language: Services to Be Performed
(Alternative B—Description Attached)

I will perform the services described in the Exhibit attached to this Agreement.

Deadlines

The agreement should also make clear when your work will be completed and delivered to the client. Make sure you give yourself enough time to complete the job. It's better to err on the side of caution and give yourself more time than you think you'll need.

Suggested Language: Deadlines

I agree to complete these services on or before [*date*].

Payment

Self-employed people can be paid in many different ways. The two most common payment methods are:

- a fixed fee, and
- payment by unit of time.

Fixed Fee

In a fixed-fee agreement, you charge an agreed-upon amount for the entire project.

Suggested Language: Payment (Alternative A—Fixed Fee)

In consideration of my performance of these services, you agree to pay me $ [*amount*].

Unit of Time

Many self-employed people, including lawyers, accountants, and plumbers, charge by the hour, day, or other unit of time. Charging by the hour does not necessarily support the idea that you're an independent contractor, but you can get away with it if it's a common practice in your field.

Suggested Language: Payment (Alternative B—Unit of Time)

In consideration of my performance of these services, you agree to pay me at the rate of $ [*amount*] per [*hour, day, week, or other unit of time*].

Clients often wish to place a cap on the total amount they'll spend on the project when you're paid by the hour because they're afraid you might work slowly just to earn a larger fee. If the client insists on a cap, make sure it allows you to work enough hours to get the project done.

Optional Language: Payment (Cap on Payment)

[*OPTIONAL:* My total compensation will not exceed $ [*amount*] without your written consent.]

Terms of Payment

Terms of payment means how you will bill the client and be paid. The client will not likely pay you for your work until you submit an invoice setting out the amount due. An invoice doesn't have to be fancy. It should include an invoice number, the dates covered by the invoice, the hours expended if you're being paid by the hour, and a summary of the work performed. (See "Getting Paid" in Chapter 7 for a detailed discussion and sample invoice form.)

Full Payment Upon Completing Work

The following provision requires you to send an invoice after you complete work. The client is required to pay your fixed or hourly fee within a set number of days after you send the invoice. Thirty days is a typical payment term, but it can be shorter or longer if you wish. When economic conditions are poor, clients may insist on a longer term.

Note that the time for payment starts to run as soon as you send your invoice, not when the client receives it. This will help you get paid more quickly.

Suggested Language: Terms of Payment (Alternative A—Payment on Completion)

I will submit an invoice after my services are completed. You will pay me within [*10, 15, 30, 45, or 60*] days from the date of the invoice.

Divided Payments

You can also opt to be paid part of your fee when the agreement is signed and the remainder when the work is finished. When you're paid by the hour, such an up-front payment is often called a retainer. The amount of the up-front payment is subject to negotiation. Many self-employed people like to receive at least one-third to one-half of their fees before they start work. If the client is new or might have problems paying you, it's wise to get as much money in advance as you can.

The following provision requires that you be paid a specific amount when the client signs the agreement and the rest when the work is finished.

Suggested Language: Terms of Payment (Alternative B—Divided Payments)

I will be paid in two installments. The first installment will be $ [*amount*] and is payable by [*due date*]. The remaining $ [*amount*] will be due within [*10, 15, 30, 45, or 60*] days after I complete my services and submit an invoice.

Optional Provisions

There are a number of other provisions you can add to a letter agreement. These aren't necessary, but they can be helpful to you. They are all discussed in detail in the first part of this chapter. They include provisions that:

- require the client to reimburse you for expenses you incur in performing the work
- require the client to provide you with materials, equipment, or facilities
- require mediation and arbitration of disputes
- allow you to obtain attorneys' fees if you sue the client and win
- require the client to pay a fee for late payments
- limit your liability to the client if something goes wrong, and
- restrict the client's ability to assign its benefits or delegate its duties under the agreement.

In addition, if your work involves the creation of intellectual property—for example, any type of work of authorship, such as an article or other written work—you should include a provision in your agreement that states who will own your work.

Putting the Agreement Together

There are two ways to handle a letter agreement. The old-fashioned way is to prepare and sign two copies and mail or deliver them to the client to sign. The client signs both copies, then returns one signed copy to you by mail or messenger and retains one copy for its records. Both copies are original, binding contracts.

Today, however, it's very common for an IC to draft a letter agreement, sign it, and then email a copy to the client. The client signs the letter and faxes or emails a copy back to you. This has the advantage of speed, but you don't have the client's original signature on the letter, only a copy.

A scanned signature is legally sufficient if you and the client don't dispute that it is a scan of an original signature. However, if a client claims that a scanned signature was forged, it could be difficult or impossible to prove it's genuine. Forgery claims are rare, however, so this is usually not a problem. Even so, it's a good practice for you and the client to follow up the email with signed originals exchanged by mail or delivery service.

Sample Letter Agreement

The following is a sample letter agreement between a self-employed public relations consultant and an oil company. The consultant agrees to create a marketing plan for the company's new oil additive called Zotz. The consultant will perform the work for a fixed fee paid in two installments.

FORM ON NOLO.COM
You can download a copy of the Letter Agreement form from this book's companion page on Nolo.com. For details on finding these and other forms on Nolo.com, which you can tailor to your own use, see "List of Forms Available on the Nolo Website" at the end of Appendix A of this book.

Maloney & Associates
1000 Grub Street
Marred Vista, Ca 90000
Maloney@marred.com

February 1, 20xx

Jerry Wellhead
Vice President
Acme Oil Co.
1000 Greasy Way
Tulsa, OK 10000

Dear Jerry:

I am pleased to have the opportunity to provide my services. This letter will serve as our agreement.

I will perform the following services on your behalf: I will create a marketing plan for the rollout of Acme's new oil additive called Zotz. The plan will include guidelines for magazine, radio, and television advertising.

I agree to complete these services on or before March 1, 20xx.

In consideration of my performance of these services, you agree to pay me $5,000.

I will be paid in two installments. The first installment will be $2,500 and is payable by February 5, 20xx. The remaining $2,500 will be due within 30 days after I complete my services and submit an invoice.

If this Agreement meets with your approval, please sign below to make this a binding contract between us. Please sign both copies and return one to me. Keep one signed copy for your records.

Sincerely,

Susan Maloney
Susan Maloney

Agreed to: Acme Oil Co.

By: _Jerry Wellhead_____
                     (Signature)
Jerry Wellhead
Title: Vice President
Date: _February 3, 20xx_____

Reviewing a Client's Agreement

Many clients have their own agreement forms they will want to use. This is particularly likely if you work for firms that often use third parties to perform services or for large companies that have their own legal departments. A client may present you with a lengthy, complex agreement, hand you a pen, and tell you to sign. You may be told that the agreement is only a standard form that all nonemployees who work for the client sign.

However, signing a client agreement is never a mere technical formality. A client agreement is not simply a bunch of words on a piece of paper. It's a binding, legal document that will have important consequences for you in the real world.

Because client-drafted agreements are usually written with the client's best interests in mind, not yours, you'll almost always be better off if you use your own agreement. A client will be more willing to do this if you:

- provide a well-drafted agreement of your own (see Chapter 19), and
- point out that if the client is audited, an IRS or other government auditor will be far more impressed by an agreement you drafted than a standard form prepared by the client. Using your agreement helps establish that you're an independent contractor, not the client's employee, and may help the client avoid assessments and penalties in the event of an audit.

If the client insists on using its own agreement, be sure to review the document before you accept the project. Read the agreement carefully, and make sure you understand and are comfortable with it before signing. If there are any provisions you don't understand, ask the client to explain them to you and rewrite them so that you do understand them.

No matter what the client may say, no agreement is engraved in stone, even if it's a "standard" agreement the client claims everybody signs. You can always request that an unfair or unduly burdensome provision be deleted or changed. If the client refuses, you have the option of turning down the project or going ahead anyway, but you lose nothing by asking.

When you review a client's agreement, you'll want to make sure it:

- jibes with the client's statements and your own oral statements
- contains all necessary provisions, and
- does not contain unfair provisions.

There may also be provisions you want to add.

Careless Doctor Done In by Unread Agreement

One emergency room physician learned the hard way that it's always necessary to carefully read and understand an agreement before signing it. The doctor, who worked on the East Coast, received an offer to work as an independent contractor for a hospital in Hawaii. The doctor agreed to take the job and signed a lengthy independent contractor agreement prepared by the hospital without reading it carefully. The agreement provided a two-year term. She thought this meant she had guaranteed work for two years and this would justify the expense of moving to Hawaii.

The doctor moved to Hawaii and started work. But within three months, she had serious disagreements with hospital officials over various clinical and administrative issues. The hospital notified her that she was being terminated. She protested, pointing out that her contract was for two years. When she took a closer look, however, she discovered that the agreement included a provision allowing the hospital to terminate her if it concluded it was necessary to do so to operate efficiently.

Make Sure the Agreement Is Consistent With the Client's Promises

Unfortunately, some clients are in the habit of telling people they hire one thing to get them to accept the project, then writing something very different in the agreements they prepare. If a client says one thing to you in person and the agreement says something else, the agreement ordinarily will control. For example, if the client tells you that your work must be completed in two months, but the agreement imposes a one-month deadline, the work will have to be done in one month.

For this reason, make absolutely sure the agreement meshes with what the client has told you and what you have told the client. If there are differences, point them out. And if they're important differences, change the document to reflect your true agreement.

How to Change an Agreement

If you want to delete all or part of a provision, you can simply cross it out. Minor wording changes can be written in by hand or typed. Both you and the client should write your initials as near the deletions or additions as possible to indicate your consent.

If you wish to add an extensive amount of new wording, it's best to redo the entire agreement to prevent it from becoming illegible or downright confusing.

Another approach is to write the changes on a separate piece of paper, called an "addendum," that you and the client sign. If you use an addendum, state that if there is a conflict between the addendum and the main contract, the addendum will prevail. (See "Addendums" in Chapter 18.)

Make Sure the Contract Covers at Least the Basics

You should also make sure that the agreement contains all necessary provisions. At a bare minimum, it should include:

- your name and address
- the client's name and address
- the dates the contract begins and ends
- a description of the services you'll perform
- how much you'll be paid, and
- how you'll be paid.

These and other standard provisions are normally included in client agreements. If the client's agreement lacks any of these provisions, you should add them. (See "Essential Provisions" in Chapter 19.)

If you're creating or helping to create intellectual property—for example, writings, photos, graphics, music, software programs, designs, or inventions—the agreement should also contain a clause making it clear who will own your work. (See "Intellectual Property Ownership" in Chapter 19.)

Provisions to Avoid

Clients' agreements sometimes contain provisions that are patently unfair to you. You should seek to delete these entirely or at least replace them with provisions that are more equitable. Examine the agreement carefully for provisions such as the following.

Indemnifying the Client

"Indemnification" is a legal word that means a promise to repay someone for their losses or damages if a specified event occurs. Some contracts may contain indemnification provisions that require you to repay the client if various problems occur (for example, if a problem with your work injures a third party who sues the client). In effect, these provisions require you to act as the client's insurer.

When it comes to indemnifying the client, your rule should be to just say "no." Examine the client's agreement carefully to see if it contains such a provision. If you find one, try to delete it. Indemnification clauses can be hard to spot and even harder to understand. They'll usually contain the words "indemnification" or "hold harmless," but not always. Any provision that requires you to defend or repay the client is an indemnification provision.

Problems With the IRS and Other Agencies

If the IRS or another government agency determines that the client has misclassified you as an independent contractor, the client may have to pay back taxes, fines, and penalties. (See Chapter 15.) Some hiring firms try to shift the risk of IRS or other penalties to the independent contractor's shoulders by including an indemnification clause in their agreements. Such provisions typically require you to repay the hiring firm for any losses suffered if you are reclassified as an employee. The following is an example of such a provision:

> If Contractor is determined to be Client's employee, Contractor will indemnify and hold Client harmless from any and all liabilities, costs, and expenses Client may incur, including attorneys' fees and penalties.

Do not sign an agreement that contains such a provision. The cost of fighting an IRS or other government audit and paying the possible penalties for worker misclassification can be enormous. This provision makes you responsible for paying all of these costs. If you are presented with an agreement containing such a provision, strike it out or refuse to sign the contract.

Injuries and Damages Arising From Your Services

Your work or services on the client's behalf may damage or injure third parties (people other than you and the client). For example, a passerby might be injured by a dropped hammer while walking by a construction project undertaken by a self-employed building contractor. Or software written by an outside programmer designed to run an elevator might fail and cause injuries. It's likely that the people injured in these situations—the passerby and the elevator passengers—would sue the hiring firm to pay for the costs of their medical care and other expenses related to their injuries.

Hiring firms often include indemnification provisions in their contracts, making the people they hire responsible for all damages and injuries that other people suffer if something goes wrong with their work. Many of these provisions are so broadly written they require you to indemnify the client even if the claim is frivolous, mainly the client's fault, or already covered by the client's insurance.

> EXAMPLE: Art, a self-employed engineer, designs and installs a new type of widget in BigCorp's factory. Art signed an agreement prepared by BigCorp's lawyers that contains the following indemnification provision:

Contractor will indemnify and hold Client harmless from any and all claims, losses, actions, damages, interest, penalties, and reasonable attorneys' fees and costs arising by reason of Contractor's performance under this Agreement.

One of BigCorp's employees alters the widget's setting without Art's permission. As a result, the widget explodes and injures a visitor at the factory, who sues BigCorp. Art has to pay all of BigCorp's costs of defending the lawsuit and any damages the injured person recovers, even though the explosion wasn't his fault. This is because the indemnification clause requires Art to repay BigCorp for any claim brought that could be said to "arise" from Art's services for BigCorp.

Most indemnification clauses are even more convoluted and harder to read than the one in the example above. The wisest course is to strike any such provision from the client's agreement.

If you must indemnify the other party, consider these strategies:

- **Beware of broad indemnity provisions.** Avoid indemnity provisions that are unusually broad. For example, stay away from a provision that indemnifies the client for any breach of the agreement. Try to rein in the indemnity clause so that it applies only to specific injuries to third parties, and to situations that you can control. For example, limit it to claims of intellectual property violations, such as copyright infringement. That way, you can avoid having to pay out on an indemnity provision by avoiding the conduct that triggers the provision.

- **Require prompt written notice of the third-party claim.** It would be unfair if the client ignored a claim or settled it secretly without your knowledge and then came after you for payment.

- **Attempt to limit indemnity to a lawsuit or even a final decision by a court.** Try to limit your obligation to situations in which a lawsuit is filed. This will prevent you from having to pay simply because somebody is threatening to sue or complaining about something. An even more protective standard would require you to pay only if you lost the legal battle with the third party.

- **Attempt to cap the indemnity.** This is perhaps the most difficult modification to get clients to agree to because it limits your liability to a specific amount. For example, you never must pay more to indemnify than you earned under the agreement.

Here's an example of an indemnification provision containing these elements:

Contractor will indemnify and hold Client harmless from any damages and liabilities (including reasonable attorney fees and costs) arising from any claim that the work produced by Contractor under this agreement violates the intellectual property rights of any third party, provided that:

- Client gives Contractor prompt written notice of any such claim
- such indemnity is applicable only in the event of a final decision by a court of competent jurisdiction from which no right to appeal exists, and
- the maximum amount due from Contractor to Client will not exceed the amounts paid to Contractor under this Agreement [*optional:* from the date that Client notifies Contractor of the existence of such a claim].

Also, make sure you have enough liability insurance to cover any potential claims. Feel free to charge the client more to cover your increased insurance costs. (See Chapter 7.)

Intellectual Property Infringement

If you create or help create intellectual property for a client, the client may seek to have you indemnify it for the costs involved if other people claim that your work infringes their copyright, patent, trade secret, or other intellectual property rights.

> EXAMPLE: Jennifer, a self-employed computer programmer, creates a program for Acme Corp. A few months later, BigCorp, Jennifer's former employer, claims that she stole substantial portions of the program from software it owned, and sues Jennifer and Acme for copyright infringement. Because Jennifer's contract with Acme contained an indemnification provision, she is legally obligated to pay Acme's attorneys' fees for defending the lawsuit and any money Acme may have to pay BigCorp as damages or to settle the claim.

Intellectual property indemnity clauses are routinely included in publishing contracts, software consulting agreements, and almost any other type of agreement involving the creation of intellectual property.

You'd be better off without such a clause —that is, less of your own money will be at risk on the job—but it's often hard to get clients to remove them. After all, the clauses are mainly aimed at ensuring proper behavior. You shouldn't commit intellectual property infringement, and clients do not to want to pay any damages if you do.

Instead of deleting the clause, your best approach may be to add a provision limiting your total liability to the client to a specified dollar amount or to no more than the client pays you.

Insurance Requirements

Look carefully to see if the client's agreement contains a provision that requires you to maintain insurance coverage. Many clients want all self-employed people they hire to have extensive insurance coverage because it helps eliminate an injured person's motivation to attempt to recover from the client for fear you won't be able to pay. It's not unreasonable for a client to require you to have liability insurance.

However, some clients go overboard and require you to obtain an excessive amount of insurance or obtain unusual and expensive policies. For example, one self-employed courier recently contracted with a courier firm to make document deliveries using his own car. The contract included an insurance clause requiring him to obtain cargo insurance. His insurance agent told him this type of coverage was usually obtained only by trucking firms and would cost several thousand dollars per year. It was ridiculous for a document courier to be required to obtain such coverage, because it provided far more coverage than the client needed and cost far more than the courier could afford to pay. The courier simply ignored the contract and never obtained the cargo insurance.

The better practice is to delete provisions requiring excessive insurance from your contract or demand substantially more compensation to pay for the extra insurance. Make it clear to the client that you have to charge more than you usually do because it's requiring you to carry so much insurance coverage.

The following is a very reasonable provision requiring you to carry liability insurance you can add to a client's agreement in place of an unreasonable insurance clause:

Suggested Language

Client will not provide any insurance coverage for Contractor or Contractor's employees or contract personnel. Contractor agrees to maintain an insurance policy to cover any negligent acts committed by Contractor or Contractor's employees or agents while performing services under this Agreement.

Noncompetition Restrictions

Businesses that hire self-employed people sometimes want to restrict them from performing similar services for their competitors. To do this, they include a noncompetition clause in a client agreement barring them from working for competitors. Try to eliminate such provisions because they limit your ability to earn a living.

At most, you might agree to the following provision barring you from performing the same services for named competitors of the client while you're performing them for the client.

Suggested Language

Contractor agrees that, while performing services required by this Agreement, Contractor will not perform the exact same services for the following competitors of Client: [*List competitors.*]

Confidentiality Provisions

Many clients routinely include confidentiality provisions in their agreements. These provisions bar you from disclosing to others the client's trade secrets, such as marketing plans, information on products under development, manufacturing techniques, or customer lists. It's not unreasonable for a client to want you to keep its secrets away from the eyes and ears of its competitors.

Unfortunately, however, many of these provisions are worded so broadly that they can make it difficult for you to work for other clients without fear of violating your duty of confidentiality. If, like most self-employed people, you make your living by performing similar services for many firms in the same industry, insist on a confidentiality provision that is reasonable in scope and defines precisely what information you must keep confidential. Such a provision should last for only a limited time: five years at the most, but preferably one or two.

Unreasonable Provision

A general provision barring you from making any unauthorized disclosure or using any technical, financial, or business information you obtain directly or indirectly from the client is unreasonable. Such broad restrictions can make it very difficult for you to do similar work for other clients without violating the confidentiality clause. The following is an example of an overbroad provision:

> Contractor may be given access to Client's proprietary or confidential information while working for Client. Contractor agrees not to use or disclose such information except as directed by Client.

Such a provision doesn't make clear what information is and is not the client's confidential trade secret, so you never know for sure what information you must keep confidential and what you can disclose when working for others.

Also, because this provision bars you from later using any of the client's confidential information to which you have access, it could prevent you from using information you already knew before working with the client. It could also bar you from using information that becomes available to the public. You would then be in the absurd position of not being allowed to use information that the whole world knows about. Always attempt to delete or rewrite such an overbroad provision.

Specifically, do not sign a contract requiring you to keep confidential any information:

- you knew about before working with the client
- you learn from a third person who has no duty to keep it confidential
- you develop independently even though the client later provides you with similar or identical information, or

- that becomes publicly known through no fault of your own. For example, you wouldn't have to keep a client's manufacturing technique confidential after it is disclosed to the public in a trade journal article written by someone other than you.

Reasonable Provision

A reasonable nondisclosure provision makes clear that, while you may not use confidential information the client provides, you have the right to freely use information you obtain from other sources or that the public learns later.

The following nondisclosure provision enables you to know for sure what material is, and is not, confidential by requiring the client to mark "confidential" any document you get in the course of that work. A client who tells you confidential information must later write it down and deliver the document marked "confidential" to you within 15 days.

Suggested Language

During the term of this Agreement and for [*6 months to 5 years*] afterward, Contractor will use reasonable care to prevent the unauthorized use or dissemination of Client's confidential information. "Reasonable care" means at least the same degree of care Contractor uses to protect its own confidential information from unauthorized disclosure.

Confidential information is limited to information clearly marked as confidential or disclosed orally and summarized and identified as confidential in a writing delivered to Contractor within 15 days of disclosure.

Confidential information does not include information that:

- Contractor knew before Client disclosed it
- is or becomes public knowledge through no fault of Contractor
- Contractor obtains from sources other than Client who owe no duty of confidentiality to Client, or
- Contractor develops independently.

Unfair Termination Provisions

Your agreement can always be terminated if you or the client breaches one of its major terms (for example, you seriously fail to satisfy the project specifications). Ordinarily, however, neither you nor the client can terminate the agreement just because you feel like it. Some clients add termination provisions to their contracts allowing them to terminate the agreements at will: for any reason or no reason at all. For example, the agreement may provide that the client has the right to terminate the agreement on ten days' written notice.

If you sign an agreement with such a provision, you lose the security of knowing the client must allow you to complete your assignment and pay you for it provided you live up to the terms of your agreement. Instead, you can be fired at any time, just like an employee.

If the client insists on such a provision, fairness dictates that it be mutual. In other words, that is, you should have the same termination rights as the client. The client should also be required to give you reasonable notice of the termination. How long the notice should be depends on the length of the project. For lengthy projects, 30 days' notice may be appropriate. For short projects, it may make sense to require just a few days' notice. Finally, the agreement should make clear that the client must pay you for all the work you performed prior to termination.

"Time Is of the Essence" Clause

Examine the client's agreement carefully to see if it contains the phrase "time is of the essence." You'll often find such clauses in the portion of the contract dealing with the project deadlines.

These simple words can have a big legal impact. Ordinarily, a delay in performance of your contractual obligations is not considered important enough to constitute a material breach of the agreement. This means the client can sue you for any damages sustained due to your lateness but is not entitled to terminate the contract.

EXAMPLE: Barney, a construction contractor, contracts to build a new wing on the AAA Motel. The contract provides that the wing is to be completed by April 1. Barney completes the new wing four weeks late. AAA may sue him for any damages caused by the delay. But because the contract does not include a "time is of the essence" clause, it may not terminate the contract and is legally obligated to pay Barney the contract price.

However, if the contract includes a "time is of the essence" provision, most courts hold that even a slight delay in performance will constitute a material breach. The client can sue you not only for damages but can terminate the contract. This means the client need not perform its contractual obligations; usually this means the client need not pay you.

EXAMPLE: Assume that Barney's contract in the above example did include a "time is of the essence" clause. This would mean that the AAA Motel was legally entitled to terminate the contract and sue Barney for breach of contract when Barney missed the completion deadline.

If you want to be able to have flexibility in your deadlines, delete any "time is of the essence" clause from the client's agreement.

One-Way Provisions

When you review a client's agreement, be on the lookout for "one-way" provisions: contract provisions that give the client rights you don't have. For example:

- an attorneys' fees clause that requires you to pay the client's fees if it wins a lawsuit to enforce the contract but doesn't require the client to pay yours if you win, or
- an arbitration provision requiring you to take any dispute over the contract to arbitration, but not requiring the client to do so.

Obviously, such one-way provisions are grossly unfair and create an uneven playing field for resolving disputes. Some states, such as California, have recognized this unfairness and automatically convert a one-way attorneys' fees contract provision into a mutual provision.

One-way provisions like these are often found unenforceable by the courts. But you don't want to rely on that possibility: Instead, try to alter or eliminate them from your contract.

Provisions to Consider Adding

There are a number of provisions that benefit you that you may wish to add to the client's agreement. These provisions are discussed in detail in "Optional Provisions" in Chapter 19 and include:

- requiring mediation and arbitration of disputes
- recognizing that the contract may have to be modified in the future and providing a mechanism to do so
- allowing you to obtain attorneys' fees if you sue the client and win
- requiring the client to pay a late fee for late payments
- limiting your liability to the client if something goes wrong, and
- restricting the client's ability to assign its benefits or delegate its duties under the agreement.

Client Purchase Orders

Not all clients use standard contracts. Instead, you may be directed to use a form that looks very different from the contracts in this book. Such a form is usually called a "purchase order." Some clients use purchase orders instead of, or in addition to, standard contracts.

A purchase order is an internal form developed by a client authorizing you to perform work and bill for it. Typically, purchase orders are used by larger companies that have separate accounting departments. Accounting departments often don't want to have to deal with lengthy or confusing client agreements.

Purchase orders are designed to provide the minimum information a company needs to document the services you'll perform and how much you'll be paid. They typically contain much of the same information as a letter agreement: a description of the services you'll perform, payment terms, and deadlines. (See Chapter 18.) The order should be signed by the client. You should include the purchase order number on your invoices and all correspondence with the client.

Some companies use purchase orders in conjunction with standard contracts or letter agreements. That is, either you or the client will prepare a contract or letter agreement, and the client will also prepare a purchase order. In this event, make sure the terms of the purchase order are consistent with your client agreement.

Other companies use purchase orders alone for small projects because they don't want to go to the trouble of drafting a client agreement. Some companies' accounting departments will not pay you unless you have a signed purchase order, even if you have a signed letter agreement or standard client agreement.

Before you start work for a client, find out if it uses purchase orders. If it does, insist on being provided a signed order before you start work. Make certain the purchase order is filled out properly. This should include an accurate description of the services you'll perform, the due date, and the terms of payment.

Below is an example of a typical purchase order for services.

Sample Purchase Order for Services

Acme, Inc.

P.O. #: 123

Vendor: Gerard & Associates
             123 Solano Avenue
             Berkeley, CA 99999
             510-555-5555

Date: 8/1/20xx

Delivery Date: 9/1/20xx

Terms: 18¢ per word translated. Total price not to exceed $6,084.

Description of Services:
Contractor will translate Acme instruction manual from the English language into idiomatic Russian using the Cyrillic alphabet. The translated material will be provided in Word format.

Authorized by: _____
             Joe Jones, Chief Financial Officer

Using the Downloadable Forms on the Nolo Website

This book comes with e-forms that you can access online at
www.nolo.com/back-of-book/WAGE.html
All the forms are RTFs which you can open, edit, save, and print with most word processing programs, such as Microsoft *Word*, Windows *WordPad*, and recent versions of *WordPerfect*.

Editing RTFs

Here are some general instructions about editing RTF forms in your word processing program. Refer to the book's instructions and sample agreements for help about what should go in each blank.

Underlines. Underlines indicate where to enter information. After filling in the needed text, delete the underline. In most word processing programs you can do this by highlighting the underlined portion and typing CTRL-U.

Bracketed and italicized text. Bracketed and italicized text indicates instructions. Be sure to remove all instructional text before you finalize your document.

Alternative text. Alternative text gives you the choice between two or more text options. Delete those options you don't want to use. Renumber any numbered items, if necessary.

Signature lines. Signature lines should appear on a page with at least some text from the document itself.

Every word processing program uses different commands to open, format, save, and print documents, so refer to your software's help documents for help using your program. Nolo cannot provide technical support for questions about how to use your computer or your software.

CAUTION
In accordance with U.S. copyright laws, the forms and audio files provided by this book are for your personal use only.

List of Forms Available on the Nolo Website

Title	File Name
Invoice	Invoice.rtf
Asset Log	AssetLog.rtf
Usage Log	UsageLog.rtf
Nondisclosure Agreement	Nondisclosure.rtf
Contract Amendment	Amendment.rtf
General Independent Contractor Agreement	IndContractorAgree.rtf
Letter Agreement	LetterAgree.rtf

Index